D1748521

Governance and Performance of Education Systems

Governance and Performance of Education Systems

edited by

Nils C. Soguel
Swiss Graduate School of Public Administration, Lausanne, Switzerland

and

Pierre Jaccard
Education Department of the Canton of Vaud, Lausanne, Switzerland

Springer

A C.I.P. Catalogue record for this book is available from the Library of Congress.

ISBN 978-1-4020-6445-6 (HB)
ISBN 978-1-4020-6446-3 (e-book)

Published by Springer,
P.O. Box 17, 3300 AA Dordrecht, The Netherlands.

www.springer.com

Printed on acid-free paper

All Rights Reserved
© 2008 Springer
No part of this work may be reproduced, stored in a retrieval system, or transmitted in
any form or by any means, electronic, mechanical, photocopying, microfilming, recording
or otherwise, without written permission from the Publisher, with the exception
of any material supplied specifically for the purpose of being entered
and executed on a computer system, for exclusive use by the purchaser of the work.

Acknowledgments

In September 2006, the conference "Educational Systems and the Challenge of Improving Results: Explaining and Enhancing Performance and Equity" was held at the University of Lausanne (Switzerland). It was jointly organised by the Swiss graduate school of public administration-IDHEAP and the General Director of the Department of Education of the canton of Vaud. The conference benefited from a grant from the Gebert Rüf Foundation that is gratefully acknowledged.

Most of this volume is the outcome of the conference. Therefore we are indebted to all the people who helped us, not only to organise the conference but also to overcome the difficulties of the second phase of this adventure, namely the completion of this book. We are especially indebted to Florian Chatagny who provided excellent organisational assistance, Lee Nicol who scrutinised the language and Béatrice Hausmann for the final preparation of the typescripts.

N.C.S & P.J.

Table of Contents

Notes on Contributors   ix

1. Introduction: Governance and Performance of Education Systems   1
   Nils C. Soguel and Pierre Jaccard

Part One   The Changing Governance of Educational Systems

2. The New Regulation Forms of Educational Systems in Europe: Towards a Post-bureaucratic Regime   13
   Christian Maroy

3. Comparing Higher Education Governance Systems in Four European Countries   35
   Harry F. de Boer, Jürgen Enders and Uwe Schimank

Part Two   Performance Monitoring and Evaluation

4. Purpose and Limits of a National Monitoring of the Education System Through Indicators   57
   Stefan C. Wolter

5. Measuring and Comparing the Equity of Education Systems in Europe   85
   Marc Demeuse and Ariane Baye

6. The Economic Benefits of Improved Teacher Quality   107
   Eric A. Hanushek

   Comments   131
   George Sheldon

7. Direct Democracy and Public Education in Swiss Cantons ... 137
   Justina A.V. Fischer

8. School Factors Related to Quality: Multilevel Analysis for Three Swiss Cantons ... 155
   Ivar Trippolini

9. Are Swiss Secondary Schools Efficient? ... 187
   Muriel Meunier

Part Three   Explaining and Controlling the Costs of Education Systems

10. Funding Schools by Formula ... 205
    Rosalind Levačić

    Comments ... 236
    Andrea Schenker-Wicki

11. A Cost Model of Schools: School Size, School Structure and Student Composition ... 247
    Torberg Falch, Marte Rønning and Bjarne Strøm

Part Four   Strategies to Encourage Performance and Equity

12. The Potential of School Information Systems for Enhancing School Improvement ... 269
    Ian Selwood and Adrie J. Visscher

13. School Autonomy and Financial Manoeuvrability: French Principals' Strategies ... 289
    Yves Dutercq

14. Finnish Strategy for High-Level Education for All ... 305
    Reijo Laukkanen

Index ... 325

Notes on Contributors

Ariane Baye

Ariane Baye is a Research Fellow at the department of Education and Training at the University of Liège (Belgium). She has been involved in several national and international projects aimed to indicators development and interpretation in the field of education and training. She has been the delegate of the French Community of Belgium for the Network A and B of the OECD/INES project. She is the National Project Manager for PISA, an international 15-year-old students assessment program. She coordinated with Marc Demeuse the Socrates project designed to build European Indicators on the Equity of the Education Systems. She has co-authored several papers on equity and indicators, and co-edited *Vers une école juste et efficace: 26 contributions sur les systèmes d'enseignement et de formation* and *Equity in European Education Systems: A Set of Indicators*.

Harry F. de Boer

Harry F. de Boer is a senior researcher at the Center for Higher Education Policy Studies of the University of Twente in the Netherlands and is lecturing and tutoring in courses in higher education management. His research topics in the field of higher education studies concern governance and steering models at macro level, institutional governance, management and leadership styles in professional organizations, strategic planning and decision-making. He has frequently contributed to studies in these areas, including articles in *Higher Education Policy, Public Administration, the European Journal of Education and Tertiary Education and Management*. Moreover, he has conducted several reports for the Dutch ministry and for national agencies.

Marc Demeuse

Marc Demeuse is Professor of Education at the Institute of School Administration (INAS, Faculty of Psychology and Education Science, University of Mons-Hainaut, Belgium). He teaches at the University of Burgundy (Dijon, France) and at the UNESCO Chair of Education in Dakar (Senegal). He is a consultant to several national and international agencies on issues like evaluation of educational systems, equity in education, school management. He has written, co-authored or edited books and articles in several journals regarding the already mentioned topics. He has been the coordinator of the European Group for Research on Equity in Educational Systems. He holds a Ph.D. in psychology from the University of Liège (Belgium) and he is also a statistician (Gembloux Agricultural University, Belgium).

Yves Dutercq

Yves Dutercq is Professor at the University of Nantes (France) and a sociologist of education. His work deals with recent transformations in educational public action, specifically with its consequences on the changing role of education administrators, and the relationship of the citizens vis-à-vis the educational services offered by the state. He is also interested in interpersonal relationships between teachers and between pupils and teachers. Yves Dutercq has conducted research on the mobilization of parents around the school and on the regulation of the educational policies. He has written several books and many articles on these various topics. Today he leads a study on the formation of future elites in France. He is co-editor of *Education et sociétés*, an international journal of sociology of education.

Jürgen Enders

Jürgen Enders is Professor and Director of the Center for Higher Education Policy Studies at the University of Twente, the Netherlands. He was previously Assistant Professor at the Centre for Research on Higher Education and Work at the University of Kassel, Germany, where he received his doctorate in political science. He is member of the editorial board of the book series *Higher Education Dynamics* and the journal *Higher Education*. His research interests are in the areas of the Political Sociology of Higher Education, Governance and Management of Higher Education and Research, Higher Education and the World of Work, and the Academic

Profession. He has written and (co-)edited numerous books and published articles in journals such as *Higher Education*, *Higher Education Policy*, *Leviathan*, *Public Administration*, *Rassegna Italiana di Sociologia*, *Scientometrics*.

Torberg Falch

Torberg Falch is Associate Professor at Department of Economics, Norwegian University of Science and Technology. He has written articles in several journals, including *Economics of Education Review*, *Education Economics*, *European Economic Review*, *European Journal of Political Economy* and *Economics of Governance*. He has been a consultant to the Norwegian government on issues of resource use in compulsory schooling, school accountability systems, early childhood education and infrastructure impact fees. He is a member of the EU think-tank "The European Expert Network on Economics of Education". He holds a Ph.D. in economics from the University of Oslo.

Justina A.V. Fischer

Justina A.V. Fischer is currently a post-doctoral researcher at the Stockholm School of Economics (Handelshögskolan i Stockholm, Sweden). She held previously visiting positions at the London School of Economics and at the University of Stanford, Hoover Institution, after having received her Ph.D. in economics from the University of St. Gallen (Switzerland) and an M.A. degree from the European University Institute, Florence. Her doctoral thesis investigates the impact of direct democracy on societal outcomes, among them public education. Her research interests are in the areas of political economy and behavioural economics with a current focus on life satisfaction outcomes. She collaborated with authors in various book publications and published articles in several journals, including *Journal of Happiness Studies*, *Public Choice*, *Social Indicators Research*, *Social Choice and Welfare*.

Eric A. Hanushek

Eric A. Hanushek is Paul and Jean Hanna Senior Fellow at the Hoover Institution of Stanford University (USA). He is also chairman of the Executive Committee for the Texas Schools Project at the University of Texas at Dallas, a research associate of the National Bureau of Economic Research and a member of the Koret Task Force on K-12 Education. He is an expert on educational policy, specializing in the economics and finance of schools. His books include *Courting Failure, Handbook on the Economics of Education, The Economics of Schooling and School Quality, Improving America's Schools, Making Schools Work, Educational Performance of the Poor, Education and Race, Assessing Policies for Retirement Income, Modern Political Economy, Improving Information for Social Policy Decisions* and *Statistical Methods for Social Scientists*, along with numerous articles in professional journals. He is a member of the National Academy of Education and an elected fellow of the International Academy of Education and of the Society of Labour Economists. He was awarded the Fordham Prize for Distinguished Scholarship in 2004. He is a Distinguished Graduate of the United States Air Force Academy and completed his Ph.D. in economics at the Massachusetts Institute of Technology.

Pierre Jaccard

Pierre Jaccard is Assistant General Director of the Department of Education of the canton of Vaud in Lausanne where he is in charge of the *Direction of organisation and planning*. He has most notably introduced the funding by formulas for schools. Mr Jaccard is currently project manager for the introduction of an information system for all schools and central offices of the Department of Education and works on all questions related to the modernization of school management. Previously, he was headmaster in an elementary school and in charge of the training of new headmasters. He holds a Master in Public Administration from the Swiss Graduate School of Public Administration–IDHEAP in Lausanne.

Reijo Laukkanen

Reijo Laukkanen is Counsellor at the Finnish National Board of Education. At the moment his work consists of international affairs but earlier he has been responsible for several major development projects of basic education and acted as head of special needs education and evaluation units of the Board. He has worked as a Counsellor in the Permanent Delegation of Finland to the OECD for 4 years covering education sector but also labour, health, public management and science policy issues. Currently he is the Finnish representative on the governing board of CERI (Centre of Educational Research and Innovation). He is also a Docent for International Education Policy at the University of Tampere. He has written, co-authored or edited several books and articles in several journals, including

Scandinavian Journal of Educational Research, European Journal of Special Needs Education, Lifelong Learning in Europe, Educational Leadership and *Administration and education*. He holds a Ph.D. in education from the University of Jyväskylä.

Rosalind Levačić

Rosalind Levačić is Professor of Economics and Finance of Education at the Institute of Education, University of London (UK). Her main research interests are school funding systems, financial and resource management of schools and the relationships between school resourcing and student outcomes. She has undertaken a wide range of consultancy work on school finance including formula funding for two English local authorities and school finance decentralization reforms in Poland, Bosnia and Herzegovina, Montenegro and Azerbaijan. Her research on school finance reforms in England was published in *Local Management of Schools: Analysis and Practice*. She has also published articles on school finance and school effectiveness in *Oxford Review of Education, Education Economics, School Effectiveness and School Improvement* and *British Education Research Journal*.

Christian Maroy

Christian Maroy is Professor of Sociology at the Department of Political and Social Sciences of University of Louvain. He is director of the GIRSEF, an interdisciplinary research group on education and training systems. Beyond a number of papers in international journals (*Journal of Education Policy, Work, Employment and Society, Education et Sociétés, Revue française de Pédagogie, Cahiers internationaux de sociologie, Formation Emploi*), he has published recently *L'enseignement secondaire et ses enseignants* and *Ecole, Régulation et Marché: Une comparaison de six espaces scolaires locaux en Europe*.

Muriel Meunier

Muriel Meunier is currently a Ph.D. student at the Department of Economics, University of Geneva (Switzerland). She is also a member of the Swiss Leading House on the Economics of Education, Firm Behaviour and Training Policies, a so-called "Excellence Centre" in the economics of education granted to the University of Geneva in 2005 by the federal office of the professional formation and technology (OFFT). Her main academic interests are the economics of education and her thesis topic is an empirical application to Switzerland. Beforehand, she wrote several articles about Quebec Province's schooling system, including dropout from and return to school, when she was at the Interuniversity Centre of Research on the Analysis of Organizations (Montréal, Canada).

Marte Rønning

Marte Rønning is employed at Centre for Economic Research at NTNU and is a Ph.D. student at the Department of Economics, Norwegian University of Science and Technology. She has been a visiting researcher at Stanford University and employed at University of Amsterdam. Her research interests are economics of education and the functioning of the teacher labour market.

Andrea Schenker-Wicki

Andrea Schenker-Wicki is Professor of Business Administration and Director of the Executive MBA Program, University of Zurich (Switzerland). Her main research interests are performance management in private and public organisations, trust and control in public and private organisations, crisis management, university management. She has published several books and diverse articles in professional journals. She completed a Ph.D. in Business Administration at the University of Fribourg and an habilitation thesis dedicated to "evaluation of universities, performance measurements and indicators" at the University of St. Gallen.

Uwe Schimank

Uwe Schimank is professor of sociology at the FernUniversität in Hagen in Germany. Besides higher education research, his research interests include sociological theory, theories of modern society, organizational sociology, sociology of sports and sociology of science. In higher education research, he is currently interested in comparative studies of governance regimes of national systems of higher education. He advised the Austrian rector's association, the German federal ministry of education and research, the VolkswagenStiftung, and participated in evaluation teams of the German Science Council and the Wissenschaftliche Kommission Niedersachsen. Besides, he is vice rector of the FernUniversität since 2002.

Ian Selwood

Ian Selwood is a Senior Lecturer in ICT in Education in the School of Education at the University of Birmingham (UK). He has worked in the field of ICT since the early 1970s, initially as head of Computer Studies in a secondary school, followed by 6 years as an advisory teacher for IT. Since 1987 he has worked in the School of Education. His research interests are mainly concerned with the use of ICT to support Educational Administration and Management and the Management of ICT in Schools. His publications not only reflect these areas of interest but also include other educational applications of ICT. Recent research projects include contributions to the DfES funded "TSW Evaluation", "ICT Testbed Baseline Study" and "Impact of Broadband on Schools" and Becta-funded research into the use of Tablet PCs. His current research is concerned with ICT and School Improvement, and ICT and personalised learning. He is Editor-in-Chief of *Education and Information Technologies* and on the editorial board of two other international academic journals, and Vice-Chair of the International Federation for Information Processing working group on IT in Educational Management.

George Sheldon

George Sheldon is Professor of Labour Economics, Industrial Organization and Applied Econometrics at the University of Basel, where he heads the Labour Market and Industrial Organization Research Unit. He has taught at the Albert-Ludwigs-University in Freiburg, the University of Berne, the University of St. Gallen and the University of Trier. He has served as a consultant to government agencies in Switzerland and Germany on issues pertaining to unemployment, technological change, education, competition and efficiency measurement. He has written, co-authored or edited several books and articles in various journals, including *Economic Letters*, *Journal of Productivity*, *Review of World Economics* and the *Swiss Journal of Economics and Statistics*. He holds a Ph.D. from the Albert-Ludwigs-University in Freiburg in economics.

Nils C. Soguel

Nils C. Soguel is professor of public finance at the Swiss Graduate School of Public Administration–IDHEAP (University of Lausanne, Switzerland). He has taught at the University College London and at the Swiss Institute of Technology in Lausanne. He has served as a consultant to several Swiss national agencies and local governments on issues like valuation of non-market goods, public finance management, school funding mechanisms, as well as fiscal federalism. He has written, co-authored or edited several books and articles in several journals, including *Journal of Risk and Uncertainty*, *Environmental and Resource Economics*, *Journal of Environmental Planning and Management*, *Revue d'économie politique*, *Politiques et management public*. He holds a Ph.D. in economics from the University of Neuchâtel.

Bjarne Strøm

Bjarne Strøm is Professor at Department of Economics at Norwegian University of Science and Technology. He has written articles in several journals, including *Economica*, *Economics of Education Review*, *European Economic Review*, *Economics of Governance* and *Scandinavian Journal of Economics*. He has been a consultant to the Norwegian government on issues such as school accountability systems, private schools and high school dropout problems. He holds a Ph.D. in economics from the University of Bergen.

Ivar Trippolini

Ivar Trippolini is research associate at the Swiss graduate school of public administration–IDHEAP (University of Lausanne, Switzerland). Former elementary school teacher, he obtained a Diploma in Political Sciences at the University of Geneva (2004) and subsequently a Masters of Public Administration at the IDHEAP in Lausanne (2006). His main fields of research and expertise cover public institutions in federal states and education policies for compulsory schooling.

Adrie J. Visscher

Adrie J. Visscher is an associate professor in the University of Twente (Faculty of Behavioural Sciences) in The Netherlands. He is interested in the factors accountable for school performance differences between schools (i.e. variance between schools in how much students learn in them) and in how quality assurance in general and school performance feedback systems and management information systems more specifically can support improving the quality of schooling. He has published about 140 publications including many articles in international scientific journals, special issues of international journals and scientific books.

Stefan C. Wolter

Stefan C. Wolter is Director of the Swiss Coordination Centre for Research in Education. He is also professor of economics of education at the University of Berne. He is currently also president of the council of the Swiss Federal Institute for Vocational Education, Swiss delegate to the Education Committee of the OECD and member of the executive bureau of the CERI (Centre for Educational Research and Innovation, OECD) governing board. He has written and co-authored several books and articles. Some two dozen articles were published in refereed journals, such as the *German Economic Review*, *Kyklos*, *Brussels Economic Review*, *Applied Economics Quarterly*, etc. He holds a Ph.D. in economics from the University of Berne.

Chapter 1
Introduction: Governance and Performance of Education Systems

Nils C. Soguel[1] and Pierre Jaccard[2]

[1]*Swiss Graduate School of Public Administration-Institut de hautes études en administration publique, University of Lausanne, Lausanne, Switzerland*
[2]*Education Department of the Canton de Vaud, Lausanne, Switzerland*

At the time of publication of this volume, education systems were experiencing a change of paradigm. The groundwork for the transformation was laid in the 1980s when the spirit of the times began to change with the movement of the so-called *new public management*. In many countries, governing by defining goals to be met by agencies rather than by stricter regulation became fashionable together with a decentralisation of the responsibility for the achievement of these goals, more citizens' choice and more competition.

These solutions were considered to be the proper answer to a growing criticism of the performance of publicly provided services. More specifically, criticisms of education systems were enhanced by the mediatisation of comparative studies and table leagues. Since the first International Study of Achievement in Mathematics in 1964, comparisons have multiplied: Third International Mathematics and Science Study (TIMSS) in 1995, Progress in International Reading Literacy Study (PIRLS) in 2001, Program for International Student Assessment (PISA) since 2000 and International Adult Literacy Survey (IALS) since 1992, just to mention the most commonly cited.

The economic downturn of the 1990s and the resulting government fiscal crisis, together with the fact that the education system represents a large share of public expenditure, reinforced the social demand for policy reforms.

As a result, the change of paradigm represented by market-oriented reforms was considered the appropriate solution. However, private-sector models cannot simply be translated to the public sector for they have not always proved to be successful in the former. Moreover, the public sector and education systems have their own characteristics which in turn make the problem all the more complex. One of these characteristics is the multiplicity of external stakeholders (parents, politicians, trade unions, private firms) and internal interests (teachers, civil servants). A further characteristic is the diversity of sometimes competing missions and goals ranging from egalitarian goals (equity of outcomes and equality of opportunities) to meritocratic goals, such as promoting the enhancement of pupils' individual attainment. One must add that the side effects of education policy for other public policies is increasingly recognised and criticised. Available evidence suggests such spillover effects in areas like functioning of democracy, economic growth, sorting mechanism for the labour market, unemployment reduction, poverty reduction, improvements in health and crime prevention. The importance of these side effects increases the pressure on education systems for an improved performance.

Through these side effects, improving educational opportunities can ameliorate both equality and efficiency in our societies. Fundamentally, it means that the education system should bring the largest number of pupils and students (and possibly all of them) to the highest possible attainment using the lowest possible amount of budget resources. As mentioned above, the first two requirements can be seen as paradoxical, not to mention the last. Nevertheless, education systems are now more than ever faced with the challenge of improving their performance and of proving that suitable measures are being taken to guarantee greater efficiency regarding equity. To various degrees in many OECD countries, the change of paradigm has encouraged competition between public and private schools, delegated authority to local authorities and schools for teacher employment, detailed curricula and teaching techniques, increased variability in the resource available to students with voucher systems and grants tailored to results, stimulated parental choice either between private and public schools or between public schools when voting with their feet.

As both spectators and actors of theses sweeping reforms, we have several related objectives for this book. The first is of course to depict the change of paradigm and to present some of the reforms in some detail. The second aim is to question the achievement of these reforms in terms of performance and equity enhancement. Several disciplines have already developed instruments for this purpose; the educational sciences have been particularly active in this field. Other disciplines, such as sociology, economics, management, information technology and political science, are also making significant contributions to the emergence of a better form of governance. Consequently, the third aim of this volume is to bring together

Introduction

contributions originating from a wide range of disciplines when most of the literature concentrates on contributions from a sole field of expertise.

The book is designed for those active in the research and management of education systems, for academics from several disciplines and for civil servants and politicians. Since it reports experience from several countries, it will also interest people in various countries.

1.1. The Changing Governance of Education Systems

The first part of the book discusses the change in governance that education systems are experiencing either at the school level or in higher education.

Christian Maroy analyses the changes in the way European countries (namely the French-speaking part of Belgium, England, France, Hungary and Portugal) institutionally regulate their school systems through the mechanisms of orientation, coordination, control, financing and balancing of the system set up by school authorities. In some countries, the long-established regulation mode based on bureaucratic processes on the one hand and the dominance of the teachers' professional expertise on the other hand has evolved toward a post-bureaucratic model. This new model of governance relies deeply on both evaluation and competition. Evaluation points mainly in the direction of "producers" (notably schools and their agents) and of the "products" of the education systems (student attainments). Competition is chiefly based on free choice by users and, more rarely, is promoted by praising the virtues of competition between schools. However, the degree of convergence between national models varies either because the educational policies refer to the new model to different extents or because the policies were developed on the basis of different contexts. In fact, the transnational change of paradigm is set in context and therefore adjusted according to political, cultural or national specificities and constraints. For example, the new model relies officially less on competition than on evaluation in most countries, with the exception of England.

Harry de Boer, *Jürgen Enders* and *Uwe Schimank* depict an identical phenomenon in the field of higher education. The authors also notice that a new form of governance of universities has emerged over the last two decades. To bring a detailed and analytical view of the change, they propose a very illustrative tool that they call the "governance equalizer". This tool allows them to compare the degree of change of university governance in England, the Netherlands, Austria and Germany according to five criteria: (a) state regulation (top-down authority), (b) stakeholder guidance through goal setting and advice, (c) academic self-governance (e.g. collegial decision-making or peer-review based self-steering), (d) managerial self-governance (e.g. internal leadership, goal setting or regulation), (e) competition for scarce resources – money, personnel and prestige – within and between universities. The most profound changes have apparently taken place in England and Austria. On the contrary, Germany seems for the moment to be the most conservative country in terms of shifts in governance, except for an increase in competitive pressures.

1.2. Performance Monitoring and Evaluation

The second part of the volume is dedicated to monitoring and evaluation. It must be considered from a double – methodological and empirical – viewpoint. First, the various contributions present some of the available methodologies to monitor and evaluate the achievement of an education system. Second, they apply the presented methodologies in order to provide us empirical evidence of the achievements of various national education systems. In turn, the results allow for the comparison of results between countries where there are differences in the governance of the systems.

Stefan Wolter presents the extent to which a national monitoring through statistical indicators is viable as a means of managing the education system. He helps the reader to understand what the limitations of such a system are. A first limitation is that a limited set of indicators cannot describe the whole complexity of the system. A second limitation is that indicators are chosen under a double constraint: the constraint of the retained analytical framework (i.e. the questions the monitoring system is meant to answer) and the information available at a reasonable cost. Furthermore, a majority of relevant statistical indicators are not self-explanatory or do not directly offer an insight into the many complex interdependencies in the education system. The author explains then how these limitations were taken into account to design the first Swiss Education Report. Based on practical examples like class size, number of lesson hours, university rankings and firms' willingness to train apprentices, he illustrates the possibilities and the problems of using indicator approaches to understand and evaluate the changes that occurred in an education system, and ultimately to learn from these transformations.

Marc Demeuse and *Ariane Baye* illustrate how difficult it is to measure and compare as complex a phenomenon as the equity of education systems with indicators. Clearly, alternative indicators lead to alternative classifications of countries with regard to equity, with the exception of countries that perform quite well or quite poorly. Therefore, the probability of biasing conclusions and policy options when using a single indicator is high. As a result, several dimensions must come into play. The authors also stress that the availability of data largely influences and even biases the seminal depiction of equity. Recent efforts designed the needed indicator set according to an intelligible model that tries to explain the results obtained while taking account of the complex structure of the different education systems. They demonstrate the process with regard to a specific dimension of equity, i.e. segregation with a model that considers two dimensions: the extent of the fragmentation of the school population in homogenous groups and the implementation of mechanisms to ensure as closely as possible a homogenous treatment of the school population, whatever school is attended. However, while implementing the model, they recognise that a trade-off must be made between the theoretical requirement and available data to obtain a feasible, reliable and useful set of indicators.

While reviewing basic evidence about two strands of literature relating to the evaluation of the quality of schooling, *Eric Hanushek* demonstrates that the shortcomings of a strict indicator approach, in terms of explanatory power, can be overcome. The first line of research investigates school achievement in connection with the labour market. The policy issue here is whether school quality – and thus quality-improving school reforms – has a positive impact on individual earnings and economic growth. Hanushek assesses these effects while giving special attention to variations across countries at different levels of development. Quoting several studies, he demonstrates that such a positive impact actually exists. Therefore, the subsequent policy issue, related to the second line of enquiry, is how a country can improve its school quality (and gain economic benefits). Past efforts to change achievement and the outcomes of schooling have shown the difficulty for policy. While standard approaches of simply providing more resources to schools have proven quite ineffective, Hanushek produces mounting evidence suggesting that improvements in teachers' quality can have a dramatic impact on student outcomes.

George Sheldon's comment sheds additional light on Hanushek's paper mainly by raising two specific controversial points. The first relates to the thesis that the quality of schooling, at least in developed countries, has a greater impact on individual incomes and economic growth than the quantity of schooling. The second pertains to the claim that no systematic relationship exists between the amount of educational resources invested and the cognitive ability of students. This latter comment clearly reveals the necessity to further investigate the various factors that can possibly explain pupils' and students' achievement and the outcomes of schooling.

The three following papers provide us with an illustration of three different kinds of techniques to achieve that objective. All of them use the data collected mainly with the OECD PISA 2000 or 2003 survey and to Switzerland, thus taking chance of the diversity of cantons' institutional settings triggered by the Swiss federalist structure.

In her contribution, *Justina Fischer* addresses the question to what extent stronger popular rights in 26 Swiss cantons affect student performance. Using a parametric technique, she estimates an educational production function where the individual student PISA 2000 score is the dependent variable (output variable), while the input variables are measured at the individual, class, school and cantonal level. They include students' socio-demographic background factors, peer performance, location and type of schools as well as economic and social characteristics of the corresponding canton. This model is augmented by a measure of the extent of cantonal direct democracy. Direct democracy is found to decrease educational spending per pupil. Moreover, stronger popular rights appear to indirectly lower attainment in both reading and mathematics (but not in natural science) through the school budget channel. Among a wide array of school resource variables, teachers' qualification appears as the most influential (and beneficial) determinant, which, in turn, is positively affected by the level of cantonal educational spending. In contrast to US studies, no evidence of a Leviathan-like school administration is detected as her analyses of the impact of direct democracy on class sizes and the instructional-to-administrative-spending ratio show.

Ivar Trippolini's paper also applies a parametric technique to model the attainment of the educational system. However, his approach is quite different in the sense that it respects the typical hierarchical or multilevel structure of educational systems. At an individual level, students have different characteristics. Then at a second level, a class has characteristics (e.g. its teacher) that are identical for all its pupils but that differ from one class to another. At a third level, all students belonging to the same school are subject to the same contextual characteristics that differ from those of other schools. He thus uses a hierarchical linear analysis to model the variance at different hierarchical levels and simultaneously estimating regression coefficients for all characteristics. In the three cantons considered, instructional conditions such as the disciplinary climate more often have a statistically significant impact on student performance than aspects of school resources and management. Thus, factors closer to the learning process within the classes are more often valid. Furthermore, his results show that the educational programmes or levels tend to be homogeneous not only for students' achievements but also for their socio-economic composition. This strong interdependence raises the question of how cantonal school systems can cope with a goal of equity in educational performance.

Muriel Meunier's contribution is illustrative of a completely different approach of the performance evaluation. Indeed, she uses a non-parametric approach, namely the data-envelopment analysis. This approach offers the ability to handle the multidimensional nature of a complex process like schooling by taking several outputs together with several inputs into consideration. Meunier considers the school as the educational production unit. The average PISA 2000 score for reading in each school and a measure of dispersion around the average are used as output measures to reflect both efficiency and equity issues. The number of hours of supervision per year, the number of teachers per pupil, the number of teachers having a teaching diploma per pupil and the number of computers per pupil are used as input measures. Her analysis of efficiency scores indicates that only a fraction of the Swiss secondary schools are efficient with only a small percentage of the pupils attending an efficient school. It seems that the proportion of efficient schools and the efficiency score increase with the school size.

1.3. Explaining and Controlling the Costs of Education Systems

The third part of the book is dedicated to the financing of the education system. Decentralising the responsibility to sub-national levels of government or to schools or universities requires simultaneously changing the way the system is financed. Most centralised systems employ a historic funding mechanism, basing allocations on the previous year's spending, which gives perverse incentives for budget recipients. Once the budget is granted, there is no point in the budget holder spending less since it would most probably lower its budget allocation next year. Another traditional method is to determine the number of teachers employed at a school according to the number of classes, which encourages schools to create as many classes as they can obtain approval for. In order to promote efficiency in the use of resources in decentralised systems, the educational management unit should be allocated a lump sum budget within which it must resource its educational provision. The issue then is how the amount of this budget should be determined. One method would be for schools to bid by submitting budget estimates, but this encourages gamesmanship for tactically inflated requirements on the part of schools. The method favoured by education systems that have decentralised financial management is to devise a formula for determining budget allocations.

Rosalind Levačić presents and analyses how a change towards funding schools by formula can ensure equity and promote efficiency. As its name indicates, such a system utilises a mathematical formula whereby a set of clearly selected criteria defines a lump sum budget for each school. The school has the responsibility for deciding how to spend for the education of its students. An increasing number of countries have introduced funding schools by formula. The chapter examines the school funding formulae of seven European countries (England, Finland, Iceland, Netherlands, Poland, Russia and Sweden) in order to illustrate some key issues in designing and operating funding formulae. The author argues that the effects of introducing a school funding formula cannot be evaluated in isolation from other key elements of the policy framework, in particular school-based management and the system of school accountability. In particular, school-based management is more likely to improve schools' efficiency, including raising attainment for a given expenditure, if accompanied by external assessment of student attainment, holding schools accountable for student outcomes and providing schools with support for improvement.

In her comment on Levačić's contribution, *Andrea Schenker-Wicki* emphasizes that funding schools and universities by formula does not automatically lead to significant gains in efficiency. In her view, the capacity of formula funding to improve political governance depends on how the transfer systems are designed, particularly when several agencies are responsible for funding (central state and member states). Eventually what matters is the quality of the overall governance of the education system to which the formula funding contributes. Nevertheless, Schenker-Wicki concludes that the technique brings horizontal transparency and equity providing that the formula takes the characteristics of a certain unit into consideration.

Torberg Falch, *Marte Rønning* and *Bjarne Strøm* argue in their chapter that it is inherently difficult to estimate a cost function that can predict how much it costs to deliver a given level of education and, as a result, would be helpful to select which variables should enter a funding equation. Indeed, the literature has not established a convincing relationship between school production and school financial resources. Instead, using data from Norway, they estimate a model relating resource use per student to school size and student composition, leaving aside school outputs from the model. They find that costs per student are diminishing within the whole range of school sizes, and they present point estimates on the costs of minority students and students with special needs.

1.4. Strategies to Encourage Performance and Equity

The fourth and concluding part of the volume exposes some strategies to encourage and develop performance and equity in school. Exploiting information technologies and especially information systems is the example of an instrumental strategy a school can implement to improve not only teaching and learning, but also school administration, management and leadership. *Ian Selwood* and *Adrie Visscher* highlight the potential that school information systems have for enhancing school improvement. They sketch out how these systems have developed in some countries, the rationale for introducing these systems and the common features of such systems. They then examine the concept of school improvement and the influence of information and communication technologies. Various aspects of school improvement are discussed including increasing efficiency of school management, raising attendance and reducing teacher workload.

Naturally, to be able to implement such instrumental strategies, schools must benefit from adequate incentives and potentially a suitable autonomy. *Yves Dutercq*'s chapter stresses the necessary consistency that must prevail between the governance of the education system and its financial system. It explains how, in France, the deconcentration of the centralized power down to different levels of regional administration has extended the autonomy of secondary institutions. Simultaneously, this change was not officially associated with an increase in financial autonomy: budgets are still narrowly earmarked and delineated. But as a matter of fact, some principals (i.e. school managers) are nevertheless able to provide their school some financial sovereignty by tweaking the standard budget and sacrificing one budgetary heading in favour of another. By doing so, the school can implement a strategy that is deliberately driven by its own priorities and institutional project. Principals also take advantage of the competition between their two supervisory authorities – the national education administration and the local or regional political authority – to broaden their autonomy and eventually increase their resources. Being the focal point for other partners gives schools an unrivalled strategic power.

Because Finnish 15-year-olds did so well in the first two PISA surveys, the Finnish education system has received plenty of attention from all over the world. Thus, a volume such as this one had to look for explanations. *Reijo Laukkanen* shows that there are many different explanations, but the most promising one stems from long-term education policy that has been based on the need to enhance equity and improve performance. Those two issues were connected together as part of the development goals when the new education system was created back in the 1970s. The paper provides details of Finnish policy including the discontinuation of streaming, the strong allocation of resources to lower secondary level, the decentralisation of decision-making, upgrading primary school teachers' education to MA level, support for weak students and cooperation with stakeholders.

Part One

The Changing Governance of Educational Systems

Chapter 2
The New Regulation Forms of Educational Systems in Europe: Towards a Post-bureaucratic Regime

Christian Maroy[1]

[1] *Groupe Interfacultaire de Recherche sur les Systèmes d'Education et de Formation-GIRSEF, Université catholique de Louvain, Louvain-La-Neuve, Belgique*

2.1. Introduction

The modes of institutional regulation of an educational system can be considered as the set of all mechanisms of orientation, coordination, control and balancing of the system set up by educational authorities. Thus, it is one of the activities of "governance" of the system alongside those related to the financing of education or the "production" of education service (Dale 1997). Our purpose is to enquire about the evolutions of the modes of the institutional regulation of the education systems in five European countries (francophone Belgium, England, France, Hungary, Portugal). More precisely, we ask whether the education policies of the past 20 years have contributed to constructing a certain convergence of the institutional regulation of the systems and, simultaneously, what important divergences remain.

This analysis is derived from the European research Reguleduc (Maroy 2004, 2006). Our analysis of the evolution of modes of institutional regulation is founded on studies of the principal morphological and institutional characteristics of the school systems of the five countries and analysis of the education policies they have applied over the last 20 years, in particular those affecting the modes of regulation of secondary schools. Each team synthesised the literature dealing with its national situation. Subsequently, a transverse synthesis (Bajomi and Barroso 2002) was done.

Our thesis is that these policies partially converge around "post-bureaucratic" governance models and regulation. Depending on the country, we can link education policies to two post-bureaucratic models promoted by transnational agencies: that of the "evaluative state" and the "quasi-market" which are largely combinable and combined. They share their opposition to the "bureaucratic-professional" model which has prevailed to varying degrees and in different versions in these countries (Barroso 2000). Still, these partial convergences in the baseline models do not necessarily imply completely identical policies, on the one hand because the policies refer to these models to different extents and on the other hand because these policies developed on the basis of different contexts from the outset. In fact, these "transnational models" are recontextualised and hybridised, according to political, cultural or national specificities and constraints. In other words, there is a "path dependency" that constrains the policies in each national context.

We first present the principal characteristics of the bureaucratic-professional model and its importance in each national context during 1960s and 1970s. Second, we look at the convergences observed and we refer them to the models of evaluative state and quasi-market. In conclusion, we discuss briefly the factors of convergences and divergences that lie behind these evolutions.

2.2. The Slow Departure of the Bureaucratic-Professional Model

The education systems under analysis are quite different. Some are decentralised (Francophone community of Belgium (FCB) and England), others are centralised systems (France, Portugal and Hungary before 1985); some have administrated enrolment (France, Portugal), some have integrated (Hungary, France, Portugal) or diversified curriculum (FCB, England). Despite these important differences in systems, the five countries have all been able to develop to varying degrees an institutional regulation of their system on the basis of the bureaucratic-professional model, which combines bureaucratic regulation and joint state–teacher regulation.

National school systems were in fact constructed in the nineteenth and twentieth centuries using an institutional and organisational model combining bureaucratic components of a nation-state responsible for the education of the people with professional components. Bidwell (1965) was one of the first authors to have described and analysed the school or the school system as a "professional bureaucracy" that is concretised to varying degrees in the different systems analysed.

In this model, to successfully socialise young generations which have become bigger, more complex and progressively diffused throughout all social classes, the state first became an educator state, taking upon itself the implementation of education service.[1] This offer of education can be organised in a more or less centralised and differentiated way, but is underpinned by increasingly standardised and identical norms for all components of the system. This goes hand in hand with a division of educational work (vertically and horizontally between levels and subjects) and facilitates an exact definition of functions, roles and the specific competencies required of everyone, which relies on written and precise rules. Additionally, the state set up a hierarchy and controlled the conformity of all agents in the system by establishing rules and procedures to follow. Based on the standardisation of rules and conformity, this organisational form was then justified in the name of rationality and the need on the nation-state scale for the greatest universality possible of rules, thus founding equal treatment and equal access to education. Thus, the bureaucratic dimension of school systems is to be found not only in its structures but also in its principles of legitimacy. According to Weber (1992), the bureaucratic model refers positively to the law as well as a valorisation of rationality in the wider sense, including "rationality in value".

Nonetheless, in view of the complexity of educational tasks to be accomplished, these bureaucratic characteristics have always been associated with a large individual and group autonomy for teachers, an autonomy founded on their expertise and professional skills. Thus, teachers have found themselves granted a wide margin of manoeuvrability their individual teaching activity, notably for coping with the "uncertainties" of their work. They are also closely associated with the management of their careers via their professional or union representatives and with the definition of programmes or pedagogy via a professional elite in charge of defining them (a body of inspectors).

---

[1] We might well have introduced many nuances into this presentation, for example by offering more detail on the chronology of the massification of schooling or by distinguishing the periods of development of primary and secondary education. The construction of standardised norms has, for example, posed more problems for the latter, insofar as most of these countries introduced more diverse types of teaching (general, technical and professional), which pre-existed in various forms and institutions.

This bureaucratic and professional model thus goes hand in hand with modes of regulation at once based on the control of agents' conformity to general rules, socialisation and the spreading of norms, values and skills of teachers and finally consultation and joint regulation of the system by the state and teachers' representatives. This model brings "state, bureaucratic, administrative" regulation and a "professional, corporative, pedagogical" regulation together (Barroso 2000), but with possible tension. In fact, in this system parents and users have practically no say in matters unless by arrangements wherein bureaucratic functioning is adapted to particular situations.

All of the countries studied share some of this model's traits, but it is undoubtedly France and Portugal that even today come nearest to it (Barroso 2000; van Zanten 2002), as well as Hungary (notably by means of its communist regime after 1948).

On the contrary, the FCB (Draelants et al. 2003) and England (Green 1990; Tomlinson 2001) are undoubtedly further removed, notably through less standardisation of norms linked to far greater freedom being granted to local initiatives and to the political and educational conceptions justifying them (a tradition of voluntary initiative and a liberal nature in England and the value of "freedom of instruction" and the room made for school initiatives of religious origins in Belgium). In these two countries, the bureaucratic-professional model has been combined with a model of "community" governance (Barroso 2000), giving legitimacy for local or religious scholastic initiatives (Weber 1922). As we have seen, this is why the countries studied remain characterised by important structural variation, as much involving the degree of centralisation, standardisation and diversification of curriculum, and the more or less strong presence of free choice.

Beyond national particularities regarding relationships established between state, school and civil society, the bureaucratic-professional model is still quite present in all the countries studied and beyond; it has been able to spread not only because of the rather general development of "mass education" but also because of "institutional mimetic" processes (Meyer et al. 1997), the development of an educator state and standard norms that have generally been associated with progress as much on the economic level (growth) as the social (social mobility).

2.3. Partial Policy Convergences Around Some Common Trends

Over the last 20 years, we have observed many significant developments in the modes of institutional regulation in the countries studied; most often they have been fostered by important legislative texts in education policy (like the Education Reform Act of 1988 in England and Wales, "the missions decree" (1997) in the FCB, the laws on decentralisation and deconcentration, as well as a law of orientation (1989) in France) or by a major political turning point like the end of the communist regime in Hungary (1989). The country where the evolutions are undoubtedly still the most modest is Portugal.

These evolutions are partially convergent and involve six trends:

1. *Increasing autonomy of schools*: The promotion (or maintenance) of a form of increasing "devolution" of responsibilities to the schools is seen everywhere (policies relative to "self-governing schools" in England and to the "autonomy of schools" in France, Portugal, Hungary and the FCB).
2. *The search for a balancing point between centralisation and decentralisation*: We observe a trend to decentralise/deconcentrate decision-making in the traditionally centralised states towards intermediate or local decision-making authorities (France, Portugal and Hungary) and a trend to reinforce centralisation in the states that were strongly decentralised at the outset, notably regarding major curricular objectives in terms of competencies to be attained (FCB, England). Furthermore, in England, reinforcement of centralisation has also focussed on the evaluation of students, schools and systems. However, these processes are accomplished with very different means, degrees and timeframes. Moreover, decentralisation and/or recentralisation can take on a rather varied significance depending on the context. Thus, decentralisation/deconcentration appears stronger in France than in Portugal, whereas English "recentralisation" is clearly stronger than that in the FCB where the curriculum centralisation has not been accompanied so far by certification procedures and more centralised evaluation.
3. *The rise of external evaluations of schools and school systems*: Increases in evaluation are above all born from the policies of the central state (either voluntarily or under pressure from users) and at times are ramped up at intermediate or local levels. The degree of development of evaluation, its technical sophistication, its instrumentation as a "steering" tool and its public exposure, however,

are rather unevenly perfected. In fact, in England (and to a lesser extent in France) these plans have been developed most and have really been put to work. Thus, in England, the creation of OfSTED and the setting up of systematic inspections have led to detailed evaluations of performances and the obligation to define plans for the improvement of all weak points, with the possibility of mandatorily closing "failing schools". With the publication of academic results obtained in external evaluation testing conducted throughout student careers (league tables), this evaluation by inspection forms the keystone of official education policy, with the explicit goal of providing important information, to local actors and notably to parents, whose school choice possibilities have actually increased. In France, and to a lesser extent in Portugal, external institutional evaluation has been promoted on a central level (with, for example, the central role of the Department of Evaluation within the French Ministry of Education between 1987 and 1997) as well as on a regional level, but with significant variations in intensity of application and follow-up on the level of academies or regional education directorships. The concrete effect of these evaluations as a regulatory "corrective mechanism" on the system and on the schools still remains minor and their impact above all symbolic (van Zanten 2002). For that matter, in France, evaluations cannot be considered totally external: the majority of evaluation reports are co-produced by the schools and the greater parts of the results remain "confidential", although three "indicators" are released to the press. External evaluation has also developed in the FCB and Hungary, but without having much concrete effect on the daily life of schools nor on public exposure.

4. *Promoting or increasing parents' choice of school*: Parents' possibilities to choose schools are reinforced or maintained in all the countries studied. This may result from a political will, from a desire to relax administrative rules, as well as from a "laisser-faire" attitude on the part of public authorities. In England and Wales, we observe a voluntarist state policy that tends to construct a quasi-market school: besides a greater liberty of choice of school by parents and students, the government has encouraged information for parents on performance. Hence, competition between schools and their increasing management autonomy are supposed to lead to greater quality and better response to the various demands and needs of families. Such a quasi-market in fact exists in the FCB. Freedom of choice of school by parents (guaranteed in the constitution) is accompanied by a mechanism that finances them in terms of the number of students. These institutional arrangements, historically constructed to guarantee philosophical and religious

pluralism, have been maintained in practice despite recognition of their perverse effects, so institutionalised and socially legitimised is "freedom of instruction".

Elsewhere, in France and Portugal it is more social pressure from parents (notably middle class) which has led to a "soft" policy that has relaxed the assigning of children to schools (politically called "desectorisation" in France, which gives parents the possibility of expressing three to five preferences for secondary schools). This policy has been applied differently depending on the academy and period. Yet, this practical or official "relaxing" takes place while seeking to preserve the egalitarian nature of offer (via a common and large curriculum and a will to preserve the social and educational mixity of schools).

In Hungary, a school district map has long co-existed with a tradition of liberalising the choice of school by parents. Thus, it is easy to request and obtain an authorisation for enrolling children outside the family's zone of residence. This tendency towards relaxing parents' choices is fed locally by contexts of demographic decline and an excess of spaces in schools and the development of active choice strategies on the part of families, notably from the middle class (see Sect. 3).

5. *Diversification of curricular offer*: We also observe a trend to accentuate, to a greater or lesser extent, the variety of curricular offer as a way of emphasising the "diversity of choices possible" for students and their parents. This is the case not only in countries where the curriculum was defined in a central and relatively standard way (Portugal, France and Hungary), but also in England, where decentralisation goes hand in hand with the comprehensive school model. In France, for example, possibilities of offering more specialised courses have been authorised, in various ways, on the middle school level: "European classes" and "specially scheduled classes" incorporating optional disciplines like sports and the arts. In England, schools can claim "specialist" status, centred around a domain (commerce, media, etc.) and benefit from increased funding; in Portugal, schools can vary the volume of class hours of different components of programmes within pre-established limits (e.g. non-disciplinary curriculum areas, creation of technological courses in secondary instruction, programmes for failing students). In Hungary, certain schools can specialise in learning foreign languages (bilingual tracks) whereas others specialise with a view to ensuring particular treatment for certain categories of students (special needs students). The policy of diversification of curricular

offer may or may not be combined with policies defining common curricular standards, which are more and more centred on some central subjects (as in England, for example). Emphasis on diversification is less significant in Belgium because of a curricular structure that has been largely diversified from the outset and structured practically into "tracks" as of the third (or even the second) year of secondary instruction.

6. *Increase in the regulation of control of teaching work*: A sixth trend is common to all countries: the trend toward erosion of the individual professional autonomy of teachers, who are subjected to more and more varied forms of supervision of their practices through training, the presence in schools of pedagogical councillors or inspectors (except in Hungary), good practice codes and pressure in favour of teamwork. This weakening of professional autonomy also affects the professional group as a whole, through a weakening of their union organisations' positions in certain countries (above all in England and Hungary).

2.4. Two Models of "Post-bureaucratic" Governance

Even if we might agree that each of these policies is underpinned by models and debates specific to each subject or each country (concerning the management autonomy of schools, the question of free choice, the promotion of a more or less standardised or diversified curriculum, the centralisation or decentralisation of systems, etc.), one can also associate them to broader governance models that cut across these various dimensions: the "quasi-market" model and the "evaluative state" model, both of which share certain "post-bureaucratic" traits that oppose them to the bureaucratic-professional model already presented. We understand by governance models, the theoretical and normative models that serve as cognitive and normative references, notably for deciders, in defining "good ways to steer or govern" the education system. These models include basic values and norms and are simultaneously instruments for interpreting the current situation and guides for action.[2]

---

[2] This idea of model is close to the concept of "référentiel d'action publique" or "policy paradigm" used in cognitive approaches to public policies, which insists on the presence of cognitive and normative references that tend to orient the definition of problems and solutions political actors propose in various areas (Jobert 1992).

2.4.1. Quasi-market Regulation

The market model, or more precisely the quasi-market model, was forged and has been widely promoted in Anglo-Saxon countries by certain neoliberal analysts critical of the bureaucratic model (Chubb and Moe 1990). For them, it is the bureaucratic character of the system that makes it inefficient, and so competitive pressure from users should be fostered to improve it. This model has been promoted by various networks of actors on the international level (international or academic organisations, experts in education policies; Halpin and Troyna 1995; Ball 1998; Whitty and Edwards 1998). Such a model has strongly inspired English policies (as well as further afield in Australia and New Zealand; Whitty et al. 1998) and has been the object of extensive critical literature in the Anglo-Saxon world (see e.g. Ball 1993; Lauder et al. 1999). In this model, the state does not disappear. It still has the important role of defining the objectives of the system and the contents of the teaching curriculum. Yet it gives autonomy to choose the proper means for carrying out these objectives to schools (or other local entities). Additionally, to improve quality and respond to the various demands of users, it installs a quasi-market system. The latter involves setting up free choice of schools by users coupled with a financing of schools relative to the student public they accept (financing on demand) (Bartlett and Legrand 1993). In other words, schools compete to carry out the task of education while referring to centrally defined objectives. Users have the capacity to choose their "school provider" which submits to a good number of rules to be henceforth centrally defined, such as definition of programmes and certification. These schools can then have various statuses, public or private. The central state, via a specialised agency, encourages informing users/clients on the performance, efficacy and efficiency of different schools in such a way that the rationality of users' choices puts pressure on the local schools to improve their ways of functioning.

2.4.2. The Evaluative State or Governance by Results

The evaluative state model (Neave 1988; Broadfoot 2000),[3] or "governance by results", also supposes that the objectives and programmes to be carried out by the education system are centrally defined and that teaching units

---

[3] This model is variously described: some authors call it steering or regulation based on "obligation of results" (Demailly 2001).

enjoy broad autonomy of pedagogical and financial management. The latter are subject to contracts. The central state negotiates goals with local entities (like schools) and delegates responsibilities and additional means for reaching these goals, all of which fit within the general objectives promoted by the public trust authorities and take into account the context of their public and the local school. Elsewhere, a system of external school performance evaluation and a system of symbolic or material incitements, or even sanctions, are set up to favour the improvement of performances and the fulfilment of the "contract" signed between the state and schools (or higher level entities).

What is aimed at then is a process of organisational and professional learning that results in improving the quality of education in these local schools. Thus, the model implies *ipso facto* an autonomy of economic and pedagogical management of schools and an optimisation of their ability to respond to requests made to them by either education control authorities or users. In any case, it involves the diffusion and acceptance of an "evaluation culture" (Thélo 1993) relying as much on institutional self-evaluation by teams seeking to improve their practice and results as on external evaluation.

2.4.3. Two Variants of Post-bureaucratic Regulatory Regime

The two models presented above can be described as "post-bureaucratic" for two principal reasons.

From the perspective of norms and values, they are no longer founded on the legitimacy of reason and rationality in value and law, typical of the bureaucratic model; results (Duran 1999) and the search for efficiency (going so far as obligatory results) are privileged in relation to the rule of law. Rationality remains valorised but is more and more reduced to instrumental rationality. Thus, that very concern for improvement in quality, valorisation of efficiency and "performativity" (Ball 2003) tend to disconnect themselves from the goals they are supposed to serve. Optimisation of instrumental efficiency takes precedence over respect for civic and social engagement and over educational goals – basically – over value rationalities that, in the bureaucratic-professional model, founded both teachers' professional autonomy and the standardisation of norms.

The modes of coordination and control set up for guiding conduct are no longer founded solely on the control of conformity of acts in relation to rules and procedures, as was typical of the bureaucratic model. Other modes of coordination are promoted, founded either on the promulgation of baseline norms (promulgation of "best practices", training sessions, accompanying projects), on contractualisation and evaluation (of processes, results or practices) or on individual adjustment and competition for the quasi-market model. Yet, these modes of coordination remain within the rule of law because an enormous amount of laws, decrees and rules are produced, seen in the fact that more and more conflicts are decided in court and that more and more precautions are taken to avoid administrative non-conformity. This is why the post-bureaucratic regime is indeed a descendant of the bureaucratic regime, even if it is also partially in rupture.

Another point common to these two models is linked to the important role of the state: it defines objectives and sees to maintaining the management of the system. For that matter, a relative autonomy is granted to the schools or local entities. Moreover, the state no longer wants to be seen as the sole offerer of legitimate instruction. Again we note that the optimisation of efficiency and performativity in these two models is matched by an increasing threat to the professional autonomy of the teaching corps unless it is framed by new systems for evaluating its practice and results. Confidence in the professionalism of teachers is slipping away and their professional autonomy no longer seems a sufficient guarantee of the quality of educational services provided (Maroy 2002).

Beyond these common points, a major difference should be underlined: in the quasi-market model, it is above all competitive pressure through the intervention of an "alerted" user-parent that pushes the school to improve the educational service rendered, whereas in the other model, regulation happens more through the evaluation of processes and results and by incitements or sanctions meted out to schools in terms of their progress and results. This system of obligatory results is supposed to serve as a lever in a process of organisational or professional learning on the part of schools. The two models are essentially opposed, then, with respect to the presence or absence of the role of competition and the market as a vector of quality education. Based on the model adopted, some policies are going to rely on the market whereas others will steer through evaluation and results.

In practice, the models of the evaluative state and quasi-market can be combined, as the English case will demonstrate. Yet, these two models intellectually seem indeed distinct to us. In fact, the promotion of the autonomy of schools coupled with an evaluative state can very easily be envisaged without a quasi-market. For that matter, the quasi-market does not necessarily imply the presence of contractualised schools or a reward- or sanction-based evaluation of their results with regard to set goals as the evaluative state model implies. Market competition and its consequences in terms of school attractiveness and the number and quality of students and professors are theoretically postulated as being a strong and sufficient incitement for promoting the improvement of educational practices and adjusting to a variety of needs and demands. Yet, the evaluation of schools' performances in order to favour users' rational choices through information is indeed part of the quasi-market model.

Let us make clear that the quasi-market and evaluative state models are not the only ones present in debates or the only ones inspiring education policies, even if they tend towards hegemony. Thus in the area of evaluation use, Lise Demailly (2001) mentions the presence of "democratic", "pluralistic" and "negotiated" uses in France, which refers to a participative and democratic version of the reform of the educator state. It is opposed to "authoritarian" uses of evaluation in the service of an evaluative state, which may become overbearing and, paradoxically, hyper rather than post-bureaucratic. Here, we have a reference system approaching what Gather Thurler (2001) calls "negotiated steering". The "community" model of governance (Barroso 2000) also finds defenders in both England and Belgium. For that matter, certain political measures can be associated with these models (e.g. the unequal and varied development of various local consultative or decision-making councils wanting to associate parents or local actors with the definition of school projects; Bajomi and Barroso 2002). These more minor models have an influence and can foster resistance to dominant policies within different societies or educational systems.[4]

Thus, paths to modernising educational systems, while open, are as we shall see a product of the system's past, the diversity of governance models and the socio-political relations within each system and nation-state. Yet, these debates and policies basically tend to place themselves in line with the bureaucratic-professional model of regulation; the governance models being compared all seek to correct, rearrange or radically transform the bureaucratic-professional model. This is why we advance the hypothesis of the post-bureaucratic regime of regulation. Within that regime, many variants or models are of course possible. In fact, the idea of a regime can

---

[4] If we do not examine these "community" and "democratic/participative" models here, it is principally because our concern is first of all comparative and we are anxious to understand the central dynamics of European convergence on the level of educational policies along with evolution in the modes of institutional regulations. These countertendencies may nonetheless exist within each national reality. For example, Lise Demailly (2003) points out the resistance and innovative social constructions existing in Lille Academy in terms of evaluation.

be taken either in the political–juridical sense placing the accent on a formal "fundamental" structure that supervises an institutional field and hopes to stabilise the margins of variability of practice, with variation being assimilated as a normal state of affairs, or in the more dynamic sense of the economists of "the French school of regulation", who aim here at a type of systemic logic resulting from the dynamic and dialectical tensions of a system, leading to not only producing regularities but also compatible with limited variations (Théret 1998).

2.5. Variations in Policies and Models

The education policies of the five countries studied are more or less inspired by the post-bureaucratic models and particularly by the evaluative state model, hence the reinforcement of the autonomy of schools and the promotion of evaluation coupled with the reinforcement of central goals and curricular standardisation in countries decentralised at the outset. Simultaneously, traits more inspired by the market model – tolerance and the promotion of free choice, the relative diversification of offer to meet the varied demands of users – have also been developed. Yet, the degree of intensity to which policies are carried out and the proportions applied among these models are very varied. The "exemplary" case of radicalism in reforms is undoubtedly England and Wales, which simultaneously promote the quasi-market and the evaluative state through an explicit and voluntarist policy.

The relative importance of the three authorities that regulate offer (the central government, local authorities and the local market) has changed greatly in England in the last 20 years. Central and market control has been reinforced to the detriment of the capacity for intervention by local authorities. Until the 1980s, the traditional organisation that regulated educational offer was centred on the control of schools exerted by Local Education Authorities (LEA). This control was realised by the definition of norms, direct financing of an ever-increasing character and supervision in the hands of local inspectors who essentially assumed a function of counselling and pedagogical support. The role of central government principally took on a character of encouragement and global policy supervision, to the extent that it influenced and defined lines of orientation for decisions taken by the LEA and by the schools themselves. The national policies striving to promote unified secondary teaching ("comprehensivism"), during the 1960s and 1970s, are an example of this flexible supervisory plan, insofar as the actual definition of concrete unification policies was left to the local level. This gave rise to numerous strategies and plans expressing the different attitudes adopted towards the governmental policy proposed, ranging from militant enthusiasm to radical opposition, from profound transformations to purely formal changes. In this context, the role of the inspection services (HMI) took on a complementary character, faced with the LEAs' intervention, in a "friendly" approach in relation to schools and the professional world of education. Beginning in the early 1980s on the initiative of Conservative governments and taken up by the Labour governments that have followed, the central government has developed a substantial policy of interventionism, encouraging competition between schools and favouring the free choice of parents, notably by means of broadening plans for external evaluation. But the development of evaluation went well beyond the simple need to inform "school consumers". Its source was a logic of regulation of schools and their agents by their results. In this regard, one of the measures crucial to the reorganisation of the HMI and the creation of a – formally independent – governmental agency was centred on the evaluation of schools (OfSTED) and a very incisive plan for their systematic inspection. This has involved detailed evaluation of performance, the obligation to define plans for improvement of all the weak points identified and the possibility of mandatory closing of schools considered in "failure" situations ("*failing schools*"). With the publication of results obtained during external evaluation tests carried out all along student careers ("league tables"), this evaluation plan by inspection forms the keystone of official education policy.

The other countries have experienced less radical evolutions and less directly the effects of voluntarist policies. External institutional evaluation has therefore developed but in a much more embryonic (Hungary, the FCB and Portugal) or rhetorical (France) fashion. They are, for that matter, less oriented by the quasi-market model. The rise of free choice is a practice more tolerated than encouraged here; it is not a matter here of a voluntarist and asserted policy (especially in Portugal and France) even if the legitimacy of parents' choice is more recognised than before in the name of the need to satisfy the various demands of users. But simultaneously in France and Portugal, competition and the market are officially rejected as opposing the valued ideals of equality of treatment for all. In Hungary, free choice is more and more encouraged in practice and has benefited from an "anti-centralising" and rather liberal political climate. In the FCB, it has long existed and generates a de facto quasi-market that is often rhetorically criticised for its ill effects without being practically called into question.

In short, the two models reinforcing the evaluative state and the market inspire the policies of these various countries to very different degrees.

2.6. Effects of Hybridisation and Recontextualisation of Models

The inspiration of education policies by post-bureaucratic governance models does not imply strictly identical policies, not only because of differences in intensity and proportion between the models already mentioned, but also because different situations at the start can lead to different policies even when the baseline models are similar. Thus, as we have seen, certain countries that were very decentralised at the outset, like England and the FCB, tend to recentralise, whereas others decentralise. This movement, which appears contradictory, can be explained by advancing the hypothesis of the rise of the evaluative state in all of the countries concerned. For such a model to emerge, the states that are decentralised at the outset need to define their basic curricular goals on a national level and, furthermore, develop evaluation while accentuating, preserving and developing an autonomy supervised by the schools. Conversely, the centralised states, which already possess a strongly standardised curriculum with national certification tests, should above all increase the autonomy of schools and develop the actors and tools capable of maintaining a close follow-up of them once they have been confronted with external evaluations.

Policies that grant schools autonomy, coupled with the decentralisation/deconcentration of responsibilities towards territorial communities or decentralised state actors, are now altogether strategic in centralised states like Portugal and France. In the FCB, the autonomy of schools was already fairly well developed for some providers and has above all been emphasised in the state schools but not in the Catholic ones. What is really at stake for the central government in England as in Belgium is knowing how to limit or instrumentally ally itself with the major community, intermediate-level actors (the various "organising powers" in the FCB and the LEA in England).

But evolution in the modes of institutional regulation cannot be reduced to *mere contamination effects* by models promoted by various networks of actors on the international level. The conditions for receiving these models should be taken into account, and we observe that governance models promoted do not spread from one country to another like an epidemic (Levin 1998) without a translation process. There is a *hybridisation* effect on these models due to the institutional and ideological contexts proper to each country. The terms in which the policies are going to develop will be largely dependent on the institutional structures, the social relationship and the actors constituting the educational system that developed throughout its history. There is then *a hybridisation* effect of models, consisting in the "superposition, the cross-breeding of different logics, language and practice in policy definition and action, which reinforces their ambiguous and composite character" (Barroso and Bajomi 2002:21). This effect can occur at the policy statement stage as well as during its implementation.

Hence, these policies are not mechanical transpositions of governance models without additional recontextualisation in terms of the material, political or symbolic constraints of the systems they are adapted to. But, as we have already pointed out, these systems are profoundly different at the outset and all contain numerous forms of tensions and contradictions. The result is that these policies are never the pure pursuit of the models mentioned, because these policies simultaneously generate and bear the marks of tensions and contradictions between actors and between the various policy orientations they impel. In other words, due to the fact that educational systems are relatively hybrid and composite at the outset and due to the policy-forming process, policy hybridisation effects develop.

These hybridisation effects can be illustrated in their various national contexts.

Hybridisation in England is first of all linked to the fact that the two models, the evaluative state and the quasi-market, were mixed up by the policies adopted. This hybridisation is partially the result of alternating policies. Thus, in 1988, the Conservative government voted in the Education Reform Act. English analysts see this as a result of the alliance between the New Right – more aware of the need to liberalise and modernise the system (whence the abandonment of school sectors, the promotion of choice and the necessity of raising levels of competence) – and the Old Right – more preoccupied with reinforcing traditional values via a reinforced national curriculum – whereby the two poles agreed on diminishing the power of unions and LEAs (Moore and Hicockx 1994). If traits of the evaluative state were already present (e.g. the possibility of imposing changes in management or teams in "failing schools"), they were reinforced by the Labour government's arrival in 1997. In fact, New Labour has not repudiated the structural reforms carried out by the Conservatives (e.g. the system's division into different types of schools, the possibility of choice by parents, the possibility of schools selecting students and external evaluation programmes) but has above all insisted on new goals to assign to the system in terms of results. It has above all been a question of promoting and raising school standards to deal with the weak results of the English system (through the School Standards and Reform Act, 1998), while developing or reinforcing certain programmes, like guidance and teacher surveillance, in order to improve their practice (Teaching and Higher Education Act). To summarise, New Labour has accentuated the central administration's interventionism (Breuillard and Cole 2003) as well as certain key traits of the evaluative state model, without calling into question various inherited features from earlier periods, except those most closely identified with the conservative ideology (e.g. financial support for "deserving" students to attend private schools; Thrupp et al. 2004).

In the FCB, education policies are always a compromise between the models and the complex, hybrid or even contradictory nature of the system of institutional regulation whose compatibility is far from being assured. A political will for reinforcing external evaluation, which is supposed to favour a better quality system, ends up being heavily constrained by existing institutions and the key policy compromises that founded the system (on freedom of instruction, notably). Thus, the FCB government is going to develop external evaluation programmes but the results will only be rendered public on the system level without publishing results for the various providers or schools, for fear of encouraging competition between them and thus favouring market logic, which the different parties and key actors categorically agree to denounce. Thus, the political actors are led to moderate the evaluative state model and account for the composite or even contradictory character of the institutions and forms of coordination in place, to build a political consensus and to respect constitutional requirements ("freedom of instruction" is in the constitution; see Draelants et al. 2003).

In France, hybridisation shows up in the insistence on developing a "culture of evaluation". The implementation of external or semi-external evaluations has in fact developed without being matched with real institutional or economic sanctions on schools. The declared goal has been that actors "internalise" evaluation as a norm and culture. This absence of sanctions may be interpreted as a measure anticipating the opposition and resistance that the teachers' unions or the teachers themselves might develop towards such a system, given their power in France. Hence, the evaluative state model has been eased to limit such oppositions and has been above all presented as a culture to be adopted.

The hybridisation of new policies with existing practices and institutions can also contribute to producing effects opposite to the goals intended.

Evaluation in France is supposed to be a key tool for correcting and regulating errors and dysfunctions in practice (notably of schools). In the eyes of teachers, it has become a supplementary bureaucratic control, for in its implementation it tends to be uncoupled from real teaching activity. The supposed post-bureaucratic logics of evaluation might in this way be reinforcing dominant bureaucratic logics (Demailly 2001; van Zanten 2002).

In Portugal, the policy of promoting the autonomy of school management finds one of its favourite enablers in the agents of Regional Education Authority who are the decentralised vectors of reforms promoted by the central state; there is thus an autonomy paradoxically promoted by the central state, which tends to relaunch the centralising dynamics already quite present.

2.7. Conclusion

Our analysis of the evolution of modes of institutional regulation is founded on the analysis of education policies that have been applied in the last 20 years, notably those which affect modes of regulation within secondary teaching, in the five countries considered. Hence, the procedure was first to summarise the existing literature. What can we retain as key results?

First of all, we see that certain convergences appear on the level of stating education policies. To different degrees and in different timeframes, everything takes place as if education policies tended to partially converge from the viewpoint of governance models and the regulations they seek to install. On the one hand, certain partial traits of an evaluative state are appearing and we are witnessing a reinforcement of the state's will for evaluation, control and follow-up over "producers" (notably schools and their agents) and the "products" of their educational systems (student attainments), notably by means of evaluation tools. On the other hand, and in a much more variable way, ingredients of a market model are being introduced through the promotion of a plan favouring free choice by users and, more rarely, by capitalising on the virtues of competition between schools. Finally, by reinforcement of their management autonomy, schools are urged to improve their functioning and results in response to the various needs of their users and the goals assigned to them by local or central authorities. The policies of the last 20 years in the countries studied therefore have certain common points: increasing autonomy of schools; the search for a balancing point between centralisation and decentralisation of decision-making; the introduction of more or fewer free choices for parents or even quasi-market mechanisms; the development of diversification in educational offer; and the introduction of evaluation mechanisms or even regulation by results.

The changes the policies have tried to advance in these different domains should not be considered in an isolated way. There are ties between them on which the regulatory and governance models presented shed light. In other words, we can advance the hypothesis that these changes may form a system and that we are undoubtedly witnessing a change in "regulatory regime". The bureaucratic-professional model of the regulation of educational systems, with important national variants, had accompanied the construction and development of the "mass" national educational systems of the 1950s and 1960s. Institutional regulation was based on arrangements such as control of conformity to rules, the socialisation and autonomy of education professionals and the joint regulation (state/teacher's unions) regarding questions of employment or curriculum. That model of regulation has since been undermined by education policies that tend to substitute or superimpose new institutional arrangements on these earlier regulatory modes based on either the quasi-market model (especially in England) or the evaluative state model. Several economic, social and political factors underlie these processes of convergence, but we can only list them without developing them fully: increasing demands by the economy on education, the neoliberal context, the crisis of welfare state legitimacy, anxiety and social demands from the middle classes concerning education and finally contamination effects of transnational models of governance (for more details, see Ball 1998; Maroy 2004).

Yet, these transformations take place with various degrees and to different rhythms and intensities, with more or less contradiction and coherence. Many factors of divergence tend to maintain differences between the various national policies: historical context (ideological, institutional) and path dependencies of the policies, as well as the political games and transactions that could influence either the conception or the implementation of policies. Important differences in education policies may first of all be due to proportions of the baseline models: the market model is used less than that of the evaluative state in most countries, except England. They also depend on the intensity with which measures are applied. Moreover, differences in policies can sometimes be explained by initial differences in systems and by the effects of the hybridisation of models with the practical or symbolic realities of the systems or societies considered. Measures that are apparently close in statement (promoting external evaluation, favouring free school choice, emphasising school autonomy) can in practice have a wide range and significance. In fact, there are some path dependencies that are intertwined with the contamination effect of the transnational models and regulation.

References

Bajomi I, Barroso J (2002) Systèmes éducatifs, mode de régulation et d'évaluation scolaires et politiques de lutte contre les inégalités en Angleterre, Belgique, France, Hongrie et au Portugal, synthèses des études de cas nationales. Deliverable 3, Reguleducnetwork, Lisboa

Ball SJ (1993) Education markets, choice and social class: the market as a class strategy in the UK and the USA. *British Journal of Sociology of Education* 14:3–19

Ball SJ (1998) Big policies/small world: an introduction to international perspectives in education policy. *Comparative Education* 34(2):119–130

Ball SJ (2003) The teacher's soul and the terrors of performativity. *Journal of Education Policy* 18:215–228

Barroso J (2000) Autonomie et mode de régulation dans le système éducatif. *Revue Française de Pédagogie* 130:57–71

Bartlett W, Legrand J (1993) The theory of quasi-markets. In: Legrand J, Bartlett W, *Quasi-markets and Social Policy*. MacMillan, Houndmills

Bidwell CE (1965) The school as a formal organization. In: March JG (ed) *The Handbook of Organizations*. Rand McNally, Chicago

Breuillard M, Cole A (2003) *L'école entre l'Etat et les collectivités locales en Angleterre et en France*. L'Harmattan, Paris

Broadfoot P (2000) Un nouveau mode de régulation dans un système décentralisé: l'Etat évaluateur. *Revue Française de Pédagogie* 130:43–55

Chubb JE, Moe TM (1990) *Politics, Markets and America's Schools*. The Brookings Institution, Washington

Dale R (1997) The state and the governance of education: an analysis of the restructuring of the state-education relationship. In: Halsey AH, Lauder H, Brown P, Wells AS, *Education. Culture, Economy and Society*. Oxford University Press, Oxford, pp 273–282

Demailly L (2001) Enjeux de l'évaluation et régulation des systèmes scolaires. In: Demailly L (ed) *Evaluer les politiques éducatives. Sens, Enjeux, pratiques*. De Boeck Université, Bruxelles

Demailly L (2003) L'évaluation de l'action éducative comme apprentissage et négociation. *Revue Française de Pédagogie* 142:115–130

Draelants H, Dupriez V, Maroy C (2003) *Le système scolaire en Communauté Française*. Centre de Recherche et d'Information Socio-Politique-CRISP, Bruxelles

Duran P (1999) *Penser l'action publique*. Libraire générale de droit et de jurisprudence (LGDJ), Paris

Gather Thurler M (2001) Au-delà de l'innovation et de l'évaluation, instaurer un processus de pilotage négocié. In: Demailly L(ed) *Evaluer les politiques éducatives. Sens, Enjeux, pratiques*. De Boeck Université, Bruxelles

Green A (1990) *Education and State Formation. The Rise of Education Systems in England, France and the USA*. Macmillan, Houndmills

Halpin D, Troyna B (1995) The politics of education policy borrowing. *Comparative Education* 31:303–310

Jobert B (1992) Représentations sociales, controverses et débats dans la conduite des politiques publiques. *Revue Française des Sciences Politiques* 42:219–253

Lauder H et al. (1999) *Trading in Futures. Why Markets in Education Don't Work*. Open University Press, Buckingham

Levin B (1998) An epidemic of education policy: (what) can we learn from each other? *Comparative Education* 34:131–141

Maroy C (2002) Quelle autonomie professionnelle des enseignants? *Revue Internationale d'Education Sèvre* 30:41–50

Maroy C (2004) Regulation and inequalities in European education systems, Final report, Reguleduc Network Research Project, Commission Européenne, 5ème PCRD. Improving socio-economic knowledge base (téléchargeable sur http://www.girsef.ucl.ac.be)

Maroy C (2006) *Ecole, régulation et marché: Une analyse de six espaces scolaires locaux en Europe*. Coll. Education et sociétés, Presses Universitaires de France, Paris

Meyer JW, Boli J, Thomas GM, Ramirez FO (1997) World society and the nation-state. *American Journal of Sociology* 103(1):144–181

Moore R, Hickox M (1994) Vocationalism and educational change. *The Curriculum Journal* 5:281–293

Neave G (1988) On the cultivation of quality, efficiency and enterprise: an overview of recent trends in higher education in Western Europe, 1986–1988. *European Journal of Education* 23:7–23

Thélo C (1993) *L'évaluation du système éducatif*. Nathan, Paris

Théret B (1998) La régulation politique: le point de vue d'un économiste. In: Commaille J, Jobert B, *Les métamorphoses de la régulation politique*. Librairie Générale de Droit et de Jurisprudence, Paris, pp 83–118

Thrupp M, Ball SJ, Vincent C, Marqués Cardoso C, Neath S, Reay D (2004) Additive and Hyper-regulation of Schooling in England: the case of Wyeham. *Recherches Sociologiques* xxxv(2):65–82

Tomlinson S (2001) *Education in a Post-welfare Society*. Open University Press, Buckingham

van Zanten A (2002) Educational change and new cleavages between headteachers, teachers and parents: global, national, and local perspectives on the French case. *Journal of Education Policy* 17(3):289–304

Weber M (1995) *Economie et société* (tome 1). Presses pocket coll. Paris. Agora (1ère édition 1922)

Whitty G, Edwards T (1998) School choice policies in England and the United States: an exploration of their origins and significance. *Comparative Education* 34:221–227

Whitty G, Power S, Halpin D (1998) *Devolution & Choice in Education. The School, the State and the Market*. Open University Press, Buckingham

Chapter 3
Comparing Higher Education Governance Systems in Four European Countries

Harry F. de Boer[1], Jürgen Enders[1] and Uwe Schimank[2]

[1]*Center for Higher Education Policy Studies, University of Twente, Enschede, The Netherlands*
[2]*Fakultät für Kultur- and Sozialwissenschaften, FernUniversität Hagen, Hagen, Germany*

3.1. Introduction

Since the 1990s, "new governance" has been at the forefront of discussions on governance in higher education and elsewhere. "Less government and more governance" has become the widely shared credo (Frederickson 1999:705). Supported by neo-liberal ideologies, authorities and powers have been redistributed across the various levels of higher education systems. In many European countries, coordination has changed from a classical form of regulation by one actor, the state, to forms in which various actors at various system levels coordinate the system ("multi-level multi-actor governance"). Coordination increasingly takes place through interconnected policy levels, ranging from the local to the global level, with a substantial number of actors who in networks of interdependent relationships influence agenda setting, policy development, policy determination, policy implementation and evaluation (de Boer 2006). Generally speaking, we witness the blend of various forms of governance, in which elements of traditional governance, with a key role of the state, self-governance, having a long tradition in higher education, and network governance are present.

In this chapter, we will take a more differentiated and analytical view on governance in four university systems. We will compare changes of university governance in England, the Netherlands, Austria and Germany over the last two decades. For this purpose, we have established what we call the "governance equalizer". After a brief introduction on governance, this analytical tool is presented in the first part of this chapter. The second part addresses broad analytical assessments, with the help of the governance equalizer, of what happened in the four higher education systems. Finally, we will draw some comparative conclusions.

3.2. Governance as the Talk of the Town

Basically the increased attention for governance in the recent years relates to government failures (Pierre and Peters 2000:50–68).

The first and most important reason to reassess governance has been the economic recessions and consequently the accompanying problems of public expenditures in continuously growing systems. More specifically, we can point to the following reasons for rethinking governance in higher education. Many higher education reforms are financially driven and are looking for savings (see in this context Pollitt and Bouckaert 2000).

Second, developments such as globalization, internationalization and Europeanization have also started questioning traditional modes of governance. Literally, "games without frontiers" require new rules and pose actors such as states for new governance questions. Moreover, new powerful actors have entered the scene (the European Union, the World Bank, the World Trade Association or the Organisation for Economic Co-operation and Development). Several of these organizations by the way support the ideological shift towards the market.

Third, we should mention the disappointed achievements of (national) governments. There has been a disillusion with and distrust of etatism. In many cases, governments could not live up to the expectations to resolving societal problems. This is due to not only the limited effectiveness of traditional governmental regulation, but also the towering high expectations. Learning from these experiences, many governments have a more modest attitude, using different ways of organizing the system.

Fourth, there has been an ideological shift towards the market. Universities are encouraged to "sell" their services at various markets. Third party funding, tuition fees and vouchers are just examples of such an incline towards the market. It requires a rethinking of various governance arrangements.

Fifth, the rise of new public management (NPM) as a new organizational approach for the public sector stimulated the rethinking of governance. According to this approach, universities should be managed in a more business-like way. By borrowing instruments and methods from the private sector, organizations should be created in which managers have the right and opportunities to manage (Pollitt 1993).

Comparing Higher Education Governance Systems

Rethinking governance has led to new institutional arrangements in co-ordinating the system. However, a shift in one direction (e.g. less state regulation) does not necessarily lead to a shift in another direction (e.g. more market orientation). This brings us to the analytical part of this chapter, the governance equalizer.

3.3. The Governance Equalizer

To illustrate our analytical perspective with respect to the shifts in governance, we will use an *equalizer* as a metaphor (see Fig. 3.1). An equalizer is an electronic device that allows attenuation or emphasis of selected frequencies in an audio spectrum. It can be used "creatively" to alter the relative balance of frequencies to produce desired tonal characteristics in sounds. In turning to the governance of university systems, we distinguish five dimensions: state regulation, stakeholder guidance, academic self-governance,

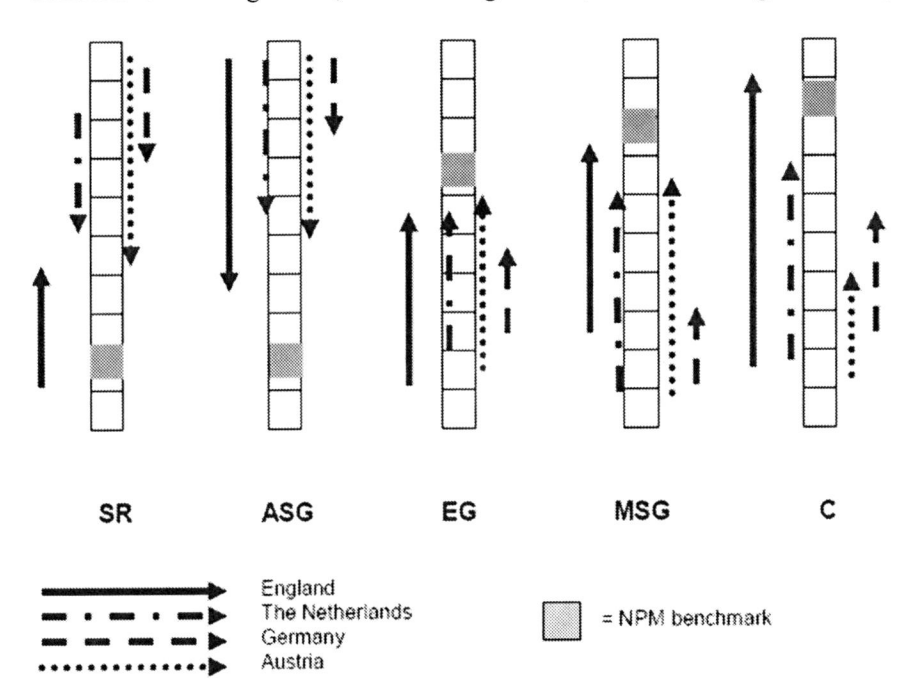

Fig. 3.1. Shifts in university governance of the four countries compared

managerial self-governance and competition. These "selected frequencies in the higher education spectrum" are derived from already existing typologies in higher education research (cf. Clark 1979; Braun and Merrien 1999; Schimank et al. 1999).[1]

- *State regulation* (SR) concerns the traditional notion of top-down authority vested in the state. This dimension refers to regulation by directives; the government prescribes in detail behaviours under particular circumstances.
- *Stakeholder guidance* (EG) concerns activities that direct universities through goal setting and advice. In public university systems, the government is usually an important stakeholder, but is not necessarily the only player in this respect. It may delegate certain powers to guide to other actors, such as intermediary bodies or representatives of industry in university boards.
- *Academic self-governance* (ASG) concerns the role of professional communities within the university system. This mechanism is institutionalized in collegial decision-making within universities and the peer review-based self-steering of academic communities, for instance in decisions of funding agencies.
- •*Managerial self-governance* (MSG) concerns hierarchies within universities as organizations. Here, the role of university leadership – rectors or presidents on the top-level, deans on the intermediate level – in internal goal setting, regulation and decision-making is at stake.
- *Competition* (C) for scarce resources – money, personnel and prestige – within and between universities takes place mostly not on "real" markets but on "quasi-markets" (Le Grand and Bartlett 1993; Bartlett et al. 1998) where performance evaluations by peers substitute the demand pull from customers.

We assume that the governance of a higher education system is made up of a specific mixture of the five dimensions at a particular point of time. The ways of governance are empirical combinations of the various dimensions of governance and these dimensions are *independent and can be*

---

[1] Clark (1979) spoke of coordination by bureaucracy, profession, politics and market, i.e. leaving out managerial self-governance. Later, in his study of entrepreneurial universities, Clark (1998) stressed the importance of executive leadership at universities as a main player in the game. Schimank et al. (1999) did not distinguish guidance by the state, as one kind of stakeholder guidance, from state regulation. Braun and Merrien (1999) as well as Enders (2002) come closest to an explicit distinction between all five mechanisms.

combined with each other in a variety of ways (see also Bradach and Eccles 1989; Wiesenthal 2000). Albeit the assumption that the five dimensions of governance can be turned up or down independently from each other, it is hard to believe that a (radical) shift in one of the dimensions does not cause any reaction in one of the others. The direction and intensity of such a re-action is, however, unknown and should be empirically investigated. Still, our basic argument is that the equalizer indicates that shifts in governance dimensions are not a zero sum game. Regulation and competition are frequently used as opposites ("if one goes up, the other goes down"), but nowadays these "rhetorical friends and deadly enemies" have become more aligned more often (Jordana and Levi-Faur 2004:5). In this respect, the equalizer provides us with a means to find unexpected combinations, as earlier spotted by Clark (1979), when he investigated four pathways of coordination:

> What strange bedfellows we find! In one case, bureaucrats and academic oligarchs work together, to ward off all political forces and to eliminate market interaction. In another, centralization means that political figures and central administrators join together to control everything as much as possible and to declare professors and market processes as unworthy coordinators. In still another, decentralization means not a strengthening of the market but appeasement of academic oligarchs and strengthening of guild-like forms of linkage. (Clark 1979:263–264)

In the subsequent paragraphs, we will use the governance equalizer for a summary description and comparison of what has happened in the four different countries under observation. By doing this, NPM will be used as a normative benchmark.[2] It is not our intention to put forward NPM as an ideal of good governance. But policy-makers in the four countries, as in other countries as well, have articulated the installation of NPM explicitly as an important goal of reform. Thus, we measure actual changes of governance by the intentions of those who initiated change.

We would characterize NPM in terms of our equalizer model in the following way:

State regulation should be rather low. Also, the role of academic self-governance should be marginal. Academics are of course of great importance in the delivery of research and teaching, but under the notion of

---

[2] See Hood (1991), OECD (1995), Ferlie et al. (1996), Pollitt and Bouckaert (2000) and Newman (2001) for different expositions of NPM.

"every man to his trade" these knowledge workers should do what they do best: to discover and transmit knowledge. At the same time, stakeholder guidance, managerial self-governance and competition should be rather dominant governance dimensions in NPM. It posits that the state should outdistance itself from direct control of universities and be primarily concerned with goal setting. Market-like competition, so it is frequently argued, is the best means to increase efficiency and to lower costs. Instead of input control, the emphasis should turn to output control, i.e. ex post evaluation and performance. It is also assumed that efficiency and effectiveness of service delivery will be achieved through the use of private-sector management techniques. To make this happen, excellent managers are needed; and they must be granted reasonable room to manoeuvre as well as the rights to manage (Pollitt 1993:3). Increased competition for resources between and within universities rests on deregulation as well as on the establishment of a new powerful institutional leadership. Greater political guidance and stakeholder involvement is supposed to provide broad long-term orientation to a university's competitive strategy. Spelled out in this way, it becomes clear that NPM is not just a bundle of loosely coupled or even disconnected changes, but rather an integrated approach towards an overall redirection of the entire university system.

3.4. Governance Changes in Four Higher Education Systems

We now turn to the four countries we have studied. For each of them, we will ask, first, where their starting point was: How did the governance configuration of their university system look like at the beginning of the 1980s? Second, we will explore their paths away from this starting point into the direction of NPM: How far have they moved by now, and have they taken at least roughly the "right" direction?

Obviously, limited space does not allow us to give detailed descriptions and interpretations of all the relevant occurrences in the countries. We can only draw very rough, but hopefully recognizable sketches based on more extensive country studies that we rely upon in the following sections. We also cannot do justice in this paper to the different dynamics over time. England was the forerunner of NPM-inspired reforms in the university sector, relatively soon followed by the Netherlands. In these two countries, changes took root in the late 1970s and early or mid-1980s. In Austria and Germany, governance reforms were discussed and implemented in dribs and drabs in the 1980s, if they were implemented at all. In Austria, changes were relatively marginal up to the turn of the century when all of a sudden Austrian universities were shaken up by massive policy changes. Finally, in Germany the arrival of changes in the configuration of governance is visible only very recently.

3.4.1. England[3]

Since the beginning of regular state funding of universities in 1919, the relationship between government and the universities in England has gone through three phases (Halsey 1992). The first one was characterized by a dominance of academic self-governance with government keeping itself at the distance.[4] The second phase which is still going on has been one of increasing state intervention, at first directed predominantly at the new universities and the polytechnics, but then extended to traditional universities as well. Finally, the third phase, overlapping with the second, is characterized by a decisive move towards a market-dominated governance configuration beginning with the 1980's reforms of Mrs Thatcher. Since then, the system has been trimmed rigorously towards NPM – with the Labour government continuing what Thatcher started.

The central point of change has been a strong impetus to increase *competitive pressure*. Motivated by the growing costs of mass higher education and the fiscal crisis of the state, government has insisted on efficiency as the overriding criterion for the spending and allocation of scarce public money. Various attempts have been made to establish "quasi-markets" in higher education and research. The state-induced quality assurance mechanisms for teaching and research have ranged from the establishment of the Research Assessment Exercises (RAE) to academic audits. These efforts have led to more accountability within universities as well as to a more prominent role of the Higher Education Funding Council in England and competition for resources among universities. Those universities which rate low in research performance no longer get any money from institutional funding which, in turn, is a strong disadvantage in the competition for third party funds from the EU or from industry. At the extreme, some universities will have become "teaching-only" institutions sooner or later.

There has been a shift towards more *regulation by the state*, especially for traditional universities. This runs counter to NPM ideals, but from a

---

[3] This section is based on Leisyte et al. (2006).

[4] According to King (2004:19), strong academic self-governance had "a peculiar British twist". Public accountability of universities was maintained through gentlemanly and informal codes of behaviour among societal elites.

starting point of very low regulation. Regulation refers not only to policies at work concerning personnel issues and budgeting, but also to academic affairs, such as research and study programmes. Especially in some focused areas that are politically salient or fashionable, an increased regulatory role of the state can be observed.

At the same time, *guidance by the state and other stakeholders* plays a more important role. Government keeps universities at "arms length" by means of accountability measures, certain pressures for performance and results-oriented management and restructuring (King 2004:19). According to Senker et al. (1999), one of the features of major policies of the English government has been that "users" must be involved in every level of policy formation in the university system. Guidance of universities is also visible in university cooperation with other actors in provision of teaching, research and services to the community as well as in the involvement of external stakeholders in university decision-making processes. In the policy agenda since the 1980s, the link between research and the British economy has been increased as can be seen in those policies that are fostering partnerships between universities and industry and businesses. They urge universities to search for matching funds for research through the creation of strategic alliances. The participation of different stakeholders in the policy-making processes at the state level is seen in respective memberships in advisory bodies, panels of RAE or the boards of research councils. The *managerial self-governance* of universities has been strengthened (Deem 2003:66). One of the major influences on internal governance structures and management was the Jarratt report of 1985 after which universities moved strongly towards corporate management structures (Henkel 2000). University top and middle management have been implementing policies while responding to the external pressures of budget cuts and quality demands. As Slowey (1995) found out, manager-academics respond to the pressures by attempts to mitigate their worst effects on the academics at universities, in other words, serving as a kind of buffer between outside pressures and internal traditional academic values and mode of work. However, it remains to be seen for how long this protective attitude prevails. *Academic self-governance* is still alive, and the voice of the academic oligarchy has not disappeared. This can be illustrated by their role in the RAE at the heart of which is a professionally operated, state-required process of peer-driven academic self-governance. The assessment panels of the RAE are composed of academics. They pass the judgments that have sincere financial consequences for the departments. However, the RAE will now be succeeded by a new, indicator-based mechanism for the allocation of research funds to universities. This will bring about a serious weakening of the academic profession.

3.4.2. The Netherlands[5]

After the Second World War, the involvement of the national government in the university system has intensified. The expanding detailed interference of the national government expressed itself in a wide range of laws, decrees, procedures, regulations and administrative supervision. At the same time, academic matters were to a large extent the domain of the professionals. In fact, academic self-governance and state regulation went hand in hand, as in Germany and Austria. At that time, the other three dimensions of governance were less present, though interest groups have always been strong. The midst of the 1980s brought a time of fundamental changes. In 1985, the government introduced the concept of "steering from a distance". Firm beliefs in the virtues of regulation were replaced by a philosophy in which the government's role is confined more to setting the general framework within which the university system is to operate (Goedegebuure et al. 1993).

This approach embodies first of all a stronger role of the government in *stakeholder guidance*. By means of deregulation and devolving authorities, the government tries to promote a higher level of self-organization of the sector. The government's focus has shifted from rather detailed ex ante measures to ex post evaluations – a shift in steering from input to output control. The universities are explicitly invited to develop their own strategic plans, though within parameters discussed, or negotiated, with the national government. Along these lines, the idea of a contractual relationship between the government and the universities has recently been put forward.

State regulation has, however, not entirely disappeared. The number of rules set by the government is still impressive and the national government is still imposing elements of reform via laws and decrees (Boin et al. 2002). Within this type of control, shifts have been taking place from strong direct regulation towards softer forms of hierarchical control. Deregulation by means of introducing framework regulations, enhancing institutional autonomy and devolving authority to intermediary organizations means that the national government does no longer prescribe in detail how the universities ought to behave. It cannot be denied that the universities have received more discretionary room in certain important issues: lump sum budgeting, administrative and financial control over property and buildings, the appointment and management of staff and the internal organizational structure.

---

[5] This section is based on a country report by de Boer et al. (2006).

At the same time, in the 1990s the tools of government increasingly changed from directives to financial incentives. Performance-based funding has been more widely used. More *competition* for students and research funds can be witnessed (Jongbloed 2003). Universities are expected to display more market-type behaviour and to establish more distinct profiles to place themselves on the market. In terms of research, the competition for grants allocated via the national research council operates "independently" from the national government; the competition for international grants especially from EU framework programs and the competition on the markets of contract research for industry and other customers have all been intensified. In terms of teaching, universities compete both for national and international students.

Another important change concerns the strengthening of *managerial self-governance* within universities. The changes already mentioned have undoubtedly facilitated the university to become a corporate actor which pursues its own strategic plans. It is particularly the role of the executives and managers that has been strengthened. The number of responsibilities and competencies assigned to the central level of the university has grown. Many non-academic matters no longer need final decisions of the ministry but are delegated to the top level of the university. At the same time, decisions about academic matters have been centralized within universities. What was once exclusively decided at the shop floor and departmental level is nowadays dealt with by university rectors or presidents.

Academic self-governance is weakened within universities. Representative bodies, where academics, non-academics and students hold seats, have become advisory instead of decision-making bodies. By the end of the 1990s, collegial decision-making within universities has lost ground. However, similar to England the academic communities continue to play a serious role in national evaluation exercises and in the development of national research programs (de Boer 2003).

3.4.3. Austria[6]

Since the late 1980s, the reorganization of the state–university relationships has been a constant theme of Austrian higher education policy. During the 1990s, the former trend of increasing regulatory state influence on universities has been reversed. Deregulation became the new buzzword for university reforms (Bessenyei and Melchior 1996). The implementation of the reform is still in progress. According to Pechar (2003), the "state

---

[6] This section is based on a country report by Lanzendorf (2006).

model" of university governance was developed even more strongly in Austria than in some other countries of the Humboldtian tradition such as Germany or the Netherlands. University professors traditionally enjoyed far-reaching decision-making powers in academic matters. Practically all non-academic and organizational aspects of university life, however, were until recently left to the discretion of the government.

With respect to *state regulation*, the present situation is thus characterized by strong deregulation. Nowadays, under the Universities Act of 2002, all universities have adopted full legal capacity and thereby have become independent public entities. In addition, the heads of administration of universities are now responsible directly to the rector and not to the Federal Ministry any more. As a corollary, the ministry will soon limit its role to a supervising function with respect to the structure and the results of universities' activities. This means, for example, that university budgets are no longer part of the government budget but are transferred to the individual universities themselves. Since 2004, universities receive public funds in the form of global budgets. Universities are also free in the way they spend the tuition fees they collect. Moreover, each university now is the employer of its staff under private law contracts.

Universities did, however, not have any choice with respect to their new legal nature and status. The state had scheduled the process and the result of the reorganization taking full legal capacity in detail. All universities had to undergo a parallel process of re-constitution, leading to an identical legal status.

As regards *stakeholder guidance*, the comprehensive deregulation that is taking place in the Austrian university sector has not led to total autonomy of universities. Through mission-based agreements, the government retains an important influence on university development. The size of university budgets is linked to performance evaluations and subsequent bargaining with the ministry. Furthermore, some of the former supervisory functions of the ministry were transferred to university councils that are staffed with personalities from outside universities and outside politics. Heads of universities now have to reach an agreement with council members about university development before they get into negotiations with the government about mission-based agreements. Overall, these relatively small and technocratic councils can primarily be understood as guardians of institutional profiling, organizational efficiency and flexibility. Also, a national advisory body on university development has been set up. This "Science Council" will observe changes in the higher education system on behalf of the Education Ministry and formulate proposals for the further development of the Austrian higher education and research system.

To increase *competition* up to now has played a minor role in reform activities. None of the provisions in the Higher Education Act does directly refer to inter-university competition. Nowadays, universities have to define their individual institutional profiles. From recent discussions on the implementation of this aspect of the new legislation the impression arises that institutional profiles are not really meant to enhance competition between universities but rather to support the ministry's country-wide development planning. As far as intra-university competition is concerned, regular evaluation mechanisms were installed in order to reach transparency with respect to the performance of the different units of universities. Rectors conclude performance contracts with deans, but it is not really clear up to now if, and to what extent, the resources of individual departments depend on actual performances. As regards *academic self-governance*, current legislation leaves the decision about the future role of academic bodies to the individual universities. The University Act regulates the state–university relation as well as the composition and tasks of the governing bodies of the universities. It makes, however, only very few provisions with respect to the internal organization of universities below the leadership level. Heads of organizational units are supposed to be university professors, appointed by the rectorate at the proposal of the chair holders of the respective organizational unit. The rectorate also has to conclude performance agreements with them. Apart from this, each university has to enact its own rules of procedure for internal governance. Common features of the new internal governance models designed by the universities are the reduction of competencies of committees at departmental and institutional level to an advisory function and the concentration of decision-making powers in the hands of the deans.

Universities have become independent legal entities. As a consequence, recent reforms introduced central elements of *managerial self-governance* by regulating the staffing, the authority and the tasks of those positions that make up central university leadership. The rectorate made up by the rector and up to four vice-rectors and managers represents the university and elaborates drafts of the main organizational documents (university statute, development plan, organization plan, annual reports). In addition, it supervises all organizational units of the university, negotiates and concludes performance agreements with the minister, acts as superior of all university staff and conducts the appointment negotiations with new professors.

The position of the deans has been strengthened as well. They will have to conclude performance agreements with the rector for their departments and also with the heads of the institutes that belong to their departments. They will also have to distribute the available resources according to the performance of the institutes and develop strategic plans for their departments.

It remains to be seen whether the deans will act according to this new role or go on behaving as before. Some doubts are plausible because it can hardly be expected that deans take tough decisions during a relatively brief period of office when they have to return to the "rank and file" professoriate afterwards.

3.4.4. Germany[7]

The traditional governance configuration of the German university system was characterized by a combination of strong state regulation and strong academic self-governance, similar to what we showed for Austria. This configuration was only complicated, but basically remained the same, when in the beginning of the 1970s other groups besides the professors – assistants, students, non-scientific staff – acquired some rights of participation in university decision-making. Reform debates started quite late in Germany. In fact, the historical chance to build up a radically modernized university system in Eastern Germany after reunification was not taken. Only since the middle of the 1990s, initiatives have been taken in some of the 16 German Länder (states) to go in the direction of NPM;[8] heated debates about whether this is the right way to go are still going on, with the majority of the professoriate being defenders of the status quo.

With respect to *regulation by the state*, the present situation is that all Länder have implemented those aspects of deregulation expected to bring about efficiency gains. They have given more room to manoeuvre to universities and professors with regard to financial resources by abandoning many features of cameralistic public budgeting, introducing, instead, lump sum budgeting.[9] In five Länder, universities can choose their legal status. They may remain public institutions, but can also opt for becoming foundations of civil law. This opens additional options in financial and organizational matters, even though universities remain bound to the public-sector salary structure and its rigid employment categories. The approval of study programmes has been delegated from the ministries to newly founded agencies of accreditation, where academic peer assessment and quality criteria have a stronger role than before. However, it is still up to

---

[7] This section is based on a country report by Kehm and Lanzendorf (2006).

[8] The German picture is especially difficult to draw because the Länder differ considerably in their policies of university reform.

[9] One major reason for granting more financial autonomy to the universities may have been to shift blame for cuts from the ministry to university leaders.

the ministry of a particular Land to decide whether a given programme at a given university fits into the overall planning of that Land.

State authorities are still reluctant to relax regulations relating to the structure and size of faculties and to the appointment of professors. A few Länder have done away with the ministry's right of approval of the appointment of professors, and have delegated this decision to rectors.

Regarding *stakeholder guidance,* since the late 1980s Länder have set up commissions to assess universities and their overall teaching and research performance. These commissions have initiated redirections in study programmes and research priorities. Recently, "management by objectives" has become institutionalized, in the form of mission-based contracts between ministries and universities. In theory, such contracts should not contain concrete recommendations, but only goal statements; in practice, this flexibility is often not granted to universities, allowing ministries to revert to regulation under the guise of NPM. For example, instead of formulating the goal that the share of female students in certain study areas shall be increased by x percent over the next 6 years, leaving the actual pursuit of this goal to each university, ministries prescribe detailed and uniform procedures as well as organizational structures of "gender mainstreaming".

The influence of external stakeholders within newly created university boards varies widely with regard to influence and position. It remains to be seen whether Länder authorities are really willing to accept their recommendations.

There has always been an important element of *competitive pressure* among individual researchers at universities, which has become stronger with increasing dependence upon funds from the Deutsche Forschungsgemeinschaft, the Federal Ministry of Research and Education, the EU and industry. Recently, in order to increase the worldwide competitiveness of the German university system, the Federal government suggested the creation of "elite universities", which it wanted to support generously with extra money to improve conditions for research as well as graduate training. Although the Länder need these additional resources very much, they continued blocking this initiative because they feared that it will lead them into a destructive competition. Finally, a compromise was reached so that now some centres of excellence and some larger research cooperations may profit from additional funding by the Federal government. Rather surprisingly, in the first round of this "excellence initiative" money was not divided proportionally over all 16 states but highly concentrated in southern Germany where, according to a general impression, research conditions indeed are better than elsewhere.

With respect to teaching, most observers expect that fees will be introduced soon everywhere. In January 2005, some Länder won a lawsuit at the constitutional court against the Federal government's prohibition of fees. Fees might result in increased competition for students. Meanwhile, other measures to increase competitive standing include a new salary scheme for professors, laid down by the Federal government and allocating about one third of salary according to performance.

In research as well as teaching, there is no direct monetary impact of demand on supply. Accordingly, because most markets within the system are but "quasi-markets" evaluations of research and teaching are necessary in order to ascertain the relative position of a university, a faculty or an individual professor. All Länder have begun evaluations; in some, e.g. in Lower Saxony, evaluation agencies have been established. Evaluation methods and criteria differ considerably. In most cases, some kind of peer review is established; but there are also examples of indicator-based formulas, mechanically used to distribute parts of public funding to universities.

Turning to *managerial self-governance*, during the 1990s the formal powers of rectors and deans increased in all Länder. Many issues can now be decided without a majority in the university senate or the faculty council. In six Länder, deans now allocate financial and personnel resources on their own.[10] Terms of office for these positions have been extended. Deans who were traditionally elected for 2 years now serve four. In five Länder, deans now need dual approval – not only from their faculty but also from the rector. They begin to be seen as important "men in the middle" who not only represent their faculty's interests to the rector but are also supposed to implement the rector's policies within their faculty – if necessary, against the will of the majority within their faculty council. All in all, the system is acquiring elements of hierarchy.

Still, *academic self-governance* stays alive in a more informal way. At the moment, most measures to build managerial self-governance remain incomplete. The consensus-oriented culture of the academic profession compels many in leadership positions to act as if they had no new powers. Thus, formal competencies remain unused, and consensus, at least among professors, is still sought by rectors and deans. One reason for this is that those in leadership positions know that one day they will return to the "rank and file", and they do not want to make enemies among those who may come into power after them. But the more important reason for "cooperativeness" is that many have internalized the traditional organizational culture of consensus during their long academic socialization.

---

[10] Excluded are resources personally dedicated to individual professors.

3.5. Conclusions

Using our governance equalizer to put all four country descriptions into one picture, several conclusions can be drawn.

Obviously, the *degree* of change varies between the four countries (the lengths of the arrows differ). The most profound changes have apparently taken place in England and in Austria. Significant shifts in England are no surprise because the Thatcher regime in the 1980s was known for its drastic measures in the public sector. Moreover, the English system has been confronted with the massification of higher education rather late. The Austrian degree of change is more remarkable. After years of standstill, many reforms have taken place in a rather short period of time. The Dutch have by and large a middle position; reforms have gradually been implemented since the midst of the 1980s. Germany seems to be the most "conservative" country, except for an increase in competitive pressures. Nevertheless, the German system is clearly in motion as well.

A second observation is that the *points of departure* have been to some extent identical. This is no surprise since three of the four higher education systems, used to be known as 'continental systems', to a large extent are based on Humboldtian notions. The English system has rather different historical roots, especially manifested in the different role of the state towards higher education.

A third observation is that some *variety* can be found for each of the dimensions of the governance equalizer among the four countries. Austria is, for instance, not always ahead of the Netherlands. Especially as regards strengthening competition in the university system, change in Austria is not very profound, whilst rather severe in the Netherlands. Another exceptional phenomenon concerns state regulation of universities in England. Traditionally governmental regulation was rather weak, and now it has actually been turned up instead of down, as it has in all other countries.

A fourth observation is that besides the differences between the countries there exist basic *similarities* as well. The governance of the university sectors in all four countries has undergone substantial change, in most respects rather gradually (with Austria as the exception). Most of the changes are going into the direction of our normative NPM benchmark.

This, however, does not mean that the picture is clear. In fact, there is a complex and somewhat disorderly mixture of the five governance dimensions in all four countries. It remains to be seen whether these are simply snapshots of an intermediary state of affairs, or whether hybrids of nation-specific traditional configurations of governance with NPM elements will permanently stay as path-dependent results of current reforms.

However, the picture certainly indicates that the "good old days" of bureau professionalism as a mode of coordination have gone. This part of the analysis underlines the observations in the beginning of our chapter where we described the fall of traditional modes of governance. State regulation and self-governance, once strong and dominant allies, are blended with other governance dimensions.

Fifth, it may appear that academic self-governance is "going down the drain". At first sight it looks as if whatever new powers the university leadership and external stakeholders win, the academic profession loses. But contrary to common belief, this is by no means a logical necessity; it is at least too soon a conclusion. Academic self-governance has been a striking feature in many higher education systems. The "fact" that they lose some of their dominance does not mean that they have completely lost their voice. Their position compared with the past may be weakened but their present-day powers are still visible. Within a university, one can imagine a coexistence of strong leadership with a strong professoriate. And we see that academics continue to play their part in the governance of the university system. The *individual* academic's influence and power to defend his own status and autonomy has weakened, as well as the formal collective power of academics in intra-university collegial bodies. But especially through mechanisms of peer review, academics have a clear *collective* impact on policies and decisions of resource allocation; and this impact will even grow because competitive pressure on "quasi-markets" depends on peer review.

Sixth, it is not only with respect to this governance dimension that we are well aware that our descriptions of the four countries so far have been confined mainly to the macro level of analysis. In this paper, we have described and interpreted political decisions and only here and there, tentatively, processes of implementation. Our bird's eye view cannot adequately capture what happens on the meso level of implementation of these decisions within universities. Perhaps, there is such a strong resistance on this level that reforms are blocked; perhaps, only facades of reform are erected on the front stage whereas on the backstage everything remains the same. Finally, identifying the real effects of implemented reforms on research as well as teaching means stepping down even further to the micro level of the day-to-day work of individual academics and research groups. It may be that big changes in the governance configuration have only very small effects on research conditions; or the other way round, small governance changes perhaps show strong effects on research. Further research should focus on the meso and micro levels in order to complement the macro findings used for this analysis.

Finally, reflecting upon the governance equalizer as a new analytical tool for a comparative approach to study governance change, we are quite satisfied with its heuristic value. At a single glance, striking similarities and differences in time or across countries become visible. Of course, each of the five dimensions is in fact made up of a number of aspects and forms a rather complex index. Ideally, we should be able to operationalize each dimension as a weighted list of indicators and to subsume concrete phenomena under a specific indicator measuring the degree of change. The task for further research is thus to move towards such a more controlled and reliable use of the governance equalizer.

Acknowledgements

This chapter presents results from a research project on "Decision making processes in management and self-governance models of universities and their consequences for research" supported by the Deutsche Forschungsgemeinschaft. The project group consists of Harry de Boer, Jürgen Enders, Barbara Kehm, Ute Lanzendorf and Uwe Schimank. The authors of this chapter would like to thank the other researchers in the project team for their project contribution.

References

Bartlett W, Roberts JA, Le Grand J (1998) (eds) *A Revolution in Social Policy: Quasi-market Reforms in the 1990s*. The Policy Press, Bristol

Bessenyei I, Melchior J (1996) *Die Hochschulpolitik in Österreich und Ungarn – Modernisierungsmuster im Vergleich*. Peter Lang, Frankfurt am Main

Boin A, Huisman J, van der Meer FM, Toonen TAJ (2002) Rearranging government. Transformation of regulation and control in the Netherlands. Paper presented at the workshop *Watchful Eyes, Oversight Explosion, and Fire Alarms? Cross-National Perspectives on Control over Government*, London

Bradach JL, Eccles RG (1989) Price, authority and trust: from ideal types to plural forms. *Annual Review of Sociology*. 15:97–118

Braun D, Merrien FX (1999) Governance of universities and modernisation of the state: analytical aspects. In: Braun D, Merrien FX (eds) *Towards a New Model of Governance for Universities? A Comparative View*. Jessica Kingsley, London, pp 9–33

Clark BR (1979) The many pathways of academic coordination. *Higher Education* 8:251–267

Clark BR (1998) *Creating Entrepreneurial Universities: Organizational Pathways of Transformation*. Pergamon Press, Oxford

de Boer H (2003) Institutionele analyse en professionele autonomie. Een empirisch-verklarende. Studie naar de doorwerking van de wet "Modernisering Universitaire Bestuursorganisatie" (MUB) (dissertatie).CHEPS, Enschede
de Boer HF (2006) Governance in het hoger onderwijs. In: van Hout H, ten Dam G, Mirande M, Terlouw C, Willems J, *Vernieuwing in het hoger onderwijs. Onderwijskundig handboek*. Van Gorcum, Assen, pp 327–340
de Boer H, Leisyte L, Enders J (2006) The Netherlands – 'steering from a distance'. In: Kehm BM, Lanzendorf U, *Reforming University Governance. Changing Conditions for Research in Four European Countries*. Lemmens, Bonn, pp 53–92
Deem R (2003) The link between teaching and research: experiences of academic staff in two university education departments. Paper read at SRHE conference *Research, Scholarship and Teaching: Changing Relationships?*, December 16–18, Royal Holloway College, University of London, Egham
Enders J (2002) Governing the academic commons: about blurring boundaries, blistering organisations, and growing demands. The CHEPS Inaugural Lectures 2002
Ferlie E, Ashburner L, Fitzgerald L, Pettigrew A (1996) *The New Public Management in Action*. Oxford University Press, Oxford
Frederickson HG (1999) The repositioning of American public administration. *Political Science and Politics* 32:701–711
Goedegebuure L et al. (1993) International perspectives on trends and issues in higher education policy. In: Goedegebuure L et al. (eds) *Higher Education Policy. An International Perspective*. IAU and Pergamon Press, Oxford
Halsey AH (1992) *Decline of Donnish Dominion: The British Academic Professions in the Twentieth Century*. Clarendon Press, Oxford
Henkel M (2000) Academic Identities and Policy Change in Higher Education, London: Jersica Kingsley
Hood C (1991) A public management for all seasons? *Public Administration* 69:3–19
Jongbloed B (2003) Marketisation in higher education, Clark's triangle and the essential ingredients of markets. *Higher Education Quarterly* 57:110–135
Jordana J and Levi-Faur D (2004) The politics of regulation in the age of governance in Jordana J and Levi-Faur D (eds.) *The politics of regulation: institutions and regulatory reforms for the age of governance,* Cheltenham UK: Edward Elgar: pp 1–28
Kehm BM, Lanzendorf U (2006) Germany – 16 Länder approaches to reform. In: Kehm BM, Lanzendorf U, *Reforming University Governance. Changing Conditions for Research in Four European Countries*. Lemmens, Bonn, pp 135–186
King R (2004) Governing universities: varieties of national regulation. Paper read at CHER conference *Public–Private Dynamics in Higher Education: Expectations, Developments and Outcomes*, September 17–19, University of Twente, Enschede
Lanzendorf U (2006) Austria – from hesitation to rapid breakthrough. In: Kehm BM, Lanzendorf U, *Reforming University Governance. Changing Conditions for Research in Four European Countries*. Lemmens, Bonn, pp 93–128

Le Grand J, Bartlett W (1993) (eds) *Quasi-markets and Social Policy*. Macmillan, Houndmills

Leisyte L, de Boer H, Enders J (2006) England – the prototype of the 'evaluative state'. In: Kehm BM, Lanzendorf U, *Reforming University Governance. Changing Conditions for Research in Four European Countries*. Lemmens, Bonn, pp 17–52

Newman, J. (2001) *Modernising Governance. New Labour, Policy and Society*. Sage, London

OECD (1995) *Governance in Transition: Public Management Reforms in OECD Countries*. OECD, Paris

Pechar H (2003) In search of a new profession: transformation of academic management in Austrian universities. In: Amaral A, Meek LV, Larsen IM (eds) *The Higher Education Managerial Revolution?* Kluwer, Dordrecht, pp 109–130

Pierre J, Peters BG (2000) *Governance, Politics and the State*. Macmillan, Houndmills

Pollitt C (1993) *Managerialism and the Public Services. Cuts or Cultural Change in the 1990s?* (second edition). Blackwell, Oxford

Pollitt C, Bouckaert G (2000) *Public Management Reform: A Comparative Analysis*. Oxford University Press, Oxford

Schimank U, Kehm B, Enders J (1999) Institutional mechanisms of problem processing of the German university system: status quo and new developments. In: Braun D, Merrien FX (eds) *Towards a New Model of Governance for Universities? A Comparative View*. Jessica Kingsley, London, pp 179–194

Senker J et al. (1999) *European Comparison of Public Research Systems*. University of Sussex. SPRU, Sussex

Slowey M (1995) Reflections on change – academics in leadership roles. In: Slowey M (ed) *Implementing Change from Within Universities and Colleges*. Kogan Page, London

Wiesenthal H (2000) Markt, Organisation und Gemeinschaft als 'zweitbeste' Verfahren sozialer Ordnungsbildung. In: Werle R, Schimank U (eds) *Gesellschaftliche Komplexität und kollektive Handlungsfähigkeit*. Campus, Frankfurt, pp 44–73

Part Two

Performance Monitoring and Evaluation

Chapter 4
Purpose and Limits of a National Monitoring of the Education System Through Indicators

Stefan C. Wolter

Swiss Coordination Center for Research in Education, Aarau and University of Bern, Bern, Switzerland

4.1. Introduction

National education systems have traditionally been areas of society and state governance exposed to heavy political and normative control. This is still true today to a varying extent in many countries. Awareness in the political community of the immense guidance and governance issues involved in the education system developed in particular in the post-World War II period with the breakneck expansion of the non-compulsory education system and the growing recognition of the social and economic importance of education. Although the widespread regulatory fervor in the industrialized nations in the 1950s and 1960s was eventually abandoned, a return to a purely normatively guided education policy was no longer imaginable in view of the significant deployment of national economic resources in the education system and the importance of human capital for national advancement and development. Under the prevailing circumstances, it would have been simply too costly to use trial and error as a guiding principle in the political governance of the education system. The same applies to normatively motivated decisions that would contradict an alternative option based on rational and objective analysis.

Although this certainly does not address the full complexity of the issues involved, it is nevertheless possible to single out one event that was crucial to the new government management paradigm in the education system and elsewhere. The Blair government was probably the first to implement a theory-based, institutionally supported philosophy of political management and administration claiming to be based on evidence.[1] Although unadulterated evidence-based policies are not viable in the face of political competition, evidence-informed policies at least represent a significant improvement in terms of the rationality of political decision-making. Incidentally, a decision on the part of governments to base their actions on evidence as far as possible is not entirely altruistic and may reap dividends despite the awareness that a reduction in policy-making freedom arising from the evidence produced may be painful for politicians.[2] It is much harder for subsequent governments to overturn evidence-based decisions than to reverse decisions that are purely normative. Hence, for those political leaders wishing to bring about a long-term and sustained impact in various political areas, the better and more comprehensive their information is regarding the current status, the interrelationships and effects and consequences in the education system, the better equipped they will be to do so.

Evidence or information-based governance and management of the education system is both more urgently needed and more workable today than was the case just two or three decades ago. This is due to a number of intermeshing trends. To meet the growing need for data about the education system, most industrialized countries invested immense sums in education statistics and in administrative information systems. In this, the OECD played an important role to standardize statistics and thus make them internationally comparable. This was paralleled by huge progress in social science empirical methodology. One very significant development was the establishment of new statistical evaluation methods which were first used in other areas of government activity and regulation such as the labor market and healthcare but which can be usefully applied to virtually any area. Improvements in data handling and interpretation methods also helped to improve the statistical basis. Nevertheless, the social science research community also came to realize that observation of real-life phenomena on its own is not a sufficient basis for investigating causal relationships or the impact of new policies. Experimental or quasi-experimental – in other

---

[1] See, e.g., "Modernising Government White Paper", 1999 (http://www.archive.official-documents.co.uk/document/cm43/4310/4310.htm), or more specific on education: "Educational Research and Development in England", Examiners Report, 2002 (http://www.oecd.org/dataoecd/17/56/1837550.pdf).

[2] This is not a new concern, as the following historical citation shows: "When the Max Planck Society was considering plans for an interdisciplinary education research institute, a German minister for education worriedly noted: 'But that would pave the way for scientifically founded criticism of the minister for education's work.'" (translated quote from Becker 1971:17).

words, deliberately constructed – variations of the kind originally employed as standard procedure in natural science and later in medicine are also necessary as a basis for exploring social phenomena. The advances in the areas of statistics and research methods that were made in the area of education research are, in turn, indispensable for policymaker acceptance of an evidence-based or even just an evidence-informed management paradigm.

This chapter is divided into five parts. Part one (Section 4.2) briefly presents the developments prompting Switzerland to build up a national reporting on the education system within an extensive education monitoring project and the circumstances under which the request to set up this system was issued. Part two (Section 4.3) specifically explores to what extent statistical indicators are viable as a means of managing the education system as well as the limitations statistical indicators are subject to. Part three (Section 4.4) explains the set-up and the thoughts and ideas underlying the first Swiss Education Report. Part four (Section 4.5) uses selected practical examples and issues to illustrate the problems and limitations of using strict indicator approaches. Part five (Section 4.6) summarizes the experience gathered while compiling the first Swiss Education Report and presents the initial conclusions, which may be of benefit in terms of future reporting on the education system.

4.2. Knowledge-Based Governance and Management of the Education System Through Monitoring

In response to the international trends outlined above, Switzerland – albeit with the country's typical tardiness[3] – decided to expand and improve its education governance system through the use of standardized tools of education monitoring and education reporting. Back in the 1990s, ongoing efforts in the area of education statistics, primarily by the Swiss Federal Statistical Office, had progressed to the point where there was a general concurrence that indicator systems should be used to lay the foundations for a better informed and hence more rational education policy. These efforts in the area of education statistics were taken up by the political community toward the end of the 1990s. The idea in some quarters was that a narrowly defined set of indicators numbering no more than a dozen would be sufficient to supply the information needed to guide and govern the

---

[3]Compared with the Anglo-Saxon countries but not with its neighboring countries.

education system.[4] Then, in 2004, the Swiss Conference of Cantonal Ministers of Education (EDK) decided to launch an education reporting program together with the federal authorities within the scope of a national education monitoring project.

Education monitoring is an extensive process involving, among other things, periodic education benchmarking using tools such as PISA and its younger Swiss counterpart, HarmoS. These individual monitoring projects are intended to generate governance information for specific educational areas and issues. The Swiss Education Report is intended to combine this knowledge with information from other sources – administrative, statistics, research – to give a composite picture. The first Swiss Education Report was published at the end of 2006 and has pilot status. The work done on this first national education report, drawn up by the Swiss Coordination Center for Research in Education (SCCRE), will provide initial and important information on whether and to what extent, and under what conditions and limitations, an entirely indicator-based information system would be able to supply the information needed as a basis for guiding and governing the education system. Without wishing to preempt the conclusions presented later in this essay, it can be stated right here and now that, as a general rule, purely statistical indicators produce governance information that is neither unequivocal nor complete. However, it must also be pointed out that monitoring is intended as a diachronic process. Hence, what matters is not only an inventory of facts at a single point in time, but also an observation of events and developments between different points in time. The education report is intended to be published at 4-year intervals. In these 4 years, the findings from the first report will be processed by the education administration, statistics and research communities and are intended to guide education policymakers in defining issues and items of special interest for the subsequent education report. Thus equipped, the next education report will then present a follow-up inventory of the new status quo, taking a close look at the relative changes versus the prior report as well as presenting the current state of the education system. In order to really be able to evaluate the importance and benefit of the education reporting system, it will hence be necessary to await the completion of at least one full report cycle, i.e. at least two reports.

---

[4]This idea was in a striking contrast to the similar and longstanding international indicator project of the OECD, which in its annual publication (Education at a Glance) already in its edition of the year 2000 counted almost 400 pages.

4.3. Indicators and Indicator Systems

According to the usual definition, indicators constitute quantitative information on the status, characteristics, proficiency or effects of a system. In other words, they constitute empirically verifiable information which, ideally, will provide a basis for theoretically founded conclusions about a given system. Although it has long been standard international practice to use indicators, in the education system as in other areas, the definition, selection and relationship between individual indicators is still fraught with unsolved issues.[5] An indicator system that satisfactorily resolves all these questions has not emerged to date. The main reasons are briefly presented below:

(a) The various indicators should be operationalized in a manner allowing an unequivocal conclusion about the matter under investigation. Indicators should go beyond the purely informational dimension of statistics (see, e.g., Kanaev and Tuijnman 2001); otherwise, they would merit the term "descriptors" rather than "indicators". To deserve being called "evaluative", indicators must meet two main conditions. First, to ensure that each of an indicator's values permits an unequivocal conclusion with regard to a prevailing state or a need for action, there needs to be a benchmark for the chosen indicator. However, absolute standards (or even consensus standards) that would permit a unique interpretation of a particular indicator value are very rare. For instance, commonly used collections of indicators (Education at a Glance of the OECD, for example) give the reader virtually no precise pointers as to how a specific value should be interpreted, just the raw statistical data (see also Thomas and Peng 2004). One of the few exceptions is international assessment tests (PISA, etc.), which, on the basis of the judgment of experts, define scales within which the observed performance values are matched to specific proficiency levels. The lack of measurable criteria for evaluating indicator values has also to do with the fact that education policymakers (intentionally or unintentionally) have neglected to define precise, i.e., operationalized, goals for what the education system is expected to perform. In the absence of precisely defined

---

[5] From the German-speaking literature, see in particular section A2 on the status of indicator research from education reporting in Germany (Konsortium "Bildungsberichterstattung für Deutschland" (2003): Bildungsberichterstattung für Deutschland: Konzeption. Frankfurt am Main/Berlin) und den Bildungsreform Band 4 Bericht (Van Ackeren 2003).

criteria for evaluating a particular indicator reading, the observer must rely either upon ipsative (or self-referential) or reference group-related outcome measures. The ipsative approach attempts, on the basis of variation over time, to at least permit a directional conclusion as to whether the indicator has improved or deteriorated since the last measurement. The reference group approach endeavors to generate findings derived from international, national, regional or inter-institutional variations in values. Compared with absolute or consensus-based standards, both these approaches are mere stopgaps as they are not a sufficient basis for truly satisfactory evaluation. Nevertheless, for want of a better alternative, the Swiss Education Report has no option but to resort to these approaches in most areas.

(b) Second, the indicator's relevance in terms of the education policy objective must be theoretically and empirically validated. In other words, the indicator must be relevant to the achievement of a particular goal or as a basis for deciding for or against a political governance option. While the absence of standards or benchmarks imposes limitations in particular on the evaluation of output and outcome indicators, the relation to the output or outcome is crucial in the case of process and context indicators. All too frequently, process or context information, which has to be controlled or taken into account by the education policy community, whose actual relevance to education output and outcome is not conclusively proven, is observed (class size is one example; this will be explored in greater detail in Section 4.5). Mere correlations, particularly on outcomes (such as health, labor market status, crime, etc.), are all too often simplistically interpreted as indicating causality, resulting in the observation of indicators which may be entirely irrelevant in terms of the desired outcome. There is also a tendency to compare and contrast individual indicators (input–output, for example) in a manner that communicates a supposedly clear cause–effect relationship, even in cases where such a relationship is only assumed but has not been proven. In most cases where a relationship with the output or outcome can be assumed to exist, the strength of the relationship is unknown. Consequently, variations in the indicator do not enable an unequivocal conclusion with regard to the change in output/outcome thus produced. If, say, very large changes in the process variables are necessary in order to produce tiny changes in output, caution should be exercised when interpreting changes in the indicator (and vice versa).

(c) At best, indicators show a need for action. However, as a general rule, they produce little information on the available options. Even more rarely do they indicate specific actions that need to be taken. If an indicator shows that the mathematics proficiency of the students of a particular country is not quite up to scratch, this information on its own neither indicates how the students' mathematics skills can be improved (see also Section 4.5), nor does it show the consequences or impact of this lack of proficiency. These limitations in terms of the meaning of indicators are not a problem as long as people are aware of them. The problem is that many indicators are communicated in a manner that creates a different impression, which may lead to poorly thought-out education policy measures.

(d) A single indicator is generally unable to present a full picture of the item in question. Indicators are therefore parts of an indicator system whose composite information needs to be taken as a basis for evaluating a system's state of proficiency. However, as soon as a number of different indicators are projected into a system, it is clear that the interrelationship between the indicators is of key importance. It is easily apparent that a number of different inputs feed into the education process. What is not so readily apparent is how these individual inputs interrelate. The impact of an input may complement that of another input, i.e., the deployment of input A also enhances the impact of input B. Conversely, the two inputs may compete with each other such that increasing input A would concomitantly reduce the impact of input B. Manifold and complex interactions between the indicators mean that the composite information generated from an indicator system must not be understood as merely constituting the sum of the information generated by the individual indicators. The problem is that so little is known about the interdependence between indicators that a greater degree of detail (i.e., more indicators) in an indicator system does not necessarily correlate with a higher degree of evidence or utility for the user.

For reasons of space, other important matters such as data quality, level of aggregation, comprehensibility of the indicator cannot be entered into in greater detail here.

The Swiss Education Report does not solve the problems inherent in using indicators and indicator systems as a basis for guiding government and public policy. However, a threefold approach endeavors to minimize the problems as far as possible:

1. Right from the beginning, it was accepted that a clearly limited small set of indicators would not be able to describe the whole of the education

system in all its complexity. Any such endeavor would have been impossible, merely in view of the multiple goals pursued with the education system. In addition, the indicator set must also be differentiated and diverse enough to reflect all the education levels and types with all their particular specificity. Finally, the indicator set must be flexible enough to keep pace with continually evolving education policy issues and challenges. Although fixed sets of indicators make intertemporal comparison easier, the fact that an indicator was measured in the past is not an adequate guarantee that it addresses an issue that is relevant to the education system in the present.

2. An analytical framework (see Section 4.4) was defined in which the indicators are integrated. However, unlike the policy pursued with most known education reports, the authors did not act according to the principle, "you show what you have". Instead, they asked themselves first which indicator would be necessary to answer the relevant question within the analytical framework. If there was no indicator that met the authors' desires (as was often the case), the indicators used, instead of the desired indicators, were described and flagged as proxy information. Accordingly, much of the information is more akin to descriptors rather than indicators. The consequence of this approach is that the report in particular highlights those areas where we know little, whereas other reports tend to highlight those areas where knowledge is abundant. However, for the first education report in a continuous monitoring project, the chosen approach is more useful in terms of building up governance knowledge.

3. Much importance is placed on using additional information from other areas as a means of improving the understanding and interpretation of the statistical information. The vast majority of relevant statistical indicators are not self-explanatory; nor is their meaning always clear in view of the plethora of complex interdependencies in the education system.[6] Therefore, research findings and education administration data have been processed in order to understand the statistical indicators, to identify their relationship with other indicators and, ultimately, to estimate their impact on the education system. In keeping with the limitations already noted, this approach also reveals what the indicator cannot do or points out potential misinterpretations that one must be beware of.

---

[6]An example is the rate of return on education as an indicator. Although the return on education is definitely a better outcome indicator than simply salary differentials between various education levels, the indicator itself is commensurately more difficult to understand (see, for example, Wolter and Weber 2005).

4.4. Framework and Objectives of the First Swiss Education Report

Like other national education systems, the Swiss education system is divided into education levels and types.[7] Institutional differences between the education levels and types and differences in education goals, level- and type-specific organization, administration and responsibilities justify structuring the education report on the basis of the various education levels and types. Finally, it is important to remember that, as a rule, statistics and research activities are also based on the specific individual education levels and types. Although this makes it easier to understand how a specific part of the education system functions, it makes it more difficult to compare the various levels. Hence, structuring the education report on the basis of education levels is logical but comes with certain limitations. One such limitation, for instance, is that individual impacts of education (outcomes), for example on people's health or social behavior, are not attributable to a specific unique education level or education type, but constitute an outcome of cumulative education processes. These aspects are, to some extent, accorded too little attention in this education report. However, it must be added that the relationship between the level of education attained by an individual or the entire population and the above-mentioned education outcomes is difficult to determine and is not always unequivocal, in particular in terms of causality.

4.4.1. Context Information

The introduction to the report as a whole gives context information of importance to the education system in general. This context information presents the exogenous framework conditions for the education system as a whole. The sections on the individual education levels and types then take a more profound look at the factors emerging from the context information that are of specific importance in the particular situation. In order to arrive at a comprehensive understanding of the education system, it is important to bear in mind that the education system cannot be evaluated from an internal perspective only. An extensive analysis and evaluation of the education system requires co-analysis of the prevailing interdependencies with other social, economic and political processes and

---

[7] Adds to that, that there is not really a Swiss educational system but 26 different systems as the governance of most parts of the educational systems lies in the hands of the cantonal authorities.

frameworks. Developments pertaining to family structures, public finances or migration policy may be just as relevant to the success or failure of the education system as the efforts of the players in the education system per se. That said, it must be stated that, for all the importance of these general context conditions in terms of how the education system operates, hard empirical facts about their actual impact on the education system are fairly thin on the ground. The availability of knowledge in this area seems to be in inverse proportion to its importance, a circumstance due not least to the exclusionary "internal-only perspective" adopted for so many years in education policy-making and research.

4.4.2. Chapter Structure

Almost all the sections concerning education types have the same basic structure. Each education level/education type is described in five subsections. The first two subsections show the framework in which the education levels/types operate. On the one hand, one has the exogenous framework conditions (contexts), i.e., the social, economic or demographic trends which have a direct impact on how the specific education level/type operates. These exogenous contexts are derived from the general context for the education system as a whole, as described in the introductory context sections. On the other hand, the internal contexts (institutions) show the institutional characteristics of the education level or type in terms of the set-up, structure, permeability or the coordination between and the decision-making authority of the individual players in each particular area. These internal contexts may vary greatly between cantons, over time, or between Switzerland and other countries. Therefore, a conclusion regarding the proficiency or weakness of an education level or type is possible and admissible only after controlling for the exogenous and endogenous contexts.

The remaining three subsections evaluate the proficiency of the education levels according to three criteria. The first of these three criteria is the *effectiveness* of the education level, i.e., the degree of target achievement of a specific education level or education type in terms of the pertinent and relevant[8] education goals. In practical terms, this involves aspects such as the number of students who achieve or surpass the defined proficiency goals. Another possible measure of effectiveness might be the number of university and technical college students and the number of apprentices in basic vocational training who make a successful transition to the labor market.

---

[8] The relevance of education goals is determined by educational policymakers.

The second criterion is the *efficiency* of target achievement. Even if there is a high degree of target achievement for a particular education goal, the limited availability of resources in the education system (as in other areas) calls for continual scrutiny as to whether target achievement was efficient, i.e., was the goal accomplished through the use of the minimum amount of resources. Or, conversely, whether an even better target achievement could have been accomplished with the same expenditure of resources. Efficiency in the education system, although rarely explicitly stated as a performance review criterion, is an aspect of evaluation that should not be neglected, also in the interests of the learners.

The third criterion is *equity* in the education system. A high average degree of target achievement and a satisfactory level of efficiency in providing an education say nothing about whether all the people being educated in the system, regardless of their background, have equal opportunities to achieve success in the education system. The fact that different students generate different learning outcomes does not serve as a sufficient indication that the equity principle is being violated. The equity principle is violated only if students' affiliation to a particular group, socioeconomic stratum or gender limits or predetermines their educational outcome.

The identical structure of all the education level sections with the same five subsections is intended to enable a differentiated analysis of the individual education levels and to facilitate comparison between the levels.

4.4.3. Determining Education Goals

It should be clear from the above that any evaluation of education system performance must be based on education goals. In summary, the key issues are: Does the education system achieve the set goals, and to what extent (effectiveness)? What resources are expended in order to realize this degree of goal achievement (efficiency)? Are specific socioeconomic strata or nationalities or is a specific gender at a disadvantage in terms of goal achievement (equity)? All the analyses focus on education goals then. Some of these education goals differ significantly between education levels and education types, which in turn justifies evaluation based on the individual levels.

However, education goals are very often unclear, incomplete or have not even been defined in many areas. And even where general education goals have been defined, they are in most cases not or not fully operationalized. As a result, there is no consensus at the end of the day on a specific and verifiable goal definition approach. Finally, each of the education levels usually pursues multiple goals at the same time. A conclusive evaluation of the overall degree of goal achievement is therefore not only extremely complex, but also a matter of political judgment. The latter is inevitable because goal hierarchies are necessary in the presence of multiple goals so that one can establish points of reference between degrees of goal achievement for individual education goals. An elementary school pupil should not only be able to read, do arithmetic and write, but also display other intellectual and social skills at the end of the compulsory schooling period. If it were necessary to express the success of education in a single variable, it would be necessary to know beforehand whether, say, performance deficits in reading can be offset by above-average mathematical skills or very good social skills, or whether indeed the latter is in fact more important. Goal hierarchies would be necessary in order to answer these and similar questions. Goal hierarchies of this kind are usually the outcome of political decision-making processes and are determined by the value-judgments prevailing in society at a given time. The authors of the pilot report were not in possession of any such goal hierarchies at the time of writing the report. Hence, both the selection and the presentation of the goals described represent the judgment of the authors and not that of the educational policy. However, the aim of a permanent monitoring process is for the political authorities to guide the process by specifying verifiable goals for future education reporting cycles.

4.4.4. Reference Variables and Dimensions

Apart from a few exceptions (see Section 4.4), education goals cannot be measured in absolute terms because the necessary outcome benchmarks have not been identified. In most cases, however, relative findings or outcomes are possible on the basis of comparisons. Suitable comparisons can be made on an intertemporal basis, between individual educational institutions or between different education systems. There are three dimensions which would be useful comparators for Switzerland and hence for this report. First, you can present the same outcome, averaged for Switzerland, at different points in time and in this manner at least determine whether goal achievement has improved or worsened over time. Second, you can compare values from one canton to another. This at least permits a relative value for each canton in terms of where it stands in relation to the best canton (which is used as a benchmark). However, this method does not generate a direct result for the best canton because this canton might still be operating far short of its theoretical potential. The same applies if you use individual educational institutions (universities, for instance) as comparators. Third, you can compare Switzerland with other countries. The same possibilities and limitations apply as for intercantonal comparisons and comparisons between educational institutions. A key aspect in all comparisons is that it is assumed that there will be no differences in the circumstances or contexts in the course of time or between institutions that will be so significant as to render a comparison of the relevant variables meaningless.

Hence, each figure can potentially be presented in a very large number of possible comparisons. This report therefore selects and presents only those comparisons which yield a relevant or conclusive finding. In a few cases, comparators/comparisons have been chosen which do not yield a true finding, but which are commonly thought to be appropriate in identifying relevant differences in order to explicitly discuss the uselessness of the comparison.

4.5. Possibilities and Limitations of Indicator-Based System Governance and Management Explained Through Practical Examples

The following part elucidates the possibilities and problems that are encountered with education monitoring and the role indicators play within this context through reference to various practical examples. The examples given are to be construed in an exemplary sense, and care has been taken to ensure that they pertained to different education levels and different areas of education policy.

4.5.1. Class Size

Class size is a classic issue, not only in the realm of education policy but also in the field of education research. It is always amazing how adamantly teachers, parents and, in the wake of these two stakeholder groups, policymakers remain fixated on the issue of class size. If education authorities decide they would like to increase the average class size even only minimally (and there are plenty of examples of this involving cantonal education policymakers), it can be certain that the entire teacher body and many of the parents will rise up in collective protest. Reducing class size will also always figure prominently in the wish lists compiled by teacher unions. Judging by the political explosiveness of the issue of class size, one could easily assume that average class size for a canton and a particular kind of school must be one of the most important indicators within the entire education system. It is also convenient that this indicator happens to be statistically well covered (although in Switzerland the corresponding data do not go back too far). But what does this indicator really stand for? Turning to educational research for an answer, which has probed this issue for decades and produced enough studies on class size to fill an entire library, the resulting findings can be distilled into one single sentence: School classes that are much too small and much too large have an equally detrimental effect on learning outcomes, but within these two poles (specialist literature mentions a range from approximately 15 to 25 students at compulsory public schools) any variation in the number of children in a school class will have no effect, or at most only a minimal effect, on student achievement (refer, for example, to Averett and McLennan 2004 for an overview of this issue). Considering this minimal effect, then, reductions in class size are in most cases not justified, simply for reasons of efficiency. One might be able to make a case for variations in class sizes by arguing that children who start school from a weak position stand to benefit from having a smaller number of children in their class (see Krueger and Whitmore 2000), but then this would also require a central planner who determines how many children are assigned to each class depending on the individual composition of the classes. Applying this indicator to the effectiveness of the education system, one can safely assume that, within the rather large range mentioned above, the number of pupils in a class does not say anything about the quality of the education provided at our schools.

What is clear, however, is that the indicator of class size is associated with two things that immediately highlight the contrast between educational policy and financial policy on the one side and the teaching body on the other. The first is that, regardless of the actual effects class size may have on student achievement, class size is an important indicator of the cost of the education system and, therefore, it serves as a significant benchmark in education funding. The second is that class size is, of course, an indicator of the work load placed on teachers, because any increase in the number of students per class means additional work for teachers both during and after classroom instruction and vice versa.

Now what should a report on education do with the universally popular indicator of class size in view of the financial-related interests and the vested interests of parents and teachers, not to mention the vast amount of research data? In the Swiss Education Report descriptive reference is made to the average class size in the cantons. According to that information, the average class sizes of all the cantons lie within a rather narrow range of about 17–21 students, so narrow then that one would not expect these differences in class size to give rise to differences in the quality of the cantonal education systems. The education report also reveals that in practically every canton that has established guidelines pertaining to average class size, these guidelines are either adhered to or the average class size is actually one to three students below the recommended range. Furthermore, in many of the cantons that have fixed a relatively low average class size there is a significant percentage of school classes that fall short of even this recommended minimum. In addition, there were several cantons that – usually for topographic reasons – set the minimum size of classes so low that one would have to say that it was already suboptimal, i.e., that the learning environment itself was detrimental to the effectiveness of the education process. Based on the differentiated information on class size in Switzerland presented in this report, one can conclude that many cantons have cost-savings potential that could be realized without seriously jeopardizing the quality of education.[9] Taking into consideration demographic projections of the school-going population in the coming decade, it appears likely that inefficiency within the education system will increase significantly if no forceful countermeasures are taken. Innovative and comprehensive measures are required and, in some cases, these will have to be implemented against the resistance of the local school organizations.

The education report also allows comparisons to be made across the various education levels, which one can do with class size by comparing recent developments at public compulsory schools and universities. If the increase in average class size at Swiss elementary schools since 1995 had been proportionately the same as the rise in the faculty/student ratio in the field of humanities and social sciences at Swiss universities, then the number of children in the average elementary class would be approximately 26 instead of approximately 20. If the average class size had risen at the same rate as the overall deterioration in the faculty/student ratio at Swiss universities, then the average elementary school class today would number more than 22 children. This comparison raises the question why any attempt to increase the average school class size by one pupil can trigger such heated political discussions about the quality of the education system when an increase six times that number in the humanities and social sciences departments of universities does not provoke any similar public outcry about the quality of university education. Could this be because it is assumed that, unlike changes in the ratio of teachers to pupils at public compulsory schools, changes in the ratio of professors to students at the universities are not relevant to the quality of a university education? This may very well be the case but then this should at least be acknowledged and the universities credited for having increased their efficiency so much over the past 15 years!

---

[9] One must, of course, also take into consideration the transportation costs that would be incurred if schools in different towns were merged.

4.5.2. The Influence of Classroom Lesson Hours on Student Achievement

Another major issue that educational policymakers and administrators are always confronted with is to what extent the number of lessons given in any one particular subject area has an impact on the scholastic skills in that subject area. Here, too, the general stance is relatively clear: the more lessons, the better. Any reduction in the number of lessons taught immediately arouses concern that student achievement will suffer and, conversely, if student achievement is to be improved in a certain subject area, then, so the general opinion, the number of lessons taught in that subject area will have to be increased. The relatively scant research evidence on how the number of lessons in a particular subject area actually affects student learning levels and learning progress contrasts starkly with the public debate on this issue. That said, this is an admittedly difficult issue to research because it would require experimental variations in the number of lessons taught and the imposition of effective controls to ensure that no compensatory measures are taken in the control group and that the same learning standards are not simply applied to the experimental group, allowing it to cover the same amount of learning material in a greater number of lessons. Natural variations in the number of lessons taught are subject to these same difficulties and lead to other problems as well. For example, the effect of mathematics lessons at upper secondary schools on mathematics skills as presented in a TIMSS study (see Ramseier et al. 1999) was based on a different number of lessons in different branches of Gymnasium. Thus the results were distorted by the fact that there was a self-selection of the students into the different branches of Gymnasium. Consequently, it is completely impossible to ascertain to what extent the better mathematics skills of the students in those branches with an emphasis on mathematics were actually attributable to the fact that these students were receiving a greater number of mathematics lessons than the rest of students in other branches of the Gymnasium.

The PISA 2003 study with its focus on mathematics revealed, however, that there apparently is a relatively strong positive correlation between the varying numbers of cumulative classroom instruction lessons given in the subject area of mathematics in each canton and the average achievement score of each canton in the PISA test. This correlation becomes even more pronounced if the two extremes, Geneva and Ticino, are excluded. While this may initially be welcomed as confirmation that more lessons apparently do have a positive effect on skill acquisition, one can use this same data to illustrate just how far we are from possessing the knowledge necessary to provide educational decision-makers with clear policy inputs. First, there is no evidence of causality between the number of lessons taught and student achievement scores. Instead, one must simply accept that the given correlation is indeed an indicator of a causal effect. Second, while the relationship between the number of lessons and PISA scores does appear to be rather linear, one must nevertheless assume that, like with any other input/output relationship, marginal returns would eventually decline as the number of lessons is further increased. It would make a difference, then, if one additional lesson were added to a subject area where two lessons a week were taught or if that same increase were made in a subject area where the number of weekly lessons was already much higher. Third, it must generally be assumed that one cannot simply increase the overall number of weekly classroom lesson hours to augment the number of lessons given in one particular subject area, so any increase in one area will always be accompanied by a reduction in classroom instruction in some other area. This makes it clear that, before deciding whether it would be worthwhile to increase the number of lessons in one particular subject area, the opportunity costs in the form of a possible loss of skills in a subject area where the number of lessons would be reduced must be calculated. Since student achievement is currently measurable in only a few areas of the school curriculum, any such decision is immediately shifted from the objective-scientific level to the political-normative level. And even if the overall number of classroom instruction hours were to be increased, the cost of an expanded school program would have to be duly taken into consideration in the decision-making process. The anticipated benefits for the state and society resulting from the increase in student competency would have to at least match the costs of the additional school lessons. This point also makes clear that an abstract variable such as an increase in student competency does not provide an appropriate information base upon which sound educational policy decisions can be reached. An appropriate information base would also always include data on the impact that student competency has in terms of personal, fiscal and social returns. Finally, it must also be noted that other alternatives besides increasing the weekly number of classroom lessons should be explored. For example, would other forms of learning or other learning technologies be more efficient in enhancing skill acquisition within the given lesson plans? The examples cited here clearly demonstrate just how far the currently available statistical information is from producing the management and governance knowledge that is required for making everyday decisions concerning the education system.

4.5.3. Willingness of Companies to Train Apprentices

The third specific example concerns basic vocational education, i.e., the educational programs offered at the secondary level II, which is still the path most Swiss adolescents take after completing their compulsory schooling. This third example is intended not least to demonstrate that education monitoring must certainly not be limited to gathering and assessing information and data on the education system itself but that other areas and stakeholders must also be monitored, depending on which education level and type are involved. Referring to the dual apprenticeship system, it is evident that this system would not even exist if companies were not willing to offer apprenticeship positions and, hence, training and employment opportunities, to Swiss adolescents. The willingness of companies to train apprentices is, therefore, a kind of *sine qua non* for the smooth functioning of the dual vocational education and training system. The question is, what information should the monitoring of this willingness to train apprentices be based on? An indicator that measures the share of companies training apprentices as a percentage of all companies active in Switzerland (which is frequently used by the Federal Statistical Office) is problematic for at least four reasons. First, the number of training firms says nothing about the number of training posts. If the number of apprentices per firm increases, a reduction in the number of training firms would not be problematic. Second, fluctuations in this indicator do not necessarily reflect changes in the willingness among companies to train apprentices, since the number of apprenticeship contracts concluded in any one period is equally dependent on the number of adolescents seeking an apprenticeship. Recent longitudinal studies clearly show that the number of training companies changes in response to demographic fluctuations in the adolescent population (see Müller and Schweri 2006). In the same context, one cannot say with certainty that the adolescents entering the market for apprenticeships always show the same level of scholastic ability and other skills that are required to successfully complete an apprenticeship program. Here, too, the latest research indicates that company willingness to hire and train apprentices fluctuates quite strongly in response to the actual or expected (from the perspective of the hiring firms) quality of school leavers (see, for example, Mühlemann and Wolter 2006). In this case, the "ceteris paribus" assumption would no longer stand and a declining indicator would not mean that companies were less willing to train apprentices. Instead, it would reflect a deterioration in the quality or qualifications of the school leavers. Third, the percentage of companies willing to train apprentices depends just as much on the aggregate number of companies active in

Switzerland as it does on the actual number of companies providing apprenticeship training. If, for example, there is a sudden increase in the aggregate number of companies while the number of adolescents remains stable, then – assuming the willingness to train apprentices is the same among the new established companies as among the older ones – this would lead to a statistically unobservable overhang of companies that want to hire apprentices but have been unable to do so.[10] Fourth, while a simple indicator like this would, despite all the limitations mentioned above, still provide some ex post information about the willingness among companies to train apprentices, educational policymakers would probably be more interested in information that is also meaningful in an ex ante sense. Information about the factors that influence this willingness to train would probably be more appropriate for meeting the latter need. As long as it was presumed to be a natural given that the willingness to train apprentices was governed primarily by the long traditions of apprenticeship training in the corporate sector as well as companies' sense of social responsibility, it seemed pointless to investigate such indicators. In the meantime, however, research has demonstrated quite clearly that, from the companies' viewpoint, the willingness to hire and train apprentices is a decision that is subject to the same business logic as any other decision with a bearing on corporate activities and performance. The cost–benefit ratio of apprenticeship training activities has thus become a decisive factor used by companies in determining whether they should even offer apprenticeship training positions (see Mühlemann et al. 2005; Wolter et al. 2006). A cost–benefit indicator is not only a quantifiable variable but also a variable whose impact on the one variable that is of particular interest to educational policymakers (the willingness of companies to train apprentices) has been scientifically examined and validated.

Another reason why the cost–benefit ratio of a training program is appropriate as an indicator of corporate willingness to provide training is because political decisions made in the field of vocational education often have a direct impact on this ratio. Consequently, continual monitoring of the cost–benefit ratio of such training programs is one means of ascertaining the cumulative effects that the complex supply and demand side factors as well as the political factors have on the willingness to provide training opportunities.

---

[10] As a matter of fact, the considerable increase in the number of firms in Switzerland, for example, is attributable to a strong increase in the number of one- and two-person companies, which are in no position to train apprentices. This means that the percentage of companies engaged in apprentice training is being measured on a false base.

This example is intended to demonstrate that obvious and easily quantifiable data do not always serve as the best indicator and that the expressiveness of more complex indicators produced through research might be superior to easily quantifiable indicators because the causal connection between the indicator and the targeted objective is proven rather than presumed.

4.5.4. University Rankings and Other Indicators Used in the Tertiary Education System

This section closes with a look at several examples of more or less viable indicators used in the tertiary education system. Comparisons at the tertiary level are generally made between individual universities rather than entire university systems because most persons knowledgeable of the system recognize that, in view of the significant variance between the universities with regard to the quality of education offered, what matters is the achievements of the individual institutions. Given the widespread popularity of national and international rankings of universities, the meticulously compiled country comparisons of university expenditure per student that many institutions use (see for example OECD Education at a Glance) seem to be out of place. What exactly is being compared in comparisons of average university expenditure per student in Switzerland and the corresponding figure in the United States? The only thing these numbers have in common is that they both have something to do with spending on persons who are attending universities. Considering, for example, that most of the university students in Switzerland are attending universities that, according to international rankings, are ranked among the top 200 universities in the world, then, assuming that quality has its price, one would have to select a completely different set of reference variables. While it is true that many of the world's leading universities are located in the United States, the vast majority of university students in America do not study at these universities and a comparison of average expenditure per student at the University of Zurich and at Stanford University would certainly produce a completely different picture than the same comparison between the University of Zurich and the University of Nebraska.

The exact same interpretative difficulties are encountered when comparing variables such as government spending on tertiary education systems as a percent of GDP or the growth rates of spending per university student over time.[11] The only thing these commonly applied indicators have in common is that they raise more questions than they resolve, not least because the input variables usually cannot be matched against corresponding reference variables for the output.

If one attempts to measure the output or the quality of universities, it is tantamount to opening a Pandora's box. Only a few thoughts on this subject will be presented here for lack of space. Whereas the individual faculties of different universities are generally compared in national rankings, and rightly so, international rankings are usually based on comparisons of entire universities. Exactly what a number of Fields medal winners[12] say about the faculty of law at a university is somewhat puzzling, though, and not only for those uninitiated in the ways of university rankings. In order to glean some meaningful information from these rankings, correlations between what should be measured and what is actually being measured must be presumed which go well beyond the limits of plausibility. These problems arise mainly because many university rankings do clearly state what is being compared but not what the results of this comparison actually mean. The validity of this point is underscored by an ancillary finding in a German study (see Büttner et al. 2003) that revealed that a comparison of all the rankings based on professors, students, personnel directors or expert opinions (CHE ranking[13]) sometimes produced a positive correlation and sometimes no correlation at all and in some cases even indicated a negative correlation. If the same things (quality!) were being measured in all the rankings, then all the correlations that were not significantly

---

[11] In these comparisons it is not even clear, for example, exactly which cost items are included in the calculations. If research expenditures are included, for example, then a university that successfully competes for research funds will become an "expensive" university in terms of spending per student. The same ambiguity can apply to the increase in spending over time if one cannot observe for which inputs and outputs more funds were appropriated. If, for example, a country neglects the funding of its universities over a longer period of time and must later compensate for this by raising spending levels, then the sudden strong increase in expenditure can be interpreted in two completely different ways. If the quality of the services provided by the universities remains at the old level, then one would have to interpret the corresponding growth figure critically as a deterioration in efficiency and a waste of money, but if quality increases, then the same figure would be a sign that the said country made important and effective investments in its tertiary education system.

[12] The Fields medal is the highest scientific award for mathematicians.

[13] For a critique of the role of this institutional evaluator (CHE, *Centrum für Hochschulentwicklung*) see, e.g., Ursprung (2003).

positive would be indicative of a problem that not even the highly popular summation of individual rankings could resolve.

Looking more closely at the indicators on the quality of universities, one encounters three basic problems. First, with some sub-indicators it is not clear why they can even be used to substantiate claims about the quality of education offered. The quality of university libraries may be important but, considering today's means of gathering information, it is not clear what causal impact libraries actually have on the quality of education given at universities. Second, there are indicators where it is not certain whether they are a cause or a consequence of quality (inverse causality). One can take the faculty/student ratios used in various rankings as an example here. Regardless of the fact that, as mentioned earlier, 20 years of research activity on class size has been unable to produce any conclusive evidence concerning the strength of the influence this ratio has on scholastic performance, the same indicator is accorded significance at the university level for ranking institutions. The problem here is the relatively long time lag before the number of professors in any particular faculty will change in response to fluctuations in student enrolment numbers, and for good reasons that require no further explanation here. In Switzerland the duration of this phase of adjustment (empirically measured from 1990 to 2002) is approximately 5 years. What's more, in Switzerland university faculties are usually so small that the creation of just one additional professorship can have a big impact on the faculty/student ratio. Under these conditions one can now imagine the following hypothetical case. Faculty X at the universities Y and Z each consist of 5 professors and 500 students at a certain point in time t. Consequently, the faculty/student ratio at both universities is equally good (or bad). The faculty at university Y is then beset with some quality problems, however, and subsequently loses half of its students to university Z over a period of 4 years. The faculty/student ratio has thus changed from 1-to-1 at the point in time t to a ratio of 1-to-3 in favor of university Y. If the faculty/student ratio is used as a measure of quality in a ranking, then the university that shows an improvement is the one whose improvement in its faculty supervision and guidance profile happens to be a consequence of its low quality![14] The third basic problem is that most rankings are based on a large number of sub-indicators, which

---

[14] See for an example the homepage of the "Swissup Ranking" of Swiss universities where for some disciplines the student/professor ratio is used as an indicator for quality (http://www.swissupranking.com/ranking-result.php?field=1&stats=1& display= ranking).

is problematic because every summarization into a single indicator rests on bold assumptions about the weighting of the individual sub-indicators.[15]

The examples given above are intended to show that the indicators regarding government expenditure on tertiary educational institutions that are so heatedly debated in political circles cannot be interpreted in any meaningful way without corresponding output parameters. However, there is a lack of hard research data that would soundly validate the use of these output parameters (especially those immensely popular rankings). Unfortunately, this is an area in which the doable dominates what would be meaningful in a manner that borders on irresponsibility.

4.6. Initial Findings from the Pilot Report on the Swiss Education System and Conclusions

As posited in the preceding sections, self-evident difficulties become apparent when one attempts to guide and govern the education system with governance knowledge derived from a system of indicators. However, this should not lead one to conclude that it would be better not to use such a system. The only alternatives to the governance and management of the education system based on indicators that are periodically and systematically gathered and interpreted would be relying on political-normative ad hoc decisions or a semi-scientific "trial and error" approach.

The fact that indicator-based governance today does not necessarily guarantee a qualitative advantage over the two aforementioned alternatives is not because an indicator-based approach is generally inferior but because the knowledge required for the successful application of indicators is fragmentary. The main reasons for the incompleteness of such knowledge are briefly explained below because they hold the key to future successful governance and management via monitoring:

(a) Although great achievements have been made in education statistics during the past two decades, major investments are still necessary, both to improve existing statistics and to extend statistical coverage to previously uncovered areas. Two examples particularly important in Switzerland will suffice here. When it comes to educational careers, statistics are still disadvantaged by the segmentation of the education system into different levels and

---

[15] Particularly resourceful producers of rankings therefore let the users of the information determine the weighting and composition of the various sub-indicators in producing an overall assessment.

different types or pathways. On the input side, monetary costs are still not comparable and there is still very little differentiation in the gathering and recording of real inputs.

(b) Apart from its participation in international achievement tests such as TIMSS or, more recently, PISA, Switzerland does not have a home-grown tradition of administering and conducting achievement tests. As such, an overview of the level of skills achievement within the education system is lacking, from both a cross-sectional and a longitudinal perspective. Participation in PISA did help to determine where Switzerland stands in an international context but, precisely because of its cross-sectional nature, PISA is unsuited as a means of producing knowledge chronicling the origins of the given proficiency levels, yet such knowledge is crucial for governance and management purposes (see also Wolter 2004). The "value-added" approaches this would require can only be implemented after data on individual achievement have been repeatedly gathered and recorded over time.

Together, these two points constitute a knowledge deficit at virtually all levels of education which imposes severe limitations on the assessment of both the effectiveness as well as the efficiency of the education system.

(a) Education research has devoted much of its attention to the internal-only view of the education system during the past decades and paid too little notice to the influence the surrounding environment exerts on the production of education and to education output, to say nothing of education outcomes. Consequently, there is a lack of empirically validated systemic knowledge, which is necessary to adequately grasp the interaction and interrelation between indicators. And that is precisely what is needed before one can even begin to speak of an indicator system.

(b) The long-standing neglect of empirical educational research (see for example Angrist 2004) is a disadvantage when setting up an education monitoring system, because it has led to a situation in which educational policymakers do not have enough knowledge about cause–effect relationships (causalities) and effect size. In real application conditions, knowledge of both is essential, however, and neither theoretical nor experience-based knowledge (expertise or historical comparisons) are a perfect substitute for such knowledge. Another consequence of this long disregard of empirical and hence social-scientific aspects in traditional educational research is that upcoming educational researchers

have received inadequate training in scientific methodology – also when compared with other social science disciplines – and, as a result, there is too little human capital available for future research purposes.
(c) Referring to quantitative-oriented researchers and the statisticians, it seemed that for a very long time they were content with what was merely doable. This led to a situation where the validity of assumptions and interpretations was not established on the basis of stringent scientific analysis but merely inferred on the grounds of plausibility. The misguided use of education indicators in many studies on education mentioned in Section 4.5 of this essay gives credence to this view. Assertions made in this conjunction have eroded the confidence of practitioners in research and statistics and are not entirely blameless for the scanty funding of educational research (again in comparison with other research fields).
(d) Referring to the educational researchers, the relationship with educational policymakers is, unfortunately, still somewhat uneasy and inhibited. A display of interest in research on the part of policymakers is often viewed as a threat to freedom of scientific research. Applied research and hence research geared to political issues was therefore often considered inferior to academic research. On the other hand, however, it is clear that responsible-minded policymakers and education administrators can improve the relationship with research only by acting responsibly when granting research contracts and when applying the findings of research activity. It is certainly possible to build a mutually beneficial relationship between researchers and policymakers, one that produces both academically outstanding quality and knowledge that is of relevance to system governance, as this has already been demonstrated by several other countries in a very convincing manner.

Reflecting on these six points – to which others could certainly be added – one might be tempted to ask whether education monitoring even makes sense under these conditions. Such doubts are justified but they are dispelled by the following two thoughts and observations:

First, a permanent and systematic monitoring and reporting process is needed to improve the knowledge and structures in those areas that constitute today's main problem areas. And this monitoring might also help to curtail the consumption of resources in those areas where unsystematic and redundant knowledge is currently being produced.

Second, one can already observe improvements in all six points mentioned above, so it appears certain that the second education report will have already filled some of the major gaps in governance and management knowledge. In the area of statistics the introduction of personal student identification numbers should enable the collection of more comprehensive data on individual educational careers. Regarding the costs of education, initial results have been produced at the university level and with regard to basic vocational education programs; further improvements will follow. The HarmoS project with the national standards and student achievement tests taken at three different times during compulsory schooling will not only enable effectiveness statements on the quality of public schools but also generate the data education researchers require to improve the understanding of education processes. Other evaluations, EVAMAR 2 for example, or large-scale pilot studies such as the *Basisstufenprojekt* in German-speaking cantons (a basic primary school project spanning 2 years of kindergarten and 2 years of primary school) are an indication of how knowledge can be generated in systematic, large-scale projects that is of practical use for governing and managing entire areas of the education system. In educational research, efforts are underway in the traditional education sciences, for example through structured and inter-university doctorate schools, and other social sciences (sociology, economics, political sciences) are displaying greater interest in education-related issues. Furthermore, one can expect that all of these developments and efforts will put a self-reinforcing process in motion that will prove to be beneficial to the quality of research and thereby strengthen the validity of research outcomes. Confidence in research findings and statistical information is, ultimately, the basic requirement that must be fulfilled before educational policymakers and education administrators will display a willingness to embrace a rational process of "evidence-based or informed policy". A final example here is the innovative research promotion instruments that are being tested in Switzerland, which should enable a more rewarding interplay between the education administration and education research. Reference is made in this regard to the concept of the so-called "Leading Houses" of the Federal Office for Professional Education and Technology, which is designed to address the needs of both researchers and administrators in a simultaneous "top-down" and "bottom-up" approach.

Before closing, the question whether better governance and management will also lead to a better education system must still be addressed. As is so often the case, better governance and management alone will not produce a better education system but it is a necessary precondition!

Acknowledgements

The author wishes to thank those who worked on the "Swiss Education Report 2006" for their input, with special thanks to Miriam Kull. All statements and any errors are the author's sole responsibility.

References

Angrist JD (2004) American Education Research changes tack. *Oxford Review of Economic Policy*, 20(2):198–212

Averett SL, McLennan MC (2004) Exploring the effects of class size on student achievement: what have we learned over the past two decades? In: Johnes G, Johnes J (eds) *International Handbook on the Economics of Education*. Edward Elgar Publisher, Cheltenham, pp 329–367

Becker H (1971) *Bildungsforschung und Bildungsplanung*. Suhrkamp Verlag, Frankfurt am Main

Büttner T, Kraus M, Rincke J (2003) Hochschulranglisten als Qualitätsindikatoren im Wettbewerb der Hochschulen. *Vierteljahreshefte zur Wirtschaftsforschung* 2:252–270

Kanaev A, Tujinman A (2001) Prospects for selecting and using indicators for benchmarking Swedish higher education. Working Paper, Stockholm

Krueger A, Whitmore D (2000) The effect of attending a small class in the early grades on college-test taking in the middle school test results: evidence from project STAR. NBER Working Paper W7656

Mühlemann S, Wolter SC (2006) Regional effects on employer provided training: evidence from apprenticeship training in Switzerland. CESifo Discussion Paper 1665

Mühlemann S et al. (2005) a structural model of demand for apprentices. CESifo Working Paper 1417

Müller B, Schweri J (2006) Die Entwicklung der betrieblichen Ausbildungsbereitschaft, Eine Längsschnittuntersuchung zur dualen Berufsbildung in der Schweiz, Zollikofen. SIBP Schriftenreihe, Band 31

Ramseier E, Keller C, Moser U (1999) Bilanz Bildung. Eine Evaluation am Ende der Sekundarstufe II auf der Grundlage der *Third International Mathematics and Science Study*. Rüegger, Chur

Thomas S, Peng WJ (2004) The use of educational standards and benchmarks in indicator publications. In: Scheerens J, Hendricks M (eds) *Benchmarking the Quality of Education*. (Official Project Report prepared for the EU commission. January 2003)

Ursprung H (2000) Schneewittchen im Land der Klapperschlangen, Evaluation eines Evaluators. *Perspektiven der Wirtschaftspolitik* 4:177–189

Van Ackeren I (2003) Entwicklung von und Forschung über Bildungssindikatoren. In: Van Ackeren I, Hovestadt G (eds) *Indikatorisierung der Empfehlungen des Forum Bildung*. Bundesministerium für Bildung und Forschung, Bonn

Wolter SC (2004) Leistungsindikatoren im Bildungsbereich. Forum der Bundesstatistik, Ökonomische Leistungsfähigkeit Deutschlands, Band 44, Statistisches Bundesamt, Wiesbaden, pp 127–136

Wolter SC, Weber BA (2005) Bildungsrendite – ein zentraler ökonomischer Indikator des Bildungswesens. Die Volkswirtschaft, Oktober, pp 38–42

Wolter SC, Mühlemann S, Schweri J (2006) Why some firms train apprentices and many others do not. *German Economic Review* 7:249–264

Chapter 5
Measuring and Comparing the Equity of Education Systems in Europe

Marc Demeuse[1] and Ariane Baye[2]

[1]*Institute of School Administration, Faculty of Psychology and Education Science, University of Mons-Hainaut, Mons, Belgium*
[2]*Education Systems and Practices Analysis Unit, Faculty of Psychology and Education Science, University of Liège, Liege, Belgium*

5.1. Introduction

Through data resulting from international surveys it has been possible to design quantitative indicators, which describe the manner in which education systems treat the young generation for which they are responsible and the manner in which they perform their task (European Group for Research on Equity in Educational Systems 2005; OECD 2005; Baye et al. 2006). Whereas the initial research work in this area put the accent on the effectiveness of education systems, an interest in equity gradually developed, at first based on the available documents – such as the OECD's Education at a Glance – then based on specific documents (Gibson and Meuret 1995; Hutmacher et al. 2001; Baye 2005).

Starting from equality of access, i.e. the right of everyone – whatever their origin – to attend school and moving then to equality of treatment, which consists in offering identical service to all, modern society has become increasingly demanding vis-à-vis its school and now expects equality of results or attainments. Thus, in most European countries, the expectations from school are that all pupils will achieve equal performances at the end of a period of education, at least in the sense of mastery of base competencies, i.e. a threshold level of competencies considered indispensable for life. Naturally, this should not restrain some, or even many, from pursuing a more or less long school career beyond compulsory education.

In the rest of this chapter, we will only be looking at education in which everyone has to participate during the period of compulsory education and from which everyone should obtain an equal benefit in terms of life skills (OECD 1999, 2003). Nevertheless, some of the data used to allow an analysis of the results at this level come from tertiary education.

5.2. Inequalities and Inequity

The dispersion of individual scores in standardised tests, such as those developed by the International Association for the Evaluation of Educational Achievement (IEA) or the OECD in its Programme for International Student Assessment (PISA), allows an appreciation of the degree of inequality between pupils within the participating countries. Notwithstanding that all the countries feature some heterogeneity of their pupils' performances, the differences are more or less pronounced. Thus, taking the divergence between the best and the weakest pupils in mathematics or reading, the inequality of results appears to be the strongest in Belgium (Baye et al. 2006:12). This, to a great extent, is what has motivated the authors and their Belgian colleagues to examine not only the problem of average performance, but also the issue of disparities between pupils.

The Belgian situation is interesting for several reasons, among which the fact that education, since 1989, is the exclusive responsibility of the three linguistic communities that make up the country – French, Flemish and German-speaking – and that the structures of these communities, initially perfectly identical, have progressively diverged. When considering Belgium in its entirety or each of its communities, the disparities between pupils are very significant. However, the average level of the pupils is not identical in the French and Flemish communities. It can thus rightly be asserted that the two education systems are both inept as regards reducing the differences in results, but it is also true that the situation for young Flemish speakers is on average more enviable than that of their compatriots in the south of the country. Whereas the young Flemish obtain, respectively, 553 points in mathematical culture, 530 in reading comprehension and 529 in scientific culture, their French-speaking counterparts only obtain, respectively, 498, 477 and 483 points in these three domains (Baye et al. 2004:49).

As pointed out by Hanushek and Woessmann (2005), it is extremely difficult, as generally demanded by users and politicians, to evaluate the impact of certain structures – such as early streaming or grade repetition – on the effectiveness or equity of an education system. International comparisons are therefore useful for both estimating the relative scale of a phenomenon and identifying the organisational structures that appear to be associated with it. Whereas inequalities exist in all the education systems studied, there are nevertheless great differences between countries/regions and "education systems are not all the same when it comes to their capacity to treat pupils in an equitable manner" (Vandenberghe 2003). With the help of a global index, Dupriez and Vandenberghe (2004) demonstrated that the Belgian French community is characterised by a more pronounced inequality, in the sense that pupils' scores in mathematics, reading and sciences are determined more than elsewhere by their families' social and cultural characteristics. At the other end of the spectrum – also as far as average performance is concerned – Finland presents results that are distinctly more favourable, that is to say, more homogeneous between pupils.

It now remains to define what level of differences in results is acceptable and conversely what level may be considered unjust, that is to say to go from the concept of inequality to that of inequity (Demeuse and Baye 2005). To do this, the European Group for Research on Equity in Educational Systems (2005), which the authors coordinated, following on from the work already undertaken by the Ad Hoc Group on Equity Issues of the OECD's Internal Education Indicators Project (INES) (Hutmacher et al. 2001), proposed a reference framework allowing the data to be organised into a coherent system of indicators (Demeuse 2004; Nicaise et al. 2005). Indeed, a set of indicators – rather than just one – is needed to grasp the complexity of education systems in regard to the very particular quality described as equity. An education system can very well show weak differences in the results of a test when considering the global school population and nevertheless concentrate the differences observed between certain groups, whether one of them corresponds to a minority or not. From this point of view, a comparison of the results of girls and boys constitutes a good example of a situation where none of the groups considered is a minority.

For the reasons already mentioned, the framework for a set of equity indicators is organised according to two dimensions. The first concerns the individuals between whom unjust differences may appear:

- In a global manner, without it being possible to associate these differences to particular characteristics of the individuals, but simply because the deviations between the weakest and the strongest are judged to be unacceptable or
- For identifiable groups of individuals (for example, girls and boys, foreigners and natives, youngsters whose parents exercise less

distinguished/less well paid/less qualified, etc. professions and other more favoured pupils) or
- For individuals, whether they belong to identifiable categories or not, who are at a particularly intolerable level (below a certain threshold, comparable to the poverty threshold in the economic area).

In the reference framework, the situation of individuals below a threshold judged to be unacceptable and for which the characteristics allow an identification is that which could be considered the most unjust.

The second dimension considers different areas where differences can appear:

- The context (external to the school) in terms of
    - individual consequences of education, such as disparities in income or social advantages,
    - economic and social inequalities, such as poverty and precarity,
    - cultural resources, such as the level of training and access to culture,
    - aspirations and feelings, such as professional aspirations or the feeling of being treated justly.
- The education process in terms of
    - quantitative differences in the education received (inequality of the length of schooling or expenditure),
    - qualitative differences in the education received (support from teachers, school segregation).
- The education system's internal results in terms of
    - competencies,
    - personal development,
    - school careers.
- The external results in terms of
    - social mobility,
    - individual benefits for the most disfavoured who may benefit, for example, from the services of the most educated,
    - collective benefits, notably towards schools or others (increased tolerance, for example).

As it is impossible to present here the full set of indicators that have been developed, the authors have privileged one dimension in particular: school segregation. This choice makes it easier to make a link between the results observed in terms of segregation and the structures of the different education systems.

Nevertheless, in order to really discuss segregation, it must be possible to associate the differences observed with attendance of different schools, classes or streams and, an aggravating factor, that such differences may be totally or partly identified with specific personal characteristics of individuals (sex, nationality, language, socio-economic level, etc.). This is what we will examine now.

5.3. School Segregation

Table 5.1, taken from the European report written by Baye and her colleagues (2006:42), allows an analysis of the segregation mechanisms that are at work in the different education systems being considered. The effects of school segregation have been estimated on the basis of data coming from PISA 2003. One of the qualities of the indicators, apart from their precision and exactitude, is that they allow a good understanding and facilitate analysis (Demeuse 2006). The authors have thus chosen a calculation method that makes the understanding of the different values rather intuitive: the proportion of pupils belonging to the target group that should change schools in order to achieve a homogenous distribution of this group in all of the schools (Gorard and Taylor 2002).

From Table 5.1, column 3, it appears that 59.2% of the Belgian pupils that are in the group of the 10% weakest in mathematics would have to be relocated to different schools in order to observe an identical proportion, i.e. 10%, of weak pupils in each school. This relocation of pupils that are weak in mathematics would only be 27.7% in Finland and 26.1% in Iceland. Column 4 shows the same type of information, but this time the target group is not the 10% weakest in the mathematics test – for which the average score is quite variable according to the country's performance level. Instead, it is the group of pupils that do not achieve level 2 (out of 5 in the global scale) in the mathematics test. This time, there are 50.4% weak pupils, i.e. below level 2 of the PISA mathematics scale, that would have to be relocated to balance their distribution among Belgian schools, whereas 33.7% of Finnish pupils and only 21.5% of Icelandic pupils would similarly need relocation.

The indicator chosen (we have just exposed two of them) is thus not insignificant: R^2 between the two methods = 0.6674 for the 25 countries for which there are data. Naturally, to interpret the numbers correctly, it is necessary to take account of the proportion of pupils below level 2, i.e. those who are in a very worrying situation, in the different education systems. There are only 6.8% in Finland compared to 15.0% in Iceland and

Table 5.1. School segregation (according to Baye et al. 2006:42)

	As a function of reading skills (10% weak) (2003)	As a function of reading skills (below level 2) (2003)	As a function of maths skills (10% weak) (2003)	As a function of maths skills (below level 2) (2003)	According to parents' profession (2003)	According to gender (2003)	According to linguistic origin (2003)	According to parents' place of birth (2003)	Inter-school variance expressed as a percentage of total variance in the country (Rho) Math 2003 (p. 383)	% pupils weak in reading (2003)	% pupils weak in maths (2003)	Average weakest decile in reading (2003)	Average weakest decile in maths (2003)
	1	2	3	4	5	6	7	8	9	10	11	12	13
Cyprus	–	–	–	–	–	–	–	–	–	–	–	–	–
Lithuania	–	–	–	–	–	–	–	–	–	–	–	–	–
Malta	–	–	–	–	–	–	–	–	–	–	–	–	–
Slovenia	–	–	–	–	–	–	–	–	–	–	–	–	–
Estonia	–	–	–	–	–	–	–	–	–	–	–	–	–
Bulgaria	–	–	–	–	–	–	–	–	–	–	–	–	–
Romania	–	–	–	–	–	–	–	–	–	–	–	–	–
Switzerland	44.9	37.9	46.1	40.8	32.4	12.0	44.1	20.7	34.2	16.7	14.5	337.9	361.1
Finland	25	32.9	27.7	33.7	30.8	7.5	65.4	45.3	4.8	5.7	6.8	407.3	409.7
Iceland	26.2	19.3	26.1	21.5	35.4	8.4	63.5	30.7	3.8	18.5	15.0	326.9	364.2
Sweden	31.4	26.8	32.3	24.5	29.3	8.5	57.9	31.6	10.5	13.3	17.3	353.8	353.3

Country											
Norway	31.8	24.1	29.9	21.1	26.6	8.4	51.0	35.7	6.6	18.1	20.8	329.2	348.1
Poland	34.5	27.7	31.8	23.3	42.5	7.8	95.5	93.9	12.6	16.8	22.0	338.9	349.3
Denmark	38.3	30.5	36.5	29.7	29.2	9.4	60.9	34.1	13.4	16.5	15.4	341.2	364.4
United Kingdom	38.4	33.7	40.7	32.8	33.9	14.9	64.5	32.4	–	14.9	17.8	349.2	360.4
Latvia	39	30.2	40.9	28.5	28.8	9.1	86.7	37	22.5	18.0	23.7	350.2	342.3
Luxembourg	39.6	32.7	39.3	32.9	21.2	13	26.2	14.2	31.6	22.7	21.7	306.6	343.6
Ireland	40.8	39.8	37.4	30.5	30.9	28.3	83.1	21.6	15.9	11.0	16.8	364.6	363.4
Spain	42.6	30.5	43.7	30.3	30.9	11.4	74.7	38.6	19.7	21.1	23.0	321.4	338.9
Greece	50.3	36.2	51	28.2	31.1	10.5	70.2	37.7	36.3	25.3	38.9	302.7	299.7
Turkey	50.8	30.6	49.5	22.9	24.9	13.0	85.0	67.5	54.9	36.8	52.2	307.5	280.8
Slovak Republic	52	37	52.4	40.8	35.9	17.4	81.3	32.4	41.7	24.9	19.9	319.8	344.8
Portugal	54.3	41.5	52.5	34	29.4	9.2	71.5	35	33.6	21.9	30.1	323.0	326.4
Czech Republic	55.3	42.6	55	46.1	40	18.8	83.7	36.8	47.8	19.3	16.6	329.1	364.3
Netherlands	56.2	54.2	56.6	55.9	33.9	10.8	55.8	33.9	58.8	11.5	10.9	375.1	384.3
France	56.3	48.3	57.5	50.4	30.8	15	57	31	–	17.5	16.6	331.2	358.7
Italy	56.5	43.6	57.6	38.1	33.6	23.5	72.2	38	52.2	23.9	31.9	301.7	310.8
Austria	59.9	50.4	55.9	47.7	31.5	28.3	47	34.6	52.9	20.7	18.8	314.1	358.0
Hungary	60.2	47	60.6	44.9	36	18.5	84.2	39.3	58.3	20.5	23.0	333.7	341.3
Belgium	61.1	49.9	59.2	50.4	38.4	17.9	55.8	34.7	46.0	17.9	16.5	306.7	332.3
Liechtenstein	63.0	62.9	63.6	61.8	32.8	5.9	17.6	16.2	42.2	10.4	12.3	378.6	360.4
Germany	64.7	48.7	62.9	49.8	36.8	12.4	52.3	37.9	51.7	22.3	21.6	301.3	326.8

16.5% in Belgium (column 11). This distribution can be further refined by community in the case of Belgium: 12% in the Flemish community, 17% in the German-speaking community and 23% in the French community (Baye et al. 2004:60).

Column 13 provides information about the average score obtained by the weakest decile, i.e. 409.7 points by the 10% weakest in Finland compared to 364.2 points in Iceland and 332.3 points in Belgium. The ranking of the countries is therefore maintained, whether the proportion of the weakest pupils (below level 2 on the global scale) or the average of the weakest 10% of pupils within each country is considered. However, the values of the indicators are different, leading to more or less pronounced narrowing of the gaps between the education systems considered.

The same reasoning can be applied for the PISA reading scale. Columns 1 and 2 show the effects of segregation when the reading test is considered. The results are very similar to those described for mathematics and thus highlight the stability of academic segregation mechanisms, independently of the discipline considered. The two methods tally even more for reading (R^2 between the two methods = 0.7531 for the same 25 countries). The results converge more when the same method and the same target groups are used (either the group of the 10% weakest pupils or the group of pupils below level 2), applied to the results obtained in the two disciplines, mathematics and reading (R^2 = 0.9779 taking account of the weakest 10%, whatever the discipline, and R^2 = 0.8946 taking account of the pupils below level 2, whatever the discipline), versus when two different methods are used for the same discipline.

Another classic method allows the same type of observation to be made, on the basis of the proportion of variance of results that can be explained by enrolment in one school rather than another. The results obtained with this method are shown in column 9 for mathematics.[1] For the 23 countries for which data are available, the concordance between the results obtained for the weakest 10% of pupils (column 3) and the proportion of variance explained by enrolment in a school is high (R^2 = 0.8554). This is not the case when the results are compared for pupils below level 2 and the proportion of variance due to enrolment in a school (R^2 = 0.4948).

The subsequent columns in Table 5.1, also based on the data collected during the PISA 2003 survey, do not look at academic segregation, i.e. the more or less confirmed existence of schools in which pupils are grouped according to whether they are stronger or weaker in terms of school

---

[1] The value of this index, supplied by the OECD (2004:383), is available neither for the United Kingdom because of the non-respect by this country of the sampling conditions nor for France (Monseur and Demeuse 2004:49–52).

results. They look at segregation on the basis of pupils' personal characteristics: parents' profession (column 5), the pupils' gender (column 6), language spoken at home – the target group being made up of those pupils that claim not to speak the language of instruction at home (column 7) – and the pupils' and parents' place of birth (column 8).

Overall, contrary to the results obtained for the different academic segregation indices, the correlations in Table 5.2 indicate a weak link (tendency) between the academic segregation indices and the segregation indices linked to profession or gender. This link can even be negative with the linguistic segregation indices (language spoken at home) or the parents' place of birth.

Still overall, the rankings thus obtained highlight a group of countries where the effects of segregation seem to be weak: Sweden, Denmark and Finland. At the opposite end of the scale are Italy, Austria, Hungary, the

Table 5.2. Correlation between the different segregation indices (columns 1–9 of Table 5.1)

	Column 1	Column 2	Column 3	Column 4	Column 5	Column 6	Column 7	Column 8	Column 9
Column 1	1.0								
Column 2	0.86779	1.0							
Column 3	0.98890	0.87107	1.0						
Column 4	0.79512	0.94581	0.81692	1.0					
Column 5	0.27357 $p<0.1858$	0.27370 $p<0.1855$	0.26648 $p<0.1979$	0.34667 $p<0.896$	1.0				
Column 6	0.41353 $p<0.0399$	0.34714 $p<0.0891$	0.36538 $p<0.0725$	0.25916 $p<0.2109$	0.14883 $p<0.4777$	1.0			
Column 7	−0.14831 $p<0.4792$	−0.36202 $p<0.0754$	−0.15657 $p<0.4548$	−0.43098 $P<0.0315$	0.33981 $p<0.0965$	0.18550 $p<0.3447$	1.0		
Column 8	−0.14487 $p<0.4896$	−0.30157 $p<0.1429$	−0.18035 $p<0.3883$	−0.36924 $p<0.0693$	0.34221 $p<0.0940$	−0.16948 $p<0.4180$	0.63143 $p<0.0007$	1.0	
Column 9	0.91824	0.75281	0.92488	0.70340 $p<0.0002$	0.20347 $p<0.3518$	0.44670 $p<0.0326$	0.44670 $p<0.0326$	−0.05580 $p<0.8003$	1.0

All the correlations are significant to $p < 0.0001$ unless stated otherwise.

Czech Republic, Germany and Belgium. It seems that the systems where segregation is not practised much at the level of schools show weak social differences and results that are relatively similar across schools. On the contrary, the systems that are more segregationist tend to increase the differences of results between social groups. From this point of view and without having to sacrifice effectiveness for equity (on the contrary!), it appears that Finland, where average results are high and not very dispersed, can be opposed to Germany, where average results are relatively weaker and their dispersion more pronounced, as pointed out by the authors of the European report (Baye et al. 2006). There are nevertheless peculiar situations. Thus, from the perspective of the language spoken at home, Finland (linguistic segregation index = 65.4) ranks lower than, for example, Belgium (55.8). This type of result, in Finland, clearly shows the influence of the concentration of certain groups, which are hardly significant at the level of the country as a whole (national minorities, for example, or foreigners in Helsinki) in certain schools, whereas these same groups can be more "diluted" when their proportion on the territory is both larger and more homogenous, as in Belgium. It is thus important, if the indicators are to be used in steering mechanisms, to take account of a rich set of information and to let the numbers speak beyond the "horse race" (to use the English expression), which attracts the attention of the tabloid press.

5.4. Structure of the Education Systems and Segregation

Several indicators have been grouped together with a view to relating the data linked to segregation with the organisation of the education systems. They are based in part on PISA data and in part on the publication "Key data on education in Europe" from Eurydice.

As for the segregation indicators, it was necessary to make some choices. The selection of data presented in Table 5.3 comes partly from a preliminary analysis study performed by one of the authors (Demeuse et al. 2001, 2005; Monseur and Demeuse 2001) and partly from a new analysis of the available data, concerning two dimensions a priori susceptible to create segregation effects: the establishment of structures that allow the separation of pupils according to academic or other characteristics (method of organisation of pre-primary education, age at the first orientation/selection, enrolment of children with special needs in different schools) and the implementation of mechanisms to ensure at least some degree of equality of treatment in all schools (e.g. uniform certification at the end of lower secondary education) or, on the contrary, that maximise the likelihood of observing specific mechanisms (share of private funding, parents' choice of the school in public education).

The first column shows the principal methods of grouping children in pre-primary education (Eurydice 2005:277, indicator E10, school year 2002/2003). The letter "S" indicates that the pupils are grouped in different classes according to age, whereas the letter "F" indicates a vertical type of grouping, also referred to as "family type" where pupils of different ages are mixed. The letter "M" refers to a mixed model. A majority of the countries have adopted an organisation by age, with the exception of the Nordic countries (Denmark, Finland and Sweden) and Germany, where the family model prevails, and 11 countries where a mixed model has been adopted. The mixed model is the most difficult to describe in particular because it can cover very different situations, including the coexistence of the two other models but in different structures. With the noteworthy exception of Italy, Austria and Cyprus, the countries where the mixed model is in operation belong to northern Europe (Norway and the Baltic countries) or to the group of new Member States that joined the European Union in 2004.

In a complementary manner to that which has been exposed for preprimary education, columns 10 and 11 show the manner in which the classes for 15-year-old pupils are made up, at least for mathematics courses. This includes, on one hand, the proportion of pupils for which the school heads indicated that the mathematics classes study the same subject matter, but at different levels of difficulty (ability grouping) (column 10), and, on the other hand, the proportion of pupils for which the school heads indicated that the mathematics classes study different content or different sets of subject matters, with a varying level of difficulty (adaptation of objectives) (column 11) (OECD, PISA 2003 database). Although these data are not complete for all participating countries and although they depend, for a large part, on the understanding that the school heads have of these two concepts (ability grouping and modification of the curriculum), it can be seen that the values are very weak for Finland, Spain, Portugal and Poland as regards adaptation of the curriculum and its objectives in function of the ability of pupils. However, this does not necessarily translate into low recourse to ability grouping: it is indeed of little significance in Finland, but much more widespread in Poland and Portugal.

The second column indicates the age at which the first possibility of an orientation/selection of pupils (streaming) occurs (Eurydice 2005:56–63, B1 and OECD, to be published, for Belgium, Switzerland and Turkey, school year 2002/2003). For this indicator, a distinction can be made

Table 5.3. Description of school structures

	Grouping methods (pre-primary)	Age at the first orientation/selection	Repeat rate at 15 years (PISA)	Norms for class passage (primary)	% of pupils with special needs in special schools	Limitation of access to tertiary education	Certification at the end of lower secondary	Integration method for allophone migrant children	% of private resources in spending on education	Distribution of 15-year-old pupils in mathematics (ability grouping)	Distribution of 15-year-old pupils in mathematics (adaptation of objectives)	Freedom of choice in public education	% of pupils educated in public education (lower secondary education)	% of 20–24 year-olds for whom the level of qualification does not permit access to tertiary education
	1	2	3	4	5	6	7	8	9	10	11	12	13	14
Austria	M	10	9.6	R	1.6	F	I	O	5.6	16.5	–	AC	92.3	15
Belgium	S	12	29.5	R	4.6	F	M	M	7	4.39	16.48	F	43.2	28.3
Bulgaria	S	14	–	R	2.2	S	I	NO	20.7	–	–	FP	–	22.5
Cyprus	M	15	–	A	0.5	S	M	O	18.8	–	–	A	–	14.7
Czech Republic	S	11	2.6	R	5	S	NO	O	8.4	7.59	8.66	AC	98.2	41.5
Denmark	F	16	3.4	A	2.3	S	I	O	3.9	21.61	13.78	AC	76.9	45.5
Estonia	M	16	–	R	4	S	M	M	–	–	–	AC	–	19.6
Finland	F	16	2.8	R	3.6	S	I	M	2.2	10.89	1.35	AC	95.8	13.8
France	S	14	38.3	C	2.2	F	M	M	8	–	–	A	78.8	40.4
Germany	F	10	20.3	R	4.8	F	I	S	18.6	23.75	11.91	AC	92.9	26.7
Greece	S	15	7.0	A	0.6	N	M	M	5.8	6.07	–	A	94.5	22.2
Hungary	S	10	9.5	R	3.9	S	I	NO	11	18.76	5.56	AC	93.7	41.3
Iceland	S	16	0.0	A	0.7	F	M	M	8.3	50.42	21.49	AC	99.1	57

Measuring and Comparing the Equity of Education Systems

Country														
Ireland	S	15	13.8	A	1.8	S	E	O	7.8	59.13	24.57	F	100	23.5
Italy	M	14	15.0	R	0.5	F	M	O	9.3	21	9.57	FP	96.6	37.1
Latvia	M	7	—	R	3.4	S	M	S	18.1	32.47	11.47	FP	—	37.3
Liechtenstein	S	11	17.3	A	1.7	F	M	M	—	21.6	11.24	A	—	m
Lithuania	M	14	—	R	1.2	S	I	M	—	—	—	AC	—	29
Luxembourg	S	12	37.9	R	1.5	F	—	M	0	4.27	18.63	A	79.3	57.6
Malta	S	16	—	R	1.3	S	M	NO	10.6	—	—	A	—	61
Netherlands	S	12	28.4	R	1.9	F	M	O	9.1	33.43	38.25	F	23.8	39.9
Norway	M	16	0.0	A	0.4	S	M	O	3.9	77.75	7.8	M(A&AC)	97.8	5.1
Poland	M	16	3.6	R	1.8	S	M	O	—	41.59	0.95	AC	98.1	39
Portugal	S	15	29.5	C	0.5	S	M	O	1.5	32.3	0.71	A	88.7	56.3
Romania	S	15	—	R	1.2	S	E	S	6.5	—	—	FP	—	44.3
Slovak Republic	M	10	2.5	R	3.6	S	NO	M	2.9	42.96	11.37	FP	94.9	33
Slovenia	M	15	—	R	1.6	S	M	M	—	—	—	AC	—	35.6
Spain	S	16	28.6	C	0.4	S	I	M	12.2	32.43	6.66	FP	67.2	35.7
Sweden	F	16	3.4	A	1.5	S	I	M	3.2	50.22	12.1	M(A&FP)	94.6	13.3
Switzerland	—	15	21.6	—	—	—	—	—	—	19.6	20.32	—	93	—
Turkey	—	11	17.3	—	—	—	—	—	—	33.22	23.46	—	a	—
United Kingdom	S	16	—	A	1.1	S	M	O	15.3	78.09	23.37	M(A&FP)	93.2	41.4
Mean			13.4		2.0				8.7	30.8	13.6		86.0	33.7

between countries that practice very early streaming (at an age between 10 and 12 years) and those that wait until pupils are at least 14 years old or more. In the first group, in addition to Turkey, can be found Austria, Belgium, the Czech Republic, Germany, Hungary, Latvia, Liechtenstein, Luxembourg, the Netherlands and the Slovak Republic. At the other extreme (streaming from 16 years), in the second group, can be found Denmark, Estonia, Finland, Iceland, Malta, Poland, Spain, Sweden and the United Kingdom.

Another way of organising pupils into groups for instruction consists in practising grade repetition. In this case, the weakest pupils, or those that do not achieve the required level at the end of a school year or cycle, are retained in the same class they were attending for one more year. This sort of practice is indicated in column 3 where it is expressed as a percentage. This percentage represents the proportion of 15-year-old pupils who reported in the PISA 2003 survey that they had already repeated at least one year (OECD, to be published, PISA 2003 database). This information allows to identify those countries where grade repetition is a frequent practice, such as Belgium (29.5%), France (38.3%), Germany (20.3%), Luxembourg (37.9%), the Netherlands (28.4%), Portugal (29.5%), Spain (28.6%) and Switzerland (21.6%). At the other end of the spectrum, repetition rates are very low for the Czech Republic (2.6%), Denmark (3.4%), Finland (2.8%), Iceland (0%), Norway (0%), Poland (3.6%), Slovak Republic (2.5%) and Sweden (3.4%).

The data in columns 2 and 3 should be put in relation: a higher frequency of grade repetition is positively associated with early streaming, except in the cases of the Czech and Slovak Republics which practice early streaming but show a low rate of grade repetition. Rather than making a choice between these two mechanisms to manage the flow of pupils according to their abilities, it seems that the systems apply either both or neither.

Column 4 provides information that partially supports that provided in the previous column. It concerns the norm for transition at the end of primary education (ISCED 1) (Eurydice 2005:296, E23, school year 2002/2003). The letter "A" indicates that transition is automatic, the letter "R" indicates that grade repetition is possible each year and the letter "C" indicates that grade repetition is not possible except at the end of the cycle. It is the Nordic countries, along with Cyprus, Greece, Liechtenstein and the United Kingdom, that present the first configuration, which naturally confirms the rates shown in column 3.

Column 5 indicates the percentage of pupils that have special education needs and are not educated in the same schools as other pupils (Eurydice 2005:130, C3; Baye et al. 2006:42, for Belgium, reference period: from

2002 to 2004). As regards this aspect, whereas 0.5% of pupils with special education needs attend special schools in Italy, they are more than nine times as many in Belgium (4.6%), which is just behind Germany (4.8%) and the Czech Republic (5%). Naturally, it is possible to not consider this as segregation, in the same manner as academic segregation or segregation on the basis of socio-economic characteristics. It is nevertheless true that the percentages observed, even though relatively weak, vary quite significantly from one country to another and, unfortunately, seem to be linked to the other indicators for a certain number of countries, e.g. Belgium, Hungary, Germany and the Czech Republic. Also, the weaker values are mostly associated with less segregationist countries as regards the other indicators, with the noteworthy exception of Finland.

In the same perspective (column 8), the integration of allophone immigrant pupils in schools (pre-primary and full-time compulsory education; Eurydice 2005:289, E19, school year 2002/2003) could also be a valid indicator of segregation mechanisms. Some countries integrate these pupils directly into ordinary classes (O), whereas others direct them towards separate classes (S). In some systems, the two models can coexist (M) and some countries, such as Bulgaria, Hungary and Malta, do not indicate any specific measures (NO). Few countries, apart from Germany, Romania and Latvia, declare that these pupils are placed in separate classes. It does not seem to be possible to easily relate the data collected up until now with those given in column 8, with respect to countries that claim to put foreign pupils into ordinary classes or on the contrary to practise a mixed model. As always when a mixed model is mentioned, unfortunately, it is difficult to apprehend its scope. It would be advisable to examine this indicator in more detail.

At the end of compulsory education, or afterwards in those countries where compulsory education is shorter, there are admission conditions for tertiary public and private grant-assisted education courses (Eurydice 2005:86, B14, school year 2002/2003). The column synthesises the different selection modes for the majority of courses. The letter "F" indicates free access to most of the courses, the letter "S" indicates a selection at the level of each individual school (according to the number of places or on the basis of national criteria) and the letter "N" indicates a selection at the national level with direct control over the selection. The distinction that is made between the two selection modes allows to identify only a single country where the level of control of access to tertiary education is really centralised: Greece. Overall, the method of access seems to be particularly open in Austria, Belgium, France, Germany, Iceland, Italy, Liechtenstein, Luxembourg and the Netherlands, at least in a majority of courses, whereas access is more restricted in other cases. It seems that here too, in comparison with other practices already identified (grade repetition and early streaming), two groups of countries can be distinguished: one in which the filters are significant in compulsory education and hardly present for entry into tertiary education and one in which the education system seems very liberal during the period of compulsory schooling, but more selective at the end of it.

The proportion of young people aged 20–24 years for whom the highest level of qualification is ISCED 0 to 2 or 3C – i.e. who do not possess the diploma required for access to tertiary education (Eurydice 2005:313, F5) – also provides a method for estimating whether compulsory education has allowed a majority of young people to attain a basic education level that enables life-long education to be pursued at the highest level. These rates are very variable, from 57.6% in Luxembourg, 57% in Iceland, 61% in Malta, 56.3% in Portugal, to 5.1% in Norway, 13.3% in Sweden and 13.8% in Finland. There does seem to be at least a partial link between the countries that practice a liberal approach during compulsory education and the high rate of young people susceptible to attend tertiary education, on one hand, and the existence of regulations for access to tertiary education, after the end of compulsory education and external to it, on the other hand. This seems to support the idea that a liberal system would not have as its central ambition to organise access to tertiary education through selection procedures (with the risk of eliminating a significant proportion of the school population underway), but rather to practise the regulation of access just before this access takes place.

In terms of evaluation during compulsory education, the certification at the end of general lower secondary education or full-time compulsory education (Eurydice 2005:302, E27, school year 2002/2003) can be performed using different methods (column 7): a certificate awarded on the basis of a final external examination (E), on the basis of marks and work throughout the year (I), on the basis of a final examination and work throughout the year (M) or no certificate (NO). The last case only applies to the Czech and Slovak Republics and the model based on an external examination (E) is only present in Ireland and Romania. The other systems are divided between the mixed model (work during the year and internal examination) and only taking account of the work during the year, without a final examination. Undoubtedly, the situation in these countries would need to be better understood in order to validly use this indicator in the majority of cases.

With regard to the dimension of "equality of treatment", a method for estimating the possible differences between schools is to consider the share of private resources (fees and all other payments to schools) in total spending on education (ISCED 0–6) (Eurydice 2005:176, D7, year 2001). These data, supplied here for information (column 9), are unfortunately not easy to interpret and point to cases that are potentially very divergent; they are thus presented as a possible track, rather than as reliable data on which it is possible to construct a model of understanding.

Column 12 provides information that is undoubtedly much easier to interpret than the preceding one. This is the degree of liberty that parents have in their choice of school in public education (Eurydice 2005:70, B5, school year 2002/2003): "F" indicates "free choice, the parents choose a school without intervention from the authorities to control the number of pupils", "AC" indicates that "pupils are allocated to a school, but the parents can demand a transfer", "A" indicates that "pupils are allocated to a school", "FP" indicates that "the parents choose a school, but the authorities can intervene if the admission capacity is exceeded" and "M" indicates that the system combines two of the preceding methods. Very few countries have a totally libertarian solution (Belgium, Ireland and the Netherlands), even adding those countries where the parents choose except where the admission capacities are reached (Bulgaria, Italy, Latvia, Romania, Slovak Republic and Spain). At the other end of the spectrum, Cyprus, France, Greece, Liechtenstein, Luxembourg, Malta and Portugal allocate the pupils to public schools, with the possibility (column 13) for parents to choose a private school to avoid this.

A complementary approach to the potential mechanisms that could favour segregation would be to consider the proportion of pupils in lower secondary education that are educated in public schools (OECD 2005:418, D5.1, year 2003). On this basis (column 13), the systems that let "market forces" operate the most can be identified. Nevertheless, it must be noted that apart from the Netherlands and Belgium, which only educate 28.8 and 43.2% of their pupils in public schools and stand out for their high segregation rates, a majority of countries are characterised by a percentage higher than 90%, with the exception of Denmark (76.9%), France (78.8%), Luxembourg (79.3%), Portugal (88.7%) and Spain (67.2%)

The analysis which has been carried out in an exploratory manner, according to an essentially univariate approach, can be completed by a tentative synthesis including both sets of variables taken into account until now. Table 5.4 shows this attempt and indicates the ranking of each country for the dimensions "segregation" (column 1) and "school structures" (column 2). The preparation of this synthesis table is based on the calculation of the average ranking of each country for the set of indicators related to each of the two dimensions, the weighting of each of the indicators being considered as equal.

Table 5.4. Average ranking of each country for the dimensions "segregation" and "school structures"

	Segregation	School Structures
Germany	22	19
Austria	21	9
Belgium	19	23
Denmark	5	10
Spain	10	14
Finland	4	2
France	13	13
Greece	15	3
Hungary	25	24
Ireland	8	15
Iceland	1	8
Italy	23	7
Latvia	9	25
Liechtenstein	16	6
Luxembourg	7	16
Norway	2	1
Netherlands	24	18
Poland	6	4
Portugal	14	11
Slovak Republic	17	20
Czech Republic	20	12
United Kingdom[a]	11	21
Sweden	3	5
Switzerland	12	17
Turkey	18	22

[a] See Footnote 1 about the reliability of the PISA data for the United Kingdom for the 2003 survey.

Despite the somewhat unpolished approach that has been proposed, the calculation of rank correlation (Spearman's Rho) leads to the identification of a link between the two dimensions which is significant ($p \leq 0.022$) but moderate (0.455). This indicates, as shown in Fig. 5.1, a certain tendency to observe higher values for the segregation indicators when the school structures are more segregationist. Thus, as shown already by the previous analyses, the Nordic countries feature both low values for the segregation indices and school structures that are not segregationist. Conversely, Belgium, Hungary, Germany, the Netherlands, Turkey and the Slovak Republic have high values for the indicators in both dimensions. Some countries, for example Latvia (school structures that are strongly segregationist, but

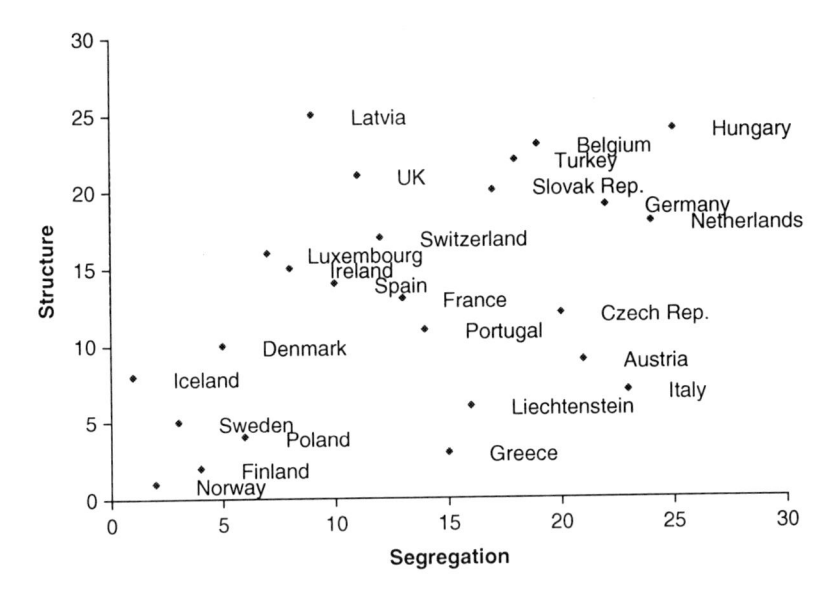

Fig. 5.1. Depiction of the average ranking of the two dimensions "segregation" and "school structures" presented in Table 5.4

segregation indices that are more average) or Greece (school structures that are weakly segregationist, but average segregation indices), show more contrasting profiles and for which it currently seems difficult to understand the relationship between these two dimensions.

5.5. Conclusions

Measuring and comparing the equity of educational systems in Europe is possible through a set of indicators, although, as we have seen, it is advisable beforehand to identify a model that allows the construction of this set of indicators. This requires making choices and clarifying them before going operational with data. The analysis of national and international publications, such as those of the OECD (Baye 2005), has shown that this type of approach is built up very progressively, after a phase during which the available data dominate the reasoning.

The idea according to which a unique variable could allow the description and classification of education systems according to an axis reflecting their greater or lesser equity should, without a doubt, be abandoned. Several dimensions come into play and it seems difficult to reduce this set to only one. From a pragmatic point of view, this is good news: the different countries cannot be classified in a univocal manner, with the exception of some that seem to be performing quite well or quite poorly whatever dimensions are taken into account, as shown by the report from the European Group for Research on Equity in Educational Systems (2005) and its extension to cover all 25 members of the European Union (Baye et al. 2006).

A more difficult task than the design of indicators according to an intelligible model is that of trying to explain the results obtained, taking account of the complex structure of the different education systems. In this chapter, we have tried this approach with regard to a specific dimension of equity, segregation, by describing the structure of the education systems through 14 indicators. The selection of these structure indicators followed the same path as for the equity indicators: on the basis of a model that takes account of two dimensions – the more or less greater fragmentation of the school population in homogenous groups and the implementation of mechanisms to ensure as closely as possible a homogenous treatment of the school population, whatever school is attended. Nevertheless, as with the implementation of the equity indicators, it was necessary to adapt to the available data and we had to conclude that some data are either missing or cannot reliably be used, notably because of the "ragbag" categories.

A significant part of the work to be performed in the future consists of improving these data and describing in more detail, quantitatively and qualitatively, the different education systems in a manner that will put into place the relationships between effectiveness and equity, on one hand, and school policies and organisation, on the other hand. The systematic work carried out by Eurydice is, from this perspective, encouraging. It is certainly advisable that it be continued, through specific studies linking the description of educational structures and the results obtained, notably via segregation indices such as those described in this text.

References

Baye A (2005) Entre efficacité et équité: ce que les indicateurs de l'OECD veulent dire. In: Demeuse M, Baye A., Straeten MH, Nicaise J., Matoul A. (eds) *Vers une école juste et efficace. 26 contributions sur les systèmes d'enseignement et de formation.* Coll. Economie, Société, Région, De Boeck, Bruxelles, pp 539–558

Baye A, Demonty I, Fagnant A, Lafontaine D, Matoul A, Monseur C (2004) Les compétences des jeunes de 15 ans en Communauté française de Belgique en mathématiques, en lecture et en sciences. Résultats de l'enquête PISA 2003. Les Cahiers du Service de Pédagogie expérimentale 19–20

Baye A, Demeuse M, Monseur C, Goffin C (2006) A set of indicators to measure equity in 25 European Union education systems. Report submitted to the European Commission, Directorate General Education and Culture, Bruxelles

Demeuse M (2004) A set of equity indicators of the European Systems. A synthesis. In: Moreno Herrera L, Francia G (eds) *Educational Policies. Implications for Equity, Equality and Equivalence*. Reports from the Department of Education. Orebro University, Orebro (Sweden)

Demeuse M (2006) Qu'indiquent les indicateurs en matière d'éducation ? In: Figari G, Mottier Lopez L (eds) *Recherche sur l'évaluation en éducation*. Problématiques, méthodologies et épistémologie, pp 109–117

Demeuse M, Baye A (2005) Pourquoi parler d'équité ? In: Demeuse M, Baye A, Straeten MH, Nicaise J, Matoul A (eds) *Vers une école juste et efficace. 26 contributions sur les systèmes d'enseignement et de formation*. Coll. Economie, Société, Région, De Boeck, Bruxelles, pp 149–170

Demeuse M, Crahay M, Monseur C (2001) Efficiency and equity. In: Hutmacher W, Cochrane D, Bottani N (eds) *In Pursuit of Equity in Education. Using International Indicators to Compare Equity Policies*. Kluwer Academic Publishers, Dordrecht

Demeuse M, Crahay M, Monseur C (2005) Efficacité et équité dans les systèmes éducatifs. Les deux faces d'une même pièce ? In: Demeuse M, Baye A, Straeten MH, Nicaise J, Matoul A (eds) *Vers une école juste et efficace. 26 contributions sur les systèmes d'enseignement et de formation*. Coll. Economie, Société, Région, De Boeck, Bruxelles, pp 391-410

Dupriez V, Vandenberghe V (2004) L'école en Communauté française de Belgique: de quelle inégalité parlons-nous. *Cahiers de recherche en Education et formation* 27:1–26

European Group for Research on Equity in Educational Systems (2005) Equity in European educational systems: a set of indicators. *European Educational Research Journal* 4(2):1–151

Euridyce (2005) *Chiffres clé de l'éducation*. Euridyce, Bruxelles

Gibson A, Meuret D (1995) The development of indicators on equity in education. *OECD Measuring the Quality of Schools*. OECD, Center for Educational Research and Innovation, Paris

Gorard S, Taylor C (2002) What is segregation? A comparison of measures in terms of strong and weak compositional invariance. *Sociology* 36(4):875–895.

Hutmacher W, Cochrane D, Bottani N (2001) (eds) *In Pursuit of Equity in Education. Using International Indicators to Compare Equity Policies*. Kluwer Academic Publishers, Dordrecht

Monseur C, Demeuse M (2001) Gérer l'hétérogénéité des élèves. Méthodes de regroupement des élèves dans l'enseignement obligatoire. *Les Cahiers du Service de Pédagogie expérimentale* 7–8:25–52

Monseur C, Demeuse M (2004) Quelques réflexions méthodologiques à propos des enquêtes internationales dans le domaine de l'éducation. Politiques d'éducation et de formation. *Analyses et comparaisons internationales* 11:37–54.

Nicaise J, Straeten MH, Baye A, Demeuse M (2005) Comment développer un système d'indicateurs d'équité au niveau européen? In: Demeuse M, Baye A, Straeten MH, Nicaise J, Matoul A (eds) *Vers une école juste et efficace. 26 contributions sur les systèmes d'enseignement et de formation.* Coll. Economie, Société, Région, De Boeck, Bruxelles, pp 337–353

OECD (1999) *Mesurer les connaissances et compétences des élèves. Un nouveau cadre d'évaluation. PISA.* OECD, Paris

OECD (2003) *Cadre d'évaluation de PISA 2003 – Connaissances et compétences en mathématiques, lecture, sciences, résolution de problèmes.* OECD, Paris

OECD (2004) Apprendre aujourd'hui, réussir demain. Premiers résultats de PISA 2003. OECD, Paris

OECD (2005) *Regards sur l'éducation. Les indicateurs de l'OECD 2005.* OECD, Paris

Vandenberghe V (2003) Iniquité scolaire: du/des concept(s) aux mesures. Premiers essais à partir de PISA. Examen des corrélations avec les mesures de ségrégation des publics et les indices d'autonomie des établissements scolaires. Note 24/2/2003. Projet REGULEDUC network.

Hanushek EA, Woessmann L (2005) Does educational tracking affect performance and inequality? Differences-in-differences. Evidence across countries. CESifo Working Paper 1415

Chapter 6
The Economic Benefits of Improved Teacher Quality

Eric A. Hanushek[1]

Hoover Institution, Stanford University, Stanford, CA, USA

6.1. Introduction

Most developed countries are acutely aware of how their students do in comparison to those elsewhere in the world. The now frequent scores on PISA and TIMSS provide direct feedback on schools.[1] But, as comparative test scores have become more plentiful, two key questions arise. First, do scores on these tests make any difference? Second, how can they be changed by any governmental policies? This chapter addresses both of these questions.

Economists are now accustomed to looking at issues of human capital. The simplest notion is that individuals make investments in skills that have later payoffs in outcomes that matter. And, in this, it is commonly presumed that formal schooling is one of the several important contributors to the skills of an individual and to human capital. It is not the only factor. Parents, individual abilities, and friends undoubtedly contribute. Schools nonetheless have a special place because they are most directly affected by public policies.

---

[1] The Programme for International Student Assessment (PISA) has been conducted in 2000, 2003, and 2006; see http://www.oecd.org/pages/0,2966,en_32252351_32235731_1_1_1_1_1,00.html. TIMSS is the Trends in International Mathematics and Science Study (formerly the Third International Mathematics and Science Study) and is a continuation of international testing begun in the 1960s; see http://timss.bc.edu/.

Much of the early and continuing development of empirical work on human capital concentrates on the role of school attainment, that is, the quantity of schooling. The revolution in the United States during the twentieth century was universal schooling. This has spread around the world, encompassing both developed and developing countries. Quantity of schooling is easily measured, and data on years attained, both over time and across individuals, are readily available. But quantity proves to be a poor measure of the skills of individuals both within and across countries.

Today, policy concerns in most corners of the world revolve much more around issues of quality than issues of quantity. This brings us back to PISA and TIMSS. Do standardized tests such as these identify qualities that have economic benefits? The next sections assess what we know about the payoff to cognitive skills for individuals and for nations. In short, there are very large payoffs to such skills. Individuals with more measured cognitive skill systematically do better than those with less. And nations with a more skilled population grow faster than those with a less skilled population.

The implications of this for policy have nonetheless been less clear. Simply providing more resources to schools has proved to be very ineffective. On the other hand, mounting evidence suggests that improving teacher quality is the one way in which student outcomes can be systematically improved. The results about the importance of teacher quality are related directly to the economic benefits of improved quality.

6.2. Impacts of Quality on Individual Incomes – Developed Countries

One of the challenges in understanding the impact of quality differences in human capital has been simply knowing how to measure quality. Much of the discussion of quality – in part related to new efforts to provide better accountability – has identified cognitive skills as the important dimension. And, while there is ongoing debate about the testing and measurement of these skills, most parents and policy makers alike accept the notion that cognitive skills are a key dimension of schooling outcomes. The question is whether this proxy for school quality – students' performance on standardized tests – is correlated with individuals' performance in the labor market and the economy's ability to grow. Until recently, little comprehensive data have been available to show any relationship between differences in cognitive skills and any related economic outcomes. Such data are now becoming available.

Much of the work by economists on differences in worker skills has actually been directed at the issue of determining the average labor market returns to additional schooling and the possible influence of differences in ability. The argument has been that higher-ability students are more likely to continue in schooling. Therefore, part of the higher earnings observed for those with additional schooling really reflects pay for added ability and not for the additional schooling. Economists have pursued a variety of analytical approaches for dealing with this, including adjusting for measured cognitive test scores, but this work generally ignores issues of variation in school quality.[2]

There is mounting evidence that quality measured by test scores is directly related to individual earnings, productivity, and economic growth. A variety of researchers document that the earnings advantages to higher achievement on standardized tests are quite substantial.[3] While these analyses emphasize different aspects of individual earnings, they typically find that measured achievement has a clear impact on earnings after allowing for differences in the quantity of schooling, the experiences of workers, and other factors that might also influence earnings. In other words, higher quality as measured by tests similar to those currently being used in accountability systems around the country is closely related to individual productivity and earnings.

Three recent US studies provide direct and quite consistent estimates of the impact of test performance on earnings (Mulligan 1999; Murnane et al. 2000; Lazear 2003). These studies employ different nationally representative data sets that follow students after they leave schooling and enter the labor force. When scores are standardized, they suggest that one standard deviation increase in mathematics performance at the end of high schools translates into 12% higher annual earnings.

---

[2] The approaches have included looking for circumstances where the amount of schooling is affected by things other than the student's valuation of continuing and considering the income differences among twins (see Card 1999).

[3] These results are derived from different specific approaches, but the basic underlying analysis involves estimating a standard "Mincer" earnings function and adding a measure of individual cognitive skills. This approach relates the logarithm of earnings to years of schooling, experience, and other factors that might yield individual earnings differences. The clearest analyses are found in the following references (which are analyzed in Hanushek 2002). (See Bishop 1989, 1991; O'Neill 1990; Blackburn and Neumark 1993, 1995; Grogger and Eide 1993; Murnane et al. 1995, 2000, 2001; Neal and Johnson 1996; Mulligan 1999; Altonji and Pierret 2001; Lazear 2003).

Murnane et al. (2000) provide evidence from the High School and Beyond and the National Longitudinal Survey of the High School Class of 1972. Their estimates suggest some variation with males obtaining a 15% increase and females a 10% increase per standard deviation of test performance. Lazear (2003), relying on a somewhat younger sample from NELS88, provides a single estimate of 12%. These estimates are also very close to those in Mulligan (1999), who finds 11% for the normalized AFQT score in the NLSY data. By way of comparison, estimates of the value of an additional year of school attainment are typically 7–10%.

There are reasons to believe that these estimates provide a lower bound on the impact of higher achievement. First, these estimates are obtained fairly early in the work career (mid-20s to early 30s), and other analysis suggests that the impact of test performance becomes larger with experience.[4] Second, the labor market experiences that are observed begin in the mid-1980s and extend into the mid-1990s, but other evidence suggests that the value of skills and of schooling has grown throughout and past that period. Third, future general improvements in productivity are likely to lead to larger returns to skill.[5]

A limited number of additional studies are available for developed countries outside of the United States. McIntosh and Vignoles (2001) study wages in the United Kingdom and find strong returns to both numeracy and literacy.[6] Finnie and Meng (2002) and Green and Riddell (2003) investigate returns to cognitive skills in Canada. Both suggest that literacy has a significant return, but Finnie and Meng (2002) find an insignificant return to numeracy. This latter finding stands at odds with most other analyses that have emphasized numeracy or math skills.

Another part of the return to school quality comes through continuation in school. There is substantial US evidence that students who do better in school, either through grades or scores on standardized achievement tests,

---

[4] Altonji and Pierret (2001) find that the impact of achievement grows with experience, because the employer has a chance to observe the performance of workers.

[5] These analyses typically compare workers of different ages at one point in time to obtain an estimate of how earnings will change for any individual. If, however, productivity improvements occur in the economy, these will tend to raise the earnings of individuals over time. Thus, if the patterns of recent decades continue, the impact of improvements in student skills could likely rise over the work life instead of being constant as portrayed here.

[6] Because they look at discrete levels of skills, it is difficult to compare the quantitative magnitudes directly to the US work.

tend to go further in school.[7] Murnane et al. (2000) separate the direct returns to measured skill from the indirect returns of more schooling and suggest that perhaps one-third to one-half of the full return to higher achievement comes from further schooling. Note also that the effect of quality improvements on school attainment incorporates concerns about dropout rates. Specifically, higher student achievement keeps students in school longer, which will lead among other things to higher graduation rates at all levels of schooling.

This work has not, however, investigated how achievement affects the ultimate outcomes of additional schooling. For example, if over time lower-achieving students tend increasingly to attend further schooling, these schools may be forced to offer more remedial courses, and the variation of what students know and can do at the end of school may expand commensurately.

The impact of test performance on individual earnings provides a simple summary of the primary economic rewards to an individual. This estimate combines the impacts on hourly wages and on employment/hours worked. It does not include any differences in fringe benefits or non-monetary aspects of jobs. Nor does it make any allowance for aggregate changes in the labor market that might occur over time.

---

[7] See, for example, Dugan (1976), Manski and Wise (1983). Rivkin (1995) finds that variations in test scores capture a considerable proportion of the systematic variation in high school completion and in college continuation, so that test score differences can fully explain black–white differences in schooling. Bishop (1991) and Hanushek et al. (1996), in considering the factors that influence school attainment, find that individual achievement scores are highly correlated with continued school attendance. Neal and Johnson (1996) in part use the impact of achievement differences of blacks and whites on school attainment to explain racial differences in incomes. Their point estimates of the impact of cognitive skills (AFQT) on earnings and school attendance appear to be roughly comparable to that found in Murnane et al. (2000). Behrman et al. (1998) find strong achievement effects on both continuation into college and quality of college; moreover, the effects are larger when proper account is taken of the various determinants of achievement. Hanushek and Pace (1995) find that college completion is significantly related to higher test scores at the end of high school.

6.3. Impacts of Quality on Individual Incomes – Developing Countries

Questions remain about whether the clear impacts of quality in the United States generalize to other countries, particularly developing countries. The literature on returns to cognitive skills in developing countries is restricted to a relatively limited number of countries: Ghana, Kenya, Morocco, Pakistan, South Africa, and Tanzania. Moreover, a number of studies actually employ the same basic data, albeit with different analytical approaches, but come up with somewhat different results.

Table 6.1 provides a summary of the quantitative estimates available for developing countries. The summary of the evidence permits a tentative conclusion that the returns to quality may be even larger in developing countries than in developed countries. This of course would be consistent with the range of estimates for returns to quantity of schooling (e.g., Psacharopoulos 1994; Psacharopoulos and Patrinos 2004), which are frequently interpreted as indicating diminishing marginal returns to schooling.

There are some reasons for caution in interpreting the precise magnitude of estimates. First, the estimates appear to be quite sensitive to the estimation methodology itself. Both within individual studies and across studies using the same basic data, the results are quite sensitive to the techniques employed in uncovering the fundamental parameter for cognitive skills.[8] Second, the evidence on variations within developing countries is not entirely clear. For example, Jolliffe (1998) finds little impact of skills on farm income, while Behrman et al. (2007) suggest an equivalence across sectors at least on theoretical grounds.

Nonetheless, the overall summary is that the available estimates of the impact of cognitive skills on outcomes suggest strong economic returns within developing countries. The substantial magnitude of the typical estimates indicates that quality concerns are very real for developing countries and that this aspect of schools simply cannot be ignored – a topic that comes up below.

---

[8] The sensitivity to estimation approach is not always the case; see, for example, Jolliffe (1998). A critique and interpretation of the alternative approaches within a number of these studies can be found in Glewwe (2002).

Table 6.1. Summary of estimated returns to a standard deviation increase in cognitive skills

Country	Study	Estimated effect[a]	Notes
Ghana	Glewwe (1996)	0.21**–0.3** (government) 0.14–0.17 (private)	Alternative estimation approaches yield some differences; math effects shown generally more important than reading effects, and all hold even with Raven's test for ability
Ghana	Jolliffe (1998)	0.05–0.07*	Household income related to average math score with relatively small variation by estimation approach; effect from off-farm income with on-farm income unrelated to skills
Ghana	Vijverberg (1999)	?	Income estimates for math and reading with non-farm self-employment; highly variable estimates (including both positive and negative effects) but effects not generally statistically significant
Kenya	Boissiere et al. (1985); Knight and Sabot (1990)	0.19**–0.22**	Total sample estimates: small variation by primary and secondary school leavers
Morocco	Angrist and Lavy (1997)	?	Cannot convert to standardized scores because use indexes of performance; French writing skills appear most important for earnings, but results depend on estimation approach
Pakistan	Alderman et al. (1996)	0.12–0.28*	Variation by alternative approaches and by controls for ability and health; larger and more significant without ability and health controls
Pakistan	Behrman et al. (forthcoming)	0.25	Estimates of structural model with combined scores for cognitive skill; index significant at 0.01 level
South Africa	Moll (1998)	0.34**–0.48**	Depending on estimation method, varying impact of computation; comprehension (not shown) generally insignificant
Tanzania	Boissiere et al. (1985); Knight and Sabot (1990)	0.07–0.13*	Total sample estimates: smaller for primary than secondary school leavers

*Significant at 0.05 level; **significant at 0.01 level.
[a] Estimates indicate proportional increase in wages from a one standard deviation increase in measured test scores.

6.4. Impacts of Quality on Economic Growth

The relationship between measured labor force quality and economic growth is perhaps even more important than the impact of human capital and school quality on individual productivity and incomes. Economic growth determines how much improvement will occur in the overall standard of living of society. Moreover, the education of each individual has the possibility of making others better off (in addition to the individual benefits just discussed). Specifically, a more educated society may lead to higher rates of invention; may make everybody more productive through the ability of firms to introduce new and better production methods; and may lead to more rapid introduction of new technologies. These externalities provide extra reason for being concerned about the quality of schooling.

The potential effect of differences in growth rates on economic well-being is easy to see. Take the expected growth of a country as given and consider how incomes would change with a marginal improvement. Figure 6.1 begins with the value of gross domestic product (GDP) per capita for a

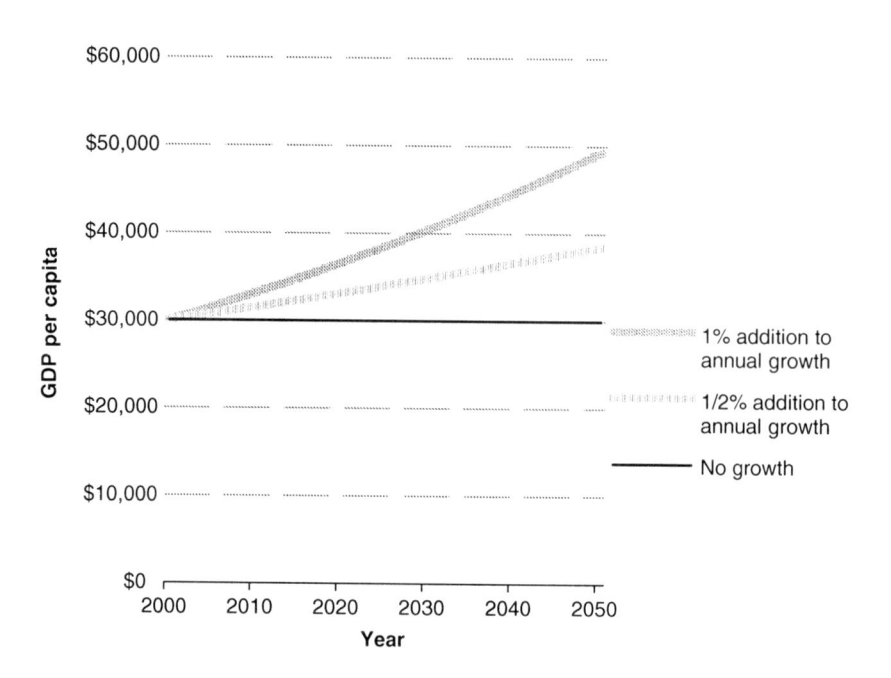

Fig. 6.1. Effect of Economic Growth on Per Capita Income

medium income European country in the year 2000 and shows its value in 2050 under different growth rates (assuming for simplicity that growth would otherwise be zero). If it grows at 1% more each year, this measure (in US dollars) would increase from $30,000 to almost $50,000 – or increasing by almost two-thirds over the period because of this marginal improvement. If it were to grow at 0.5% per year, it would still exceed $38,000 in 2050. Small differences in growth rates have huge implications for the income and wealth of society.

The current economic position of the United States, for example, is largely the result of its strong and steady growth over the twentieth century. Economists have developed a variety of models and ideas to explain differences in growth rates across countries – invariably featuring the importance of human capital.[9]

The empirical work supporting growth analyses has emphasized school attainment differences across countries. Again, this is natural because, while compiling comparable data on many things for different countries is difficult, assessing quantity of schooling is more straightforward. The typical study finds that quantity of schooling is highly related to economic growth rates. But, quantity of schooling is a very crude measure of the knowledge and cognitive skills of people – particularly in an international context.

Hanushek and Kimko (2000) go beyond simple quantity of schooling and delve into quality of schooling.[10] We incorporate the information about international differences in mathematics and science knowledge that has been developed through testing over the past four decades. And we find a remarkable impact of differences in school quality on economic growth.

The international comparisons of quality come from piecing together results of a series of tests administered over the past four decades. In 1963 and 1964, the International Association for the Evaluation of Educational Achievement (IEA) administered the first of a series of mathematics tests to a voluntary group of countries. These initial tests suffered from a

---

[9] Barro and Sala-i-Martin (2004) review recent analyses and the range of factors that are included.

[10] Barro and Lee (2001) provide an analysis of qualitative differences that also includes literacy. Others have also investigated quality and growth; see Barro (2001), Bosworth and Collins (2003), Wößmann (2002), and Jamison et al. (2006).

number of problems, but they did prove the feasibility of such testing and set in motion a process to expand and improve on the undertaking.[11]

Subsequent testing, sponsored by the IEA and others, has included both math and science and has expanded on the group of countries that have been tested. In each, the general model has been to develop a common assessment instrument for different age groups of students and to work at obtaining a representative group of students taking the tests. Using these test data, it is possible to track performance (aggregated across the age groups and subject area of the various tests) over time.[12] The United States and the United Kingdom are the only countries to participate in all of the testing.

There is some movement across time of country performance on the tests, but for the one country that can be checked – the United States – the pattern on international tests is consistent with other data. The National Assessment of Educational Progress (NAEP) in the United States is designed to follow performance of US students for different subjects and ages and shows a sizable dip in US student performance in the 1970s, a period of growth in the 1980s, and a leveling off in the 1990s – exactly the pattern on international tests.

Kimko's and my analysis of economic growth is very straightforward. We combine all of the available earlier test scores into a single composite measure of quality and consider statistical models that explain differences in growth rates across nations during the period 1960–1990.[13] The basic statistical models, which include the initial level of income, the quantity of schooling, and population growth rates, explain a substantial portion of the variation in economic growth across countries.

---

[11] The problems included issues of developing an equivalent test across countries with different school structure, curricula, and language; issues of selectivity of the tested populations; and issues of selectivity of the nations that participated. The first tests did not document or even address these issues in any depth.

[12] The details of the tests and aggregation can be found in Hanushek and Kimko (2000) and Hanushek and Kim (1995).

[13] We exclude the TIMSS and PISA tests from 1995 on because they were taken outside of the analytical period on economic growth. We combine the test measures over the 1965–1991 period into a single measure for each country. The underlying objective is to obtain a measure of quality for the labor force in the period during which growth is measured.

Most important, the quality of the labor force as measured by math and science scores is extremely important. One standard deviation difference on test performance is related to 1% difference in annual growth rates of GDP per capita.[14]

This quality effect, while possibly sounding small, is actually very large and significant. Because the added growth compounds, it leads to powerful effects on national income and on societal well-being. One needs only to return to the calculations presented in Fig. 6.1 to understand the impact of such skill-based improvements in economic growth.

Extensions of this work by Jamison et al. (2006) to 2000 show a very similar pattern of quality on growth. Importantly, building on the construction of new quality information from recent testing by Hanushek and Woessmann (2007), adds considerably more countries to the sample for the growth analysis – and the results hold.

6.5. Importance of Quality

The frequent focus of governmental programs has been increasing school attainment and expanding on the years of schooling of the population. The previous discussion, however, highlights the central importance of quality. While years of schooling attainment are important, that holds only if quality is maintained.

The impact of improved quality can be calculated from the considerations of how quality affects growth rates for economies. Consider the effects of beginning a successful school improvement program in 2005. Of course, school reform takes time. And, even if successful, it takes some time before the school graduates work their way into the labor force and thus some time before the impact will be felt.

Figure 6.2 illustrates the impact that reform could be expected to have over time if it is successful at achieving moderately strong knowledge improvement (corresponding to a 0.5 standard deviation increase

---

[14] The details of this work can be found in Hanushek and Kimko (2000) and Hanushek (2003b). Importantly, adding other factors potentially related to growth, including aspects of international trade, private and public investment, and political instability, leaves the effects of labor force quality unchanged.

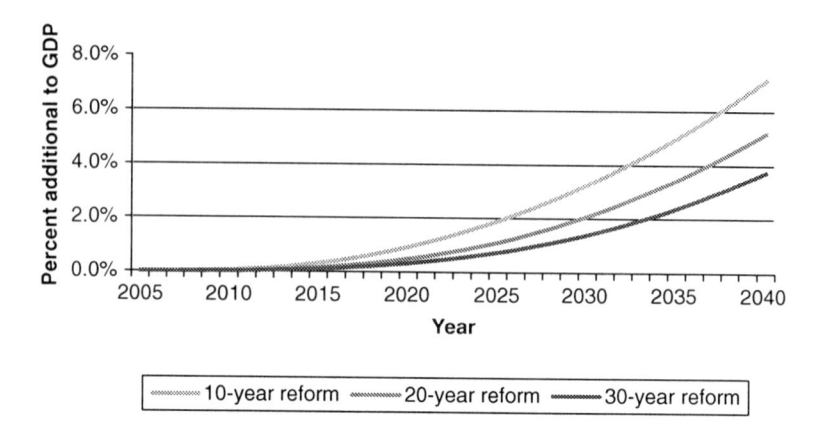

```
                Percent additional to GDP
8.0%
6.0%
4.0%
2.0%
0.0%
    2005  2010  2015  2020  2025  2030  2035  2040
                        Year

········ 10-year reform  ──── 20-year reform  ▬▬▬ 30-year reform
```

Fig. 6.2. Improved GDP with Moderately Strong Knowledge Improvement

in test score achievement).[15] The curves sketch out the path of GDP improvement that would occur with a reform plan that reaches its improvement goal within 10, 20, or 30 years.

Consider just the slow improvement of schools over a 30-year period. In 2040, the GDP would be almost 4% higher than projected without the schooling reforms. Of course, faster reforms would yield even greater gains in GDP. This magnitude would cover total school spending in most countries of the world.

6.6. Causality

One common concern in analysis such as this is that schooling might not be the actual cause of growth but, in fact, may just reflect other attributes of the economy that are beneficial to growth. For example, the East Asian countries consistently score very highly on the international tests, and they also had extraordinarily high growth over the 1960–1990 period. It may be

---

[15] These calculations are calibrated to scores on international mathematics and science exams. The "moderately strong" improvement implies an increase in scores by 0.5 standard deviations across the international comparisons. This is equivalent of bringing a country at the 31st percentile of performance up to the median for the world.

that other aspects of these East Asian economies have driven their growth and that the statistical analysis of labor force quality simply is picking out these countries. But in fact, even if the East Asian countries are excluded from the analysis, a strong – albeit slightly smaller – relationship is still observed with test performance. This test of sensitivity of the results seems to reflect a basic importance of school quality, a factor that contributes also to the observed growth of East Asian countries.

Another concern might be that other factors that affect growth, such as efficient market organizations, are also associated with efficient and productive schools – so that, again, the test measures are really a proxy for other attributes of the country. In order to investigate this, we concentrate on immigrants to the United States who received their education in their home countries. We find that immigrants who were schooled in countries that have higher scores on the international math and science examinations earn more in the United States. This analysis makes allowance for any differences in school attainment, labor market experience, or being native English-language speakers. In other words, skill differences as measured by the international tests are clearly rewarded in the United States labor market, reinforcing the validity of the tests as a measure of individual skills and productivity.

Finally, the observed relationships could simply reflect reverse causality, that is, that countries that are growing rapidly have the resources necessary to improve their schools and that better student performance is the result of growth, not the cause of growth. As a simple test of this, we investigated whether the international math and science test scores were systematically related to the resources devoted to the schools in the years prior to the tests. They were not. If anything, we found relatively better performance in those countries spending less on their schools.

In sum, the relationship between math and science skills on the one hand and productivity and growth on the other comes through clearly when investigated in a systematic manner across countries. This finding underscores the importance of high-quality schooling.

6.7. Why has US Growth been so Strong?

The United States has not been competitive on an international level in terms of tests. It has scored below the median of countries taking the various tests. Moreover, the performance on tests of US students is much stronger at young ages but falls off dramatically at the end of high school

(Hanushek 2003b). Understanding how this matches with growth is important for understanding the broader policy implications.

Earlier, we introduced the discussion of the importance of growth by recounting United States' successful economic growth during the twentieth century. Yet, this is contrasted with the fact that the United States has been at best mediocre in mathematics and science ability. Regardless of the set of countries taking the test, the United States has performed in the middle of the pack or below. Some people find this anomalous. How could math and science ability be important in light of the strong US growth over a long period of time?

The answer is that quality of the labor force is just one aspect of the economy that enters into the determination of growth. A variety of factors clearly contribute, and these factors work to overcome any deficits in quality. These other factors may also be necessary for growth. In other words, simply providing more or higher-quality schooling may yield little in the way of economic growth in the absence of other elements, such as the appropriate market, legal, and governmental institutions to support a functioning modern economy. Past experiences investing in less developed countries that lack these institutional features demonstrate that schooling is not itself a sufficient engine of growth.

Indeed, some have questioned the precise role of schooling in growth. Easterly (2002), for example, notes that education without other facilitating factors such as functioning institutions for markets and legal systems may not have much impact. He argues that World Bank investments in schooling for less developed countries that do not ensure that the other attributes of modern economies are in place have been quite unproductive. As discussed below, schooling clearly interacts with other factors, and these other factors have been important in supporting US growth. They are also surely relevant for other countries.

It is useful to describe some of the other contributing factors to US growth. This is done in part to understand more fully the character of economic growth, but more importantly to highlight some important related issues that are central to thinking about human capital policies.

Almost certainly the most important factor sustaining the growth of the US economy is the openness and fluidity of its markets. The United States maintains generally freer labor and product markets than most countries in the world. The government generally has less regulation on firms (in terms of both labor regulations and overall production), and trade unions are less extensive than those in many other countries. Even broader, the United States has less intrusion of government in the operation of the economy – not only less regulation but also lower tax rates and minimal government production through nationalized industries. These factors encourage investment, permit the rapid development of new products and activities by firms, and allow US workers to adjust to new opportunities. While identifying the precise importance of these factors is difficult, a variety of analyses suggest that such market differences could be very important explanations for differences in growth rates.[16]

Over the twentieth century, the expansion of the education system in the United States also outpaced that around the world. The United States pushed to open secondary schools to all citizens. With this came also a move to expand higher education with the development of land grant universities, the G.I. bill, and direct grants and loans to students. In comparison with other nations of the world, the US labor force has been better educated, even after allowing for the lesser achievement of its graduates. In other words, more schooling with less learning each year has yielded more human capital than found in other nations that have less schooling but learn more in each of those years.

Finally, the analysis of growth rates across countries emphasizes quality of the elementary and secondary schools of the United States. It did not include any measures of the quality of US colleges. By most evaluations, US colleges and universities rank at the very top in the world. No direct measurements of quality of colleges across countries exist. However, there is indirect evidence. Foreign students by all accounts are not tempted to emigrate to the United States to attend elementary and secondary schools – except perhaps if they see this as a way of gaining entry into the country. They do emigrate in large numbers to attend US colleges and universities. They even tend to pay full, unsubsidized tuitions at US colleges, something that many fewer US citizens do.

6.8. Generalizing to Developing Countries

The previous discussions have concentrated considerable attention on the United States and on other developed countries. Most developing countries look very dissimilar to these. Do these results generalize?

The modeling of economic growth in Hanushek and Kimko (2000) relied upon the direct measures of math and science achievement that unfortunately included relatively few developing countries. The analysis did, however, work to extend the modeling to a large number of countries not included in the direct testing. This was done by modeling test scores and

---

[16] See, for example, Krueger (1974); World Bank (1993); Parente and Prescott (1994, 1999).

then projecting the results to other countries. The analysis did not, however, consider all countries. It excluded countries whose predicted scores fell outside the range of observed tests. This exclusion applied to a number of developing countries.

Within the set of countries with observed or projected test data, the growth models appear rather robust. A variety of tests indicate that the modeling applies to the range of countries. This is reinforced by the additions to the sample by Jamison et al. (2006).

Questions remain, however, about the wider range of countries. Clearly, many of the arguments made by Easterly (2002) obviously apply to the most destitute countries – those which also tend to lack a good structure of laws, which tend to have a variety of restrictions on labor and product markets, and so forth. These countries may not be able to fruitfully use schooling investments if the labor markets will not accommodate skilled workers.

The tentative conclusion would be that the previous results generalize if the other conditions for growth also exist. If they do not, it is much more uncertain. But it is also true in the latter cases that investment in quantity of schooling is unlikely to be productive either.

6.9. Improving Quality

Much of school policy is traditionally thought of as an exercise in selecting and ensuring that the optimal set of resources, somehow defined, is available. Matched with this policy perspective has been a line of research considering the relationship between resource usage and student performance. If the effectiveness of different resources or combinations of resources were known, it would be straightforward to define an optimal set of resources. Moreover, we could often decide about policies that would move us toward such an optimal set of resources. Unfortunately, this alludes us.

Schools in the United States have been the focus of extensive research. Both aggregate data about performance of schools over time and more detailed school and classroom data point to a simple conclusion: There is a lack of any consistent or systematic effect of resources on student achievement. While controversial, partly because of the conflict with existing school policies, the evidence is very extensive (Hanushek 2003a). Most other countries of the world have not tracked student performance over any length of time, making analyses comparable to the US discussion impossible. Nonetheless, international testing over the past four decades permits an overview of spending across countries. The simplest overview

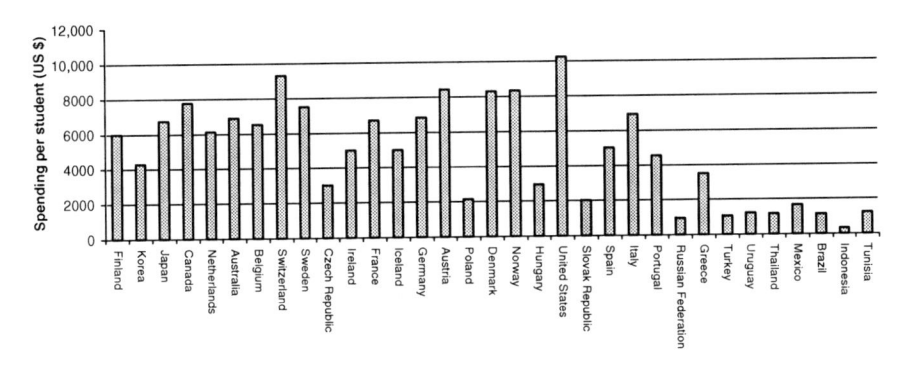

The Economic Benefits of Improved Teacher Quality

Fig. 6.3. Expenditure per Sutdent at All Levels (countries ranked by combined PISA 2003 scores)

comes from the most recent PISA tests. Figure 6.3 ranks countries by performance on PISA, and the height of the bars gives the spending per pupil in each (on a purchasing power parity basis). Instead of a simple declining pattern, one sees essentially no correlation until reaching the least developed countries.

Seven different mathematics and science tests (the data for the growth analysis) were given between the early 1960s and 1995 to students at different grade levels in a varying set of voluntarily participating nations. Performance bears little relationship to the patterns of expenditure across the countries. Hanushek and Kimko (2000) estimate models that relate spending, family backgrounds and other characteristics of countries to student performance for the tests prior to 1995. This estimation consistently indicates a statistically significant negative effect of added resources on performance after controlling for other influences. Similar findings hold for the OECD countries.

Existing statistical analyses in less developed countries have shown a similar inconsistency of estimated resource effects as that found in the United States (Hanushek 1995). In general, a minority of the available studies suggests much confidence that commonly identified resources – class size, teacher experience, and teacher salaries – positively influence student performance. There is generally somewhat stronger support for these resource policies than that existing in US analyses, hinting that the importance of resources may vary with the level of resources. Nonetheless, the evidence does not indicate that pure resource policies can be expected to have a significant effect on student outcomes.

In sum, a wide range of analyses indicate that overall resource policies have not led to discernible improvements in student performance. It is important to understand what is and is not implied by this conclusion. First, it does not mean that money and resources *never* matter. There clearly are situations where small classes or added resources have an impact. It is just that no good description of when and where these situations occur is available, so that broad resource policies such as those legislated from central governments may hit not only some good uses but also bad uses that generally lead to offsetting outcomes. Second, this statement does not mean that money and resources *cannot* matter. Instead, as described below, altered sets of incentives could dramatically improve the use of resources.

The evidence on resources is remarkably consistent across countries, both developed and developing. Had there been distinctly different results for some subsets of countries, issues of what kinds of generalizations were possible would naturally arise. Such conflicts do not appear particularly important.

Many countries have of course attempted to improve their schools. While some have succeeded, many have not. One explanation for past failure is simply that insufficient attention has been given to teacher quality. By many accounts, the quality of teachers is the key element to improving student performance. But the research evidence also suggests that many of the policies that have been pursued around the world have not been very productive. Specifically, the chosen policies of individual countries may have led to changes in measured aspects of teachers such as degrees or teacher qualifications, but they have not tended to improve the quality of teachers – at least when quality is identified by student performance.[17]

Rivkin et al. (2005) describe estimates of differences in teacher quality on an output basis. Specifically, the concern is identifying good and bad teachers on the basis of their performance in obtaining gains in student achievement. An important element of that work is distinguishing the effects of teachers from the selection of schools by teachers and students and the matching of teachers and students in the classroom. In particular, highly motivated parents search out schools that they think are good, and they attempt to place their children in classrooms where they think the teacher is particularly able. Teachers follow a similar selection process (Hanushek et al. 2004). Thus, from an analytical viewpoint, it is difficult to

---

[17] For a review of existing US literature, see Hanushek and Rivkin (2004). This paper describes various attempts to estimate the impact of teacher quality on student achievement. Similar studies are currently much less available in other countries.

sort out the quality of the teacher from the quality of the students that he/she has in his/her classroom. The analysis of teacher performance in Rivkin et al. (2005) goes to great lengths to avoid contamination from any such selection and matching of kids and teachers.

Estimates show that the differences in annual achievement growth between an average and a good teacher are large. Within one academic year, a good teacher can move a typical student up at least four percentiles in the overall distribution (equal to a change of 0.12 standard deviations of student achievement).[18] From this, it is clear that having a series of good teachers can dramatically affect the achievement of any student. In fact, a series of good teachers can erase the deficits associated with poor preparation for school.

It is also possible to see what these results imply for improving student achievement in the aggregate. Perhaps the simplest policy is to replace teachers who leave the profession with new, higher-quality teachers. While turnover of teachers differs across countries, a description of the implications for the US school system illustrates the general points. In the United States, around 7% of all teachers exit teaching each year; another 6% change schools. To give some sense of the leverage hiring has on the system, this range (7–13%) is used to identify the replacement possibilities.

Figure 6.4 displays the annual hiring improvement that is necessary to achieve a 0.5 standard deviation improvement under a 10-, 20-, and 30-year reform plan and based on applying it to either just those exiting or the higher turnover rates that include transfers. As is obvious, the stringency of the new hiring is greater when there is a shorter reform period and when fewer new (higher-quality) teachers are brought in each year. Achieving a 0.5 SD boost in achievement in 10 years by upgrading just those who exit each year implies hiring at the 61st percentile, but this declines to the 52nd percentile for a 30-year plan where the higher turnover population is subject to these new hiring standards.

These calculations are meant to illustrate two points. First, existing research into student achievement and teacher quality shows that teachers have significant leverage on performance. By implication, if better teachers can be hired and retained, significant changes in student achievement

---

[18] In another attempt to estimate the variation in teacher quality, we analyze variations across classrooms within a large school district in Texas (Hanushek et al. 2005). In this, we match individual teachers and students and look at achievement-based quality measures of each teacher compared to all of the teachers in the district or, alternatively, all of the other teachers in each school. On a basis comparable to the prior estimates, we obtain an estimate of teacher quality between 0.15 and 0.18 standard deviations of student achievement.

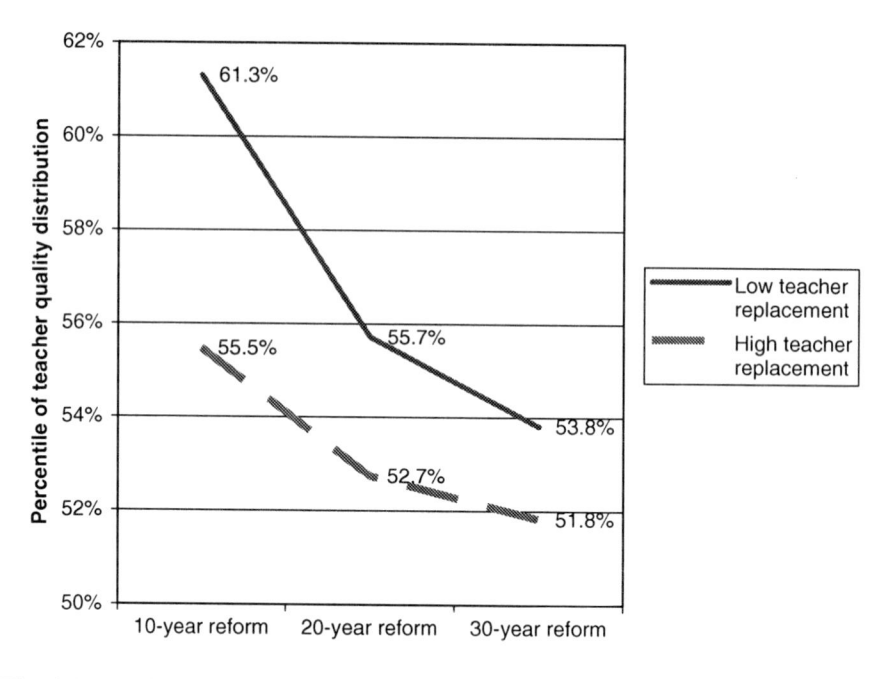

Fig. 6.4. Required Quality Percentile for New Teaches (0.5 s.d. Reform)

can be obtained. Second, without dramatic changes in policies about teacher retention, feasible reform will take a quite long period of time. Specifically, unless larger numbers of current teachers are fired and replaced, changing the character of the teaching force takes time.

6.10. Conclusions

School quality is directly related to decisions about attending schools and to promotion through schools. High-quality schools raise student achievement and speed students through primary (and perhaps secondary) schools, thus conserving on costs. Thus, studies of the rate of return to schooling which only consider quantity of schooling produce a misleading estimate of the potential gains. Estimation of the rate of return to schooling that does not account for quality differences will systematically overstate the productivity gains that are associated with additional years of schooling, because the estimates will include quality differences that are correlated with quantity. If policy simply pushes people to stay in school longer, without changing the fundamental quality of the schools, the newly induced school completers will only get the returns associated with years of schooling and not with quality. Thus, they will not be able to gain as much as the rate of return estimates suggest.

Policy makers who concentrate on quality of schools are frequently stopped, however, when they begin considering how to improve quality. There has been a huge amount of work on various approaches, but the record of accomplishments is modest.

Recent work underscores the importance of high-quality teachers. While the evidence is limited to US schools, teachers appear to have a very strong impact on student outcomes. Unfortunately, teacher quality is not simply measured by such things as experience or teacher education. Thus, developing policies to implement this finding will take some effort.

Nonetheless, the potential economic gains from improvement also suggest that there is considerable room for aggressive policies to attract and retain good teachers. With a suitable planning horizon, it appears feasible to upgrade the teaching force, yielding truly large gains for students and for nations.

Acknowledgment

Lei Zhang provided valuable research assistance.

References

Alderman H, Behrman JR, David R, Sabot R (1996) The returns to endogenous human capital in Pakistan's rural wage labor market. *Oxford Bulletin of Economics and Statistics* 58:29–55

Altonji JG, Pierret CR (2001) Employer learning and statistical discrimination. *Quarterly Journal of Economics* 116:313–350

Angrist JD, Lavy V (1997) The effect of a change in language of instruction on the returns to schooling in Morocco. *Journal of Labor Economics* 15:S48–S76

Barro RJ (2001) Human capital and growth. *American Economic Review* 91:12–17

Barro RJ, Lee J-w (2001) International data on educational attainment: updates and implications. *Oxford Economic Papers* 53:541–563

Barro RJ, Sala-i-Martin X (2004) *Economic Growth* (second edition). The MIT Press, Cambridge, MA

Behrman JR, Kletzer LG, McPherson MS, Schapiro MO (1998) The microeconomics of college choice, careers, and wages: measuring the impact of higher education. *Annals of the American Academy of Political and Social Science* 559:12–23

Behrman JR, David R, Sabot R (2007) Improving the quality versus increasing the quantity of schooling: estimates of rates of return from rural Pakistan. *Journal of Development Economics.* Article in press

Bishop J (1989) Is the test score decline responsible for the productivity growth decline? *American Economic Review* 79:178–197

Bishop J (1991) Achievement, test scores, and relative wages. In: Kosters MH (ed) *Workers and Their Wages.* The AEI Press, Washington, DC, pp 146–186

Blackburn, ML, Neumark D (1993) Omitted-ability bias and the increase in the return to schooling. *Journal of Labor Economics* 11:521–544

Blackburn, ML, Neumark D (1995) Are OLS estimates of the return to schooling biased downward? Another look. *Review of Economics and Statistics* 77:217–230

Boissiere MX, Knight JB, Sabot R (1985) Earnings, schooling, ability, and cognitive skills. *American Economic Review* 75:1016–1030

Bosworth BP, Collins SM (2003) The empirics of growth: an update. *Brookings Papers on Economic Activity* 2:113–206

Card D (1999) Causal effect of education on earnings. In: Ashenfelter O, Card D (eds) *Handbook of Labor Economics.* North-Holland, Amsterdam, pp 1801–1863

Dugan DJ (1976) Scholastic achievement: its determinants and effects in the education industry. In: Froomkin JT, Jamison DT, Radner R (eds) *Education as an Industry.* Ballinger, Cambridge, MA, pp 53–83

Easterly W (2002) *The Elusive Quest for Growth: An Economists' Adventures and Misadventures in the Tropics.* The MIT Press, Cambridge, MA

Finnie R, Ronald M (2002) Minorities, cognitive skills, and incomes of Canadians. *Canadian Public Policy* 28:257–273

Glewwe P (1996) The relevance of standard estimates of rates of return to schooling for educational policy: a critical assessment. *Journal of Development Economics* 51:267–290

Glewwe P (2002) Schools and skills in developing countries: education policies and socioeconomic outcomes. *Journal of Economic Literature* 40:436–482

Green DA, Riddell WC (2003) Literacy and earnings: an investigation of the interaction of cognitive and unobserved skills in earnings generation. *Labour Economics* 10:165–184

Grogger JT, Eide E (1993) Changes in college skills and the rise in the college wage premium. *Journal of Human Resources* 30:280–310

Hanushek EA (1995) Interpreting recent research on schooling in developing countries. *World Bank Research Observer* 10:227–246

Hanushek EA——— (2002) Publicly provided education. In: Auerbach AJ, Feldstein M (eds) *Handbook of Public Economics.* Elsevier, Amsterdam, pp 2045–2141

Hanushek EA (2003a) The failure of input-based schooling policies. *Economic Journal* 113:F64–F98

Hanushek EA (2003b) The importance of school quality. In: Peterson PE (ed.) *Our Schools and Our Future: Are We Still at Risk?* Hoover Institution Press, Stanford, CA, pp 141–173

Hanushek EA, Kain JF, O'Brien DM, Rivkin SG (2005) The market for teacher quality. Working Paper 11154, National Bureau of Economic Research

Hanushek EA, Kain JF, Rivkin SG (2004) Why public schools lose teachers. *Journal of Human Resources* 39:326–354

Hanushek EA, Kim D (1995) Schooling, labor force quality, and economic growth. Working Paper 5399, National Bureau of Economic Research

Hanushek EA, Kimko D (2000) Schooling, labor force quality, and the growth of nations. *American Economic Review* 90:1184–1208

Hanushek EA, Pace R (1995) Who chooses to teach (and why)? *Economics of Education Review* 14:101–117

Hanushek EA, Rivkin SG (2004) How to improve the supply of high quality teachers. In: Ravitch D (ed.) *Brookings Papers on Education Policy 2004*. Brookings Institution Press, Washington, DC, pp 7–25

Hanushek EA, Rivkin SG, Taylor L (1996) Aggregation and the estimated effects of school resources. *Review of Economics and Statistics* 78:611–627

Hanushek EA, Woessmann L (2007) The role of education quality for economic growth. Policy Research Working Paper Series 4122, The World Bank. Washington

Jamison EA, Jamison DT, Hanushek EA (2006) The effects of education quality on mortality decline and income growth. International Conference on the Economics of Education, June 20–23, Dijon, France)

Jolliffe D (1998) Skills, schooling, and household income in Ghana. *World Bank Economic Review* 12:81–104

Knight JB, Sabot RH (1990) *Education, Productivity, and Inequality*. Oxford University Press, New York

Krueger AO (1974) The political economy of the rent seeking society. *American Economic Review* 64:291–303

Lazear EP (2003) Teacher incentives. *Swedish Economic Policy Review* 10:179–214

Manski CF, Wise DA (1983) *College Choice in America*. Harvard University Press, Cambridge

McIntosh S, Vignoles A (2001) Measuring and assessing the impact of basic skills on labor market outcomes. *Oxford Economic Papers* 53:453–481

Moll PG (1998) Primary schooling, cognitive skills, and wage in South Africa. *Economica* 65:263–284

Mulligan CB (1999) Galton versus the human capital approach to inheritance. *Journal of Political Economy* 107:S184–S224

Murnane RJ, Willett JB, Braatz MJ, Duhaldeborde Y (2001) Do different dimensions of male high school students' skills predict labor market success a decade later? Evidence from the NLSY. *Economics of Education Review* 20:311–320

Murnane RJ, Willett JB, Duhaldeborde Y, Tyler JH (2000) How important are the cognitive skills of teenagers in predicting subsequent earnings? *Journal of Policy Analysis and Management* 19:547–568

Murnane RJ, Willett JB, Levy F (1995) The growing importance of cognitive skills in wage determination. *Review of Economics and Statistics* 77:251–266

Neal DA, Johnson WR (1996) The role of pre-market factors in black–white differences. *Journal of Political Economy* 104:869–895

O'Neill J (1990) The role of human capital in earnings differences between black and white men. *Journal of Economic Perspectives* 4:25–46

Parente SL, Prescott EC (1994) Barriers to technology adoption and development. *Journal of Political Economy* 102:298–321

Parente SL, Prescott EC (1999) Monopoly rights: a barrier to riches. *American Economic Review* 89:1216–1233

Psacharopoulos G (1994) Returns to investment in education: a global update. *World Development* 22:1325–1344

Psacharopoulos G, Patrinos HA (2004) Returns to investment in education: a further update. *Education Economics* 12:111–134

Rivkin SG (1995) Black/white differences in schooling and employment. *Journal of Human Resources* 30:826–852

Rivkin SG, Hanushek EA, Kain JF (2005) Teachers, schools, and academic achievement. *Econometrica* 73:417–458

Vijverberg WPM (1999) The impact of schooling and cognitive skills on income from non-farm self-employment. In: Glewwe P (ed) *The Economics of School Quality Investments in Developing Countries: An Empirical Study of Ghana.* St Martin's Press (with University of Oxford), New York

World Bank (1993) *The East Asian Miracle: Economic Growth and Public Policy.* Oxford University Press, New York

Wößmann L (2002) *Schooling and the Quality of Human Capital.* Springer, Berlin

Comments

George Sheldon[1]

[1]*Director of the Industrial Organization and Labor Market Research Unit (FAI), Department of Economics, University of Basel, Basel, Switzerland*

Eric Hanushek's chapter reviews two strands of literature relating to the quality of schooling. One line of research pertains to the impact of school quality on individual earnings and economic growth and uses standardized achievement test scores in place of years of schooling as proxies for human capital in Mincer wage equations and international growth regressions. The second direction of enquiry focuses on the factors determining the level of school quality and employs test scores too, albeit as dependent variables – instead of explanatory variables – in educational production functions intended to explain the variation of achievement test scores across participants. In assessing the research results, Hanushek concludes (1) that the quality of schooling has a strong impact on individual earnings and economic growth and (2) that the amount of educational resources invested in schooling has no systematic effect on the quality of schooling. He qualifies the latter albeit by noting that recent research suggests that at least teacher quality has a statistically significant impact on students' cognitive abilities.

Hanushek provides a very clear and enlightening overview of current research, and I can subscribe to much of what he has to say. Only in two instances do I have any serious reservations. The one case pertains to his claim that no systematic relationship exists between the amount of educational resources invested and the cognitive ability of students, and the other to his thesis that the *quality* of schooling, at least in developed countries, has a greater impact on individual incomes and economic growth than the *quantity* of schooling.

I begin with my first point of contention: the apparent lack of a systematic relationship between the amount of educational resources invested and students' level of cognitive skills. I do not wish to belabor this point, however, as many other authors have already questioned Hanushek's stance on this issue, as he himself knows. Besides, I generally agree with Hanushek's judgment that throwing money at an educational problem does not necessarily solve it and that educational policy is often economically inefficient. What I wish to bring to mind here are two other points. First of all, the assessment that no systematic relationship exists between the level of educational inputs, and the output of cognitive skills they engender generally rests on a simple comparison of the number of educational production function regressions that yield positive, negative, or statistically insignificant results without considering whether the results are multiple estimates pertaining to the same sample of data and without taking the ranking of the journal of publication into account. Other authors[19] have shown that one can reach quite different conclusions when the latter two factors are regarded.

Secondly, it is important to consider what an apparent failure to find a systematic relationship means or implies. It could indicate that a relationship does in fact not exist or, instead, that the educational process was inadequately modeled, the data were poor, or the empirical methodology was inappropriate. Todd and Wolpin (2003) provide reasons to believe that not only the non-existence of a relationship, but faulty research as well is the cause.

I turn now to my second point of contention, the claim that the *quality* of schooling is the central educational issue today and not the *quantity* of schooling. Hanushek bases his judgment largely on the observation that standardized achievement test scores are better able to explain individual income differences and international economic growth disparities than the number of years spent in school, i.e., than the level of educational attainment. Cognitive skill levels, which standardized achievement test scores are intended to measure, are not solely the product of the quality of schooling, however. In fact, as Hanushek himself notes, cognitive abilities not only depend on the quality of schooling, but among other things also on the level of educational achievement, parental upbringing,[20] cultural differences, and innate ability. Hence it is basically unknown what the determining factors are that lie behind the cognitive skills that enter into these regressions. School quality is but one possibility.

What the better predicative power of achievement test scores really tells us is that years of schooling are a poorer measure of cognitive ability than standardized achievement test scores and that the economic impact of hu-

---

[19] See for instance Hedges et al. (1994) or Krueger (2003).
[20] Wössmann (2004), for example, finds that the explanatory power of parental background dwarfs the effects of school inputs and institutional features on educational achievement.

man capital increases noticeably when the latter is more accurately measured. That is good news for economists as it underscores the importance of the economic study of education.

The distinction between the quantity and quality of schooling is not merely a matter of semantics either. The critical issue in the United States may indeed be one of school quality, as evidenced by the trend decline in achievement test scores despite increasing spending on education. But in Europe, the quantity of schooling, especially the low educational attainment of foreign youth, is a major issue as well. Many young foreigners in Europe are the children of low-skilled guest workers recruited to perform menial tasks that natives find unattractive to do. Given the low intergenerational educational mobility in Europe, a disproportionate share of young foreigners are thus concentrated in remedial and unchallenging paths of study that offer little opportunity for educational and economic advancement. As a consequence youth unemployment in Europe is particularly high among foreigners.[21] A large stock of low-skilled labor is an educational issue that Europe cannot afford to ignore. Given the skill bias of technical progress and the ongoing export of low-skilled manufacturing jobs to developing countries, it threatens the international competitiveness of Europe's economies.

But why is academic attainment among foreign youth so low in Europe? Recent evidence in Switzerland suggests two possible causes. One of the reasons appears to be the comparatively early selection of students into different educational paths of study. In many cantons in Switzerland, and in most of Germany as well, the decision by the school authorities to allow young persons to pursue a course of studies permitting later entry into college is often based on a student's marks in fourth grade and without the aid of standardized test scores. Bauer and Riphahn (2005) show that early selection significantly lowers the intergenerational educational mobility of foreign youth in Switzerland. In the canton of Ticino, for example, where selection does not occur until after eighth grade, the intergenerational educational mobility among foreign youth is much higher.

A further cause of the low academic path of foreign youth appears to be statistical discrimination. Research presently being carried out at my institute at the University of Basel points in this direction.[22] Statistical discrimination arises in the educational system when the school authorities – for lack of more objective information – use proxies for cognitive ability in placing students of different capabilities into different levels of course study. Nationality could serve as such a proxy as foreign students in Swit-

---

[21] Cf. OECD (2001).
[22] See Bauer (2006).

zerland score lower on the PISA test on average than observably identical natives. Note that statistical discrimination differs from other forms of discrimination in that it is statistically fair on average. Any injustices arising from incorrect placement result from inadequate information and not from personal prejudices.[23]

Our research indicates that school grades, upon which school placement is based in Switzerland, are a poor predictor of cognitive ability as measured by PISA test scores, showing that the school authorities are indeed subject to informational uncertainty when making their placement decisions on the basis of school grades. Secondly, we find that the predictive ability of grades improves significantly when the nationality of a student is additionally taken into account. Hence it is statistically fairer to include a student's nationality when trying to assess his or her cognitive abilities on the basis of school grades. And finally we discover that teachers do not discriminate against foreigners in setting grades. Thus the lower educational placement of foreigners is not due to personal prejudices, as some Swiss fear.

A simple means of eliminating statistical discrimination of course exists. The solution is to introduce mandatory standardized achievement tests nationwide. Achievement test scores would eliminate quality uncertainty allowing the authorities to place students in accordance with their true cognitive capabilities.

The benefits of standardized achievement test scores are not limited to the elimination of statistical discrimination in school placement, however. As Hanushek's survey clearly points out, achievement test scores also provide the requisite empirical basis for measuring accurately the economic benefits of education, which according to his survey are substantial, and for determining which educational policy instruments are the most effective in which settings. The availability of achievement test scores is also essential for assessing the economic efficiency of the educational system and thus to ensure that scarce educational resources are being put to full use. In short, test score information is vital for forging an educational policy intended to serve the interests of both the instructed and society as a whole. That is to my mind the central message that Hanushek's chapter has for European educational policymakers. Hopefully it will be heeded.

---

[23]Cf. Phelps (1972) or Aigner and Cain (1977).

References

Aigner D, Cain G (1977) Statistical theories of discrimination in labor markets. *Industrial and Labor Relations Review* 30:175–187

Bauer P (2006) Are school grades a good signal for skills? Industrial Organization and Labor Market Research Unit (FAI), (Mimeo), University of Basel

Bauer P, Riphahn R (2005) Timing of school tracking as a determinant of intergenerational transmission of education. *Economics Letters* 91:90–97

Hedges L, Laine R, Greenwald R (1994) Does money matter? A meta-analysis of studies of the effects of differential school inputs on student outcomes. *Educational Researcher* 23:5–14

Krueger A (2003) Economic considerations and class size. *Economic Journal* 113:F3–F33

OECD (2001) *Employment Outlook*. Paris

Phelps E (1972) The statistical theory of racism and sexism. *American Economic Review* 62:659–661

Todd P, Wolpin K (2003) On the specification and estimation of the production function for cognitive achievement. *Economic Journal* 113:F3–F33

Wössmann L (2004) How equal are educational opportunities? Family background and student achievement in Europe and the United States. CESifo Working Paper 1162, University of Munich

Chapter 7
Direct Democracy and Public Education in Swiss Cantons

Justina A.V. Fischer

London School of Economics, London, UK and University of St Gallen, St-Gallen, Switzerland

7.1. Introduction

The unexpectedly mediocre performance of Switzerland in the international PISA study in 2000 has rekindled discussion about improving its educational system.[1] At the same time, cuts in the federal, cantonal, and local budgets have become necessary due to the economic recession, which have also affected the financial means available for public education. The ongoing debates about school reforms are complicated by the fact that the Swiss voter has an important influence on fiscal and budgetary issues through direct legislation. In general, direct legislative institutions restrict the financial means available to the sub-federal government for the provision of schooling (Schaltegger 2001; Fischer 2005b,c). The underlying question is whether people's control over the school budget necessarily leads to a lower quality of this public good or not. Since Swiss cantons are heterogeneous with respect to the degree of direct democracy, and quite autonomous in their policies on public education, Switzerland appears to be especially suitable for such an analysis.

This chapter aims at contributing to these recent discussions in Switzerland by summarizing the most recent findings on the impact of direct democracy on educational spending in general, school budget components in specific and, finally, the quality of public education. The data used in these

---

[1] The average Swiss test score in reading with 499 was statistically not different from the international mean of 494 for the PISA 2003 study. The highest score was observed for Finland (543), and the lowest for Tunisia (375). See also Table T 15.03.02.01 available through http://www.bfs.admin.ch/.

studies are government spending and class size information provided by the Swiss Federal Statistical Office and individual data on Swiss ninth graders' test performances collected simultaneously with the OECD PISA data collection in 2000.

The rest of this chapter is organized as follows: first, in Section 7.2 some information on the political and public educational system in Switzerland is briefly presented. In the subsequent section, recent research on the impact of direct legislation on educational spending (in total and by various components) and class size is described (Section 7.3). Then the results when estimating an educational production function augmented by the political institution for student performance in the three test subjects – reading, mathematics, and natural science – are discussed (Section 7.4). In Section 7.5, the relationship between teacher qualification, educational spending, and direct democracy are analysed. Finally, Section 7.6 concludes with some policy recommendations.

7.2. Institutional Background

When discussing educational issues with respect to Switzerland it is important to be aware of the institutional framework and the organization of public education in this country. More specifically, two aspects need to be briefly introduced: first, the division of financial responsibilities for public schooling among the government tiers, and second, the issue of decision-making decentralization in the policy area relating to schooling. Implicitly, both aspects raise the question to what extent citizens' influence through direct legislation affects the various areas and aspects of public education. A concise overall introduction to the Swiss educational system can be found in Freitag and Bühlmann (2003), while the following section describes the organization of compulsory education, the quality of which was assessed by the OECD PISA 2000 study. In Switzerland, compulsory education finishes with the ninth grade, usually at the age of about 15.

Switzerland is a three-tiered federal state with one central, 26 cantonal (state), and about 3000 local (communal) governments. As stipulated in its federal constitution (Art. 3), public education is among the core jurisdictions of the cantons in which local autonomy remains unchallenged by the central government (Germann 2002). As regards compulsory education, Swiss cantons bear a two-fold responsibility: they have the ultimate authority in school organizational issues including the determination of school curricula and design of the school system, and they also bear the main financial burden for its provision including the costs of instruction and educational investment. The consequences are manifold: first, the central government exerts no decisive political or financial influence on schooling issues; second, this cantonal autonomy gives rise to 26 distinct school systems with school types that are incomparable across cantons; and finally, at the sub-federal level, a strong link between educational spending and schooling outcomes can be presumed.

As regards the overall costs of compulsory education, the federal government contributes only 0.2%, whereas the cantons bear 38.8% and the communes 61.1%.[2] With respect to the communes, they mostly finance primary schools. Although there are as many school systems as there are Swiss states, all cantons share the general characteristics that two types of advanced education can be distinguished: basic education and education to meet advanced requirements (e.g. university preparation). Usually, the second type can only be entered on a selective basis. Nowadays, Swiss cantons' school curricula in primary and secondary stages of education are harmonized to a great extent through inter-cantonal agreements.[3]

Also included in cantonal authority is the general responsibility for the education of teachers, particularly of those for primary and secondary I schools, which takes place in specialized teacher seminaries. At the time when the PISA 2000 study was conducted, more than 100 teacher seminaries run by cantonal departments of education issued teacher licences that were valid only for the corresponding canton, creating a serious obstacle to teacher mobility. A requirement for entry to these institutions was a secondary I degree (obtained after the ninth grade), while the teacher licence itself constituted a secondary II degree. In contrast, training of prospective secondary II school teachers took place at Swiss universities, and teacher candidates had to meet the identical admission criteria as any other student. Thus, these teachers entered university with a secondary II (high school) degree, received a tertiary education, and graduated with a master's degree in a particular subject complemented with additional pedagogical courses. As a consequence, in Switzerland there is a huge gap in education between these two types of teachers, contrasting the teaching requirements prevalent in other countries. A more detailed description of the

---

[2] Information on this issue can be found at www.educa.ch, the Federal Statistical Office, www.bfs.admin.ch or in the annual issues of the *Statistisches Jahrbuch der Schweiz*, Bundesamt für Statistik (ed.), Neue Zürcher Zeitung.

[3] Such a curriculum includes the cantonal main language, a first foreign language, mathematics, writing, religion, history and civics, natural sciences, applied arts, needlework, music, and sports.

organization of education of Swiss teachers at the time of the PISA 2000 study is provided in EDK (2001).

The fundamental regulations of public education are laid down in various cantonal laws on education. These concern all aspects of public education ranging from school organization to financing, the latter including the split of investment or instructional costs between the Swiss canton and its communes.

Turning to the political institutions, Switzerland is shaped by a so-called (semi-)direct democratic political system, namely a representative system complemented by direct democratic institutions that exist at all three levels of the state (federal, cantonal, and communal).[4] While statutory initiatives provide the electorate with an agenda-setting power, the corrective influence on policy outcomes preferred by politicians, which is exerted through fiscal or legislative referenda, is of a reactive nature. Furthermore, Switzerland is characterized by a very strong fiscal decentralization; therefore, in the 26 Swiss cantons a direct institutional link between the power to tax and the power to spend exists. For this reason, through direct democracy citizens exert political influence on both sides of the sub-federal budgets. Since cantons (and communes) differ with respect to their degree of direct democracy, it is possible to analyse the impact of these differences on a particular policy outcome (Feld and Kirchgässner 2001), such as the provision of schooling.

At the state level, political influence through institutions of direct legislation can be exerted through statutory initiatives, statutory referenda as well as fiscal referenda.[5] The first two institutions are broader in their scope than the latter as they affect directly the cantonal laws on education and thus, indirectly, anything that relates to the cantonal school system. In contrast, the fiscal referendum affects solely major spending decisions that meet the constitutional financial threshold, e.g. costs triggered by the construction of a new school building.

To summarize, Switzerland is extremely decentralized in the provision of public education, and the local electorate exerts a strong influence on policy outcomes in this area. This feature of Switzerland has been exploited in various studies on educational outcomes.

---

[4]Forms of semi-direct democracies are also present in about half of the states in the USA (at the state level) and in various American counties and municipalities.

[5]Certainly, institutions of direct legislation that affect amendments to the cantonal constitutions may exert an additional, albeit extremely indirect impact.

7.3. Direct Democracy and Educational Spending in Swiss Cantons

A first generation of studies investigated the impact of direct legislation at the state level on the sub-federal expenses for public education using time-series cross-sectional panels of combined state and local government spending data provided by the Swiss Federal Statistical Office. These contributions focused on total revenue and expenditures only, comprising outlays for all state and locally provided public goods including health care, security and culture, and identified a strong restraining impact of popular rights on both sides of the budget (e.g. Feld and Kirchgässner 2001; Feld and Matsusaka 2003). In these and the following papers, public finance models that view government spending as a function of political factors, government structure features, and socio-demographic characteristics were estimated.[6] In these models, one of the focal variables is the degree of cantonal direct democracy that is commonly measured by an index ranging from 1 (minimum) to 6 (maximum) (for a detailed description of its construction see Stutzer 1999), reflecting the availability of these institutions to the cantonal electorate. That the mere presence of institutions of direct legislation exerts an impact on the policy chosen by politicians has already been shown in various theoretical models of game theory, as they serve as credible threat (e.g. Gerber 1996; Besley and Coate 2001; Feld and Kirchgässner 2001). Thus, even in the case that no initiative is launched and no referendum is taken by the electorate, policy outcomes may differ between cantons with stronger or weaker popular rights.

The first analysis of various budget components was carried out by Schaltegger (2001), who reports a limiting influence of direct democracy on overall spending, particularly in those policy areas in which sub-federal autonomy is present to a great extent. These areas include – besides health, security, culture, and administration – public education. A related study is the one by Freitag and Bühlmann (2003), whose contribution is valuable with regard to the richness of their public finance model and the included spending determinants. Contrasting previous findings, however, their results do not support the view that direct democracy restrains spending on public education. This difference in outcome may be explained by two factors: first, the alternative measure of direct democracy they employed and second, the different spending data they used. More specifically, in the tradition of political scientists, the number of referenda and initiatives

---

[6] See Feld et al. (2006) for a more detailed description of these spending models and predictions for each of their determinants.

actually held is included in their model, potentially understating the effective impact of direct legislation. Furthermore, their spending data contain cantonal expenses solely, omitting the contribution of the local level. However, due to the differences across Swiss cantons with respect to the split of the financial burden between the communes and the state, restricting the analysis to cantonal spending provides only a fairly incomplete picture.[7] Using sub-federal educational spending per pupil rather than per capita as in Schaltegger (2001), Fischer (2006) finds that the spending restraint impact of popular rights becomes even more pronounced.[8]

Dividing the budget component "educational spending" into further categories, an analysis by type of spending (current/investment) and school type was carried out by Fischer (2005a). Given that a major proportion of current educational spending, in some cantons up to 80%, comprises spending on instruction such as wage payments for teachers and instruction material, current spending serves as good proxy for instructional spending.[9] In general, direct democracy does not appear to affect investment spending for the different school types in any systematic way, potentially because of its rather erratic occurrence over time. In contrast, current spending on the school administration appeared significantly lowered in more direct democratic cantons. The picture for current expenses by school type is more differentiated: on overall instructional spending, a restraint impact resulting from stronger popular rights is identified that is congruent with previous studies. As regards school types, the financial resources for not only professional secondary II schools in particular but also secondary I education appear negatively affected, while no impact on current expenses is observable for, e.g. primary schools. Furthermore, a lowered spending effect is equally identified when the total expenses for compulsory education are investigated; in this specific case, this finding holds also for its single components, namely investment or current/instructional spending (Fischer 2006). In light of the definition of the OECD PISA sample, which includes

---

[7] Grob and Wolter (2005) analyse the socio-demographic determinants of educational spending but omit the influence of time-invariant political institutions that is disguised in the state fixed effects of their model.

[8] Model misspecification and potential simultaneity might distort results. However, using different sets of instruments and assuming endogeneity of various determinants do not change the basic findings for the effects of direct democracy (see Fischer 2005a–c, 2006 for such variations).

[9] See e.g. Bundesamt für Statistik (2000), pp. 22–23.

students at the end of compulsory education (namely secondary I), the latter finding is particularly noteworthy.[10]

Determined by and thus linked to educational spending are class sizes and remuneration of teachers. As these two constitute potentially decisive inputs in the so-called educational production function (Figlio 1997a; Krueger 2002), the question to what extent direct democracy affects these two elements of school spending may be of some importance. For Switzerland, however, data on wages for teachers are not readily available, and information on class size has been collected only since 1999. Nevertheless, as regards wages, it should be borne in mind that in Switzerland more than 60% of current spending reflects wage payments for teachers, which is congruent with levels of educational spending in the USA, which is primarily determined by the number of teachers hired (Krueger 2002). As regards class size, preliminary analyses for five different school types over the period of 1999–2002 suggest that, as a general tendency, there is no influence of institutions of direct legislation on this production factor (Fischer 2005a). In particular, *ceteris paribus*, classes in both primary and secondary I schools that offer compulsory education are of comparable size across cantons, regardless of the cantonal degree of direct democracy.

Theories of bureaucracy give rise to the conjecture that constraining an administrator's budget, e.g. through popular rights, leads to an adaptive or even manipulative behaviour as her/his reaction (Figlio and O'Sullivan 2001). More specifically, given that not only a growing budget but also an increasing number of personal staff are conducive to her/his well-being (Williamson 1964; Niskanen 1975), the school administrator might deliberately choose to shift resources from the instructional budget component to the administrative component. Expressed differently, if such behaviour was indeed present, the ratio of instructional to administrative spending should be negatively associated with the political institution that limits budget size or growth. Indeed, US studies on the effect of tax limits on local school budget components suggest that such Leviathan behaviour is triggered by these spending restraining institutions (e.g. Figlio 1997, 1998). In contrast, for Swiss cantons no such effects induced by institutions of direct legislation is identified (Fischer 2005a). Moreover, for most types of schools, instructional spending appears to have increased relative to administrative spending. It remains an open question to what extent this differential behaviour of school administrators in Switzerland

---

[10] There is a branch of US literature on the effects of local tax limits that is often viewed as related as this institution equally constrains local government revenue and (educational) spending (e.g. Card and Payne 2002; Shadbegian 2003). For the effect of US state initiatives on state spending, see e.g. Matsusaka (2005).

can be attributed to incomparability of the focal variables (tax caps in the US districts versus direct democracy in Swiss cantons) or general cultural differences between the two countries.

7.4. Direct Democracy and Performance of Swiss Students in Reading, Mathematics, and Natural Science

The impact of direct democracy on student performance in the core subjects of reading, mathematics, and natural science is assessed by estimating an educational production function using the national sample of the OECD PISA 2000 data (Fischer 2005b,c, 2006). Such a production function includes "inputs" at the school, class, and individual level that are conjectured to determine student performance. At the individual level, commonly employed variables are age, gender, citizenship, mother tongue, family income, and other social background factors. These are augmented not only by class-level determinants such as peer effects (namely the performance of the student's classmates), grading rules, and frequency of homework assignments, but equally by factors at the school level such as the type of institution of education as well as its location or selectivity.

For analysing school budget-specific aspects of student performance, an important subgroup of school- and class-level inputs are those whose quality and/or quantity are determined by the school's financial resources. These include, among others, factors not only relating to physical capital (instruction material, heating, size of class room, equipment with PCs) but equally those relating to human capital, namely teacher quality and teacher qualification.

In order to assess the impact of direct democracy on student performance, the direct democracy measure is included as an additional factor in the educational production function model. The only strand of literature that explores a similar question using comparable data, models, and methods are empirical studies on the impact of the fiscal institution "tax cap" on students' test scores at the US district level. In most of these contributions, these revenue-driven input factors have been replaced with an indicator variable of the institution in question, assuming that the effect of the latter is fully mediated through the first (e.g. Downes and Figlio 1997; Figlio 1997). In contrast, in the various contributions by Fischer a mediatory effect of the budget-driven variables is directly tested by estimating the augmented educational production function in two versions: the first, with the revenue-driven variables excluded and then the second, including them. A comparison of the estimates for the direct democracy variable and their significance levels across the two models gives an indication of (a) whether these budget-driven school inputs work as direct democracy's transmission channel, and (b) the direction of the institutional impact through the school budget, in case there is one. A detailed description of these two different model specifications and a discussion of how their outcomes are to be interpreted are given in Fischer (2005b,c, 2006).

The empirical studies on student performance employ a specific subset of the OECD PISA 2000 data. Jointly with the OECD PISA 2000 survey, the Swiss government collected a "national sample" that includes ninth graders at the end of compulsory education, in contrast to the PISA survey that samples 15-year-old students. However, the tests and background questionnaires used were identical, and there is a substantial overlap between the two survey samples.[11] The so-called Swiss or national sample has two advantages over the original OECD data: first, it allows for the construction of class-specific peer variables since either all students or a random sample were selected from each participating class.[12] In all empirical analyses conducted by Fischer, peer effects appear as strong predictors of academic achievement that thus should not be omitted from the model. The second advantage is that the national sample provides a more accurate picture of the student population in the 26 Swiss states than the OECD PISA data in which the smaller cantons are particularly underrepresented. The main focus of the PISA survey is on reading performance, but a fraction of the participating students had to answer additional test questions in mathematics and natural science. Qualitatively, the reading test score is said to measure more the know-how abilities than the know-that abilities.

Student performance is reflected in the so-called PISA test scores that are calculated for each test subject separately. This score represents a weighted likelihood estimate of student attainment that takes into account the difficulty of the question (Warm 1989). In other words, the PISA score does not simply equal the share of correct replies, and a student solving one difficult problem might perform equally well as another one who answered several, but "easy" questions correctly. The mean of the reading

---

[11] As in the PISA study, the national sample provides background information about the pupil and his or her school not only by the *student questionnaire*, but also by the *computer familiarity questionnaire*, the *CCC questionnaire*, and a *school questionnaire*. The latter had to be filled in by the school principal.

[12] Entire classes were sampled in the French-speaking regions while in the German-speaking regions random samples were drawn.

test score was originally normalized at a score of about 500 with a standard deviation of 90 for the whole national data set.[13]

Turning to the results of the empirical investigations presented in Fischer (2005b,c, 2006), the most important finding is that direct democracy exerts an indirect test score-lowering impact that is mediated through the revenue-driven school inputs. This observation is made for student performance both in reading and mathematics, while the results for natural science are not sufficiently robust to arrive at a final conclusion. As regards the size of the impact, a one-point increase in the composite index of direct democracy lowers student performance in reading by nine test score points (Fischer 2006). The magnitude of this institutional effect, however, varies slightly across alternative model specifications so that this value should be taken with a grain of salt (e.g. Fischer 2005c, reports a value of about –8). That restraining the school budget through specific politico-fiscal institutions exerts a deleterious impact on student performance has also been revealed by research on US district-level tax limit effects using individual student data (e.g. Downes and Figlio 1997; Figlio 1997; Downes et al. 1998).

Another important outcome for Swiss student performance in reading and mathematics is that there is no (direct) test score-lowering influence of direct democracy that goes beyond its (indirect) budgetary impact, namely that is not already fully captured by inclusion of the budget-driven school input factors in the educational production function (see Fischer 2005b,c, 2006).[14] This result contrasts a corresponding finding in the American literature on the effects of tax limits that identified a decreasing impact on academic achievement even when taking into account current school input levels (Downes et al. 1998).[15] This remarkable observation becomes relevant again when the presence of a Leviathan school administration is discussed in the next section.

Finally, exploring the potential importance of the single revenue-driven school input factors for student achievement in reading and mathematics, most of these do not appear influential. This observation pertains

---

[13] Due to elimination of some observations the regression sample mean differs (see Fischer 2005b,c).

[14] It should be noted that the residual (direct) impact of direct democracy on mathematics test scores appears to be even performance improving. This result is interpreted as a response to median voters' preferences in Fischer (2006).

[15] The budget-driven input factors in their study are student–teacher ratios in the district, mean teaching experience of teachers, and the fraction of teachers with a BA as highest degree, opposed to those with a postgraduate degree (MA, MSc, etc).

particularly to those determinants relating to the quality and/or quantity of physical capital, namely availability and quality of instruction material, existence of a well-equipped school library as well as the state of the school building and availability of space. Only "having no access to a PC at school" is significantly associated with lower student test scores in reading, contrasting the corresponding albeit insignificant finding for mathematics. For both subjects, the number of total hours of schooling appears equally irrelevant. As regards the human capital aspect of educational production, teacher shortage does not prove to be decisive in determining student performance in mathematics or reading.[16] However, in all three test subjects the fraction of teachers with a university-level education appears to increase students' test scores – with considerable marginal impacts. In fact, the estimated coefficients are among the largest observed in the regressions (in a absolute terms), suggesting that an increase in the share of highly qualified teachers by 1 per cent point raises an average student's PISA test score between 22 and 28 points. Testing for the sensitivity of these values to variations in model specification proves that teacher qualification remains a dominating predictor.[17]

That teacher qualification matters to student performance in Switzerland is a crucial insight. Indeed, previous empirical literature, using data from different countries, has reported quite ambiguous results (for a survey and meta-analysis, see Hanushek 2002). However, Meunier (2006), using the full Swiss sample of the OECD PISA 2000 data, identifies independently a strong and decisive impact of average teacher qualification on students' test scores in all three test subjects. Since Meunier's empirical analysis differs with respect to model specification and estimation technique from the various contributions by Fischer, the finding of the importance of teacher qualification can be seen as quite robust.

To explain, teacher training in Switzerland is unique in comparison with how it is organized in other countries: first, before teacher candidates start their training, the gap in education between the two types of prospective teachers, the ones who attend teacher seminaries and the others who are educated at universities, is already large and easily amounts to 4 years of schooling. Furthermore, using minimum high school final grade point averages as entry requirements for studying at universities serves as some

---

[16] In the natural science regressions, however, both a lack of instruction material and a subject-specific teacher shortage lower students' test scores.

[17] In Fischer (2006), other sources of misspecification that might have inflated the estimates are discussed and ruled out. They include selection issues, specification variations, and choice of data samples.

kind of intelligence-based selection criterion. Finally, prospective teachers studying at universities are exposed to up-to-date scientific knowledge, while training in teacher seminaries focuses on transfer of basic knowledge necessary for teaching at primary and secondary I schools.

7.5. Teacher Qualification as Transmission Channel of Popular Rights

Repeating previous results, direct democracy appears to lower student performance with its impact working through the budgetary channel. Among the revenue-driven school input variables, the proportion of teachers with a university-level education turns out to be a more or less exclusively decisive determinant of student performance, exerting a robust and sizable impact on students' test scores. This finding pertains to academic achievement in all three test subjects: mathematics, reading, and natural science. Moreover, this influence is exerted, on the one hand, by the share of highly educated *subject-specific* teachers in all three test subjects and, on the other, by the share of teachers with a university-level education in the *overall* teaching staff, particularly in natural science and reading.[18] The decisiveness of teacher qualification for student performance is reported both in Fischer (2005b,c, 2006) and in Meunier (2006).

Based on these results it is most likely that the impact of direct democracy works not only through the school budget in general, but even more specifically through the average qualification of the teaching personnel. However, such conjecture should not remain empirically unchallenged. Indeed, as Fischer (2006) shows, the simple correlation between the extent of popular rights and the share of subject-specific teachers with a university education is considerably negative. More convincing, however, is the regression outcome when a model of demand for school resources is estimated that yields the partial correlation and causal effect, exploiting variation across about 150 schools of the Swiss national PISA 2000 sample. In such a model, based on Figlio (1997), Hoxby (2000), and Poterba (1997), the demand for teachers with a university degree is viewed as a function of direct democracy, school characteristics, and socio-demographic determinants

---

[18] As regards statistical significances, the effects of subject-specific teacher qualification are significant at the 5 and 1% levels, respectively, while the impact of the qualification of the overall teaching body is statistically weaker for reading and mathematics test results but stronger for academic achievement in natural science.

at the school and cantonal levels (e.g. location of school, selectivity of school, cantonal shares of impoverished persons or foreigners).[19] In a variation of this model, the institutional variable of interest is replaced with a proxy for the level of teachers' wages that most likely works as popular rights' transmission channel. That stronger popular rights decrease, ceteris paribus, instructional spending for compulsory education has already been reported in Section 7.3.

Estimating this model of demand for school resources yields two important outcomes: first, higher spending for compulsory education per student is strongly and positively associated with a larger proportion of teachers with a university-level education. Second, analogously, the reverse effect is observable for direct democracy: stronger popular rights reduce the average qualification of the teaching personnel. Overall, the effects are strongest for the overall teaching body and mathematics teaching personnel, and still substantial for reading teachers, but rather weak for natural science staff.[20] Admittedly, given that these estimations use data of a cross-sectional nature, they exploit inter-cantonal variation only.

7.6. Conclusion

To provide a short summary, several studies on the impact of direct democracy on school spending and student attainment in Swiss cantons yield the following picture: on the one hand, stronger popular rights restrain educational spending, specifically that for compulsory education. Obviously, the spending lowering impact is directly linked to worse teacher qualification, which, in turn, exerts a deleterious impact on student performance, particularly in the two core subjects reading and mathematics. (The results for natural science, a subject that is introduced in the school curriculum at a much later stage, are rather inconclusive in that respect in comparison with mathematics and reading, which are taught from the very beginning of compulsory schooling.) However, on the other

---

[19] Hanushek et al. (2004) report that a school's attractiveness is determined by average student performance, racial composition of student body, and students' average wealth. Figlio (1997a) and Clotfelter et al. (2006) emphasize the importance of teacher salaries.

[20] A point of critique might be reversed causality particularly in the model that includes spending on compulsory education. To mitigate its effect, the focal variables "spending on compulsory education" and "direct democracy" have been averaged over the preceding 10 years.

hand, empirical research for Switzerland suggests that the test score decreasing influence is not caused by a Leviathan-like school administrator, as observed in other countries. Particularly, the insignificant findings for class size, student–teacher ratio, and ratio of instructional to administrative spending point in that direction, as well as the fact that for no test subject a performance-lowering impact going beyond the one working through the budget channel could be identified, contrasting evidence for the US (Downes et al. 1998). Overall, in Swiss cantons a non-benevolent attitude of school administrators does not appear to be part of the problem.

Do these results imply that direct legislation is deleterious to the quality of locally provided public goods such as public education? Not at all. Indeed, recent research has also shown that the direction of the effect of institutions of direct democracy does depend on voters' preferences. In particular, the spending restraint impact identified in many empirical studies on Swiss sub-federal budgets most probably indicates that the Swiss people are (currently) fiscally conservative, but does not constitute an effect of the institution per se. Indeed, Matsusaka (1995) has shown for US states that in some periods of American history voters used institutions of direct legislation to expand government spending. In other words, what is needed in Switzerland is an open discussion on the scopes and objectives of public education and the necessary means for achieving them. The Swiss electorate is called to use this "new" information to re-assess its optimal point in policy space, re-formulate and re-prioritize policy goals in public. In such case, already the mere availability of institutions of direct democracy will then induce politicians to respond and change education policies accordingly. Nevertheless, extremely strong policy alterations may have to be directly initiated by the people through exerting their popular rights.

Since the OECD PISA 2000 study, this discussion process has already started and proposals for reform have been made. Given the decisiveness of teacher qualification for student attainment in Switzerland, identified independently by Meunier (2006) and Fischer (2005b,c), teacher training appears to be one of the levers Swiss politicians might use. In this light, the ongoing reforms of the Swiss teacher training system, now requiring a university-level degree for all teachers and abolishing education at cantonal teacher seminaries, is possibly the right step to take. In addition, the Swiss public might consider taking further action to make the teaching profession more attractive to high-quality candidates, through policies raising its reputation in society rather than through measures consuming vast financial resources.

References

Besley T, Coate S (2001) Issue unbundling via citizens' initiatives. Discussion Paper 2857. Centre for Economic Policy Research, London

Bundesamt für Statistik (2000) Oeffentliche Bildungsausgaben: Finanzindikatoren 1998, under the collaboration of Egloff M, Muehlemann K. Bundesamt für Statistik, Neuchâtel

Card D, Payne AA (2002) School finance reform, the distribution of school spending, and the distribution of student test scores. *Journal of Public Economics* 83:49–82

Clotfelter C, Glennie E, Ladd H, Vigdor J (2006) Would higher salaries keep teachers in high-poverty Schools? Evidence from a policy intervention in North Carolina. Working Paper 12285, NBER

Downes TA, Figlio DN (1997) School finance reforms, tax limits and student performance: do reforms level up or dumb down? Discussion Paper 1142-97, Institute for Research on Poverty

Downes TA, Dye RF, McGuire TJ (1998) Do limits matter? Evidence on the effects of tax limitations on student performance. *Journal of Urban Economics* 43:401–417

EDK (2001) Schweizer Beitrag für die Datenbank Eurybase – the Information Database on Education in Europe. EDK Schweizerische Konferenz der kantonalen Erziehungsdirektoren and Bundesamt für Bildung und Wissenschaft (eds) Information Dokumentation Erziehung Schweiz, Bern

Feld LP, Kirchgässner G (2001) The political economy of direct legislation: direct democracy in local and regional decision-making. *Economic Policy* 33:329–367

Feld LP, Matsusaka JG (2003) Budget referendums and government spending: evidence from Swiss cantons. *Journal of Public Economics* 87:2703–2724

Feld LP, Fischer JAV, Kirchgässner G (2006) The effect of direct democracy on income redistribution: evidence for Switzerland. Working paper 1837, CESifo, Munich

Figlio DN (1997) Did the tax revolt reduce school performance? *Journal of Public Economics* 65:245–269

Figlio DN (1997a) Teacher salaries and teacher quality. *Economic Letters* 55:267–271

Figlio DN (1998) Short-term effects of a 1990s-ERA property tax limit: panel evidence on Oregon's measure 5. *National Tax Journal* 51:55–70

Figlio DN, O'Sullivan A (2001) The local response to tax limitation measures: do local governments manipulate voters to increase revenues? *Journal of Law and Economics* 44:233–257

Fischer JAV (2005a) Do institutions of direct democracy tame the leviathan? Swiss evidence on the structure of expenditure for public education. Working paper 2005-22, Department of Economics, University of St. Gallen

Fischer JAV (2005b) The impact of direct democracy on society. Doctoral Thesis 3074, University of St Gallen, http://www.biblio.unisg.ch/www/edis.nsf/wwwDisplayIdentifier/3074/$FILE/dis3074.pd

Fischer JAV (2005c) The impact of direct democracy on public education: performance of Swiss students in reading. Working paper 2005-10, Department of Economics, University of St Gallen

Fischer JAV (2006) The impact of direct democracy on public education: evidence for Swiss students in reading, mathematics and natural science. Mimeo, Hoover Institution, University of Stanford

Freitag M, Bühlmann M (2003) Der Einfluss sozioökonomischer Bedingungen, organisierter Interessen und politischer Institutionen auf die Bildungsausgaben im kantonalen Vergleich. *Schweizerische Zeitschrift für Politikwissenschaft* 9:139–168

Gerber E (1996) Legislative response to the threat of popular initiatives. *American Journal of Political Science* 40:99–128

Germann RE (2002) Die Kantone: Gleichheit und Disparität. In: Klöti U et al. (eds) *Handbuch der Schweizer Politik 3*, überarbeitete Auflage. NZZ Verlag, Zürich, pp 385–419

Grob U, Wolter SC (2005) Demographie und Bildungsausgaben. Discussion paper 7, Department of Economics, University of Bern

Hanushek EA (2002) Publicly provided education. In: Hanushek EA, Welch F (eds) *Handbook of Public Economics*, Vol. 4. Elsevier Science, Amsterdam, pp 2045–2141

Hanushek EA, Kain JF, Rivkin SG (2004) Why public schools lose teachers. *Journal of Human Resources* 39:326–354

Hoxby CM (2000) Does competition among public schools benefit students and taxpayers. *American Economic Review* 90:1209–1238

Krueger AB (2002) Economic considerations and class size. Working Papers 8875, National Bureau of Economic Research, Inc, NBER

Matsusaka JG (1995) Fiscal effects of the voter initiative: evidence from the last 30 years. *Journal of Political Economy* 103:587–623

Matsusaka JG (2005) Direct democracy works. *The Journal of Economic Perspectives* 19:185–206

Meunier M (2006) Fonctions de production éducationelle: le cas de la Suisse. *Swiss Journal of Economics and Statistics* 142:579–615

Niskanen W (1975) Bureaucrats and politicians. *Journal of Law and Economics* 18:617–643

Poterba JM (1997) Demographic structure and the political economy of public education. *Journal of Policy Analysis and Management* 16:48–66

Schaltegger CA (2001) The effects of federalism and democracy on the size of government: evidence from Swiss sub-national jurisdictions. *Ifo Studien* 47:145–162

Shadbegian RJ (2003) Did the property tax revolt affect local public education? Evidence from panel data. *Public Finance Review* 31:91–120

Stutzer A (1999) Demokratieindizes für die Kantone der Schweiz. Working Paper 23, IEW, University of Zurich

Warm TA (1989) Weighted maximum likelihood estimation of ability in item response theory. *Psychometrika* 54:427–450

Williamson OE (1964) *The Economics of Discretionary Behavior: Managerial Objectives in a Theory of the Firm*. Prentice-Hall, Englewood Cliffs, NJ

Chapter 8
School Factors Related to Quality: Multilevel Analysis for Three Swiss Cantons

Ivar Trippolini[1]

[1]*Swiss Graduate School of Public Administration-Institut de hautes études en administration publique, University of Lausanne, Lausanne, Switzerland*

8.1. Introduction

What influence do schools and the educational system have on students' performance? How should schools be organised to ensure equal opportunities for students independently of their origin? What school characteristics impacting students' outcomes are easily amenable to educational policies? Launched by the Organisation for Economic Co-operation and Development (OECD), the Programme for International Student Assessment (PISA) offers a framework for analysis and a unique database for offering answer to questions of this kind. Since 2000, OECD member states like Switzerland as well as other associate countries have participated every 3 years in a survey. Their aim is to examine and compare knowledge and skills acquired by students at completion of compulsory education (e.g. OECD 2001, 2004).

In the Swiss federal system, education is in major part under the jurisdiction of the cantons (member states of the federal state) and municipalities. Consequently, it is worthwhile not to limit research to an international comparison but to examine the regional and cantonal levels too. Hence, under the aegis of the Swiss Federal Statistical Office (SFSO) and the Swiss Conference of cantonal Directors for Education (SCDE), an important series of common studies analysed and discussed Swiss students' results (e.g. SFSO/SCDE 2001, 2002, 2003a, 2004, 2005). The analysis led by the SFSO and the SCDE covered a broad range of determining factors of students' performance. However, among the explanatory variables, the policy-amenable school factors have often been neglected, especially in the studies of French-speaking cantons. Concretely, we are interested in policy-amenable school characteristics that at the same time impact students' performance in these cantons. Thus, taking as a reference a current international multilevel study (OECD 2005a), we will seek to shed light on the conditions for learning in the schools within the educational systems of the three French-speaking cantons located around Lake Leman (the cantons of Geneva, Vaud and Valais). We hope to subsequently raise a number of issues useful for the practice of educational policies at school level.

This chapter is divided into five sections. In the following section, we first give an overview of the main branches of school effectiveness research. This allows us to define our explanatory model and our corresponding hypotheses. The third section specifies the method and the data as well as certain limitations of the analysis. The fourth section presents and interprets the estimated results for the three above-mentioned cantons. Finally, the main findings are summarised in the concluding section.

8.2. Three Main Branches of School Effectiveness Research

The question of the role of schools and their capacity to transmit knowledge is probably as old as the institutionalisation of education itself. However, the last 30 years have witnessed an upswing never seen before of research programs investigating the factors, at educational systems level, that influence the performances of pupils. This strong increase in the number of studies was partly a reaction to the results provided by a survey carried out in the United States,[1] its principal result being that "schools do not make the difference". Others explain the rise of studies on school impact as a natural prolongation of traditional studies concerning educational processes (Creemers 1995:106). In any case, the theoretical and conceptual framework has been greatly developed since the 1960s and one speaks henceforth of the field of *educational effectiveness research*, better known under the name of *school effectiveness research*. In our study, we use this second terminology, which seems more precise with regard to our object of study.

In school effectiveness research field we distinguish three main branches, each having its origin in a different scientific disciplines (Scheerens and

---

[1] Commonly known as the "Coleman Report": Coleman et al. (1966) *Equality of Educational Opportunity*. US Department of Health, Education and Welfare, Washington, DC.

Bosker 1997:36ff; OECD 2005a:13ff): *the economic approach of school effectiveness,* centred on the educational production function; *the educational–psychological approach of school effectiveness,* which studies the teaching strategies and the instructional conditions within classes; and *the narrow-sense school effectiveness approach,* which is interested in the organisational and managerial characteristics of schools. These approaches obviously did not develop in completely independent ways. In the first part of this section it is, however, primarily their diversity and much less their interactions and points of convergence that interest us.

Each discipline defines school effectiveness differently. In this study the use of the term effectiveness simply refers to the relationship between a desired objective and the obtained results (Schedler et al. 1998:13). Nevertheless, the definition of the objectives as well as the results and the way to measure them depend on the chosen research approach.

8.2.1. The Economic Approach of School Effectiveness

The first studies on school effectiveness were dominated by the economic approach (Reynolds et al. 2000:4), also known as *economics of education.* The theoretical base of education economics draws on the *theory of human capital* (Becker 1964).

By introducing the value of individual skills, the theory of human capital describes a phenomenon such as growth and income distribution placed within the neo-classical model of production including the factors of production, capital and work. Since all individuals do not have the same skills, they will not have the same productivity in a given working position.

Hence, the most qualified will be more productive and will consequently be better remunerated. As with investing in a free market, it becomes rational for *homo economicus* to invest in education as long as the costs incurred are covered by the resulting benefits. It is thus interesting to compare the *inputs* (or *costs*) of education with the *outputs* (or *benefits*) in order to justify an investment in human capital. Consequently, the educational economics approach looks at this relationship between inputs and outputs of educational systems.

At an empirical level, among studies analysing educational inputs and outputs, the publication *Does Money Matter? – The Effect of School Resources on Student Achievement and Adult Success* edited by Gary Burtless (1996) contains contributions by researchers who are among the most recognised in the field of educational economics. The book covers two types of analysis on school system effectiveness: *external efficiency,* which looks at the effects of investment in education on non-educational benefits, and *internal efficiency,* which evaluates the benefits measurable at the institutional level. In the publication, these two approaches are mainly addressed as meta-analyses of current research. The results of these contributions are ambivalent. If the studies on external efficiency show a rather positive impact of a rise of resources allocated to education, studies on internal efficiency do not lead to the same conclusions. Hence, "the contradiction between the two sets of findings is deeply puzzling" (Burtless 1996:17). Thus, if investment in human capital does not impact students' performance, there will be no productivity difference related to their education. Furthermore, differentials in remuneration should not be explained by educational inputs. Either the first or the second results should be questioned or else both do not measure the same thing. It is hence not surprising that the authors are very (auto-) critical especially with regard to the operationalisation of the different dimensions and their costs and benefits (cf. Betts 1996:183; Hanushek 1996:58ff; Hedges and Greenwald 1996:88ff).

8.2.2. The Educational–Psychological Approach of School Effectiveness

The second approach that we will consider is the *educational–psychological approach*, which emphasises factors that are the closest to the student's learning process. In fact, this approach finds its roots in psychology and educational sciences. Until the mid-twentieth century, the stream of *behaviourism* with psychologists such as Thorndike (1922) and Skinner (1957) impregnated theories on the learning process. The core idea advocated a learning process according to the following principle: If an individual's responsiveness to a stimulus from his/her environment is followed by encouragement, then his/her responsiveness will reproduce in future similar situations. The link between the stimulus and the response becomes increasingly strong after repeating the exercise. Consequently, the teachers' role was to give stimuli and then encouragement in order to develop and shape students' behaviour and learning. Nevertheless, this approach did not consider individuals' internal processes. In other words, it was a *non-cognitive* approach (Knoers 1996:317ff). The epistemologist and psychologist Piaget (1947) was among the first authors to fill this gap by emphasising the active role played by the individual in the learning process using cognitive skills such as reasoning, perception or attention. However, this new approach raised significant questions on the importance of the teacher and the teaching process as such. It focused much less on practices able to improve education in school. It was Carroll (1963) with his publication *A model of school learning* who managed to integrate the cognitive and behaviourist approaches in a single model explaining learning in school (Scheerens and Bosker 1997:40). Carroll's model is hence a significant contribution in putting into practice theories stemming from psychology. This model is based on the idea that students have different characteristics such as intelligence, aptitude or motivation and consequently need different ways of teaching, particularly concerning quality and duration of the learning opportunity (for instance, an unfavourable climate of discipline shortens the duration of the opportunity to learn). Based on this conceptual framework, a series of other models have been conceived to enable the analysis and implementation of an optimal balance between school success and students' differing capacities and the teaching conditions from which they benefit. The main object studied was therefore the learning process in the classroom. Researchers mainly focused on the role of the teacher, the teaching method and the way to adapt to the learning rhythm of the different students (e.g. Creemers 1994).

At the empirical level, the significance of the impact of the factors close to the student has been demonstrated several times (Walberg 1984; Fraser et al. 1987). In the broadest meta-analysis to date, Wang et al. (1993) come to the conclusion that the more the factors are close to the students' learning process, the bigger will be the impact on their performance. "Proximal variables like psychological, instructional, and home environment variables have more impact on learning than most of the variables studied and should be part of an effective strategy to promote student learning" (Wang et al. 1993:276).

8.2.3. The Narrow-Sense School Effectiveness Approach

The third approach to school effectiveness concentrates on schools as the objects of study. This is why we talk about a narrow-sense school effectiveness approach. This approach, which scrutinises organisation modalities and institutional management, finds its roots in theories and concepts around organisations. In his book *Organizations: Rational, Natural and Open Systems* (1981, 4th edition. 1998) Scott suggests a judicious synthesis and perspective on scholars interested in organisations. He distinguishes three main perspectives or schools of thought that theorise and conceptualise the functioning of organisations: *organisations as rational systems* (e.g. Taylor 1911; Fayol 1919; Weber 1922; Simon 1945), *organisations as natural systems* (human relations stream, e.g. Mayo 1945) or *organisations as open systems* in continuous interaction with their context (e.g. van Bertalanffy 1956; Wiener 1956).

Developed at the end of the 1970s, the narrow-sense school effectiveness approach was inspired by the three perspectives on organisations mentioned by Scott. Scheerens and Bosker (1997:13, 22) suggest an overview of this approach. They advance a conceptual framework on school effectiveness (as organisations) constituted of eight principal concepts. Each one of these concepts can be related to at least one of the three perspectives by Scott.

Four of the eight concepts clearly refer to the rational perspective on organisations. In the centre of the narrow-sense school effectiveness thinking, we find the question on *finality* or *objectives*. Inherent to the concept of effectiveness (see Sections 8.1 and 8.2), the definition of the *outputs* to achieve by schools is essential. We can add to it the question on the *content* of skills to pass on, what Scheerens and Bosker name the *primary process*. The third and fourth concepts drawn from the rational perspective are those of *structure* and *control*. Both refer to a clear definition of tasks and responsibilities to achieve within the school. Thoughts of the kind abated, for example the idea that schools need to be led by a principal.

The concept of *procedures* within schools refers both to the rational and natural perspectives on organisations – rational, because it deals with the formalisation of a number of procedures such as logistics and planning of school functioning, and natural, because it also considers all aspects of human resource management, namely a number of informal procedures. In the same way, we consider the *cultural concept* among these informal procedures. Often defined as the assemblage of shared opinions or the assemblage of informal and collective rules (Dean et al. 2000:22ff), culture within school covers, for example, questions such as the climate or the dynamic between teachers.

The seventh concept is inspired by the open systems perspective. Researchers of school effectiveness demonstrated the importance of the *environment* in which every school evolves. Worth mentioning are not only social context considerations, but also reform aspirations coming from national or, in our case, cantonal education ministries. In the same way, the concept of *contingency* predicts that there is not only one good way for the organisation, but depending on the environment, several ways can lead to similar results.

8.2.4. Integrated, Multilevel School Effectiveness Model and Hypotheses

The general explanatory model that we apply in our study consists of a combination of the three approaches on school effectiveness that we discussed above. Our aim is thus to integrate the economic, the educational–psychological and the narrow-sense school effectiveness approaches into a single model (Fig. 8.1).

The first models attempting to combine these three approaches on school effectiveness appeared at the beginning of the 1990s (Scheerens 1992; Stringfield and Slavin 1992; Creemers 1994). This resulted partly from the development of statistical methods in that period that allowed testing these complex models. Indeed "Research on school effects has been plagued by both methodological and conceptual problems. In our view, the two are closely related. The available analytic models tend to limit conceptualization to what can be empirically be tested through such models. There is a natural hesitancy to form conceptualization when it remains unclear how to test the fruits of that conceptualization" (Raudenbush and Bryk 1986:15). As a first step to conceive the integrated models, researchers started with the basic assumption of the economic approach that schools are production entities that convert inputs into outputs. Then, based on the conclusions met by the educational–psychological approach, the processes occurring within this production

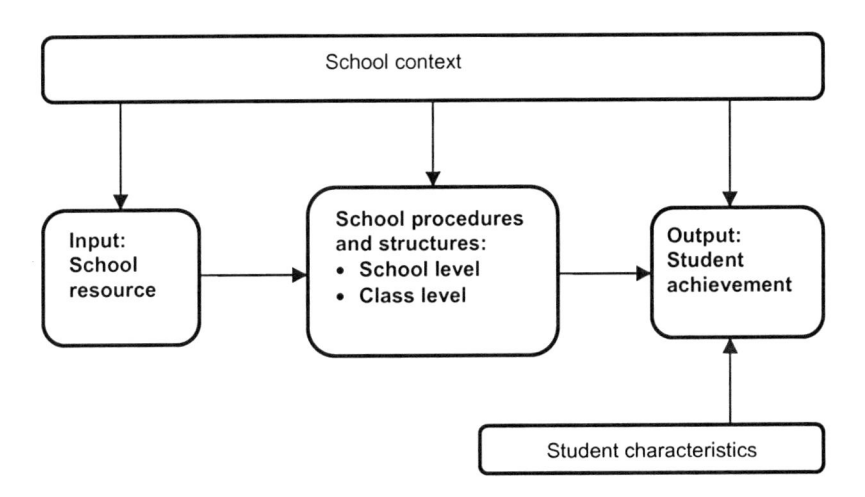

Fig. 8.1. Integrated model on school effectiveness (adapted from OECD 2005 by the author)

entity were added to the model. The last step consisted in taking into account the assumptions identified by the narrow-sense school effectiveness approach, that is to conceive a model as an entity following procedures and structures in one hand and to see the whole as an open system in interaction with its context. Finally, we must not forget that students' individual characteristics are very important control variables for the analysis of school effectiveness; they need to be considered in every study.

Until now, with the debate on the three approaches of school effectiveness, we addressed mainly the identification of causes (independent variables) and much less the effects or results of schools (dependent variables). With regard to the dependent variable *school results*, we first need to look at the *content* of the objectives for schools to achieve. We assume that the principal responsibility of schools is to transmit skills to students.[2] Thus, it is students' performance within schools that interests us. Second, we have to examine the way in which these key skills are *distributed* in the school population. Do we aim in an educational system for an average students' performance to attain the highest possible level ("high quality") or is a system with the smallest dispersion of students' results preferable ("high equity")? *Quality* and *equity* are concepts inherent to education's objectives that might not only compete but also complement each other (Meuret 2005). However, for feasibility reasons we need to limit our field of study and we will in consequence restrict ourselves to the study of quality.[3]

Hence, we suggest three hypotheses to test the validity of our analytical model. Each hypothesis rests on one of the three approaches of school effectiveness:

- *Hypothesis I*: The more the school resources are developed, the better are students' average achievements (controlling the effect of individual characteristics and the school context).

- *Hypothesis II*: The more favourable are the instructional conditions, the better are students' average achievements (controlling the effect of individual characteristics and the school context).

---

[2] For an in-depth discussion and a framework for the essential knowledge and skills necessary for students for full participation in society, see the OECD's Definition and Selection of Competencies (DeSeCo) Project (e.g. Rychen and Salganik 2001).

[3] Nevertheless, it is important to notice that a large research project from the European Union helps to conceptualise equity and offers a large number of indicators to measure it (e.g. GERESE 2003).

- *Hypothesis III*: The more favourable are the school management factors, the better are students' average achievements (controlling the effect of individual characteristics and the school context).

Inherent to this explanatory model is the hierarchical or multilevel structure that links the various explanatory variables. The educational system serves as a good example of such a structure. In fact, at the first individual level we find the students who all have different characteristics (e.g. socio-economic origin). At the second level, the class characteristics (e.g. its teacher) are identical for all its students but they differ from one class to another. At the third level, all students belonging to the same school are subject to the same contextual characteristics (e.g. cultural composition of the school population) that differ, however, from those of other schools. At the fourth level, a national or regional educational system subjects all its students to the same conditions (e.g. curriculum). The latter can nonetheless differ from one country to the next or, in our case, from one canton to the other. Finally, today the idea to conceptualise the efficiency of educational systems by integrating the different approaches and consequently also its hierarchical modelling is favoured by a large consensus (Reynolds et al. 2000:11, OECD 2005a:12). Nevertheless, what appears logical and plausible at a conceptual level proves to be very complex to operationalise at an analytical level. We will follow up on this challenge in the methodological section hereafter.

8.3. Method and Data

8.3.1. Multilevel Analysis

As we have just clarified, the integrated models of school effectiveness research follow a clearly hierarchical structure. In order to take into account the sources of variability and the effects of the different levels of analysis, we will use a statistical method known as "multilevel analysis" (for an introduction see Snijders and Bosker 1999; Jones and Gould 2005) or "hierarchical linear models" (Bryk and Raudenbush 1992). Multilevel models make it possible to analyse individual and contextual factors simultaneously – attributes that are more difficult to obtain with other methods (for an in-depth discussion see e.g. Bühlmann 2004, 2006; Rasbash et al. 2004). Formally speaking, as Bühlmann and Freitag (2006:25) summarise briefly and well, "the underlying principle of multilevel modelling is quite simple: intercepts of common linear square (OLS)-regression analysis are allowed to vary". According to this, the basic variance components model can be written as:

$$y_{ij} = \beta_0 + \beta_1 X_{1ij} + \cdots + \beta_n X_{nij} + \alpha_1 W_{1j} + \cdots + \alpha_n W_{nj} + \varepsilon_{ij} + \mu_{0j}$$

where – if we take our case study – the response variable is the achievement in mathematics of the student i within the school j (y_{ij}) explained by a so-called *fixed part* which consists of the overall achievement mean (β_0), the students' characteristics ($\beta_1 X_{1ij} + \cdots + \beta_n X_{nij}$) as well as the school factors ($\alpha_1 W_{1j} + \cdots + \alpha_n W_{nj}$) and a *random part* with individual (ε_{ij}; within-school variation) as well as contextual (μ_{0j}; between-school variation) variation of the residuals. Both variations are assumed to have a normal distribution with a mean of zero and a variance of σ^2.

Thus, statistically speaking, multilevel analysis can be described as a combination and synthesis of three large branches of statistics (Delaunay 2003). The *fixed part* corresponds to the traditional analysis of regression, which makes predictions for a dependent variable with one or more independent variables. Then, the *random part* of the multilevel model refers to the variance analysing approaches. Finally, to model the variation of the random part, the multilevel analysis is based on a stochastic approach taking into account the assumptions related to the random variations of basic units known from Bayesian modelling.

To analyse and interpret the relative impact of the different levels (students, schools) and the different groups of variables (school resources, instructional conditions, school management) we focus at first on the analysis of the variance or the so-called *random part* of the multilevel model. Only in a second step will we turn our attention to the fixed effect of each single variable. As multilevel analysis and also following the modelling strategy of the OECD study *School factors related to quality and equity* (OECD 2005a), we fit at first an *empty* or *null model* without any explanatory variable. This model gives us information about the distribution of the total variance at the respective levels. Furthermore it is our reference model. As a next step we add different explanatory variables at the level of students and schools and we compare the different models hierarchically. This means that we compare the residual variance of the different models to measure how much variance is explained by the added explanatory variables at the different levels. Table 8.1 gives an overview of our models run in the analyses.[4] We

---

[4] All estimations have been calculated by means of the software MLwiN (version 2.0), which was developed by the Center of Multilevel Modelling at the Institute of Education of the University of London (Rasbash et al. 2004). All our multilevel models were estimated with the RIGLS estimation method (Restricted Iterative Generalized Least Squares).

Table 8.1. Models run in the analyses

Model	Factors	Gross or adjusted or effects
Model 1	Empty or null model	–
Model 2	Student characteristics	–
Model 3	Student characteristics, school context	–
Model 4	Student characteristics, educational programme	–
Model 5	Student characteristics, educational programme, school context	–
Models 6a–c	School resources (a), instructional conditions (b), school management (c)	Gross effects
Models 7a–c	School resources (a), instructional conditions (b), school management (c)	Adjusted for student characteristics, institutional selection, school context
Model 8	All school variables model (school resources, instructional conditions, school management)	Gross effects
Model 9	All school variables model (school resources, instructional conditions, school management)	Adjusted for student characteristics, institutional selection, school context

fitted all 13 models for every canton separately. The calculation of the percentage of variance explained by the added variables is equal to: Variance restricted model – Variance extended model/Variance restricted model.

8.3.2. PISA 2003 Database

All data used to test our assumptions comes from the OECD Programme for PISA surveys, which collects information about students and schools in compulsory education every 3 years. For the second PISA survey in 2003, students were tested in reading, mathematical and scientific literacy as well as problem solving. The primary focus was on mathematical literacy. In addition to the assessments, PISA included student (filled out by the students) and school questionnaires (filled out by the school principals) to collect social, cultural, economic and educational background and context data. Aside from the *international sample* (15-year-old students), Switzerland[5] has drawn a second *national sample* from the population which includes

---

[5] The whole proceeding is a collaboration between the SFSO (Swiss Federal Statistical Office) and the SCDE (Swiss Conference of Cantonal Directors for Education). We wish to thank these two institutions for providing the data and specially Thomas Holzer from the SFSO for his helpful instructions.

all students in the ninth grade which is the last year of their compulsory education. Moreover, in the *national sample* 12 cantons (member states of the Swiss federal state) provided representative samples for their own territory.[6] For our study we have chosen three which have French-speaking schools and which are located around Lake Leman: the cantons of Geneva, Vaud and the French speaking part of Valais (Table 8.2).

8.3.2.1. Three Cantons with Three Different Systems of Educational Selection: Variables Used for Adjustment for Student Characteristics and School Context

It is particularly important to control for the context in federal countries like Switzerland where the federal structure enabled the establishment and the maintenance of 26 educational systems. The differences are especially significant when considering selection system after the six first years of primary school. Thus, at the compulsory secondary education level, the canton of Vaud has a school structure with three different programmes (bachelor, general, vocational) with homogeneous classes according to

Table 8.2. National sample PISA 2003: cantons of Geneva, Vaud and Valais

Cantons	Schools	Classes	Tested students				Scores in mathematical literacy[a]		
	No. schools	No. classes	Min.	Max.	Mean	No.	Mean	SE
Geneva	17	94	9	24	18.6	1669	507.9	(2.4)
Vaud	24	91	5	24	19.1	1634	524.4	(2.0)
Valais (fr)	25	89	12	25	20.1	1745	548.9	(1.9)

Source: OECD PISA database, national sample – SFSO/SCDE (2004).
[a] To compensate for non-participation of schools and students, student weights were applied. As suggested by the SFSO we used the new post-stratified weights (SFSO/SCDE 2005:144).

---

[6] Similar to the international sample, a two-stage sampling procedure was carried out in each canton. First, schools were drawn and thereafter, in contrast to the OECD, classes (and not students) within schools (SFSO/SCDE 2005:12).

students' performances.[7] The educational systems of the cantons of Geneva[8] and Valais[9] have similarities in the sense that they are both in mixed systems. One part of their students follow selective programmes with classes of homogeneous performance, and another part of the students follow comprehensive programmes with heterogeneous classes with the exception of classes in certain principal subjects, which are divided into three levels. In order to take these differences into account, we included the variable of students' school selection according to the coding provided by SFSO/SCDE (2003b). The other variables or indices used for *student characteristics* are: gender, age, socio-economic status (SES) and immigration background. For the *school context* we used: class average socio-economic status, class average immigration background and size of school location.

8.3.2.2. School Output Variable: Mathematical Literacy

We previously raised the question of defining the school output in the theoretical section. Thus, we limit our analysis to the main domain tested by PISA 2003: mathematical literacy.[10] To overcome the conflicting

---

[7] At the end of elementary school, the students of Vaud are oriented and selected for one of the three following programmes: "Voie secondaire baccalauréat" (VSB, upper programme), "voie secondaire générale" (VSG, general programme) and "voie secondaire à options" (VSO, lower programme).

[8] After elementary school, students in Geneva follow two different educational systems: The first system distinguishes between an upper programme "A" (homogenous classes) and a lower programme "B" (heterogeneous classes, but two levels for some subjects). The second system is comprehensive and groups the students in heterogeneous classes with a distinction of three levels for principal subjects. For further details see Soussi (2005:70ff).

[9] In the canton of Valais, after elementary school, all students follow a two-year programme with heterogeneous classes grouped by sections or levels for some subjects according to their performances. Afterwards, the students are selected either in a homogenous upper-level programme or in the comprehensive programme with three levels for principal subjects. For further details see Menge (2005:95ff).

[10] "Mathematical literacy is an individual's capacity to identify and understand the role that mathematics plays in the world, to make well-founded judgments and to use and engage with mathematics in ways that meet the needs of that individual's life as a constructive, concerned and reflective citizen" (OECD 1999:49).

demands of the assessment field's broad coverage and limited testing time for students, the PISA survey used the *Item Response Theory*[11] (IRT) to get the proficiency scores. This proficiency measures are generally subject to measurement error. Therefore, to include this feature in the analysis model, the PISA database provides five *plausible values*[12] for each test score in each domain. They have been standardised so that the average of the subjects is equal to 500 and the standard deviation equals 100 for all the participating countries. Correct results are obtained with the use of all five plausible values. For that reason we integrate the five plausible values for mathematical literacy as an extra level in our analyses (cf. Rasbash et al. 2004:162ff; OECD 2005a:110).

8.3.2.3. Variables Used for the Policy-Amenable School Characteristics

For each one of our three hypotheses, the PISA 2003 surveys provide between six and nine indicators. An important part of them was drawn from the questionnaire filled out by the school principals. The rest were built based on students' questionnaires. In Table 8.3, we indicate for each variable the point of view (students' or principals') from which it is to be interpreted. When we speak about "index", we refer to the indices built by the OECD on the basis of weighted maximum likelihood estimates (Warm 1985; OECD 2005b:375).

8.3.2.4. School Factors Analysed at Class Level: Limits of the Database and Other Precautions

After having been guided along the characteristics of our database, it is important to underline the limits of our analysis. According to us, the four most important points are as follows:

1. Ideally, it would be necessary to lead analyses at three levels (individual, class and school). However, first, such analyses are technically complex and, second, considering the limited number of principals questioned, we are constrained to limit ourselves to two levels of

---

[11] For a straightforward introduction to Item Response Theory see OECD (2005b:54ff).

[12] For a straightforward introduction to plausible values see OECD (2005b:72ff).

Table 8.3. PISA variables and indices used for the policy-amenable school characteristics

School factor	Questionnaire
School resources	
Index of quality of schools' physical infrastructure (SCMATBUI)	(school principal)
Index of quality of schools' educational resources (SMATEDU)	(school principal)
Availability of computers (RATCOMP)	(school principal)
Shortage of mathematics teacher (SC08Q01)	(school principal)
Student/mathematics teacher ratio (SMRATIO)	(school principal)
Class size (CL_SIZE)	own calculation
School size (SCHLSIZE)	(school principal)
Instructional conditions	
Index of teacher support in maths lessons (TEACHSUP)	(student, class mean)
Index of disciplinary climate in maths lessons (DISCLIM)	(student, class mean)
Index of student behaviours (STUDBEHA)	(student, class mean)
Index of student–teacher relations at school (STUREL)	(student, class mean)
Index of student morale (STMORALE)	(school principal)
Index of teacher–related factors affecting school climate (TEACBEHA)	(school principal)
Index of attitudes towards school (ATSCHL)	(student, class mean)
Index of sense of belonging to school (BELONG)	(student, class mean)
Late for school (ST28Q01)	(student, class mean)
School management	
Index of school autonomy (SCHAUTON)	(school principal)
Number of assessments per year (ASSESS)	(school principal)
Index of teacher participation (TCHPARTI)	(school principal)
Index of mathematics teacher consensus (TCHCONS)	(school principal)
Index of teacher morale (TCMORALE)	(school principal)

Source: OECD PISA database, national sample – SFSO/SCDE (2004).

analysis: the students and class levels. Consequently, we apply the data of schools to classes. In other words, we "pull down" the variables from the third level (collected from the principals) to the second level. It follows, for those variables, that all the classes within the same school will have the same values and no variance will be measurable. This will decrease the general variance between all classes and will create groups of variables that can skew the total results in one direction or the other.

2. The data at the centre of interest for this study are mainly those collected at school level. They come from questionnaires filled out by the school directors. Thus they can only deliver a general opinion on the entire school and not for each class. In order to have information on the instructional conditions within the various classes of a school, it is possible to create indicators based on the answers given by the students. However, the class teachers were not questioned.
3. For practical reasons, all students were questioned within their basic class. Several cantons (e.g. two of our three cases) have a school system where students are grouped in the same basic class but then, for the principal subjects, they are set out again in levels according to their performances. Thus, by measuring the impact of (basic) class characteristics on the performances in mathematics, it may be that certain students follow the mathematic courses apart from the basic class and the learning conditions are consequently not the same as in the basic classes. Nevertheless, one can also argue that students spend the major part of their school time in their basic class and consequently, the impact of the instructional conditions in the basic class is more important.
4. Last but not least, PISA is not a longitudinal survey in which one can follow the changes of the different variables and consequently definitively establish the causes and the effects of a phenomenon. As in any analysis of a transversal survey, the interpretation of causalities must be made with caution (OECD 2005a:17).

Finally, considering all these remarks about the method and the data, our multilevel models have the structure given in Fig. 8.2.

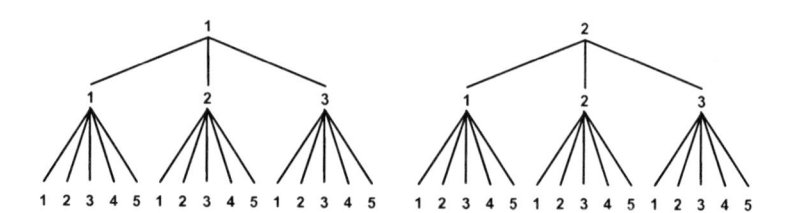

Level 3: Classes
Level 2: Students
Level 1: Plausible values in mathematics

Fig. 8.2. Multilevel design of the models run in the analyses

8.4. Results by Cantons

In order to test our hypotheses, we will use two aspects of the multilevel method. In the first part of the analysis, we are interested in the proportion of variance in students' results attributable to school resources, instructional conditions and school management. Then, in the second part, we will estimate the impact that each variable of the three dimensions can exert on students' performance.

8.4.1. School Characteristics Influencing the Variance of Performance Between Classes

8.4.1.1. Variance Between Classes and Variance Within Classes

As observed above, the structure at the level of compulsory secondary education differs strongly according to the canton. These different educational structures have a visible impact on the distribution of total variance in students' test scores in mathematics (Table 8.4). Thus, the canton of Vaud (VD) – in which secondary level students are grouped in homogeneous classes according to their performance – accounts for about 42% of explained variance between classes. In contrast, this *between-classes variance* remains among 20 and 25% in the cantons of Geneva (GE) and Valais (VS), which have mixed systems. On the contrary, the *within-class* variance rises to more than three quarters of the total variance in the cantons of Geneva and Valais and remains at about 58% in the canton of Vaud. Hence, we notice that the dispersion of performances *within classes* is much more important in systems with classes having heterogeneous requirements, whereas the dispersion of performances *between classes* is much more important in systems with homogeneous classes.

Table 8.4. Students' performance in mathematics: between-class and within-class variances

Canton	Between-class variance %	Within-class variance %
Geneva	19.7	80.3
Valais	24.4	75.6
Vaud	41.9	58.1

Source: OECD PISA database, national sample – SFSO/SCDE (2004).

8.4.1.2. Partitioning of the Between-Class Variance

Since we are principally interested in school factors related to quality, we will focus our coming analysis on the variance between classes, which as we saw in the methodological section, also includes the between-school variance.

The final model that includes all the variables of our study demonstrates the preponderant importance (between 49 and 85.7%) of the variable that takes into account the educational programme or the level of requirements in which the student finds himself/herself (Fig. 8.3). This result by canton certainly corroborates a number of studies made at the level of Switzerland as a whole (Moser and Berweger 2004:57). In turn, the variables specifically of interest to us – school resources, instructional conditions and school management – explain between 1.4% (GE) and 9.6% (VS) of the variance between classes. On a purely comparative basis, in the similar study made by the OECD with data from PISA 2000, about 6.7% of the variance between schools is explained by this kind of variables (OECD 2005a:118).

The biggest effect of the variable "educational programme and/or levels" necessitates some explanation. It has been demonstrated many times that a strong correlation exists in Switzerland between social origin and students' performances (OECD 2001, 2004; SFSO/SCDE 2005). This effect is noticeable not only at the level of individual characteristics but also at the contextual level such as the socio-economic composition of the class (Moser and Berweger 2005). Thus, students with similar background follow often the same educational programme. This has as a consequence that the

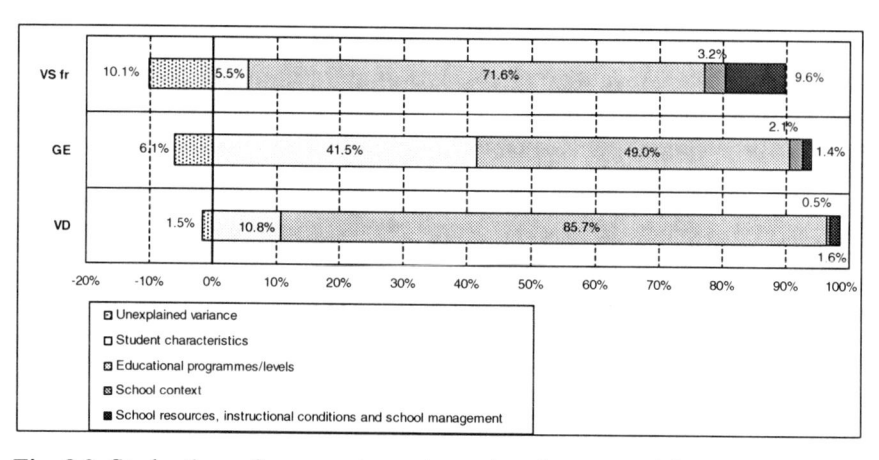

Fig. 8.3. Student's performance in mathematics: factors explaining the between-class variance

inclusion of variables of students' programmes/levels "eats up" a big part of the effect caused by individual characteristics, the context and their interactions. In order to illustrate this effect we calculated a model containing uniquely context variables without the programmes/levels and a second model with them (Table 8.5). If in the first model the social composition (average SES within the class) has an important effect on students' performances in the three cantons (between 59.7 and 75.9 additional points in mathematics), the impact is completely cancelled in the model with the programmes/levels for the cantons of Vaud and Valais and strongly reduced for the canton of Geneva. Hence, in order to capture the effect of the interaction between the social composition of the class and the school characteristics, we will include the variables of the programmes/levels in the group of context variables for the future set of analysis.

Table 8.5. Performances in mathematics: impact of the socio-economic composition of the class and the educational programmes or levels

	Model 3						Model 5 (adjusted for programmes / levels)					
	Geneva		Vaud		Valais fr		Geneva		Vaud		Valais fr	
	Effect	S.E.	Effect	S.E.	Effect	S.E.	Effect	S.E.	Effect	S.E.	Effect	S.E.
Constant	**511.2**	(6.02)	**538.0**	(5.74)	**571.7**	(5.55)	**477.3**	(5.62)	**537.4**	(3.17)	**563.3**	(5.44)
Student characteristics												
Gender	**−27.9**	(3.91)	**−37.0**	(2.90)	**−38.6**	(2.76)	**−27.6**	(3.75)	**−38.0**	(2.82)	**−38.6**	(2.53)
Socio-economic status (SES)	**10.8**	(1.84)	1.6	(1.62)	**6.9**	(1.91)	**8.3**	(1.79)	1.6	(1.62)	**4.7**	(1.98)
Immigration status	**−15.0**	(3.41)	**−13.5**	(3.46)	**−17.5**	(4.93)	**−17.5**	(3.47)	**−13.6**	(3.46)	**−13.8**	(4.39)
Age	**−28.8**	(3.29)	**−13.5**	(2.52)	**−13.9**	(2.62)	**−24.0**	(3.13)	**−13.5**	(2.58)	**−10.4**	(2.57)
Class context												
Class average SES	**59.7**	(7.71)	**75.9**	(7.05)	**74.0**	(8.01)	**21.4**	(6.19)	10.5	(6.58)	5.3	(10.55)
Class average immigration status	−2.7	(20.77)	−50.5	(27.74)	11.9	(27.08)	3.7	(13.98)	−23.0	(16.77)	−30.6	(22.47)
School location (<3,000 inhab)	–	–	1.0	(8.24)	−5.1	(11.38)	–	–	−1.1	(3.86)	−3.4	(8.85)
School location (>15,000 inhab)	−1.9	(6.37)	**20.0**	(8.42)	−9.9	(6.74)	−6.0	(4.74)	3.6	(5.11)	**−13.1**	(4.96)
Educational programme/level												
Programme/level: upper (homog.)							**65.7**	(5.71)	**70.0**	(5.78)	**61.3**	(7.23)
Programme/level: upper (heterog.)							**54.9**	(6.91)			**29.1**	(3.95)
Programme/level: low							**−20.5**	(6.24)	**−44.9**	(5.34)	**−39.7**	(2.76)

Source: OECD PISA database, national sample – SFSO/SCDE (2004).
The person of reference is a boy having a socio-economic status corresponding to the average in the French-speaking part of Switzerland; he is not born from a migrant family; he is 15 years and a half and goes to school in a location with 3000–15,000 inhabitants; his class has a cultural and socio-economic composition corresponding to the average in the French-speaking part of Switzerland and he follows a general (middle) educational programme/level. Effects printed in bold are significant at $p < 0.05$.

8.4.1.3. Hypothesis I: Variance Explained by School Resources

With regard to school resources, the dispersion of results in mathematics between classes explained *jointly*[13] by school resources, students' characteristics and the context is remarkably high (Fig. 8.4). There is probably a strong positive interdependence between the two groups of variables. This could indicate an unequal distribution of educational resources according to the school composition or the origin of the students. However, knowing that the size of the classes belongs to the variables measuring school resources (see Table 8.3) and having included the variable of the programmes/levels, we can presuppose that a big part of the interdependence is explained by the fact that in the Swiss educational systems the size of classes is adapted to the level of requirement of the programme/level; in order to compensate students' learning difficulties in programmes/levels having low requirements, such classes have reduced sizes (see also Moser 2005:123). Finally, the difference between classes explained uniquely by the material and personal resources of schools remains small and is about 1% for the cantons studied.

	Proportion of between-class variance explained by student characteristics and context	Proportion of between-class variance jointly explained by school resources, student characteristics and context	Proportion of between-class variance explained by school resources
VD	62.5%	34.4%	0.2%
GE	24.8%	65.0%	1.4%
VS fr	30.1%	50.2%	1.0%

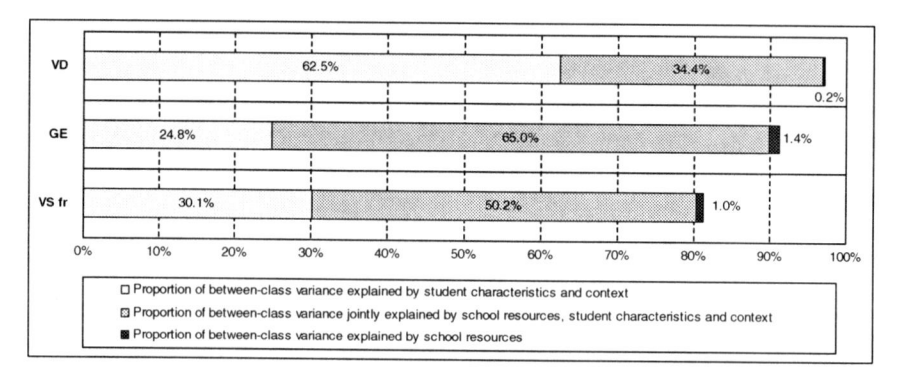

Fig. 8.4. Student's performance in mathematics: differences between classes explained by school resources

---

[13] Methodologically, we forgo a deeper discussion on this issue of joint effect and refer to the detailed explanations in the OECD report *Schoolfactors related to quality and equity* (2005a:112ff).

8.4.1.4. Hypothesis II: Variance Explained by the Instructional Conditions

Even though it is much less important than in the case of the resources, the dispersion of students' performances explained jointly by the instructional conditions and the individual/contextual variables remains important and is situated between 6% in Geneva and 15% in Valais (Fig. 8.5). The interpretation of this reciprocal relation can go either way. For instance, students originating from a family with a high socio-economic level can contribute to more favourable instructional conditions with a positive attitude towards school, or on the contrary, good instructional conditions in a certain school can encourage parents with privileged conditions to send their children to that school. If we look at the effect on performances exclusively explained by the instructional conditions, we observe that in the canton of Valais, with about 4%, the impact is relatively big compared to the two other cantons (VD: 0.5%, GE: 1.4%).

8.4.1.5. Hypothesis III: Variance Explained with the School Management

The autonomy of the school, the recourse to regular evaluations and the features of staff management explain only a small proportion of the dispersion of performances in mathematics between classes of the cantons of Vaud and Geneva (Fig. 8.6). Even when taking into account the possible interaction effects with the context and students' characteristics, the measures of school management seem to have little impact. In those two

VD	88.3% / 8.6% / 0.5%
GE	86.6% / 6.0% / 1.4%
VS fr	65.0% / 15.2% / 4.1%

☐ Proportion of between-class variance explained by student characteristics and context
☐ Proportion of between-class variance jointly explained by instructional conditions, student characteristics and context
■ Proportion of between-class variance explained by instructional conditions

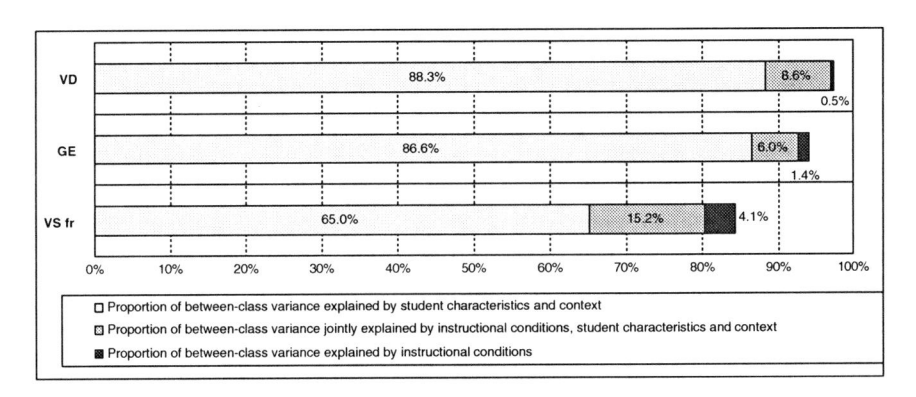

Fig. 8.5. Student's performance in mathematics: differences between classes explained by instructional conditions

```
          VD ████████████████████████████████████ 94.9% █ 0.6%
                                                         0.7%
          GE ██████████████████████████████████ 89.5%  ██ 2.2%
                                                         0.4%
          VS fr ████████████ 46.6% ██████████ 33.7%  █ 2.4%
          0%   10%  20%  30%  40%  50%  60%  70%  80%  90%  100%
```

☐ Proportion of between-class variance explained by student characteristics and context
☐ Proportion of between-class variance jointly explained by school management, student characteristics and context
■ Proportion of between-class variance explained by school management

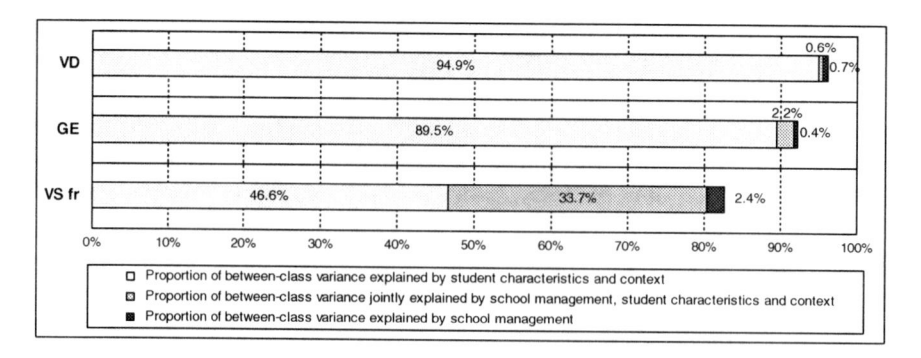

Fig. 8.6. Student's performance in mathematics: differences between classes explained by school management

cantons, about 90% of the variance between classes is jointly explained by the students' characteristics and the school context. On the contrary, in the canton of Valais the dispersion of performances is to a large extent (34%) explained by the interaction between school management on the one hand and students' characteristics and the context on the other.

8.4.2. Characteristics of Schools Having an Impact on Students' Performances

It is now interesting to know in greater depth in what way and with what intensity each factor at the school level influences students' performances. In general, we expect that the effect of school factors and the effect of context variables (students and classes) will go in the same direction, namely, that the model that adjusts results according to context will have less important values. However, the necessity to consider the programmes/levels (and their strong influence on performances) in our context variables can also completely cancel an effect or reverse it. This is the case when an effect can only be explained by the fact that all schools with a certain programme/level are, for example, subjected to management directives differing from those of schools of another programme/level.

8.4.2.1. Hypothesis I: Impact of the School Resources

From estimations done for the *canton of Geneva*, we observe that two of six factors analysed at the level of school resources are significant in the first model (Table 8.6, model 8). It appears that a strong shortage of

School Factors Related to Quality 177

Table 8.6. Effects of school resources, instructional conditions and school management on student performance in mathematics (gross effects and adjusted for student characteristics and context)

	Canton of Geneva						Canton of Vaud						Canton of Valais (fr)					
	Model 8			Model 9			Model 8			Model 9			Model 8			Model 9		
	Effect	SE	s.	Effect	SE	s.	Effect	SE	s.	Effect	SE	s.	Effect	SE	s.	Effect	SE	s.
Constant	500.3	12.1	**	508.4	48.4	**	513.6	23.6	**	552.3	10.6	**	635.4	17.3	**	571.3	18.4	**
Student characteristics																		
Gender				−26.7	3.9	**				−37.7	3.0	**				−39.0	2.5	**
Socio-economic status (SES)				7.6	2.0	**				2.7	1.8					5.6	1.9	**
Immigration status				−16.5	3.9	**				−12.0	3.8	**				−11.5	4.1	**
Age				−21.9	3.4	**				−11.6	2.9	**				−10.7	2.5	**
Class context																		
Class average SES				8.2	9.8					3.0	6.3					15.4	10.8	
Class average immigration status				−11.3	19.4					15.7	22.9					11.8	28.3	
School location (<3,000 inhab)				empty						−14.6	9.9					−0.6	9.2	
School location (>15,000 inhab)				−54.1	38.0					−6.7	8.1					−37.0	11.0	**
Educational programme/level																		
Programme / level: upper (homog.)				76.9	15.9	**				78.5	5.4	**				48.1	17.4	**
Programme / level: upper (heterog.)				56.7	8.9	**										29.0	4.1	**
Programme / level: low				−11.3	7.7					−53.8	5.7	**				−37.0	3.0	**

(Continued)

Table 8.6. (Continued)

	Canton of Geneva						Canton of Vaud						Canton of Valais (fr)					
	Model 8			Model 9			Model 8			Model 9			Model 8			Model 9		
	Effect	SE	s.	Effect	SE	s.	Effect	SE	s.	Effect	SE	s.	Effect	SE	s.	Effect	SE	s.
School resources																		
Schools' physical infrastructure	−4.9	8.9		−24.8	24.8		22.2	11.1		**4.7	6.4		−7.8	4.2		*4.3	4.4	
Schools' educational resources	−10.1	12.2		14.2	22.9		−7.7	8.3		−7.1	5.3		28.6	5.7		**8.5	5.1	*
Student/mathematics teacher ratio	−0.6	0.6		−0.4	0.8		out	out		out	out		−0.5	0.2		**−0.3	0.2	
Shortage of mathematics teacher	−17.1	10.1	*	−11.3	8.5		−3.5	12.6		6.5	5.1		−14.4	17.2		36.0	11.8	**
School size	0.1	0.1		0.0	0.1		out	out		out	out		0.1	0.0		**0.1	0.0	**
Class size	9.5	0.7	**	0.8	1.6		8.4	1.1		**−0.3	0.6		2.3	1.0		**1.9	0.9	**
Instructional conditions																		
Teacher behaviour	−39.2	13.3		−18.1	10.1	**	−27.8	11.7	*	**−5.0	5.1		−4.8	9.4		10.0	7.0	
Student–teacher relations	−2.6	12.9		4.4	8.2		−2.1	5.7		1.0	3.8		15.3	9.8		−7.8	10.1	
Student morale and commitment	−8.8	11.7		34.2	21.3		28.6	13.8		**13.1	5.6	**	−4.5	4.8		−1.1	4.2	
Teacher support in mathematics	7.6	16.0		−18.1	17.1		32.6	14.9		**4.8	7.7		−31.9	6.2		**−12.9	4.9	**
Student behaviour	−7.2	7.0		−3.8	4.5		−4.8	5.3		3.8	3.2		−4.8	7.2		4.0	5.6	
Disciplinary climate in mathematics	8.5	5.6		7.0	4.2	*	0.1	3.2		3.6	2.4		**14.6**	5.9		**6.9	4.1	**
Late for school	−19.5	3.9	**	−13.9	3.8		−12.2	5.9	**	−10.3	6.1	*	−22.9	7.3		**−17.4	6.9	*
Students' attitudes towards school	−2.7	1.8		−0.2	1.8		−5.0	1.8		**−2.6	1.6		−1.8	1.9		−0.1	1.5	

Students' sense of belonging to school	110.5		11.4			-1.8		9.8		3.0		5.8		0.8		4.6	
															0.4	10.4		0.3	7.7

School management

Variable																	
Mathematics teacher consensus	-8.5		7.9			-0.2		7.8		-6.6		6.1		-1.2		2.0		21.2	2.7		**11.3	4.1	**
Teacher morale and commitment	-3.1		7.4			-15.6		6.8	**	-7.9		11.7		4.9		3.4		-6.1	4.3		-5.9	3.7	
Teacher participation	-33.0		7.8	**		19.6		15.1		-4.6		13.3		7.1		6.8		9.1	6.4		16.3	5.4	**
Assessments per year (20–39)	out		out			out		out		-5.3		21.4		-10.7		11.2		-66.8	14.4	**	**6.5	10.1	
Assessments per year (>40)	out		out			out		out		-68.9		47.5		-26.3		19.5		-32.6	11.8	**	**9.1	9.0	
School autonomy	2.3		10.9			-46.7		19.2		-17.9		19.0		-12.0		10.4		0.8	9.1		-22.3	10.4	**

Variance

(3) Class level	467		111	**		140		41	**	**5,318		615		**141		77	*	306	68		**159	43	**
(2) Student level	9,436		390	**		7,711		300	**	**12,410		615		**10,660		565	**	4,806	234	**	**3,462	199	**
(1) Plausible values	799		20.6	**		804		20	**	**811		20		**806		20	**	781	15	**	**782	15	**

Deviance (RIGLS)

-2*loglikelihood	69,217		65,020		69,344		66,656		84,429		82,167

Cases (students)

Cases in use	1,352	1,275	1,349	1,304	1,664	1,630
Total cases	1,669	1,669	1,634	1,634	1,745	1,745
Missings	317	394	285	330	81	115

Source: OECD PISA database, national sample – SFSO/SCDE (2004).

The effects show the regression coefficients which indicate to what extent the score on student performance in mathematical literacy tends to go up (positive effect) or down (negative effect) by an increase of one standard deviation on the specified explaining variable, while all other variables are constant; Missings: all our estimations have been calculated without the cases of non-answers, non-valid or missing answers; Sign. statistics: ** $p < 0.05$; * $p < 0.1$; "empty" = variable does not exist; "out" = non-used variable due to too much missings.

mathematics teachers has a negative impact on performances for students going to a school with recruitment problems. On the other hand, this effect loses its statistical significance if we consider the school context and the individual characteristics. We detect the same loss of significance for the variable measuring the impact of the class size. In the *canton of Vaud*, it seems that the school infrastructure differs from one school to another and that favourable infrastructure has a positive impact on students' performances. The effect retains its positive value in the adjusted model but loses its statistical significance. The same happens with class size. Furthermore, the positive effect of class size – observable in the three cantons studied – confirms the comments made concerning interdependences between context and resources (see Section 4.1). The situation in the *canton of Valais* shows a surprising result. It seems that the more that qualified mathematics teachers are in shortage, the better are the students of that school (+36 points). In order to give a reasonable explanation to this positive relationship, it would be necessary to do more in-depth research on the difficulty of recruiting teachers for a specific programme/level.

8.4.2.2. Hypothesis II: Impact of the Instructional Conditions

From the nine factors that served to operationalise the instructional conditions, six have a significant impact in one or more cantons. Across *all cantons*, students that are often late to school have a tendency to obtain lower grades than classmates that are only occasionally late to school. This can also serve as an indicator of environment and discipline within a school. Indeed, a good learning environment in mathematics classes has a positive effect in the *cantons of Geneva and Valais*. In the *canton of Vaud*, it is the motivation and commitment of the students in a school that have a positive impact on the results in mathematics. Already observed at the Swiss level (Moser and Berweger 2004:59) and in German-speaking cantons (Brühwiler and Buccheri 2005:80), the negative relationship between teachers' behaviour and the performances in mathematics is also confirmed in the cantons of Geneva and Vaud. After controlling for the context and the students' characteristics, however, this effect is reduced by half or even becomes insignificant. This indirectly indicates – considering the strong correlation between context and programmes/levels – that the appreciation of teachers' behaviour is linked to the requirements level of schools and classes. For example, in classes with low requirements, a bigger emphasis is given to aspects such as individualised teaching and good relations with students. Apparently in the canton of Valais this type of explanation also applies in relation to the appreciation of students' behaviour.

8.4.2.3. Hypothesis III: Impact of the School Management

The fixed effects of the five variables used to measure the influence of school management on performances in mathematics give significant estimations only in the cantons of Geneva and Valais. In the *canton of Valais*, the aspects linked to the management of human resources and to the relations within the teaching body have a positive impact on students' performances. When increasing the level of consensus between mathematics teachers by one unit – specifically the one measuring teachers' participation in school management – the performance of students in those schools raises from 11 to 16 points. In turn, the influence of the school autonomy index becomes negative (–22) after integrating control variables. We observe the same effect in the *canton of Geneva* where the negative impact of a bigger autonomy results in –47 points. This result confirms previous studies at the national level (Moser and Berweger 2004:56) and the international level (OECD 2005a:42). Hence, it disproves the hypothesis that school autonomy, as measured with our data, has a stimulating impact on students' performances.

8.5. Conclusions

To answer our initial question – What influence do schools and the educational system have on students' performance? – we made a broad review of the literature focusing on education systems. At the origin of the *school effectiveness research* are very distinct scientific disciplines such as economics, pedagogy and psychology as well as theories on organisations. First, this enabled us to distinguish three approaches that together form the integrated model of school effectiveness. Second, it also highlighted the hierarchical structure that exists between the various explanatory variables on the level of students, classes, schools and context. At the same time, we deducted from our three hypotheses, the impact on the students' performances, by (1) the school resources, (2) the instructional conditions and (3) the school management.

To test our assumptions empirically and taking a current OECD study (OECD 2005a) as a reference, we used multilevel analysis methods which allow for modelling the variance at different hierarchical levels and simultaneously estimating regression coefficients for all the factors in question.

We chose the three French-speaking cantons of Switzerland where such school factors-centred analysis has been neglected until today. As a result of Swiss federalism, compulsory education differs from one canton to another and therefore cantonal comparative analysis makes sense. We took the three French-speaking cantons located around Lake Leman (the cantons of Geneva, Vaud and Valais) which have drawn representative samples for the OECD PISA surveys. The three cantons have more or less selective education systems which group the students, according to their performance, in different programmes (Vaud) or levels for some subjects (Geneva, Valais). Therefore, the important effect of educational programmes/levels on the students' performances is not particularly astonishing. It explains between 49% (Geneva) and 86% (Vaud) of the between-class variance of the students' performances in mathematical literacy. However, we were able to show that the programmes/levels tend to be homogeneous not only for the students' performances but also for their socio-economic composition. Consequently, there is a strong interdependence (with mutual causalities) between the two types of variables. Thus, at first, in the variance analysis of our three hypotheses, we also calculated the variances between classes jointly explained by the school factors on the one hand and the student characteristics, the school context as well as the programmes/levels on the other hand. This jointly explained variance exceeds in all cantons the unique variance explained by school factors and it is a particularly high proportion in the case of school resources (34–65%). This fact is narrowly linked to the educational programme/level because, for instance, the cantons adapt the class size to take into account the requirements of the programme/level. Secondly, to estimate how each school factor influences student performance, we adjusted the effects not only for student characteristics and school context but also for programmes/levels. Our results show that the instructional conditions such as, for example, the disciplinary climate, have more often statistically significant impact on student performance than aspects of school resources and management. Thus, among all the school characteristics that have an impact on the performances of the students and that are at the same time policy-amenable, the factors closer to the learning process within the classes are more often valid in all three cantons. They consequently deserve greater attention from the experts and political leaders in the field of compulsory education. Nevertheless, the major challenge for the three cantonal school systems is how to cope with the high interrelations between the educational programmes/levels and the socio-economic composition of the classes. Therefore, the question of *equity* in educational performance needs more attention of researchers and policy makers.

Acknowledgments

The author would like to thank Pascal Sciarini and Nils Soguel from the IDHEAP (Swiss Graduate School of Public Administration), Thomas Meyer from TREE (Transitions from Education to Employment) and Thomas Holzer from the SFSO (Swiss Federal Statistical Office) for their helpful comments.

References

Becker GS (1964) *Human Capital*. Columbia University Press, New York
Betts JR (1996) Is there a link between school inputs and earnings? Fresh scrutiny of an old literature. In: Burtless G. (ed.) *Does Money Matter? The Effect of School Resources on Student Achievement and Adult Success*. The Brookings Institution, Washington, DC, pp 141–190
Brühwiler C, Buccheri G (2005) Merkmale der schulischen und unterrichtilichen Lernumgebungen. *PISA 2005 Deutschschweiz/FL*. PISA 2003: Analysen und Porträts für Deutschschweizer Kantone und das Fürstentum Liechtenstein – Detaillierte Ergebnisse und methodisches Vorgehen. Kantonale Drucksachen- und Materialzentrale, Zürich, pp 73–103.
Bryk AS, Raudenbush SW (1992) *Hierarchical Linear Models: Applications and Data Analysis Methods*. Sage Publications, Newbury Park, CA
Bühlmann M (2004) Die Mehrebenenanalyse: Funktion, Anwendung und Probleme. Handout journées méthodologiques 3ème cycle CUSO, Lausanne.
Bühlmann M (2006) *Politische Partizipation im kommunalen Kontext*. Haupt, Bern
Bühlmann M, Freitag M (2006) Individual and contextual determinants of electoral participation. *Swiss Political Science Review* 12/4:13–47
Burtless G (1996) Introduction and summary. In: Burtless G (ed.) *Does Money Matter? The Effect of School Resources on Student Achievement and Adult Success*. The Brookings Institution, Washington, DC, pp 1–42
Carroll JB (1963) A model of school learning. *Teachers College Record* 64:722–733
Creemers Bert PM (1994) *The Effective Classroom*. Cassell, London
Creemers Bert PM (1995) Process indicators on school functioning and the generalisability of school factor models across countries. In: OECD, *Measuring the Quality of Schools*. OECD, Paris, pp 103–119
Dean GJ, Peter M, del Prete T (2000) *Enhancing Organizational Effectiveness in Adult and Community Education*. Krieger Publishing Company, Malabar, FL
Delaunay D (2003) Présentation générale de l'analyse multiniveau. Centre Population et Développement/Institut de Recherche pour le Développement (Handout), Paris

Fayol H (1970, 1ère publication 1919) *Administration industrielle et générale: prévoyance, organisation, commandement, coordination, contrôle*. Dunod, Paris

Fraser BJ, Walberg HJ, Welch W, Hattie JA (1987) Syntheses of educational productivity research. *International Journal of Educational Research, Special Issue* 11(2), pp. 145–252

Frederik WT (traduction française 1967, 1ère publication 1911) *La direction scientifique des entreprises*. Marabout, Verviers

GERESE (Groupe Européen de Recherche sur l'Equité des Systèmes Educatifs) (2003) *L'équité des systèmes éducatifs européens. Un ensemble d'indicateurs*. Commission Européenne, Bruxelles

Hanushek EA (1996) School resources and student performance. In: Burtless G (ed.) *Does Money Matter? The Effect of School Resources on Student Achievement and Adult Success*. The Brookings Institution, Washington, DC, pp 43–73

Hedges LV, Greenwald R (1996) Have times changed ? The relation between school resources and student performance. In: Burtless G (ed.) *Does Money Matter? The Effect of School Resources on Student Achievement and Adult Success*. The Brookings Institution, Washington, DC, pp 74–92

Jones K, Gould M (2005) Mutlilevel analysis: practical applications. Handout for the Essex Summer School in Social Science Data Analysis. University of Essex, Essex

Knoers A (1996) Paradigms in instructional psychology. In: De Corte E, Weinert FE (eds) *Developmental and Instructional Psychology*. Pergamon, Oxford, pp 317–321

Mayo E (1945) *The Social Problems of an Industrial Civilization*. Graduate School of Business Administration, Harvard University, Boston, MA

Menge O (2005) Description du système scolaire. In: IRDP. *PISA 2003: Compétences des jeunes romands – Résultats de la seconde enquête PISA auprès des élèves de 9e année*. Institut de recherche et de documentation pédagogique, Neuchâtel

Meuret D (2005) L'équité des systèmes éducatifs: mieux construire la notion. Conférence à Genève, 31 mai 2005

Moser U (2005) Kontextmerkmale des Bildungssystems und ihre Bedeutung für die Mathematikleistungen. *PISA 2005 Deutschschweiz/FL*. PISA 2003 Analysen und Porträts für Deutschschweizer Kantone und das Fürstentum Liechtenstein – Detaillierte Ergebnisse und methodisches Vorgehen. Kantonale Drucksachen- und Materialzentrale, Zürich, pp 106–140

Moser U, Berweger S (2004) Einflüsse des Bildungssystems und der Schulen auf die Mathematikleistung. *SFSO/SCDE*. PISA 2003 Kompetenzen für die Zukunft – Erster nationaler, Bericht, pp 45–62

OECD (1999) *Measuring Student Knowledge and Skills – A New Framework for Assessment*. OECD, Paris

OECD (2001) *Connaissances et compétences: des atouts pour la vie. Premiers résultats du programme international de l'OECD pour le suivi des acquis des élèves (PISA) 2000*. OECD, Paris

OECD (2004) *Apprendre aujourd'hui, réussir demain. Premiers résultats de PISA 2003.* OECD, Paris
OECD (2005a) *School Factors related to Quality and Equity – Results from PISA 2000.* OECD, Paris
OECD (2005b) *PISA 2003: Data Analysis Manual for SPSS Users.* OECD, Paris
Piaget J (1947) la psychologie de l'intelligence, A. Colin. Paris
Rasbash J, Steele F, Browne W, Prosser B (2004) *A User's Guide to MLwiN Version 2.0.* Centre for Multilevel Modelling, Institute of Education, University of London, London
Raudenbush SW, Bryk AS (1986) A hierarchical model for studying school effects. *Sociology of Education* 59(1):1–17
Reynolds D, Teddlie C, Creemers B, Scheerens J, Townsend T (2000) An introduction to school effectiveness research. In: Teddlie C, Reynolds D (eds) *The International Handbook of School Effectiveness Research.* Falmer Press, London, pp 3–25
Rychen DS, Salganik LH (2001) *Defining and Selecting Key Competencies.* Hogrefe und Huber, Göttingen
Schedler K, Bossi H, Hochreutener MA, Stäger L, Stauffer T (1998) *Kostenrechnungsmodell für Bildungsinstitutionen.* Schweizerische Erziehungsdirektorenkonferenz, Bern
Scheerens J (1992) *Effective Schooling. Research, Theory and Practice.* Cassell, London
Scheerens J, Bosker RJ (1997) *The Foundations of Educational Effectiveness.* Pergamon, Elsevier Science Ltd, Oxford
Scott RW (1998) *Organizations: Rational, Natural and Open Systems* (fourth edition). Prentice Hall, Upper Saddle River, NJ
SFSO/SCDE (2001) Préparés pour la vie? Les compétences de base des jeunes – Synthèse du rapport national PISA 2000. SFSO/SCDE, Neuchâtel
SFSO/SCDE (2002) Préparés pour la vie? Les compétences de base des jeunes – Rapport national de l'enquête PISA 2000. SFSO/SCDE, Neuchâtel
SFSO/SCDE (2003a) PISA 2000 – Synthèse et recommandations. SFSO/SCDE, Neuchâtel
SFSO/SCDE (2003b) PISA 2003 Schulprogramme für die Schweiz und Liechtenstein. SFSO/SCDE, Neuchâtel
SFSO/SCDE (2004) PISA 2003 Compétences pour l'avenir – Premier rapport national. SFSO/SCDE, Neuchâtel
SFSO/SCDE (2005) PISA 2003 Compétences pour l'avenir – Deuxième rapport national. SFSO/SCDE, Neuchâtel
Simon HA (1976, first publication 1945) *Administrative Behavior: A Study of Decision-Making Processes in Administrative Organization* (3ème edition). Collier Macmillan, London
Skinner BF (1957) *Verbal Behavior.* Copley Publishing Group, Acton
Snijders TAB, Bosker RJ (1999) *Multilevel Analysis: An Introduction to Basic and Advanced Multilevel Modelling.* Sage Publications, London

Soussi A (2005) Le système genevois dans le secondaire I. *IRDP*. PISA 2003 Compétences des jeunes romands – Résultats de la seconde enquête PISA auprès des élèves de 9e année. Institut de recherche et de documentation pédagogique, Neuchâtel

Stringfield SC, Slavin RE (1992) A hierarchical longitudinal model for elementary school effects. In: Creemers BP, Reegzigt GJ (eds) *Evaluation of Effectiveness*. ICO, Gröningen

Taylor FW (1911) The Principles of Scientific Management. Harper Bros. New York

Thorndike EL (1922) *The Psychology of Arithmetic*. MacMillan, New York

van Bertalanffy L (2001, first publication 1956) *General System Theory: Foundations, Development, Applications*. Braziller G, New York

Walberg HJ (1984) Improving the productivity of American schools. *Educational Leadership* (41): 19–27

Wang MC, Haertel GD, Walberg HJ (1993) Toward a knowledge base for school learning. *Review of Educational Research* 61:249–294

Warm TA (1985) Weighted maximum likelihood estimation of ability in item response theory with tests of finite length. Technical Report CGI-TR-85-08. US Coast Guard Institute, Oklahoma City

Weber M (1980, first publication 1922) Wirtschaft und Gesellschaft. Grundriß der Verstehenden Soziologie. Mohr Siebeck, 5. Auflage, Tübingen

Wiener N (1956) *The Human Use of Human Beings: Cybernetics and Society*. Doubleday, Garden City, NY

Chapter 9
Are Swiss Secondary Schools Efficient?

Muriel Meunier

Department of Economics and Swiss Leading House on the Economics of Education, Firm Behaviour and Training Policies, University of Geneva, Geneva, Switzerland

9.1. Introduction

Since the disappointing performance of Switzerland in the year 2000 PISA survey, carried out by the OECD,[1] the quality of schools in Switzerland has become a particularly sensitive issue. The concern about the efficiency of educational production is now a key point raised in debates about schools. The aim of this paper is to measure the efficiency of Swiss secondary schools in order to make an academic contribution to this topic. The Data Envelopment Analysis (DEA) method was used to define the efficiency scores and production frontiers (Charnes et al. 1978).

The relationship between efficiency and size of school has also been given special attention (Kirjavainen and Loikkanen 1998; Bradley et al. 2001; Barnett et al. 2002). Interest in this question is motivated by the fact that the organisation of education in Switzerland is going through a process of complete transformation. Given that in Switzerland not one but 26 different scholastic systems[2] coexist on the same territory, in attempts to

---

[1] *Programme International pour le Suivi des Acquis des élèves* (Programme for International Student Assessment). In an international comparison of 32 participating countries (classification in reading): Finland (1st) had an average score of 547, France (14th) scored 505, Switzerland (17th) 494, Italy (20th) 488, Germany (21st) 484, Brazil (last) 396, and the average score of OECD countries was 500.

[2] Switzerland is a federal state with a three-tier political structure: the (federal) Confederation, the (regional) cantons (26), and the (local) communes. The Constitution only grants a very limited number of tasks in educational matters to the

develop a national education system, the question of harmonising public state education[3] recurs again and again (Swiss Confederation 2006). In fact, this leads to and will continue to lead to the making of numerous decisions.[4] The question of the optimum size of schools might be one of these. The results show that the larger the size of the school, the larger the percentage of efficient schools.

This chapter is organised as follows. The next section presents the DEA model, after which the database is explained in Section 9.3, followed by the selection of outputs and inputs in Section 9.4. The results are analysed in Section 9.5. The final section concludes with the implications for public political choices and possible future research.

9.2. Methodology

Educational researchers have been implementing the DEA methodology that began development in the United States in the early 1980s (Charnes et al. 1981; Bessent et al. 1982, 1984). DEA is a mathematical technique that estimates a frontier (Charnes et al. 1978). This frontier is determined by defining for each observation variables as either inputs (resources used in production) or outputs. The idea of efficiency, as defined by Farrell (1957), is the success (of a firm) "in producing as large an output as possible from a given set of inputs".

Let X_i be a vector of inputs and Y_i a vector of outputs for the school i ($i = 1,...,N$). Suppose X_0 and Y_0 are, respectively, the inputs and outputs of school 0 whose efficiency score needs to be determined. The measurement of efficiency for school 0 may be defined as follows:

Confederation. It is the cantons who control the structure and content of training and education (art. 62 of the federal Constitution).

[3] In late May 2006, the Swiss people took part in a popular vote aiming to change the articles in the Constitution governing education and (vocational) training. One issue in this vote was the harmonisation of state education. For the first time the majority of voters (85%) voted yes to national involvement of the federal state in education (voter participation rate: 27%).

[4] For example, harmonisation of the new school year. Until the mid-1980s, the cantons in favour of the autumnal new school year were opposed to those defending the spring start of the new school year. Following the results of the popular vote of 22 September 1985, the start of the new school year was finally set between mid-August and mid-September throughout the country.

$$\text{Min } \eta_0 \tag{9.1}$$

s.t.

$$\sum_{i=1}^{n} \theta_i Y_{ij} \geq Y_{0j} \qquad \forall \; j = 1,\ldots,s \tag{9.2}$$

$$\sum_{i=1}^{n} \theta_i X_{ik} \leq \eta_0 X_{0k} \qquad \forall \; k = 1,\ldots,m \tag{9.3}$$

$$\sum_{i=1}^{n} \theta_i = 1 \tag{9.4}$$

where η_0 represents the efficiency score of school 0 and θ_i the weight given by the school i in order to dominate school 0, j represents the outputs and k represents the inputs. Optimal η_0 cannot be greater than 1. If the score of school 0 is equal to 1 ($\eta_0 = 1$), then the school is efficient whereas if it is less than 1 ($\eta_0 < 1$), the school is inefficient.

In order to illustrate this in graph form, an example composed of four schools (A, B, C, and G) is now considered in which only one input (X) is used so that only one output (Y) is produced. Figure 9.1 represents the two dimensions of a plane on which the four schools are positioned. Schools A, B, and C are efficient as they are situated on the frontier. On the other hand, school G is inefficient. The degree of inefficiency can be measured (graphically) in two ways: either as the vertical distance between point G

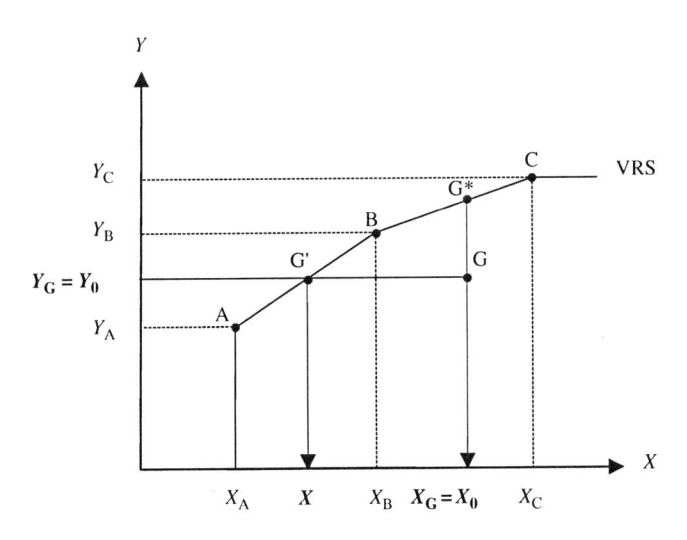

Fig. 9.1. The DEA frontier

and point G* (output oriented) or the horizontal distance between point G and point G' (input oriented). The output-oriented measurements indicate the amount by which the outputs must be proportionally increased in order to reach the frontier while keeping inputs constant. The input-oriented measurements indicate the amount by which inputs could be proportionally reduced while keeping output quantities constant.

If it is considered that the aim of school headmasters is to obtain the best results possible using the resources available (over which they exercise little or no control), the output-oriented version is appropriate (Mancebón and Bandrés 1999). On the other hand, if the goal is that schools minimise the use of inputs while keeping their output level constant, then it is better to opt for an input-oriented model (Kirjavainen and Loikkanen 1998). In this chapter, we share the view that because of difficult budgetary context, educational policies are aimed at improving the use of resources (Diagne 2006). The results are therefore input oriented, that is to say, a school is not efficient if an input can be reduced without increasing another input and decreasing the output (Charnes et al. 1981).

To determine the (in)efficiency score of school G, then:

$$X_G = X_0 \tag{9.5}$$

and

$$Y_G = Y_0 \tag{9.6}$$

$\sum_{i=1}^{n} \theta_i Y_{ij}$ represents the weighted sum of Y_i, i.e. $\theta_A Y_A + \theta_B Y_B + \theta_C Y_C + \theta_G Y_G$ with $\theta_A + \theta_B + \theta_C + \theta_G = 1$ (hypothesising variable returns to scale). Assuming that:

$$\sum_{i=1}^{n} \theta_i Y_i = Y_0 \tag{9.7}$$

$\sum_{i=1}^{n} \theta_i X_i$ represents the weighted sums of X_i and assuming that:

$$\sum_{i=1}^{n} \theta_i X_i = \eta_0 X_0 = X \tag{9.8}$$

The efficiency score is:

$$\eta_0 = \frac{X}{X_0} \tag{9.9}$$

If η_0 is 0.8, the inefficiency of school G is 20% (1 – 0.8=0.2). In other words, school G must decrease its input by 20% if it is to become efficient, that is to say, to be placed on the segment of the frontier linking school A and school B.

Initially, Charnes et al. (1978) assumed the scale returns were constant (CRS). In a production process constant returns to scale indicate that production varies in the same proportion as the production factors involved. If all the schools perform optimally, then the CRS hypothesis is appropriate. Banker (1984) then modified the CRS model in order to account for situations in which the returns to scale are variable (VRS). This hypothesis means a more flexible frontier can be estimated.

Figure 9.2 shows the distinction between technical inefficiency (starting measuring from the VRS frontier) and the scale inefficiency (starting measuring from the CRS frontier). The technical inefficiency corresponds to the inefficiency defined in Eq. 9.9. However, it seems that at point G', the productivity ratio Y_G/X is weaker than the maximum ratio Y_G/X_A of school A. Even though its technical efficiency places it at point G', the size of school G means it cannot have the maximal average production per factor unit. Compared to the latter, which is situated at the optimal size, school G suffers from scale inefficiency measured by the relationship $X_{G''}/X$. Its total inefficiency combines the two forms of inefficiency and is measured by the relationship $X_{G''}/X_G$.

One advantage of DEA is that by using several inputs and outputs, it considers the multidimensional characteristics of education. Another advantage is the non-parametric character of the method. However, the results are sensitive to choice of inputs and outputs and since a non-stochastic method is used, the classic statistical tests do not allow the specifications used to be tested.

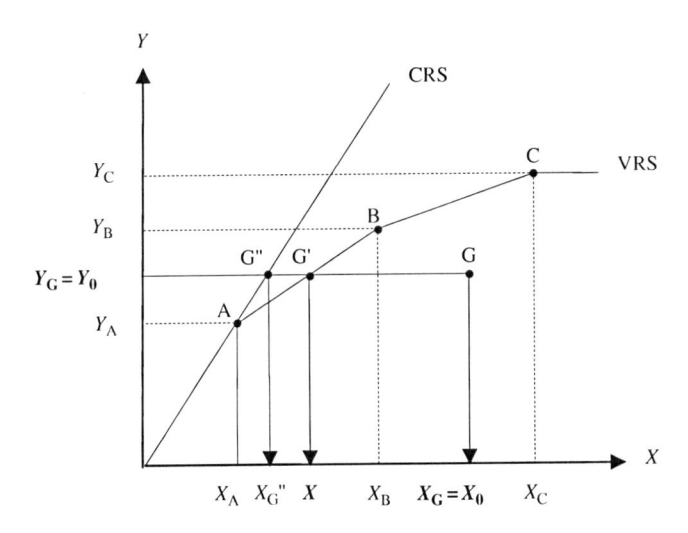

Fig. 9.2. The technical efficiency and the scale efficiency

9.3. The Data

The data used in this study were obtained from the PISA survey national sample for Switzerland. This survey was carried out by the OECD in the year 2000 (OECD 2002). The aim of this survey was to test the ability of pupils so that the educational achievement of the young could be compared. Three fields were examined: reading, mathematics and science. The sample population was defined in agreement with the school year. The final obligatory year of schooling in the Swiss scholastic system is Year 9.[5]

Representative samples in the three large linguistic regions in Switzerland were taken by the PISA survey national management (i.e. the Swiss Confederation and the cantons).[6] In the first stage, the schools were sorted on the basis of the 1998/1999 school data of the Swiss Federal Statistical Office (SFSO). In the second stage, the pupils were randomly selected from the schools considered. Therefore, not all pupils participated in the PISA survey, and only certain pupils in certain schools took the tests.

The sample used in this study only treats the schools in which less than 20 pupils took part in the PISA survey. This was the case in 156 schools in 22 cantons.[7] This number is based on the average number of pupils per class (only for state schools) which was 19.1 in Secondary 1 in 1999–2000 (SFSO 1999). In order to verify that there was no attrition bias, the descriptive statistics from this sub-sample were compared to those of the total sample (243 schools).

9.4. Selection of Outputs and Inputs

Considering schools as companies specialising in educational production, Schultz (1963) opened the way to evaluation of production frontiers and

---

[5] Compulsory schooling lasts 9 years and is composed of the primary and secondary I levels. In most cantons, primary education lasts 6 years (from 6/7 years old to 11/12) and secondary I lasts 3 years (from 12/13 years old to 14/15). For more details on the Swiss education system see the CDIP web-site (http://www.ides.ch/umfrage2003/mainUmfrage_F.html).

[6] It concerns German (spoken by 64% of the resident population as mother tongue), French (20%), and Italian (7%). The remaining 9% use other languages to express themselves.

[7] Two cantons (Uri and Appenzell Rhodes-Intérieur) did not take part in the PISA and the schools in the cantons of Glaris and Nidwald did not reply to certain questions.

the measurement of efficiency in education. The school is therefore considered to be an entity carrying out a production process (in this case educational) by transforming inputs into outputs (Thanassoulis and Dunstan 1994). Given the present state of knowledge concerning this process of acquisition, the school is generally considered to be a black box. In addition to measuring inputs and outputs, the conceptualisation also forms part of recurring problems found in numerous studies (Mancebón and Bandrés 1999).

9.4.1 The Outputs

The educational output should represent the aim of the school. As an institution, the school has the essential function of transmitting a curriculum. This formal curriculum is what is officially designated and supposed to be transmitted to the students (mainly composed of cognitive abilities). But the school is situated in a world of socialisation meaning the pupils also learn what some sociologists call the hidden curriculum: affective abilities (Duru-Bellat and van Zanten 1999). The whole problem lies in the multidimensional nature of education, in other words, the multiplicity of aims pursued by the school cannot be aggregated into one single measurement (Bessent et al. 1982). Furthermore, it is not always easy to measure educational production. And yet, if one wishes to analyse the production of the schools, it is nevertheless essential to employ appropriate measurements of the outcomes.

From the moment when the subject selection decisions of the students are taken, which are theoretically based on school criteria objectives such as the marks obtained by the students, these represent a measure recognised by the institution itself. In most Swiss cantons, the average mark obtained at the end of the academic year forms the basis for provisional or definitive promotion to the class above (CDIP 2001). The majority of studies in the literature use standardised test scores (Bradley et al. 2001). This output fulfils one of the essential aims of schools: obtaining knowledge for guidance and therefore selection within the education system. The score for reading in the PISA 2000 test is used as the output (READ) in this study. This means the arithmetic average of pupils taking part in the survey by school. The school is therefore the educational production unit. The pupils taking part in the 2000 survey all answered the questionnaire on reading. Unfortunately, this was not the case in mathematics or science, which resulted in considerable attrition of the data.[8] Consequently, only the reading results are used in this paper.[9]

In order to measure the homogeneity of pupil performances within the establishments, the inverse standard deviation (by school) of the reading score (INVRSD) was used. This variable takes the dispersion of results inside the school into account. The greater the value, the more homogeneous the results of the pupils within the school, that is to say, concentrated around the average of the school considered. In addition, particular attention needs to be given to the idea of equity. In fact, if two schools having the same average score are considered, the one in which all the pupils are concentrated around the average will be preferable to that in which the pupils are split into a wider spectrum, with the good on the one side and the poor on the other. Seldom present in the literature, this consideration deserves more attention from those who do research into efficiency.

Figure 9.3 illustrates the relationship between the two outputs used in the DEA. The degree of pupil homogeneity correlates positively with the average performance level in reading (the coefficient of correlation is 0.6009). There are two possible interpretations. The first is that the level of performance within the establishments leads to homogenisation of pupil results, i.e. performance and equity are not contradictory. The second is that the schools situated in a homogeneous environment obtain the best results. The causality between performance and equity is therefore the inverse of the first explanation.

9.4.2 The Inputs

As accurately as possible, the selected inputs must represent the characteristics of the educational system impacting on the process of educational production. However, this selection is restricted by the availability of information in databases. There is no unanimous choice of inputs in the literature (Hanushek 1986).

---

[8] Of all the students in the original sample taking the reading test (7997 pupils) only 2653 replied to the questions on both reading and science, 2647 to those on reading and mathematics, and 1804 on reading, mathematics, and science, and 893 on reading only.

[9] The correlation coefficients between the subjects studied by the 1804 pupils who replied to the three questionnaires were: reading and mathematics (0.8120), reading and science (0.8983), and mathematics and science (0.7979).

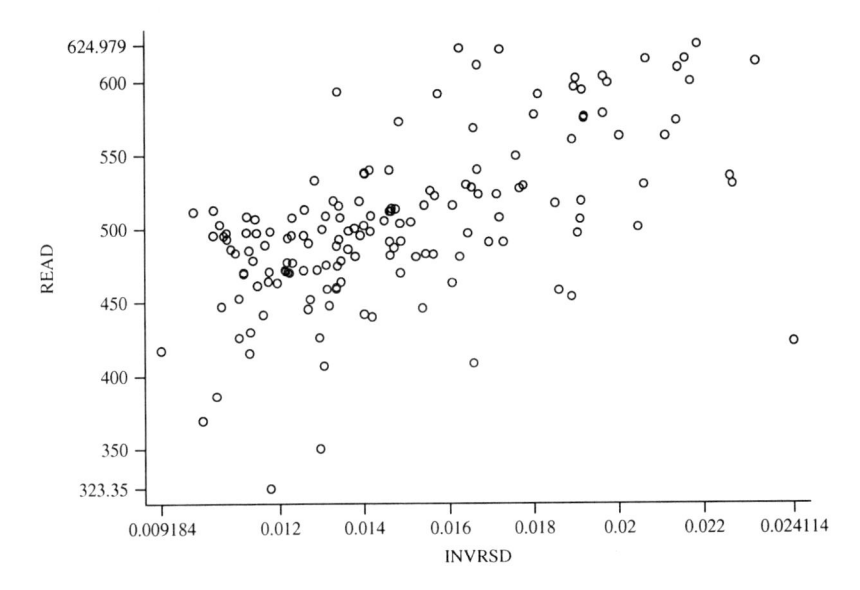

Fig. 9.3. The two DEA outputs (READ and INVRSD)

In that the DEA results are sensitive to the inputs used, this forms an important stage in the modelling. There is a methodological divide in the literature resulting from the precise choice of inputs made. On the one hand, there are the studies that suggest using only discretionary inputs in the DEA, i.e. under the control of the schools (Charnes et al. 1981; Bessent et al. 1982, 1984; Kirjavainen and Loikkanen 1998; Mancebón and Bandrés 1999; Diagne 2006). On the other hand, there are studies simultaneously using discretionary and non-discretionary inputs, such as environmental or socio-economic inputs (Ray 1991; Ruggiero 1996).

The choice of methodology has empirical implications. Studies which introduce only discretionary inputs into the DEA use the non-discretionary inputs in a second stage (OLS or tobit) in order to explain the distribution of efficiency scores (Bradley et al. 2001). The others generally use the econometric method of stochastic frontiers (Barrow 1991; Cooper and Cohn 1997).

In order to understand the resources allocated to teaching from a quantitative point of view,[10] the inputs of human capital considered in the analysis

---

[10] The importance of class size to scholastic performance has been highlighted in literature (Summers and Wolfe 1977; Arias and Walker 2004). It is therefore unfortunate that this variable does not appear in the PISA, all the more when considering the virulent debate surrounding this problem (Krueger 2003).

presented in this chapter include the number of teachers per pupil[11] (TEACHER). They also include the number of hours of supervision per year (TOTHRS) so as to take the annual time available for teaching pupils into consideration. This input is important in the Swiss case since there is a great variation between establishments because the responsibility for setting the Secondary 1 study plan lies with the cantonal authorities. For example, during the course of their obligatory schooling a pupil in the canton of Fribourg attends school for at least 700 h more than a pupil in the canton of Geneva (CDIP 2001). Finally, in order to quantitatively consider the resources allocated to teaching, the number of teachers per pupil having a teaching diploma (QUAL) was also taken into consideration. While the Coleman report (1966) concludes that the experience of teachers makes only a marginal contribution, the results of Summers and Wolfe (1977) and Goldhaber and Brewer (1997) disagree with Coleman. In the Swiss case, given that the teacher training system is governed by cantonal legislation, this input is also important.[12] The working conditions of teachers, salary level, and type of post are also fixed by the cantons (CDIP 2001). Unfortunately, this information is not available in the PISA survey.

Following Ruggiero (1996) we consider an input in physical capital as well.[13] The number of computers per pupil (COMPUTER) provides an approximate idea of the availability of information technology equipment, and so the financial commitment of the school to new technology can be measured. The descriptive statistics of the variables used are presented in (Table 9.1) along with the correlation matrices (Table 9.2).

---

[11] The quantity of available educational resources can be measured in different ways: the number of professionals per 100 pupils (Bessent et al. 1982), the number of teachers per pupil (Mancebón and Bandrés 1999; Diagne 2006), or the pupil/teacher ratio (Mizala et al. 2002). With regard to homogeneity, the pupil measurements for all the variables were considered.

[12] Since 2005 all teacher training has been carried out to university degree level. The hautes écoles pédagogiques (HEP) were created for this (Universities of Teacher Education).

[13] Ruggiero (1996) also uses the number of classrooms per pupil as an input to measure capital.

Table 9.1. Descriptive statistics

Variables		Mean	Std. Dev.	Min	Max
Outputs	READ	503.5198	54.4640	323.35	624.98
	INVRSD	0.0148	0.0033	0.0092	0.0241
Inputs	TEACHER[a]	0.0875	0.0214	0.0203	0.1751
	TOTHRS	987.4615	80.6980	579	1261
	QUAL[a]	0.5734	0.3309	0.01	1
	COMPUTER[a]	0.1158	0.0723	0.018	0.571
Others	SCHLSIZE	409.8077	295.0303	35	1715

Source: PISA 2000.
Sample size $N = 156$ schools. [a] Variables measured *per pupil*.

Table 9.2. Correlation matrices of the variables used in the DEA

	READ	INVRSD	TEACH	TOTHRS	QUAL	COMP
READ	1.0000					
INVRSD	0.6009	1.0000				
TEACH	0.0397	0.0390	1.0000			
TOTHRS	0.1149	0.0706	0.1194	1.0000		
QUAL	0.4151	0.2121	−0.1025	0.1123	1.0000	
COMP	−0.0019	0.1035	0.2954	0.1995	0.2023	1.0000

Source: PISA 2000.
Notes: $N = 156$ schools. TEACH = TEACHER, COMP = COMPUTER.

9.5. Results

The production frontiers were determined using the DEA model and the Efficiency Measurement System software (Scheel 2000). The basic specification included two outputs (READ and INVRSD) and four inputs (TEACHER, TOTHRS, QUAL, and COMPUTER). Table 9.3 shows that when variable scale returns are used, the average efficiency score is 0.8348 (standard error of 0.1147). This means that on average the schools could reduce their resources by approximately 16% while maintaining the same level of educational production. The minimum efficiency score is 0.5264 and the number of efficient schools is 24 (out of 156), i.e. 15% of the sample.

When constant scale returns are used, the average efficiency score is lower (0.8043 with a standard error of 0.1194). The minimum efficiency score is also lower (0.4421) and the number of efficient schools is no more than 16 (out of 156), i.e. 10% of the sample. In terms of effectiveness, the

Table 9.3. Average efficiency score, minimum and maximum scores and percentage of efficient schools (CRS and VRS)

	Mean	Minimum	Maximum	% of efficient schools
CRS	0.8043	0.4421	1.0000	10% (16/156)
VRS	0.8348	0.5264	1.0000	15% (24/156)

Source: PISA 2000.

16 efficient schools are attended by only 851 of the 5870 pupils attending the 156 schools in the sample (14.5%). The average size of the 16 efficient schools is much higher (579) than the 140 inefficient schools (390.47). Figure 9.4 represents the distribution of schools classified in order of increasing efficiency when constant scale returns are used.

One question which deserves attention is whether school size matters for efficiency. This topic is frequently discussed in the literature but the authors do not agree on the link between size and efficiency. For example, the results of Barnett et al. (2002) show that the performance of schools correlates positively with their size. On the other hand, Kirjavainen and Loikkanen (1998) remark that efficiency scores correlate less with the size

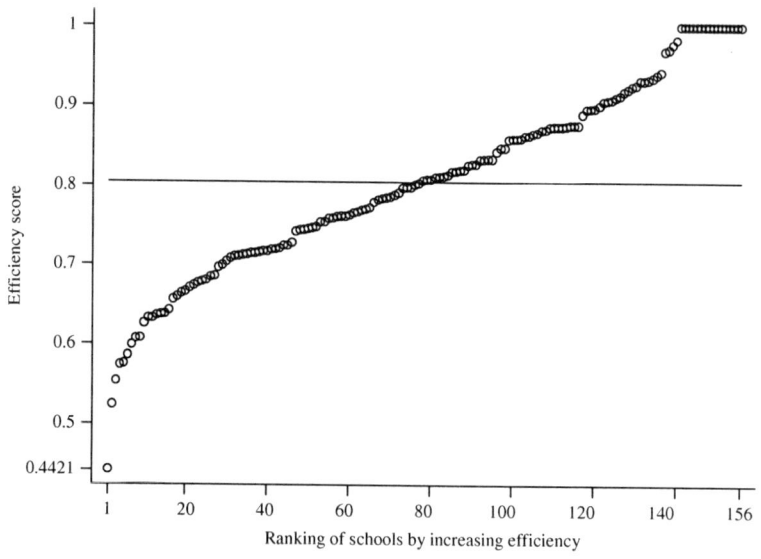

Fig. 9.4. The efficiency distribution of input-oriented DEA model (CRS is assumed)

of the school and more positively with class size.[14] According to Bradley et al. (2001) the greater is the degree of competition between schools and pupils, the more efficient the schools tend to be. There will be a contradictory effect between the fact that the larger the schools the more the efficiency and the fact that the more numerous the schools are (and therefore small in size), the more they compete against each other and are efficient.

Figure 9.5 represents the efficiency scores of the 156 schools by size of school. The average size is approximately 410 pupils and it is quite clear that the more the size of the school increases, the more the dispersion of the school efficiency scores decreases (the coefficient of correlation is 0.3545). Analysis of the quartiles (Table 9.4) also shows that when schools situated in the 1st quartile are compared to the 4th quartile, the number of efficient schools increases (from 2.6% for the 1st quartile to 18% in the 4th

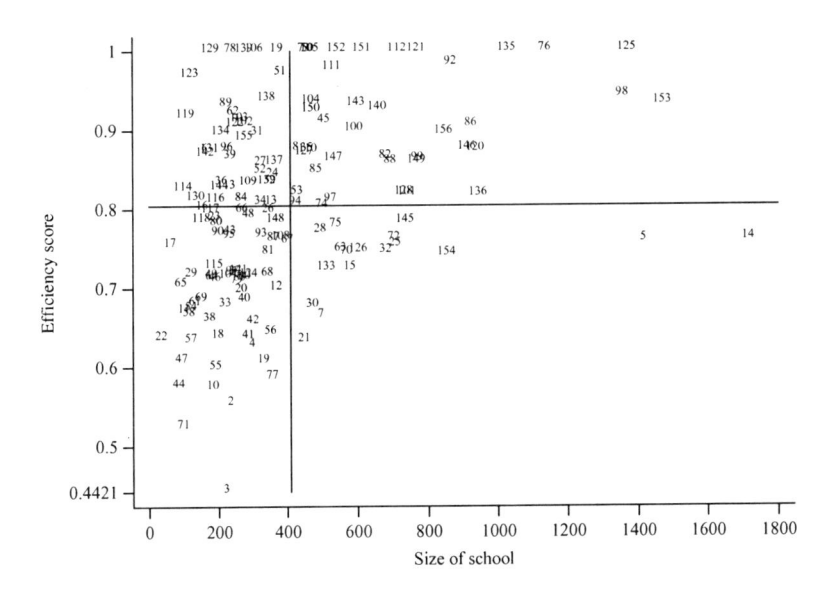

Fig. 9.5. Efficiency scores and size of school (CRS is assumed)

---

[14] Barnett et al. (2002) do not control for the class sizes. According to the results of Kirjavainen and Loikkanen (1998), inefficiency initially increases with class size then decreases from an average class size of 11 pupils (inefficiency is minimised when average class size is 27 pupils).

Table 9.4. Efficiency (CRS) according to size of school

Size of school	n	Efficient (%)	Reading mean	INVRSD mean	Efficiency mean	Total
1st quartile	1	(2.56)	496.7762	0.0149	0.7460	39
2nd quartile	3	(7.69)	492.1934	0.0138	0.7865	39
3rd quartile	5	(12.82)	491.2368	0.0143	0.8192	39
4th quartile	7	(17.95)	533.8729	0.0162	0.8655	39

Source: PISA 2000.
1st quartile (less than 213), 2nd quartile (213 to 326.5),
3rd quartile (326.5–516.5), 4th quartile (more than 516.5).

quartile).[15] The average efficiency score also increases with size of school (0.7460 for the 1st quartile to 0.8655 for the 4th quartile).

The explanation of this result is probably inherent to the notion of returns to scale. Indeed, having a critical mass of pupils enables the school to save money on some items; indeed, we can reasonably assume that there exists an optimum school size. However, as Bradley et al. (2001) suggest, while closing a school can certainly lead to a reduction in public expenditure, it can also reduce competition between schools.

9.6. Conclusion

The analysis of efficiency scores obtained using the DEA method highlights the fact that out of 156 Swiss secondary schools in the national sample taken in the PISA 2000, only 10% are efficient (when the scale returns are assumed to be constant). This figure is low not only in terms of schooling but also in terms of effectiveness since only 14.5% of the pupils in the sample attend an efficient school.

It seems that the more the size of the school increases, the greater is the proportion of efficient schools (2.65–18%), and the average efficiency score (0.7460–0.8655) also increases. Moreover, the closure of a school can have a contradictory effect on efficiency. On the one hand, increase in size of establishments (for a given class size) means the school can benefit from economies of scale and increased efficiency. On the other hand, the closure of several establishments reduces competition among schools and the incentive to be efficient.

---

[15] Tests were carried out to compare the averages of the reading scores and the efficiency scores of schools in the 1st and 4th quartiles. These are significantly different (to 1%).

One limit of this research was that DEA was applied to the data in cross-section. If the efficiency of Swiss secondary schools is going to be understood and each school advised individually, repeated information needs to be available. Only annual national evaluation (for example in the final year of obligatory schooling) will mean the performance of Swiss schools can really be followed. An effective redistribution system would then be able to take place between the schools. Analysis of efficiency of the sample group data would also make it possible to consider frontier displacements.

References

Arias JJ, Walker DM (2004) Additional evidence on the relationship between class size and student performance. *Journal of Economic Education* 35 (4):311–329

Banker RD (1984) Estimating most productive scale size using data envelopment analysis. *European Journal of Operational Research* 17:35–44

Barnett RR, Glass JC, Snowdon RI, Stringer KS (2002) Size, performance and effectiveness: cost-constrained measures of best-practice performance and secondary-school size. *Education Economics* 10:291–311

Barrow MM (1991) Measuring local education authority performance: a frontier approach. *Economics of Education Review* 10:19–27

Bessent A, Bessent W, Kennington J, Reagan B (1982) An application of mathematical programming to assess productivity in the Houston independent school district. *Management Science* 28:1355–1367

Bessent A, Bessent W, Elam J, Long D (1984) Educational productivity councils employs management science methods to improve educational quality. *Interfaces* 14:1–8

Bradley S, Johnes G, Millington J (2001) The effect of competition on the efficiency of secondary schools in England. *European Journal of Operational Research* 135:545–568

Charnes A, Cooper WW, Rhodes E (1978) Measuring the efficiency of decision making units. *European Journal of Operational Research* 2:429–444

Charnes A, Cooper WW, Rhodes E (1981) Evaluating program and managerial efficiency: an application of data envelopment analysis to program follow through. *Management Science* 27:668–697

Coleman JS (1966) *Equality of Educational Opportunity*. US GPO, Washington, DC

Confédération Suisse (2006) Modification des articles de la Constitution sur la formation. Votation populaire du 21 mai 2006, Explication du Conseil fédéral

Conférence suisse des directeurs cantonaux de l'instruction publique (2001) Contribution suisse à la base de données Eurybase – la base de données sur les systèmes d'enseignement en Europe. IDES Information Documentation Suisse, Berne

Cooper ST, Cohn E (1997) Estimation of a frontier production function for the South Carolina education process. *Economics of Education Review* 6:313–327

Diagne D (2006) Mesure de l'efficience technique dans le secteur de l'éducation: une application de la méthode DEA. *Swiss Journal of Economics and Statistics* 142:231–262

Duru-Bellat M, van Zanten A (1999) *Sociologie de l'école*. Armand Colin

Farrell MJ (1957) The measurement of productive efficiency. *Journal of the Royal Statistical Society, Series A (General)* 120:253–290

Goldhaber DD, Brewer DJ (1997) Why don't schools and teachers seem to matter? Assessing the impact of unobservables on educational productivity. *Journal of Human Resources* 32:505–523

Hanushek EA (1986) The economics of schooling: production and efficiency in public schools. *Journal of Economic Literature* 24:1141–1177

Kirjavainen T, Loikkanen HA (1998) Efficiency differences of Finnish senior secondary schools: an application of DEA and Tobit analysis. *Economics of Education Review* 17:377–394

Krueger AB (2003) Economic considerations and class size. *Economic Journal* 113:34–63

Mancebón MJ, Bandrés E (1999) Efficiency evaluation in secondary schools: the key role of model specification and of ex post analysis results. *Education Economics* 7:131–152

Mizala A, Romaguera P, Farren D (2002) The technical efficiency of schools in Chile. *Applied Economics* 34:1533–1552

OECD (2002) Programme for International Student Assessment (PISA). Manual for the PISA 2000 Database. OECD Publishing

Office fédéral de la statistique (1999) Les indicateurs de l'enseignement en Suisse, 1999. 15 Education et science, Neuchâtel

Ray SC (1991) Resource-use efficiency in public schools: a study of Connecticut data. *Management Science* 37:1620–1628

Ruggiero J (1996) Efficiency of educational production: an analysis of New-York school district. *The Review of Economics and Statistics* 78:499–509

Scheel H (2000) EMS: efficiency measurement system user's manual. Mimeo, Operations Research und Wirtschaftsinformatik, University of Dortmund

Schultz TW (1963) *The Economic Value of Education*. Columbia University Press

Summers A, Wolfe B (1977) Do schools make a difference? *American Economic Review* 67:639–652

Thanassoulis E, Dunstan P (1994) Guiding schools to improved performance using data envelopment analysis: an illustration with data from a local education authority. *The Journal of Operational Research Society* 45:1247–1262

Part Three

Explaining and Controlling the Costs of Education Systems

Chapter 10
Funding Schools by Formula

Rosalind Levačić

Institute of Education, University of London, London, UK

10.1. Introduction

Over the last two decades, an increasing number of countries have introduced funding schools by formula. Per student funding systems are also being promoted by the World Bank for transition states (e.g. Bulgaria, Montenegro and Azerbaijan, where I have worked on proposals for their introduction[1]). The move to formula funding is generally associated with decentralised financial management for state schools. Under this system each school is allocated a lump-sum budget, which it decides how to spend for the education of its students. Consequently, a mechanism is needed for determining how much budget each school is allocated. A funding formula, which is a set of clearly defined criteria for determining budget allocations, has the merits of being objective and transparent, ensuring equity and promoting efficiency – given that it is appropriately designed.

The purpose of this article is to examine the school funding formulae of seven European countries in order to illustrate some key issues in designing and operating funding formulae. A school funding formula is restricted here to one that allocates funding directly to schools: it does not include

---

[1] Though the World Bank has been promoting per student funding for schools in these regions, there is no single paper produced by the bank, which contains this as a policy recommendation (personal communication). A conference was held in January 2005 on Educational Finance and Decentralization at which papers on mainly successful examples were presented (see https://register.rti.org/EducationFinance/background.cfm#fiscal).

formulae for funding local authorities or other state agencies that maintain schools. Though school funding formulae are technical constructs they are inherently instruments of policy, as is emphasised by Ross and Levačić (1999), and are designed with differing degrees of importance given to efficiency and equity considerations.

The chapter starts by briefly defining the scope of a school funding formula and proceeds to examine the relative advantages of funding schools by formula compared to alternative mechanisms. The main body of the chapter is concerned with presenting seven examples of school funding formula in European countries. In each case, their design maps to the four components of a school funding formula developed in Ross and Levačić (1999). The different importance given to the four components in the formulae reflects the relative emphasis given by policy makers to the market, directive and equity functions of a formula. Some key policy issues in designing school funding formulae are discussed and illustrated with examples drawn from the seven countries' formulae.

10.2. Funding Schools by Formula and by Alternative Methods

10.2.1. Alternative Funding Methods

Formula funding comes within the first of two main methods of resource allocation to schools as defined by the European Commission (Chap. 3) (Office for Official Publications of the European Communities 2001):

- A systematic common rule
- Administrative discretion of the authority concerned

There are two types of systematic common rule. The first is a *conversion rule*. This converts the number of students in each grade at a school to the number of teachers required, given regulations on class size, student lesson hours stipulated in the curriculum and teachers' work load. Other resources may also be allocated by conversion rules relating to the physical area of the school, its condition, types of student or location. Transition states still largely use very detailed conversion rules dating back from the time of communist planning.

The second type of systematic rule distinguished by the European Commission is a *mathematical formula.* This contains a number of variables (items such as number of pupils in each grade, area of school, poverty and learning need indicators, location of schools), each of which has attached to it a cash amount. The funding formula thus determines the annual budget revenue of each school in the education authority for which the formula applies.

The second method – administrative discretion – describes education authorities that do not use any systematic rule but determine the needs of schools by an individual assessment of each school. This includes using historic spending to determine next year's allocation. This method may have the advantage relative to a systematic rule of delivering more accurately the amount of resources each school needs, but this accuracy can only be achieved by a relatively small authority or one with small sub-units where officials have good knowledge of each school.

Schools may be funded by a mixture of conversion rules, formula and discretion. For example, conversion rules determine staff allocations, while a simple formula delivers a per student amount for learning materials and administrative discretion determines other operational costs, such as maintenance.

10.2.2. Efficiency Incentives

Formula funding, so long it has appropriate indicators, provides better efficiency incentives than the alternative methods.[2] Historic funding gives perverse incentives as there is no point in a school spending less on an item since this results in a lower budget allocation next year. Bidding by submitting budget estimates encourages gamesmanship on the part of schools, which submit inflated bids. The result is often a counteracting cut in the estimates by the funding agency. Conversion rules, since they often have some flexibility, encourage schools to obtain approval from their authority for the maximum possible number of classes and hence teachers.

In unreformed educations systems in transition states conversion rules are adhered to rigidly. They specify the number of teachers and non-teaching staff in great detail in relation to the number of classes and other factors, for example the number of stoves, size of school yard, etc. (Republic of Azerbaijan Cabinet of Ministers 1994; Tuzla Canton (Federation Bosnia and Herzegovina) Minister of Education 1997).[3] In transition states

---

[2] Efficiency is further encouraged by formula funding if schools can carry forward budget savings from one financial year to the next.

[3] A brief selection from Azerbaijan should suffice to illustrate the detailed prescription. A cloakroom attendant position is defined for winter if there is a special place for keeping clothes. An additional 0.5 cleaner is defined for every two classes in schools, which have more than 30 classes. A further additional cleaner position is defined if one cleaner's cleaning area is more than 400 m² on condition that there cannot be more than one cleaner to each 400 m². A yard-keeper

education funding in real terms fell significantly after the collapse of communism. Consequently, the numbers of staff specified in the norms could only be sustained by having low salaries and very little of the school budget spent on non-staff items. For example, in Azerbaijan, Bosnia and Montenegro, between 2 and 10% at most of a school's recurrent spending is on non-staff expenditure compared to an average of 19% in OECD countries (OECD 2005).[4] As a consequence the physical condition of schools and their learning resources are abysmal. Schools are unable to shift from expenditure on staff to non-staff expenditure because the method of resource allocation prevents this. A rigid line-by-line budgeting system, which forbids money being switched from one narrowly defined line to another, means that schools cannot even reallocate between non-staff expenditures.[5]

Efficiency incentives are provided when schools are funded by a formula, which allocates a lump-sum budget for the school to determine how to spend, though it is still necessary to ensure that the formula does not include any indicators that have perverse incentives. The school decides how many classes to form, how many teaching hours to employ and the number and kinds of non-teaching staff posts to have, subject to regulations on curriculum standards, teachers' and other staff's terms and conditions of work and health and safety laws.

Another advantage of formula funding is that it is transparent: it draws attention to the cost of educating an individual student and to differences in this between schools and localities. Traditional budgeting methods do not calculate the cost per student so this remains hidden from view. Once per student cost differences between schools become evident, questions are then asked as to whether these are justified. Such transparency promotes reviews of the school network, followed by closing or amalgamating costly small schools, where their existence is not justified by the need to maintain access to students in rural areas.

---

position is defined according to norms for the swept area. If a school has an orchard or decorative tree area of not less than 1.5 hectares, a gardener position can be established instead.

[4] Data are from the years 2003 to 2005.

[5] An extreme example is a school in Alibayramli (Azerbaijan) which received money in its budget for gas heating but had no gas supply: the money could not be spent on anything else.

10.2.3. Equity

Funding formulae are in general better at ensuring equity in the allocation of resources to schools than administrative discretion which, over time, leads to the accretion of anomalies between schools as some school principals are more successful than others at negotiating higher levels of resourcing. Both formulae and conversion rules achieve horizontal equity – schools with the same characteristics as reflected in the formula are funded at the same level. Funding by formula may be less equitable in circumstances where schools have differential per student costs due to particular features of their buildings, location or function when these are not adequately reflected in the formula.

Funding formulae are well able to address vertical equity by allocating additional resources to students who are judged to need these (Hill and Ross 1999). Schools can be funded additionally either by including in the formula indicators that predict the incidence of students with special educational needs or by indicators that identify the number of students with specific forms of special educational need which attract given amounts of extra funding.

There is an inevitable trade off between, on the one hand, the complexity created by including in the formula various indicators of special educational need and of differences in schools' structural costs (i.e. costs that the school cannot influence) and, on the other, the simplicity of a formula with only a few indicators, which is easier for stakeholders to understand and hence more transparent.

10.3. A Framework for the Analysis of School Funding Formulae

Ross and Levačić (1999) proposed a framework for analysing school funding formulae that first differentiates between the three major policy functions of a formula and second, decomposes the structure of funding formulae into four components that could be applied to all the case-studies included in the book.

10.3.1. Market, Equity and Directive Functions

Since funding formulae are policy instruments they invariably reflect the orientation of their policy context. If priority is given to operating state schools within a quasi-market or, in addition, to supporting private-sector schools with state funding, the formula serves the "market" function of setting the price of a student. When a funding formula serves only a market function then there are no additional elements for vertical equity or school structural cost differences. Schools have to survive in the market as best as they can, receiving just the market price for educating a student of a given age.

If policy makers are concerned with vertical equity then the formula will be designed so that students with defined special needs have specific prices attached to them to compensate schools for incurring additional costs and to encourage them to recruit special needs students.

The third function that a funding formula can serve is a directive function when the state funding agency wishes to promote specific education policies by providing additional funding. Examples are preserving high-cost small schools in rural areas or promoting schools specialising in particular areas of the curriculum or providing enhanced educational opportunities.

10.3.2. Funding Formula Components

The four components are set out below.

Component 1: basic pupil allocation by grade level

This is made up of two sub-components:

- A basic per pupil allocation
- A grade level supplement, which provides differentiated supplementary funding by grade level, year group or age level

Component 2: curriculum enhancement

This is additional funding for enhanced or different curricula for certain pupils or schools. These programs usually focus on specific subjects: for instance music, sport, languages or vocational studies. Component 2 serves the directive function when funding differentials are used to promote certain areas of the curriculum or modes of delivery.

Component 3: pupil-specific factors: special educational need

Some pupils require additional resources in order to provide them with similar access to the curriculum to that enjoyed by the majority of pupils of their age. The equity function is of particular salience in designing component 3 of a formula to allocate additional resources for special educational needs.

Component 4: school-specific factors

This component allocates additional money to schools for having above-average site-related costs due to structural factors that a school cannot alter. Equity considerations justify modifying the fixed allocation per pupil in component 1 to reflect structural differences in school site costs.

10.3.3. Component Dimensions

The relative importance of the components in a specific formula reflects the emphasis given to the equity, directive and market functions. A formula could include only one function. For example, if education policy were restricted to market regulation of schools, then the formula would contain just the first component. The more a formula is designed in the context of social policies for supporting the particular needs of communities and individuals, the more it will encompass components 3 and 4. In contrast, the more a formula is designed to support change towards certain curriculum areas the more it will concentrate on component 2.

Given the four main components of the formula, the next step is refining them in order to deliver finance adequate and appropriate for each of the included components. This requires more precise definition of each component – referred to as its dimensions – and specifying the unit of funding.

For component 1, the unit of funding is usually full time equivalent enrolled students, differentiated by age and/or grade. Alternative units are students who attend or complete, or funding courses taken and/or completed rather than students. For component 2, those areas of the curriculum that will attract additional funding need to be identified. The dimensions of component 3 relate to different sources of special educational need, in particular socio-economic disadvantage, disabilities and learning difficulties. The dimensions of component 4 concern various aspects of the school site such as:

- School size in terms of pupil numbers
- Isolation of the school and its community
- Physical characteristics of the building and the school
- Regional cost variations

A well-designed school funding formula should both promote efficiency in schools' use of resources and ensure an equitable distribution of resources between schools that vary in their expenditure needs. Efficiency requires that schools take decisions about those cost factors that they can control, such as class size, staff numbers and use of utilities and materials. A formula that is equitable and efficiency promoting must include indicators and coefficients for those costs that schools cannot influence while avoiding indicators that encourage schools to inflate their expenditures in order to obtain more funding.

10.4. School Funding Formulae in Seven European Countries

This section considers examples of formula funding of schools in selected European countries that have adopted this system either nation-wide or locally. The main source of comparative information on European school finance is the Office for Official Publications of the European Communities (2001) *Key Topics in Education (finance and resourcing)* but this does not give direct information on which countries actually fund schools by formula. However, European Commission: Eurydice (2001) provides a set of financial flow profiles which indicate countries where there is delegation of resource management to school level. This is almost invariably accompanied by formula funding in order to allocate a budget for schools to manage. This source indicates 13 countries with financial delegation at school level,[6] from which seven countries were selected for detailed study of their school funding formulae. The Netherlands was chosen because the Ministry of Education, Science and Culture provided detailed documents on school formula funding.[7] Personal contacts enabled me to visit Sweden[8]

---

[6] Belgium, Czech Republic, Denmark, Estonia, Finland, Hungary, Latvia, Netherlands, Poland, Portugal, Spain, Sweden, UK. Two – Belgium and Spain – did not delegate decisions on teaching establishments to school level and so would not have teaching staff allocated within a funding formula.

[7] I would like to thank Lucile Moquetter and Mr Van Oijen of the Ministry of Education, Science and Culture for supplying me with documents on school funding formulae (Ministry of Education C a S (2003) *Financial Summary Memoranda,* Ministry of Education, Culture and Science, Zoetermeer) and Julian Ross for translation into English.

[8] I am grateful to Professor Holger Daun (University of Stockholm), Dr Karl Slenning (National Agency for Education), Bjorn Soderkvist (School Principal, Nacka) and Eva-Lena Arefall (Swedish Association of Local Authorities) for interviews and documents about school financing in Sweden.

and Finland[9] in 2003 and Iceland[10] in 2005 to interview municipal and national agency officials. Information on Poland was taken from a case-study by Herczynski (2004) and that on Russia from an unpublished paper by Godfrey (2003). Information on England was obtained from government and local authority publications[11].

In the Netherlands and England school formula funding is nation-wide whereas in Sweden, Finland, Iceland, Poland and the Russian Federation it is practised in certain education authorities only. The Swedish examples are taken from the municipalities of Nacka and Sigturna, in Poland from the cities of Kwidzyn and Swidnik, from Reykjavik in Iceland and the oblasts of Yaroslavl and Churvash in the Russian Federation. In the Netherlands the Ministry of Education allocates resources directly to schools via formula, while in England local education authorities are required to use a formula, which they devise within central government guidelines. In Finland, Sweden, the Netherlands and Poland independent schools are funded by a formula that is equivalent to that used for state-sector schools.[12] The Finnish formula allocates a per student amount to each municipality and the same per student amount to private schools within the municipality. The municipalities get different per student allocations depending on a range of student needs and cost factors which are converted into a per student tariff. Some municipalities, for example Helsinki, use a formula to allocate budgets to schools.

In all seven countries, while there are differences in emphasis on the equity, directive and market regulation functions of the formula, it can be decomposed into the four components outlined above. The formulae examined are summarised under the four components in Table 10.1. In

---

[9] I would like to thank Timo Ertola (National Board of Education) for supplying me with much of the information about Finland and for arranging a short study visit for me to Helsinki and also the Helsinki Education Department for information on their funding system.

[10] I wish to thank Gutti Hannesson for his help and the Municipality of Reykjajvik for providing me with information on the Reykjavik school funding formula.

[11] As well as personal knowledge as a school governor.

[12] In Poland, private schools can obtain 50% of the per student allocation to municipalities (Herczynski 2004).

Table 10.1. Formula components and related dimensions in selected European countries

Dimensions of components	Netherlands	England	Finland: unit price for all providers	Sweden (Nacka and Sigtuna)	Poland (Kwidzyn and Swidnik)	Russia (Yaroslavl and Chuvash)	Iceland (Reykjavik)
Component 1: basic allocation							
Basic funding	Number of pupils Staff and operations budgets calculated separately	Number of pupils At least 75% of school budget must be allocated by number and ages of pupils	Number of pupils	Number of pupils Up to 95% of budget in some municipalities	Number of pupils	Number of pupils	Number of pupils: teaching hours per pupil. Actual salaries. Operational costs – per pupil. Grades 1–7 and grades 8–10 are funded differently
Grade level supplements	Primary: age 4–6 weighted more than ages 8–12 Secondary grade supplements	Fine gradations from grade 1 to 13, dependent on local authority Secondary weights higher than primary	Comprehensive schools: grades 1–6 weighted 1 and grades 7–9 1.75. Upper secondary: about 1.6 of grades 7–9	Grade funding bands: 1–3 = 1 4–6 = 1.1 7–9 = 1.3 or 1.4	Kwidzyn: primary weight = 1, secondary = 1.2 Swidnik: primary = 1, secondary = 1.13	Distinguished by phase of education	
Component 2: curriculum enhancement							
	Supplement for teaching Friesian language in Friesland. Secondary weights for school type	Grants to specialist schools for technology, arts, languages, sports and other programmes	Additional grants to schools with an "educational mission" or subject specialism; also for Swedish language track	None	Swidnik: extra for folk dance group	Chuvash: specific subjects and home tuition	
Component 3: pupil-specific factors							
Socio-economic status	Parents' educational level and if child or parent born abroad	Free school meals used in 90% of formulae, pupil mobility in 30% of formulae		Used in other municipalities' formulae, e.g. Botkyrka			No additional allocation
Non-fluency in language of instruction	Extra funding for Dutch as an additional language	Lack of English fluency in 25% of formulae	Immigrants funded separately from unit price	Swedish as additional language			New immigrant children funded outside formula

Funding Schools by Formula

Low educational attainment	SEN children in mainstream primary schools funded additionally	Tests of cognitive ability used in one third of formulae		
Learning impairments		3.5% children receive statements of special educational need with funding prescribed by the	Handicapped receive twice average unit price and severely handicapped 3.5 times	SEN funding allocated to individual pupils outside the formula	Kwidzyn: extra for integrated special needs unit	Extra funding for disabled and sick pupils	Special schools not included in formula

Component 4: school-specific factors

Small school roll	Fixed element in the teaching allocation	Lump sum for small schools or tapering allowance Split site allowances	Number of small schools in municipality	Not included	Kwidzyn: Three small schools get supplements	Five size bands determine weights for components 1–3 Rural schools funded extra
Location			Municipality population density and islands	Not included		Fixed allocation of teaching hours
Building running costs	Allocated by municipality on a school basis	Allocated by pupil numbers supplemented by floor and grounds area, building type	Allowed for in municipality funding to schools	Not included in formula: reflected in differential rent charges	Heating paid for by local authority directly. Extra for swimming pools and sports halls	Maintenance and utilities funded separately on reimbursement basis	Additional allocations for facilities e.g. sports halls

order to focus on key issues in formula funding of schools I will not describe each country context and formula in detail but instead concentrate on particular aspects of a country's formula which illustrate specific issues.[13]

In order to illustrate how a formula decomposes into the four components I will use the English example as this is a very comprehensive formula, which includes funding for the full range of recurrent expenditures of schools as well as an allocation for capital expenditure.

England (population 49 million) is by far the largest of the four countries that make up the United Kingdom. It has a unitary form of government with relatively weak local government. Most state-funded schools are administered by the 150 local authorities (LAs), which are part of local government units responsible for other local services as well. About 90% of state schools' funding is provided via their local authority and around 10% comes directly from the national level Department for Education and Skills (DfES) in the form of specific grants.

Local authorities finance three quarters of their expenditures from central government block grants and the rest mostly from a tax on residential property. LAs must fund schools by a formula, approved by the DfES. The major element of the formula is component 1 (basic entitlement). LAs are required to allocate at least 75% of their total budget for schools according to the number and ages of pupils. This gives formulae a strong market function. Curriculum enhancement (component 2) does not feature in the LAs' formulae. However, around 74% of secondary schools were specialist schools by 2006, specialising in a particular curriculum area for which they received an extra £129 per pupil from the DfES.

Component 3 is included in all LAs' formulae though some give more emphasis to compensatory funding for social disadvantage or other forms of learning need than others. The most common indicator used for additional educational need is the number of pupils at a school eligible for free school meals (FSM). Over 80% of LAs use at least two indicators of additional educational need. Other indicators used are National Curriculum Assessments (31% of LAs), standardised educational tests (27%) and English as an additional language (25%) (Marsh 2002). LAs provide additional funding for individual pupils entitled to a statement of special educational need.

---

[13] Details of the individual formulae can be provided by the author (Levačić R (2005) Funding Schools by Formula in 6 European Countries, mimeo).

Component 4 is also included in LAs' formulae. When formula funding was introduced, the DfES stipulated that historic costs could not be used in formulae as this would not give schools incentives to be efficient in their management of operational costs (Thomas and Levačić 1991). Only differences in schools' costs due to size or type and location of buildings can be included. Most formulae have two elements for component 4:

- A fixed amount regardless of school size to support small schools which have a higher proportion of fixed costs in their total costs
- Indicators, which relate to the costs of operating the school building and grounds (size, condition, split-sites, special facilities, etc.).

Since 2002, post-16 pupils in schools and other institutions are funded by a government body called the Learning Skills Council (LSC) which operates its own funding formula (Learning and Skills Council 2001). The main driver of LSC funding is the number of courses provided by the school or college (component 1) differentiated by type of course (component 2). The formula includes an indicator for component 3 (student-specific needs) and for school-specific costs (component 4).

The LSC formula has five elements:

1. A national base rate reflecting the length of a programme of study
2. A programme weighting in three bands to reflect course cost differences: Band A = 1; Band B = 1.12; Band C = 1.3
3. 10% of the funding from (1) and (2) depends on the student obtaining a qualification
4. An additional amount for social disadvantage, measured by socio-economic indicators attached to students' home address post-codes
5. Area costs to reflect higher costs in London and related areas

An assumed student retention rate of 95% is built into the formula and adjusted later against actual school records.

The LSC formula differs from the LA formulae in that it is designed with stronger in-built efficiency incentives: funding reflects differences in course costs and not all the funding is input based – a modest proportion depends on the school's output of completed qualifications.

English LA formulae not only have a relatively strong market regulation function, imposed by central government, but also include a vertical equity element, which varies with local political preferences. The various dimensions and indicators for component 3, as well as for component 4, make for complex formulae with many individual terms. LAs with rural schools protect them through a fixed cost allocation or one that tapers off with size.

10.5. Efficiency and Equity Issues in Formula Design

In this section a number of key issues related to formula design are considered and illustrated using examples from the seven countries' formulae summarised in Table 10.1.

10.5.1. How Comprehensive is the Formula?

The comprehensiveness of a funding formula refers to the proportion of the expenditure on resources used by schools that are allocated by formula and delegated to schools to fund out of their own budget. To be suited to allocation by formula, an expenditure item should recur annually and be reasonably predictable or if not predictable, then relatively small so fluctuations can be absorbed by the school budget. Items that are uneven in their incidence across schools, like large capital expenditures, are not suited to being allocated by a formula. Costs for sick pay and parental leave or redundancy payments are also uneven in their incidence. However, these are included in English LA formulae as schools can take out insurance — an option not available in countries without well-developed markets. Some items may be prohibitively expensive, such as insurance on school buildings in areas where arson and vandalism are rife, in which case it is cheaper for the local authority to bear the risk out of its own revenues. If the local authority is providing a monopoly service, for example for financial accounting, personnel management, estate management and architectural and building survey advice, then there is no point placing these in the formula.

As one of the major efficiency benefits of formula funding derives from the presumption that schools are better judges of their expenditure needs than their funding authorities and will choose the best value purchases in order to gain the benefits for the school (Gertler et al. 2006), then the more resources are included within the formula the greater the efficiency gains are likely to be. Removing the local authority monopoly of service provision by enabling schools to purchase services on the open market should also generate better value services, as was the case in England (Levačić 1995, 1998).

The English formulae are the most comprehensive of the seven countries as they include capital expenditure (excluding large capital works), sick pay and parental leave and all services since schools have the choice of purchasing them from private providers or a local authority. All funding for special needs students is also now delegated to schools. This very comprehensive formula took almost a decade to emerge fully. As schools become more experienced with financial self-management and the system proved popular with school managers, it was gradually extended to include more items, such as devolved capital expenditure and all services.[14]

The treatment of salaries within a formula is a crucial issue. Salaries are the largest element of costs in a school budget, varying from around 65 to over 90%. For this reason I have only selected as examples of school funding formulae in Table 10.1 those that include salaries. Whether or not salaries are included in the funding formula for schools has been a sticking point in some countries where per student funding has been introduced for materials and/or operational expenses. Sri Lanka is one example where with World Bank funding a norm-based unit cost resource allocation mechanism was introduced in 2000 to allocate money for materials and inexpensive equipment to all state schools using a per student formula (Balasooriya 2004; World Bank 2005). This was extended in 2005 but staff allocation was kept out of the formula due to concerns that this would be unpopular with teachers and with politicians who win political support by influencing teacher appointments. Thailand has also introduced per student funding for non-staff expenditures, but had made no progress so far with including staff in the funding formula (Punyasavatsut et al. 2005). Another example is Bulgaria where about 40 out of 264 municipalities have introduced delegated budgets to schools, often using formula but these do not include staffing (Club Economika 2000 2005).

A unified funding formula is one that includes in the student unit amount the costs of both staff and non-staff items. The school receives its budget worked out in terms of the student amount (differentiated by grade) multiplied by the number of students plus other elements in the formula that are attached to other indicators. There are therefore no restrictions on how much of the allocation is spent on teacher costs, non-teaching staff costs and other expenditures, unless maximum class size or student–staff ratios are stipulated. This is for the school to decide. Consequently, teachers and other staff are not protected by having a portion of the formula-funded budget earmarked for staff costs. Some countries

---

[14] An important factor for establishing such a comprehensive formula is that this kind of formula had been created in 1988 for grant-maintained schools, which were able to leave their local authority and become funded directly by the Department for Education. When the Labour Government abolished GM schools in 1998 they extended the very comprehensive formula to all maintained schools.

have implemented a divided formula – the staffing formula is separate from the other items allocated in the formula. The Netherlands primary school formula is an example of a divided formula, as is the formula used in New Zealand (Pole 1999).

Another vexed question is what unit to use to measure the salary costs allocated to a school. A market-oriented formula uses the system-wide average costs of teachers (and non-teaching staff), while the school pays the actual cost of its staff. This approach is known as average-in-actual-out salaries. It may create financial problems for some schools if there is a wide range between the bottom and top of the teacher salary scale, usually due to automatic annual increments for experience. Under the average-in-actual-out approach, schools with a higher than average proportion of more experienced teachers are likely to be unable to afford their existing staffing complement and have to reduce the number of teaching posts. The extent of the salary differential by experience across countries is quite varied. For example, in England the time it takes to reach the top of the main teacher salary scale has been reduced to 6 years, after which salary increments depend on performance. In other countries, such as Thailand, it can take 30 years to reach the top of the scale.

The average-in-actual-out approach is more equitable than the alternative of actual-in-actual-out because schools in favoured locations or with easier-to-teach students have more experienced and long-serving staff and therefore higher funding per student, whereas inner city schools and remote rural schools with poor facilities have high teacher turnover and therefore younger staff and lower per student funding. Another advantage of the average-in-actual-out method is that it encourages schools to take into account teacher salaries when recruiting teachers and weighing these costs against the likely benefits of the appointment. However, it should not be introduced suddenly as schools with higher than average teacher costs need time to adjust. When formula funding and local management of schools were introduced in England starting from 1990 schools were given 4 years to adjust: it took 4 years for the difference between a school's actual funding prior to local management and the amount the school was allocated by formula to be fully implemented.

Of the seven countries in Table 10.1, the Netherlands has a divided formula with staffing allocated separately for the primary sector. The two Polish municipalities also had a divided formula as schools' operational costs were allocated outside the formula and based on historic costs. Formula allocations were based on average teacher salaries in all the examples except Netherlands (primary) and Iceland (Reykjavik). However, the average-in-actual-out approach has been modified in England to the extent that the new performance-related upper spine payment introduced in

2000 is still not paid out of the formula but out of a specific grant based on the actual salary amounts involved. The Netherlands primary formula and Reykjavik formula allocate school budgets according to actual teacher salary costs.

10.5.2. Average-In-Actual-Out Approach to Teacher Salary Costs: Nacka and Sigturna Municipalities in Sweden

The two Swedish municipalities practice average-in-actual-out salary allocations. Municipalities in Sweden have extensive powers and responsibilities with a high degree of discretion in execution. There are 290 municipalities ranging in size from 3000 to 685,000 inhabitants. Among the services for which municipalities are responsible is primary and secondary education. Compulsory schooling is from the ages of 7 to 16 in comprehensive schools, followed by an upper secondary phase.[15] Independent schools also have the right to be funded by the municipality on the same basis as state schools. Over two thirds of local government expenditure is funded from local taxation, which includes a supplementary income tax. Fiscal equalisation transfers occur between municipalities outside the central government's budget. Resource equalisation ensures that each municipality gets between 98 and 101% of the average municipal tax revenue per inhabitant. There are also inter-municipality transfer payments to reflect differences in expenditure needs.

Municipalities can determine the methods they use for financing schools. About half practise some form of formula funding, which tends to be favoured by larger municipalities and those with right-of-centre political leadership. Nacka and Sigturna provide good examples of market-orientated formulae. Nacka is a prosperous neo-liberal municipality. Since 1992 it has operated a quasi-voucher system with parental choice of school. If there is excess demand for a school, pupils are selected by the municipality according to the distance between home and school.

The Nacka formula acts as a quasi-voucher. Revenue from the voucher has to cover all the school's costs including capital works. Since 2001 schools can borrow from the municipality at 5–6% interest rate and pay back over 10 years or so. Sigturna is less extreme and does not delegate

---

[15] Information on the financing of Swedish municipalities was obtained from the Swedish Association of Local Authorities and from a report by PriceWaterhouseCoopers (2000) Local Government Grant Distribution: an International Comparative Study, undertaken for the UK Department for the Environment, Transport and the Regions.

capital expenditure. In 2002 Sigturna retained 14% of its education budget of 447 million SEK, to spend on central services, pre-school, youth and cultural services, health and special needs.

In both municipalities component 1 (basic needs) dominates the formula. Both municipalities' formulae for comprehensive schools differentiate by three grade ranges. The amounts allocated per pupil are shown in Table 10.2. Allocations are totally pupil based. Each school receives the same allocation per pupil within the specified grade range, therefore teacher salaries are allocated on the average-in-actual-out principle.

Component 3 does not appear in either formula as in both municipalities special educational needs are funded outside the formula. Schools have to make a case for each pupil deemed in need of additional resources. Component 4 is not included directly in the Nacka and Sigturna formulae. Instead, differences in the costs of running school buildings are to some extent taken into account in the rent charged for them.

In Nacka there is no national or municipal imposed teacher salary scale. Teachers' salaries are agreed individually between the teacher and school principal when the teacher is recruited. Teachers in shortage subjects consequently get paid more and salaries have risen because of teacher shortage. Annual salary increases have to be agreed between the unions, municipality and principals.

10.5.3. Actual-In-Actual-Out Approach to Teacher Salaries: Netherlands' Primary Formula

The Netherlands, with a population of 15.5 million, is a unitary state. Local government consists of 21 provinces and 538 municipalities, which vary in size from 1000 to 590,000 inhabitants.[16] The unitary nature of the state is reflected in the low proportion of funding for local services that

Table 10.2. Cash allocations per pupil by grade level in Nacka and Sigturna municipalities

	Nacka 2003		Sigturna 2002	
	SEK per pupil	Grade weighting	SEK per pupil	Grade weighting
Grades 1–3	45,500	1	33,742	1
Grades 4–6	50,200	1.1	36,802	1.1
Grades 7–9	64,700	1.4	42,874	1.3

---

[16] The 1998 figures from PriceWaterhouseCoopers (2000) Local Government Grant Distribution: an International Comparative Study, PWC, London.

comes from local revenue sources – 16% – with the rest coming from central government general and specific grants.

Primary education is from 4 –to 12 years and secondary, which consists of three tracks (academic, technical and vocational) is from 13 to 19 years of age. Primary and secondary education is the responsibility of central government, but it uses local government to deliver some educational services, in particular:

- Primary and secondary school buildings
- School advisory services
- Compensatory education policy
- Modern minority languages

Article 23 of the constitution requires the government to provide and finance good-quality education, regardless of the denomination of the school concerned. Schools are run by management boards, which are either private – mainly Catholic or Protestant denominational schools – and attended by 70% of students or municipal. More than half the school boards – 1060 – manage only one school.

In order to contain school expenditures and provide schools with efficiency incentives the government introduced formula funding for secondary and primary schools. Since the early 1990s secondary schools have been allocated a global budget to manage as they choose. Primary schools have been funded by a different formula for staff and non-staff resources with restrictions on the movement between these budget headings. The government began to introduce global budgeting for primary schools in 2004, starting with those school boards that volunteered (Ministry of Education 2003, Chap. 4).

The primary formula is an example of a divided formula: it is calculated in two parts – staff and operational costs – and these are allocated separately. Staffing is allocated in terms of staffing units rather than money. Each type of post attracts a certain number of staffing units. A school can convert staffing units into cash or transfer them to another school. The school can appoint staff within its staffing unit allocation but not exceed it; the government reimburses actual salaries. The funding for staff also includes an additional amount for replacement staff and redundancy pay. To fund this, schools pay a premium into the Replacement Fund and the Participation Fund, respectively. In anticipation of the introduction of lump-sum funding, since August 2001 primary schools have been given a school budget for staff paid in cash rather than staffing units – the cash allocation being calculated using the actual salaries of the school staff.

The budget for operational costs is allocated separately and cannot be used for staffing. This part of the budget is designed to cover things such as teaching materials, building maintenance, furniture, ICT facilities, etc. It is paid on a calendar year basis and is related to the number of pupils and is adjusted annually to accommodate price changes.

10.5.4. Actual-In-Actual-Out Approach to Teacher Salaries: Iceland – Reykjavik Formula

Another example of a formula that allocates staffing units comes from Reykjavik. In Iceland compulsory schooling is from grade 1 (age 6) to grade 10. Most schools teach all grades. In 1995 education was decentralised to municipalities, which can determine their own method of allocating resources to schools. Reykjavik introduced funding by formula in 2001.

The formula allocates teacher costs to schools in the form of lesson hours per week per student, which vary by grade. Smaller schools are assisted by means of a fixed 10 lesson hour allocation for each grade regardless of the size of the school. Teacher salary costs vary quite considerably between schools. One reason for this variation is that newly qualified teachers and teachers over the age of 54 teach fewer lesson hours a week – 24 rather than 28.[17] The salary part of the formula is calculated as the number of lesson hours allocated to the school by the formula multiplied by the school's actual average teacher salary cost per lesson hour. There are further allocations for non-teaching staff posts depending on the size of the school, with actual salary costs determining the cash amount allocated.

School are given their budget allocation in cash, which covers both staff and non-staff expenditures, the latter being allocated mainly on a per student basis. The actual composition of the formula in terms of the cost components that make it up is no longer revealed to schools since when this was done schools stuck to the formula allocations rather than make their own independent decisions about allocating the budget.

10.5.5. Actual-In Versus Average-In Salaries

The average-in-actual-out approach provides better efficiency incentives than actual-in-actual-out as schools are forced to consider the costs of individual teachers in relation to the anticipated returns from employing them. This is what teacher unions generally dislike about the approach, ar-

---

[17] Teachers aged 60–70 teach only 19 h per week.

guing that it is wrong to consider the cost of teachers, that it penalises older teachers and induces schools to forsake quality for cheaper younger teachers. The average-in-actual-out approach is much easier to implement if there is not a long extended salary scale up which teachers move automatically with experience. This type of salary scale is not conducive to providing efficiency incentives for teachers as experience, after the first few years of teaching, is not related to teacher effectiveness (Wayne and Young 2003; Rivkin et al. 2005).

When first introduced the average-in-actual-out affects schools differentially depending on the salary structure of their teachers and other staff. Some schools receive more than they need to cover existing salary costs and others less. Clearly this would be inequitable because it reduces the non-staff resources available to students in high-cost teacher schools if the higher cost teachers are not more effective teachers than the lower paid ones. Hence a few years of adjustment are required. Once schools have adjusted to the new incentive signals then average-in-actual-out is more equitable since schools with a high turnover of young staff still receive the same average staff costs as schools with stable experienced staff.

However, a formula which uses the actual-in-actual-out salary approach still provides better efficiency incentives than conversion rules or discretion since these give schools a perverse incentive to maximise the number of classes and teaching hours in order to expand staff and hence expenditure. When a formula allocates teaching hours to a school, the managers need to decide what is the best class organisation to create. Even better efficiency incentives are provided if schools can transmute teaching hours into cash and use the money on non-staff expenditures.

10.6. How Funding Formulae Deliver Vertical Equity

As already noted, formulae are highly influenced by their education policy context. Consequently some are more oriented to the equity function than others. The formulae in the Netherlands and England (already described) include several types of special educational need – those related to social disadvantage, specific indicators of low attainment and various forms of learning difficulties. The Netherlands funding rules are designed to encourage inclusion. Finland includes funding for students with learning difficulties but not social disadvantage: Swedish minority students receive additional funding for being taught in Swedish. The two Russian oblasts include funding for disabled and sick children. The two Polish municipalities have no special educational needs funding within the formula. One school with a unit for integrating special needs children into mainstream provision receives separate additional funding. A general feature of transition states is lack of awareness of social disadvantage as a justifiable reason for giving students additional funding.

10.6.1. Funding for Special Educational Needs in the Netherlands Formula

The Netherlands provides a particularly good example of the use of component 3 of a funding formula. The secondary school formula is calculated in two parts – staff and operating costs. Staff costs are divided into three categories – management, teachers and support staff. Components 1 (basic entitlement), 2 (curriculum) and 3 (special educational need) are combined in the calculation of the amount of budget allocated for the three types of staff, expressed as full time equivalents. The number of teaching posts allocated consists in part of a fixed amount regardless of the size of the school. This is a component 4 element, which protects smaller schools. The rest of the teaching establishment depends on the number of students times a number of weights for different types of school and pupil. For example, additional weighting is given to pupils from ethnic minorities. The full time equivalent posts for management and for support staff are the number of students weighted for school and pupil characteristics. In order to determine the amount of money schools receive for these staffing numbers they are multiplied by a "price" which is average staff costs for the type of school and category of staff. Prices include allowances for the replacement of absent staff and for payments to staff who are made redundant or dismissed. Operating costs are a fixed sum of money plus the number of pupils times the price. The fixed sum (reflecting components 2 and 4) depends on the type of school and the price on the type of pupil (reflecting component 3).

In the primary school formula, the amount per pupil that a school receives for staffing and operational costs depends on the school weighting which takes into account the learning needs of the pupils. Component 3 (special educational needs) thus features strongly in the formula. Each school's formula weighting is derived from the weightings given to individual pupils, based on parents' education level and country of origin.

Funding to cover the costs of teaching Dutch to non-native speakers is paid separately to eligible primary schools, based on the number of eligible pupils at each school. If schools have been allocated additional staff, for example because of the presence of bargees' children and/or disabled pupils, they receive supplementary funding, which is not part of the main staff budget.

The municipalities also have responsibilities for delivering education programmes for socially disadvantaged children, for which they receive specific central government grants. Schools receive money, depending on their weightings, to implement the municipal compensatory education plan for socially disadvantaged children. Municipalities also receive a fixed amount per pupil to broaden the range of modern languages taught.

Inclusion is encouraged by the funding rules. The funding of primary and secondary special education varies depending on the type of school (for the deaf, hard-of-hearing, physically disabled, etc.). If a pupil with an indication for a particular type of special school in fact attends a mainstream school, this generates additional funding for both the mainstream school and the special school, which plays a supporting role. Staffing establishments at special primary and secondary schools are determined on the basis of number of minutes per pupil per type of post (group teacher, caretaker, classroom assistant, etc.) and differ by type of school (for the deaf, physically disabled, etc.).

The "Back to School Together" scheme has incentives to encourage regular primary schools to offer a customised care and education package to as many special needs children as possible. If more than 2% of the pupils in a co-operative network of schools are enrolled at special primary schools, part of the staffing allowance is shifted from the mainstream schools in the network to the special primary schools.

10.7. Efficiency Incentives in Funding Formulae

In order to ensure that funding formulae provide incentives for schools to use resources efficiently a number of principles need to be adhered to. Schools must not be able to manipulate indicators in the formula so as to receive more money. When schools provide data for indicators this needs to be independently verified to prevent inaccurate or fraudulent reporting – a particular concern in transition states. Elements in the formula that are funded according to historical costs give no incentives to schools to economise and should be replaced by indicators of cost drivers.

10.7.1. Non-manipulatable Indicators

It is the indicators in the formula and the cash values attached to them that provide incentives for schools. This is a particularly important consideration when schools can select pupils either when recruiting them or when influencing dropping out or expelling students that are the most difficult to educate. The issue of appropriate indicators is the most problematic for component 3 dimensions. The desirable properties of a special needs indicator are that it identifies or predicts the incidence of special needs students well, that it is cheap to administer and not subject to schools being able to manipulate it in order to obtain additional funding.

Some forms of special educational need, arising from physical, mental or emotional conditions, are identified for individual children. This requires a professional assessment by qualified staff external to the school, which, being costly, is usually limited to a relatively small proportion of children.[18] Internal school assessment of students with special needs, if it attracted additional funding, would stimulate growth in the number of students thus identified. Some instances of special need, such as students who lack fluency in the language of instruction because they come from immigrant families, can be relatively easily identified and their status verified.

However, for other students, whose own language is the language of instruction and who have relatively mild special needs, their incidence can be predicted at school level rather than individually identified and additional resources provided to the school, which are not earmarked for individual students. Therefore, some measure of the incidence of lower attaining students who need additional resources to improve their outcomes is needed. Careful consideration needs to be given to selecting appropriate indicators. For example, if low attaining students receive additional funding, then to use a measure of low attainment that is taken after the students have attended the school for a year or more would give perverse incentives for schools to have low scores. Measures of attainment taken on entry to school are also subject to manipulation as students can be encouraged to make little effort in the tests.

Therefore, prior attainment tests taken at the school attended at the previous stage of education are much better indicators for funding purposes since they cannot be manipulated or give rise to perverse incentives. Prior attainment indicators can only be created and collected for schools in the second or subsequent stages of education in systems where students transfer at a particular grade to a different school. The alternative to attainment tests is using those indicators of socio-economic status that correlate well with students' attainment. However, to be economical to use, these need to

---

[18] In England nationally 3% of students have statements of special educational need, which attach specified resources to a student that are then usually delegated to the school.

be readily available because they are already collected for other purposes. For example, in the United Kingdom, students' eligibility for free school meals is used as an indicator of poverty and correlates quite well at school level with examination results and predicts lower examination results at pupil level. Nevertheless, free school meals eligibility is criticised because not all who are eligible register and some who are not eligible do claim so the error between the true number and actual number of free meals students differs between schools. A more reliable indicator may be obtained in countries where the characteristics of the area where the student lives are a relatively good predictor of the student's socio-economic status and hence educational attainment. In this event post-codes linked to population census data on the socio-economic characteristics of a neighbourhood provide good indicators for compensatory funding for socio-economic disadvantage – as recommended by Ross (1983) on the basis of research in Australia. Indicators of special need collected by the school, such as the school's assessment of parental education or income, are undesirable since they are open to manipulation or even falsification.

10.7.2. The Student Number Count

When and how the number of students that is used to calculate a school's budget allocation is counted needs to be clearly specified. Schools need to be informed of their budgets before the start of the financial year in order to plan next year's budget and this requires the use of either a count of students in the previous year or a forecast of the number in the following year. However, the number of students enrolled in the previous financial year may be different from the number enrolled a few months later in the new financial year, or when the new school year starts someway through the financial year. Some authorities, for example Reykjavik, adjust the student numbers each term and adjust funding accordingly. For authorities making in-year adjustments to the student count for funding purposes, schools with falling student numbers are faced with having sums of money clawed back, which may result in a deficit budget. In England the DfES has now required all authorities to fund according to the number of pupils recorded in the annual school census in January. Having one fixed count per year is justified by the fact that schools' marginal cost are generally falling (except when a new class has to be formed) so that it is easier for rising rolls schools to accommodate more students out of an unchanged budget than it is for falling rolls schools to reduce costs when their budget decreases.

10.7.3. What Is funded? Output or Performance?

Economic theory (specifically principal-agent theory) predicts that schools are better motivated to maximise output (in particular the educational attainment of students) and hence operate efficiently if they were paid in relation to the output produced by the school. However, the majority of funding formulae allocate according to the number of students enrolled and not according to the students' attainments. Funding students does provide greater efficiency incentives than funding resource inputs – as is done by alternative resource allocation methods based on staffing norms or historic funding of operational costs. Some formulae for post-compulsory stages of education fund for courses taken rather than the number of students, for example the LSC formula for post-16 students in school and colleges in England and "taxameter" formula used in Denmark to fund vocational education colleges (Jespersen 2002). The Learning Skills Council formula also has a small element for rewarding performance measured in terms of course completion.

The problem of devising a formula that would pay for school output gives rise to the moral hazard problem (Dixit 2002) of accurately measuring the school's output when student attainment is influenced by many factors beyond the control of the school. To measure the school's actual output accurately one would need to control correctly for all the variables that influence students' attainment and are beyond the control of the school. Even with the amount of pupil level data now collected in the English National Pupil Database and the DfES value-added school indicators now derived from these data, it is doubtful that measuring the school's contribution to its students' attainment can be done sufficiently accurately to risk making school funding dependent on such measures. One of the remaining important sources of bias in value-added estimates of school performance is that students are not randomly allocated to schools: parents select schools and schools – some more than others – select students. More able and less able students are selected into particular schools and we do not know to what extent the unobserved characteristics of students that are associated with the schools they are selected into actually contribute to their attainment. So we may mistakenly attribute value-added output to the school that is really due to the unobserved characteristics of their students. For performance-related funding to stimulate improved school efficiency not only do we need to be able to measure schools' outputs without bias, but it is also necessary that teachers and managers in schools are motivated by the prospect of receiving additional funding. As Dixit (2002) points out, if economic agents in public-sector organisations are motivated to perform in the interest of their clients by professional values rather than monetary gain then financial incentives may not induce better performance and could even undermine existing non-monetary motivations. Funding value-added output would also create the problem of worsening the financial situation of poorly performing schools and make it even more difficult for them to improve.

Given the moral hazard problems of constructing school funding formulae to reward performance, it is better to restrict efficiency incentives to more easily measurable outcomes such as course completion and school attendance, provided that records are not likely to be falsified to gain additional funding. Also schools with lower completion rates and attendance, which are related to the socio-economic background of their students, would need to receive sufficient compensatory funding in the third component of the formula to offset their poorer predicted completion and attendance rates compared to schools with socially advantaged students.

10.8. Does Formula Funding Raise Student Attainment?

By itself, unaccompanied by other policies, the mechanism by which formula funding could raise student attainment is via the more efficient use by schools of a given amount of funding. This reallocation is more likely to have a discernible impact on student attainment, the larger it is as a proportion of the schools' budgets and the more impact a given amount of spending on educational resources has on attainment. In developed countries, with already adequate levels of spending on education, the evidence from research on the education production function is that the effect of additional expenditure per student is sometimes positive but relatively small (Jenkins et al. 2006) or according to other views non-existent (Hanushek 1997). There is more convincing evidence that additional expenditure on improved learning materials and school facilities does have a positive effect on student attainment in developing countries (Pritchett 1997).

It is difficult to test the hypothesis that formula funding as part of a policy of school-based financial management will improve attainment since a number of countries that have introduced it have done so nation-wide so there are no control schools with which to make comparisons. Comparisons of changes in attainment scores over time are unsatisfactory tests since other policies aimed at improving attainment, in particular accountability and high stakes testing polices, have been implemented at the same time – as in England. A further restriction on such research in England is that national pupil level attainment data only became available from 2000 onwards, long after formula funding and local management of schools was introduced in 1990–1994. Qualitative research studies of the early years of school-based financial management in England in the main concluded that schools had responded by becoming more cost efficient (Levačić 1995, 1998). Schools were actively seeking and obtaining better value when spending money and were making judgements about how different ways of allocating their resources could benefit teaching and learning. The only quantitative study (Bradley and Taylor 1998) to address changes in efficiency in England concluded that the introduction of the quasi-market, which included school performance management policies, increased school competition as well as formula funding, had led to a substantial improvement in efficiency for secondary schools as measured by examination results at school level.

In order to test whether school-based financial management (which is usually associated with formula funding) on its own would have a positive impact on student attainment it would be necessary to have data for a set of contrasting educational jurisdictions, some with and some without school financial autonomy, as well as good pupil level data on attainment and control variables and school context variables. One such data set is the TIMSS third international study. Using these data Wößmann (2003) found that school autonomy did contribute to higher student attainment but only in the presence of an external examination system.

10.9. Conclusion

Formula funding of schools is usually a necessary accompaniment to school-based management, since once schools have delegated budgets an objective method of determining budgets for schools to manage is required. A school funding formula is, by its very nature, horizontally equitable and, if appropriately designed, promotes efficiency in schools' use of resources and can deliver vertical equity by additional funding for defined categories of special educational need. School funding formula from seven European countries illustrate a range of policy orientations, from almost exclusively market-oriented formulae in the cases of the two Swedish and two Polish municipalities to the Netherlands formula which gives much greater emphasis to equity.

In designing a formula, the treatment of salaries is a particularly salient issue. Funding formulae that exclude salaries are weak at promoting improved efficiency and greater equity since such a large proportion of school expenditure is on staff. Comprehensive formulae, which include salaries, differ in whether salaries are combined with other resources so that the formula allocates a single lump sum or whether the formula divides salaries and non-salary items into separate pots. The actual-in-average-out approach to calculating the notional staffing allocation within a funding formula provides better incentives for efficiency in the remuneration and deployment of teachers than average-in-average-out. The former is less easy to operate when the teachers' position on the salary scale is determined by experience only and there is automatic progression over many years. The average-in-actual-out approach is more attuned to teacher salary scales in which pay reflects teacher performance and the labour market values of specific subjects and where schools have some flexibility in positioning teachers on the pay scale.

It is not possible to evaluate the effects of introducing school funding formula in isolation from other key elements of the policy framework, in particular school-based management and the system of school accountability. Evidence to date (Wößmann 2003; de Grauwe 2005; Hanushek 2005) indicates that school-based management is more likely to improve schools' efficiency, including raising attainment for given expenditure, if accompanied by external assessment of student attainment, holding schools accountable for student outcomes and providing schools with support for improvement.

References

Balasooriya J (2004) An evaluation of the impact of school-based resource management and formula funding of schools on the efficiency and equity of resource allocation in Sri Lanka. Unpublished PhD thesis, Institute of Education University of London, London

Bradley S, Taylor J (1998) The effect of school size on exam performance in secondary schools. *Oxford Bulletin of Economics and Statistics* 60:291–324

Club Economika 2000 (2005) Analysis and assessment of delegated school budgets in Bulgarian municipalities. Local Government Initiative (Research Triangle International), Sofia

de Grauwe A (2005) Improving the quality of education through school-based management: learning from international experiences. *Review of Education* 51:269–287

Dixit A (2002) Incentives and organizations in the public sector: an interpretative review. *Journal of Human Resources* 37:696–728

European Commission: Eurydice (2001) Financial flows in compulsory education in Europe (diagrams for 2001). www.eurydice.org., Brussels

Gertler P, Patrinos H, Rubio-Codina M (2006) Empowering parents to improve education: evidence from rural Mexico. Working Paper 3935 June. World Bank Policy Research, pp 29

Godfrey M (2003) The education reform project and per capita financing of schools in the Russian Federation: an overview. World Bank Internal Mimeograph

Hanushek EA (1997) Assessing the effects of school resources on student performance: an update. *Education Evaluation and Policy Analysis* 19:141–164

Hanushek E (2005) *Economic Outcomes and School Quality*. International Institute of Educational Planning, Paris

Herczynski J (2004) Formulae for allocation of funds to individual schools in Poland. In: Levačić R, Downes P (eds) *Formula Funding of Schools, Decentralization and Corruption: A Comparative Analysis*. IIEP-UNESCO (forthcoming publication), Paris

Hill P, Ross K (1999) Issues in funding pupil specific factors related to supplementary educational need. In: Ross K, Levačić R (eds) *Needs Based Resource Allocation in Education Via Formula Funding of Schools*. IIEP, Paris

Jenkins A, Levačić R, Vignoles A (2006) Estimating the relationship between school resources and pupil attainment at GCSE. DfES, Research Report 727: 85

Jespersen C (2002) The taxameter system. In: Dohmen D, Cleuvers BA (eds) *Financing Further Education and Lifelong Learning*. Forschunginstitut für Bildungs- und Sozialökonomie, Köln

Learning and Skills Council (2001) School sixth forms: new funding arrangements. Learning Skills Council, Coventry (www.lsc.gov.uk/news_docs/6thforms.pdf)

Levačić R (1995) *Local Management of Schools: Analysis and Practice*. Open University Press, Buckingham

Levačić R (1998) Local management of schools: results after six years. *Journal of Education Policy* 13:331–350

Marsh AJ (2002) *Resourcing Additional and Special Educational Needs in England: 10 Years On (1992–2002)*.National Foundation for Educational Research, Slough

Ministry of Education C a S (2003) *Financial Summary Memoranda*. Ministry of Education, Culture and Science, Zoetermeer

OECD (2005) *Education at a Glance*. OECD, Paris

Office for Official Publications of the European Communities (2001) Key topics in education, vol 2: the financing and management of resources in compulsory education in Europe – trends in national policies. Brussels

Pole N (1999) Formula funding of schools in New Zealand. In: Ross K, Levačić R (eds) *Needs Based Resource Allocation in Education Via Formula Funding of Schools*. IIEP, Paris

PriceWaterhouseCoopers (2000) *Local Government Grant Distribution: An International Comparative Study*. PWC, London

Pritchett L (1997) Where has all the education gone? Policy Research Working Paper 1581. Human Development Department, World Bank, pp 1–64

Punyasavatsut C, Mongkolsmai D, Satsanguan P, Khoman S (2005) *Technical Consultancy for Country Development Partnership Program in Education in Thailand, Component 1: School Finance Reforms*. Thammasat University, Bangkok

Republic of Azerbaijan Cabinet of Ministers (1994) Approving Republic of Azerbaijan general education schools' exemplary regulations. Resolution N 109 (March 12). Government of Azerbaijan, Baku

Rivkin S, Hanushek E, Kain J (2005) Teachers, schools and academic achievement. *Econometrica* 73:417–458

Ross KN (1983) *Social Area Indicators of Educational Need*. Australian Council for Educational Research, Hawthorn, Victoria

Ross K, Levačić R (1999) (eds) *Needs Based Resource Allocation in Education via Formula Funding of Schools*. International Institute of Educational Planning, Paris

Thomas G, Levačić R (1991) Centralizing in order to decentralize? DES scrutiny and approval of LMS schemes. *Journal of Education Policy* 6:401–416

Tuzla Canton (Federation Bosnia and Herzegovina) Minister of Education, E, Culture and Sports (1997) Pedagogical standards for elementary schools, educational institutions for children with special needs and homes for pupil without parents. Article 56 of Law on Cantonal Administration (Official Gazette of Tuzla Canton 1/99) and Article 8 of Law on Elementary Schools (Official Gazette of Tuzla – Podrinje Canton 4/96, 9/97) and (Official Gazette of Tuzla Canton 9/99).

Wayne AJ, Young P (2003) Teacher characteristics and student achievement gains: a review. *Review of Educational Research* 73:89–122

World Bank (2005) *Treasures of the Education System in Sri Lanka*. World Bank Human Development Unit South East Asia Region, Colombo

Wößmann L (2003) Schooling resources, educational institutions and student performance: the international evidence. *Oxford Bulletin of Economics and Statistics* 65:117–147

Comments

Andrea Schenker-Wicki

Institut für Strategie und Unternehmensökonomik, University of Zürich, Zürich, Switzerland

1. Principles of Funding Mechanisms

In the past decade, education policy has undergone a paradigm change in many countries: state government and control has been replaced by supervision. The educational institutions have been granted a larger degree of autonomy combined with lump-sum budgets, contract management and target-oriented funding. Responsible for this change were new trends in public management based on institutional economics and theories of social choice.[19]

Within this context, the paper of Rosalind Levačić gives a detailed insight into different funding methods for budgeting schools in seven European countries (the Netherlands, England, Finland, Sweden, Poland, Russia and Iceland), describing "some key issues in designing and operating formula funding" and comparing "the relative advantages of funding schools by formula" to the traditional administrative discretion approach. While the traditional approach should lead to an inefficient allocation of resources, the formula funding is assumed to lead to a more transparent allocation of resources and to allow gains in efficiency.

With respect to formula funding, a number of variables – characterising a specific educational institution – are taken into account. This could be the number of pupils in different grades, poverty and learning, the need for indicators or the location of schools, for instance. To obtain a better general view of the different mathematical formula funding systems, Levačić suggests a classification scheme involving the following components: basic allocation (component 1), curriculum enhancement (component 2),

---

[19]Schenker-Wicki and Hürlimann (200673–91).

pupil-specific factors (component 3) and school-specific factors (component 4), whereby the issue of appropriate indicators for the pupil-specific factors is the most difficult one.

In England, for instance, there is a strong emphasis on component 1. Components 3 and 4 are also utilised whereby component 2 is not featured at all. Generally speaking, the English formula system seems to be the most comprehensive one. In the Swedish example, component 1 dominates the formula, component 3 is not considered and component 4 is only considered indirectly. The funding system acts as a "quasi"-voucher for schools.

With respect to mathematical formula funding, three areas of controversy are raised by Levačić: namely, the issue of how to determine the costs of a school (including salary, infrastructure and teaching materials), the issue of non-manipulatable indicators and the debate concerning funding input versus performance. Finally, the incentives and impacts of the different funding methods are discussed in brief but not empirically validated.

Even though a number of different points could be raised for discussion, I shall concentrate on the following ones:

- Does formula funding really enhance efficiency as proposed in the paper?
- Is formula funding suitable for political governance? Does it help to reach political objectives?
- What are the advantages and disadvantages of formula-based funding?

Finally, I would like to present very briefly a new funding mechanism for educational institutions on the tertiary level based on standard cost accounting.

2. Does Formula-Based Funding Enhance Efficiency?

Definition: Efficiency is a performance indicator and defined as an output/input relation. In the education system, student numbers, infrastructure and teacher salaries are often used as input factors. For output you can either use factors directly resulting from the education production process such as the number of diplomas or retention rates or you can base it on the outcome. The outcome of the education process is the quality of education. To calculate the efficiency of a system, there are two possibilities: you can calculate either the output efficiency or the outcome efficiency.

Output efficiency: concerning Levačić, formula funding appears to provide more efficiency than other funding methods based on the assumption that the allocation of resources by a lump-sum budget generates more efficiency due to increased financial flexibility. This efficiency gain should be due primarily to the notion that an organisation is better motivated and able to regulate its internal matters than a distant ministry. Unfortunately we do not have any data from the schools analysed in the seven European countries to test this hypothesis. To cope with this difficulty and to give the reader an idea whether efficiency gains are possible in the educational system, we quote a study from the university sector, in which the output efficiency of the Swiss universities was analysed for the years 2000–2003.[20] As the Swiss universities have enjoyed more autonomy since the late 1990s, it should be possible to make gains in efficiency visible over the course of time.

The method used to analyse efficiency behaviour was a DEA method, which calculates efficiency based on an optimisation process. As the DEA method allocates optimum weights to all input and output factors, the maximum weight is attached to those factors in which a university performs better in comparison with others. The DEA methods are benevolent due to optimisation of weightings and the fact that decision units are always compared to decision units with similar objectives and preferences.

The question as to whether autonomy for the Swiss universities has paid off could not be finally cleared. Taken on a whole, the behaviour of the universities was too heterogeneous and the results were not significant: only 40% of the universities showed small increases in efficiency, 30% of the universities reduced their efficiency and 30% showed no change in efficiency behaviour.[21] With respect to these heterogeneous results, it is assumed that an increase in autonomy does not lead per se to an increase in efficiency. In order to achieve gains in efficiency, not only autonomy but also internal organisational reforms, which affect both processes and structures, are demanded and last but not least a change in university culture is necessary. In reality, all universities, which were able to increase their efficiency, have been confronted with major changes and restructuring processes.

Due to the fact that only universities were analysed, it would be of interest to find out whether the results are homogenous for the whole educational system (primary, secondary and tertiary level) or if there are any differences.

---

[20] Schenker and Hürlimann (2006:73–91).

[21] These universities were efficient during the observation period.

Outcome-efficiency: A study which analyses outcome efficiency for schools is the Wössmann study. Wössmann analysed education quality by means of cognitive performance tests and discussed the input–outcome relation.[22] The empirical results clearly show that[23] neither financial autonomy nor more resources have led to better education quality.[24] In contrast to the frequently used political argument that more resources and more autonomy automatically lead to better outcomes, other factors have been identified to enhance school performance in a sustainable and significant manner such as:

- Competition within educational institutions (private and public sector).
- Autonomy, but coupled with centralised examinations. Based on the results of the TIMSS and TIMSS-Repeat study, Grundlach and Wössmann found a positive central examination effect of approximately 1 year to be effective.[25]
- A high number of private schools coupled with a high level of public funding.

Saving (efficiency) incentives: It is often assumed that traditional funding results in perverse incentives as less spending regularly results in a lower budget in the next year and therefore all the available resources are spent to keep the budget at the same level. But, this could also be true for formula-funded units. If formula-funded units save money and are not allowed to retain their savings, they will also spend their whole budget. Incentives for saving money are only given if savings can be retained and reserves built up independently if the units are historic or formula-based funded. However, in the public sector it is difficult to build up reserves and the reason why is obvious: building up reserves with taxpayers' money is politically a very delicate matter.

3. Is Formula Funding Suitable for Political Governance (Vertical Equity)?

As formula-based funding is a policy instrument, it should give incentive to schools to develop in a certain manner, which is determined by politics.

---

[22] Wössmann (2006:417).
[23] idem.
[24] Fuchs and Wössmann (2004a,b); Hanushek and Raymond (2004).
[25] Gundlach and Wössmann (2003).

For the measurement of the impact of the incentives, effectiveness could be analysed by measuring the achievement of a target. Unfortunately, we know very little about targets and the achievement of targets in the seven European countries described in the Levačić paper.

Even though we do not have data from the schools analysed, concerning the seven European countries I should like to discuss very briefly some results we obtained from an effectiveness analysis of the Swiss university funding system. To calculate the governance impact of the formula-based funding, the central state subsidies were examined for the period 2000–2003.[26] In order to determine the behaviour of the universities, the relative changes in the individual universities were identified by analysing the most important indicators, derived from the main targets of the University Funding Law such as:

- 1st target: reducing study times *indicator: number of foreign students*
- 3rd target: intensifying research activities *indicator: research months per professor granted by state research promotion institutions*
- 4th target: increasing the acquisition of private funds *indicator: private funds acquired in CHF*

Based on the results of the years 2000–2003, the impact was found to be rather weak. Whether formula-based funding by the central state can really prove to be effective could not be judged conclusively.[27] Of particular note is that payment according to norm study times has not brought any positive change in the sense of reducing study times although both the central states and the member states use the same type of incentive system. One reason for the failure could be that the universities have been hesitant to introduce the necessary regulations – for example, significantly higher study fees for long-term students – to support this target.

Based on these results, it has to be assumed that formula-based funding, especially in subsidiary allocation systems, is not a very powerful instrument for political governance. This is especially true for a funding system involving several objectives. The results from this study are in line with the results of Burke and Minassians, who also found only a moderate impact resulting from formula-based funding and contract management.[28]

---

[26]Schenker-Wicki and Hürlimann (2006:73–91).

[27]One of the reasons could be the relatively brief period of time since the new University Funding Law was put into effect (4 years).

[28]Vgl. Burke and Minassians (2002).

4. The Advantages and Disadvantages of Formula-Based Funding

Horizontal equity: One of the most important advantages of formula-based funding is the transparency and equity with which it is associated. It is true that, using formula-based funding, all institutions are treated equally and there is no negotiation advantage of more or less skilled principles. But one of the remaining problems is the problem of fairness. If the formula is not comprehensive and does not involve a satisfying number of a school's characteristics, formula funding becomes unfair. On the other hand, if the formula considers too many parameters, it would be difficult to explain it to Parliament and the sensitivity of the system will be low (inert system). This reduces the impact given by this type of funding.

Vertical equity: Vertical equity means that schools will receive a higher price for students with defined special needs. This should compensate schools for additional costs and encourage them to accept students with special needs. Even though vertical equity is assumed to be important in many of the countries analysed, we do not know if vertical equity has been paid off by the formula funding system. As already mentioned before, the results from the Swiss university system show a rather weak impact.

Fairness: Very little is known about the fairness perceived by the schools with respect to formula-based funding. It would be very interesting to know how schools have reacted and how much time they needed to adjust from traditional funding to formula-based funding.

Side effects of formula funding (perverse incentives): Even though there is large number of different funding practices, we do not know which ones induce positive and which ones induce perverse effects. Nor do we know how schools have developed after the formula-based funding system was introduced. The positive and negative effects of different funding incentives in a given context would be a topic of interest to make sure that the educational institutions learn from each other and develop in a favourable way.

Performance-based funding versus input-oriented funding: Performance-based funding has been one element which was introduced with paradigm change in the public management systems. Performance-based funding involves contract management, lump-sum budgets and output-oriented funding. In very rare cases, outcome is funded but, due to the complexity of the social systems, outcome is difficult to determine and can be influenced by many factors beyond the control of a certain public institution.

The examples in Rosalind Levačić's paper are all more or less based on an input-oriented funding system. It is surprising that, on the primary school level, performance-based funding has not really entered the system compared with university funding, where contract management and output-oriented funding (including target-oriented funding) become more and more important (see Table 10.3). Even though there is a basic budget nearly everywhere, which is input-oriented funded, contract management and output-oriented funding are used widely.

5. New Aspects of Formula-Based Funding in Swiss Universities: Standard-Cost Accounting

University funding – at least in Switzerland – is slightly different from the funding of the primary and secondary school level due to our federally organised state. In Switzerland, the member states (cantons) are the legislative bodies for the universities and therefore largely responsible for their funding. The central state has merely a secondary allocation function, the so-called vertical financial equalisation. In addition to vertical financial

Table 10.3. Funding systems of universities[29]

Country	Basic budget: input-based, number of students (different weights)	Contract management	Output-oriented
England	Yes	Yes	–
Austria	Yes	Yes	Yes
Baden-Württemberg	Yes	Yes	Yes
Bavaria	Yes	No	Yes: small part 1.5% of the whole budget
United States: Tennessee	Yes	No	Yes: small part – 2–6% of the whole budget
Australia	Yes	Yes: very rudimentary	Yes: but only for research
Netherlands	Yes	Yes	Yes: 37% of the whole budget
Denmark	No	No	Yes: taxameter system, weighted with respect to different study domains
France	Yes	Yes: 1/3 of the budget	No

---

[29] This funding mode is considered for teaching activities. Research activities are funded separtely. In: CHEPS 2001.

equalisation, there is also a horizontal one, resulting from non-university cantons payments for their students to the university cantons. These payments are de facto political prices and do not reflect the real costs which students create during their study time. This situation is not at all satisfactory because the political prices are estimated to be too high or too low depending on the field of study. Based on this fact, the author was mandated by the central state and the university cantons to develop a standard cost accounting system, which should help to determine the "right" prices.

Standard-cost accounting is defined as a cost accounting system based on full costs and standard capacities.[30] It is a widely used method in the business environment, but not in the university sector. This is due to the fact that there is often no management accounting as such at the universities. Additionally, standard-cost accounting is conceived as being difficult to be defined due to the lack of an ideal production function as a benchmark for standardisation. This difficulty has to do with the different profiles and activities which universities want to achieve and might be one reason why there are no empirical data for standard-cost accounting at universities.

With respect to the definition in the former paragraph, it is evident that standard-cost accounting, resulting from industrial production, cannot be directly implemented in the university system. Despite the differences, there are two elements, which can be applied both in industry and universities: full-cost accounting based on actual costs and the so-called standard capacities. Whereas the actual costs (full costs) do not have to be discussed in detail, the second component – the standard capacity – has to be analysed further. The question as to what standard capacity – no too great or too low capacity – means to a university can be answered by using a so-called standard faculty–student ratio, whereas a high faculty–student ratio is related to a good interaction with the faculty staff and to outstanding education quality. Due to that, the faculty–student ratio has been chosen as a pendant to standard capacity in the industrial production process.

To determine a ratio suitable for standardisation, different ratios derived from literature were analysed, but nobody was satisfied with the results. In the end, it was agreed to enhance the simple ratio and to design a new model, which is better suited to reflect the workload of the system. The new model is based on supply and demand capacities and students and staff were asked to give their ideal norms to allow us the calculation of a benchmark for standardisation. For the time being, the data from the first run were evaluated and we are optimistic to find a valuable benchmark.

---

[30]http://www.manalex.de/d/standardkostenrechnung/standardkostenrechnung.php.

6. Conclusion

In the seven European countries, which form the basis for the Rosalind Levačić study, different mechanisms to finance educational institutions are analysed. In practically all countries, formula-based funding has asserted itself whereby the greatest part of resources is still allocated input-oriented and not output-oriented. If the efficiency is analysed, it has been shown that formula-based funding (coupled with a lump-sum budget) does not automatically lead to significant gains in efficiency although this is a frequently used political argument in this connection. Also the question as to whether political governance by means of formula funding is possible cannot be answered without further ado in particular in those cases in which different political bodies are responsible for funding (central state and member states).

If it is assumed that not the funding mechanism but institutional factors are responsible for outstanding education quality, the discussion about the advantage of formula funding methods compared with traditional administrative methods loses its importance, at least in the western countries where schools are sufficiently equipped with staff and have an adequate infrastructure.

But, although the introduction of formula-based funding has – up to now – not led to major changes, this kind of funding is, despite everything, preferable to the traditional administrative discretion approach as it is based on targets or objectives to be achieved and not on ownership level guarantees. And last but not least, undisputable advantages of formula-based funding are horizontal transparency and equity – as long as the formula takes the characteristics of a certain unit into consideration.

References

Burke JC, Minassians H (2002) *Performance Reporting: The Preferred "No Cost" Accountability Program – The Sixth Annual Report*. The Nelson A. Rockefeller Institute of Government, New York

Fuchs T, Wössmann L (2004a) What accounts for international differences in student performance? A re-examination using PISA Data. CESifo, Working Paper 1235, München

Fuchs T, Wössmann L (2004b) Computers and Student learning: bivariate and multivariate evidence on the availability and use of computers at home and at school. Working Paper, Ifo Institute for Economic Research at the University of Munich, Munich

Gundlach E, Wössmann L (2003) Bildungsressourcen, Bildungsinsvestitionen und Bildungsqualität: Makroökonomische Relevanz und mikroökonomische Evidenz: revidierte Fassung

Hanushek EA, Raymond ME (2003) The effect of school accountability system on the level and distribution of student achievement. *Journal of the European Economic Association* 2(2–3) pp 406–415

Schenker-Wicki A, Hürlimann M (2006) Wirkungssteuerung von Universitäten – Erfolg oder Misserfolg, eine ex post Analyse. In: Weiß M (ed.) *Evidenzbasierte Bildungspolitik: Beiträge der Bildungsökonomie*. Duncker & Humblot, Berlin

Wössmann L (2006) Bildungspolitische Lehren aus den internationalen Schülertests: Wettbewerb, Autonomie und externe Leistungsüberprüfung. *Perspektiven der Wirtschaftspolitik*, vol 7. Blackwell, Oxford

Chapter 11
A Cost Model of Schools: School Size, School Structure and Student Composition

Torberg Falch[1], Marte Rønning[1] and Bjarne Strøm[1]

[1]*Department of Economics, Norwegian University of Science and Technology, Trondheim, Norway*

11.1. Introduction

This chapter analyses the relationship between school resources and school and student body characteristics. School mergers and school district consolidation have been a controversial issue in several countries, including the United States, United Kingdom and Norway.[1] To have measures of financial benefits of such policies one needs estimates of the economies of scale in education. The available literature indicates sizable potential cost savings of consolidation, see for example Andrews et al. (2002) and Taylor and Bradley (2000). A separate argument, why economies of scale in education are important, is the existence of maximum class size rules, which is common in many countries. A reduction in the number of students does not necessarily affect the number of teachers simply because it does not need to affect the number of classes.

State aid to school districts typically tries to take not only objective cost differences into account, related to scale economies, but also differences due to variation in student composition. Students from certain demographic groups, for example students from ethnic minorities, may be more costly than other students, and it is usually argued that school districts with a large share of these types of students should for equity reasons be compensated with higher state aid, see for example Downes and Pogue (1994)

---

[1] In Norway the issue of school mergers has for some time been more controversial than the issue of school district mergers.

and Ladd and Yinger (1995).[2] In order to do so, one needs measures of the economies of scale and the extra costs related to specific groups of students. In addition to these cost and demand arguments, in several countries, national legislation gives students with special needs and students from ethnic minorities legal rights to extra resources. For instance, according to the Norwegian legislation, students whose parents speak a foreign language have the right to additional language instruction until they have a good command in the Norwegian language.[3] However, the extent to which such legal requirements for special groups of children are fulfilled or implemented will typically vary between school districts due to the budgetary situation, priorities within the local political entity and the political power of the parents representing these special groups of students.

With reference to the arguments above, a common question is: What does it cost to deliver a given level of education to our children? And related to student composition: What does it cost to bring certain demographic groups to reach a certain level of education? While simply framed, in reality, such questions are very hard to answer. A natural point of departure for an economist is to use a "cost function" approach. Assuming an underlying well defined production technology and that school owners minimize costs for every output level, a structural cost function relating total costs to input prices and output, and possibly exogenous environmental factors as school size and student composition, can be established. Such a relationship will describe how much it will cost to increase student performance.

Several problems arise when trying to establish such a relationship in education. First, how is output defined? A conceptually important distinction was introduced in the seminal paper by Bradford et al. (1969). They distinguish between services directly produced (D-output) and results of primary interest for the users (C-output). Within education, C-output can be defined as the level of valuable skills acquired by the students or the competencies paid off in the labor market, while D-output for example can be defined as the effective numbers of hours with learning in schools.

The problem is that C-output, in contrast to D-output, is not easily observed. Bradford et al. (1969) considered C-output to be at least partly determined by D-output and discuss whether measures of D-output can be

---

[2] Falch et al. (2005) provide a discussion for Norway.
[3] More details on the system in work up until 2003 can be found in Bonesrønning et al. (2005).

used as proxies of C-output.[4] This illustrates that it is not easy to estimate underlying structural parameters of educational costs and production. In a cost function approach the effect of output level on costs is of interest, while in a production function approach the effect of inputs (which determines the costs) on output is of interest. Strong assumptions are needed in order to empirically distinguish between cost function parameters and production function parameters. The output level is endogenous in the cost function. In addition, it is reasonable to consider education as producing many kinds of skills, and the output is therefore multidimensional. A cost function must include all outputs if it shall describe a cost-minimizing production process.

Further, it is by no means clear that the school owners' objective is to produce skills in a least cost way as assumed in the cost function approach. Several authors suggest that public-sector agents have other objective functions than simply cost minimization, following the seminal contribution by Niskanen (1971). One interpretation of the weak link between resource use in schools and student achievement is that the schools do not simply seek to maximize outputs, see for example Hanushek (2002). Accordingly, papers that try to estimate cost functions often get small and insignificant effects of output on costs, see for example Downes and Pogue (1994) and Duncombe and Yinger (2005), indicating that costs must increase considerably to achieve a minor increase in student performance.

To cope with these problems, several authors have tried to derive cost function parameters from the estimation of what they call "expenditure functions", see for example Ratcliffe et al. (1990) and Downes and Pogue (1994). The expenditure function is a reduced form model in the sense that determinants of school outputs are included in the model instead of the outputs themselves. However, the identification of underlying cost parameters from this approach requires strong assumptions about the political process transforming individual demand into community demand for education. In most countries, allocation of resources is taken by local governments subject to various restrictions given by the central authorities. In Norway, the local governments allocate the budget between several sectors such as education, health care and technical infrastructure. This allocation depends on income, the preferences of the local decision makers (politicians) and on the unit costs of services provided by the different sectors.

---

[4] On a more basic level, outputs are determined by inputs. Purchased inputs in schools include for example teachers, buildings and teacher material, which can be summarized by total cost.

Thus, school expenditures in a district are determined both by cost factors and the demand for public school services. This implies that knowledge of the decision-making process in the school districts is necessary to identify the parameters of interest and to distinguish between demand and cost factors in an expenditure function approach, see the discussion in Downes and Pogue (1994).[5]

In this chapter, we use information at the school level from Norway to estimate the relationship between resource use, student composition and school size net of these confounding effects. In light of the discussion above, our estimated relationship cannot be interpreted as a cost function in the meaning of the traditional economic textbook because we do not include output into the model. Including output will introduce all the problems described above, making it very hard to interpret the estimated coefficients. Our model can be seen as a reduced form model in the sense that both costs and output are determined by the same factors.

Our contribution to the literature is that we condition in our empirical model on school district fixed effects, that is, we only utilize variation between schools within districts to estimate the effects of school size and student composition on resource use. All demand factors common for all schools in a district are differentiated out of the model. In effect, we are removing from the model the district-level role of policy decisions, local preferences, political power of parents representing special student groups and the priority of spending on schools in relation to other services in the district. Thus, an alternative interpretation is that we estimate how the school districts distribute a given school budget between the schools. In that sense, our model can be considered as an "allocation model".

---

[5] Studies of the demand for school services include Poterba (1997), Falch and Rattsø (1997, 1999) and Grob and Wolter (2005). Analyses of school costs have to a large extent focused on the economies of scale in education, see Fox (1981) and Andrews et al. (2002) for reviews of this literature. The literature on school cost models can be divided into three groups. The first group includes papers that use school-level data within one large school district, see for example Summers and Wolfe (1976), Roza and Hill (2004). The second group consists of a small number of papers that use school-level data for multiple districts in the analysis, see for example Cohn (1969), Kenny (1982), Taylor and Bradley (2000), but none of these papers condition on school district fixed effects as in the present paper. The last group of papers uses data at the school district level, see for example Downes and Pogue (1994), Duncombe et al. (1995), Duncombe and Yinger (1997, 2005), Duncombe (2002) and Imazeki and Reschovsky (2003).

In Norway, the maximum class size rule was terminated before the school year 2003/2004. The idea was that teaching could be made more efficient when organized in a more flexible way, with larger student groups in some subjects than in other subjects. One reasonable hypothesis is that economics of scale in education became less important under the new flexible system. We will investigate whether this regulatory change affected the economics of scale in the allocation of the school budget across schools. To our knowledge, this article is the first to examine empirically the consequences on school resource use from removing a maximum class size rule.

Section 11.2 gives a short description of our methodology, while Section 11.3 presents the institutional setting for Norwegian schools and the data we will use. The empirical results are presented in Section 11.4. Within our allocation model we find that costs per student is diminishing within the whole range of school size in Norway. Further, we find that a minority student costs almost twice as much as an average student, while students with special needs cost more than twice as much as an average student. Section 11.5 offers some concluding comments.

11.2. Methodological Issues

The approach in this chapter is to consider the actual allocation of educational services and inputs across schools and to study how this distribution depends on school size and student composition. Even within such a reduced form approach, problems remain as to the identification of the causal effect from student demographics on the distribution of school resources.

Consider a stylized case where the local governments allocate the budget between several sectors. As an example, consider two local governments, A and B, with an equal number of students to be given compulsory schooling. Both local governments are restricted by a maximum class size rule, say 30 students. In A, the students are distributed between two schools while in B, the students are distributed between five schools because of exogenous topographical reasons. The lower average school size in B implies that the necessary resources in terms of teachers are higher than in A simply because B is less able to fill up the classes to the maximum allowed.

Since the average class size is smaller in local government B than in local government A, the unit cost of education is higher in B than in A. Higher unit costs give, all else equal, B incentives to spend less on education than A for a given overall budget. In addition, the budget and spending decisions will depend on local preferences and the political power of different interests, including parents representing special student groups. Thus, the resulting distribution of resources across schools in different local governments may arise as a mixture of exogenous topographical and demographic factors, local preferences and the local decision-making processes.

To provide a more systematic discussion of the empirical challenges, consider a linear equation relating school resources C in school i in local government j at time t to school size Q, student composition P and a vector of variables at the school district level Z:

$$C_{ijt} = a_0 + a_1 Q_{ijt} + a_2 P_{ijt} + a_3 X_{ijt} + a_4 Z_{jt} + u_{ijt} \quad (11.1)$$

If we want to isolate the effect of school size on C from the exogenous demographic factors, we need to specify the vector Z. This is not an easy task given the complex and, for the researcher, unknown way local preferences are translated into local decisions through the political process. If omitted elements in Z are correlated with the school-specific variables Q or P, the estimated effect of these variables will be biased away from their true value.

Our way of handling this problem is to substitute Z with time-varying local government fixed effects as in Eq. 11.2:

$$C_{ijt} = a_0 + a_1 Q_{ijt} + a_2 P_{ijt} + F_{jt} + v_{ijt} \quad (11.2)$$

The fixed effects F control for all omitted variables at the local government level which affect school resources at particular schools. This model is therefore better suited than Eq. 11.1 to obtain unbiased estimates of the causal effects of school size and student composition on the allocation of resources across schools. Thus, in the empirical part of the chapter several versions of the basic model outlined in Eq. 11.2 will be estimated. As a robustness check, we also estimate a version of the model with fixed school effects.

11.3. Institutions and Data

Primary schools (grades 1–7) and lower secondary schools (grades 8–10) in Norway are run and owned by multipurpose local governments.[6] Private schools do not provide a realistic alternative to public schools because less

---

[6] The local governments are multipurpose institutions that provide other services in addition to schooling, for instance elderly care, day care and preschool educa-

than 3% of the students are enrolled in private schools. The number of schools varies to a great extent within the school districts (from 1 to 124) because of variation in population size and settlement pattern. Parental school choice between public schools for given residence is not allowed. Most schools are primary schools because lower secondary schools tend to include more students at each grade. About 25% of the schools are so-called combined schools which offer both primary and lower secondary education.

Before the school year 2003/2004, the maximum class size rule was removed from the school law and replaced by the following formulation: "Students can be divided in groups by requirements. The groups cannot exceed a level that is justified by pedagogical or security arguments" (§2.8 in the school law). One issue in this chapter is to investigate to which extent this change in the law changed the way resources are allocated across schools.

Usually accounting data are not available at the school level, but only at the school district level. This is also the case in Norway. Instead of using total costs, we use measures of the amount of teacher input, which accounts for about 70% of the total costs. We use school-level data from the Norwegian Ministry of Education which cover the school years 2001/2002–2005/2006. As a measure of resource use in the schools we will mainly use teacher hours per student. Teacher hours is a measure on how many hours the teachers interact with students, either in the classroom or as extra education to specific students (mostly disadvantaged students and minority students). Teacher hours can be regarded as the most accurate measure of the teacher resource use in schools.

Table 11.1 presents a descriptive overview of teacher hours per student as well as the teacher–student ratio. The number of schools (observations) slightly declines over time because of some school mergers. Teacher hours per student declined in the school year 2003/2004, thereafter stabilizing at an intermediate level. The same is true for the teacher–student ratio. The standard deviation is relatively large, indicating large variation across schools. The relationship between teacher hours per student and the teacher–student ratio is strong, the correlation coefficient is equal to 0.94, and is illustrated in Fig. 11.1.[7]

---

tion and infrastructure. Spending on education consists of about 30% of total spending.

[7] Below, we will present empirical results only for teacher hours per student. Results using the teacher-student ratio as alternative dependent variable are very similar.

Table 11.1. Teacher hours per student and teacher–student ratio

Year	Teacher hours per student			Teacher–student ratio		
	Mean	Standard deviation	Observations	Mean	Standard deviation	Observations
2001/2002	84.3	28.4	3069	0.099	0.034	3070
2002/2003	84.3	29.6	3054	0.097	0.035	3058
2003/2004	82.6	28.4	3008	0.093	0.032	2977
2004/2005	83.8	28.2	2987	0.094	0.031	2993
2005/2006	83.7	28.5	2944	0.094	0.032	2948

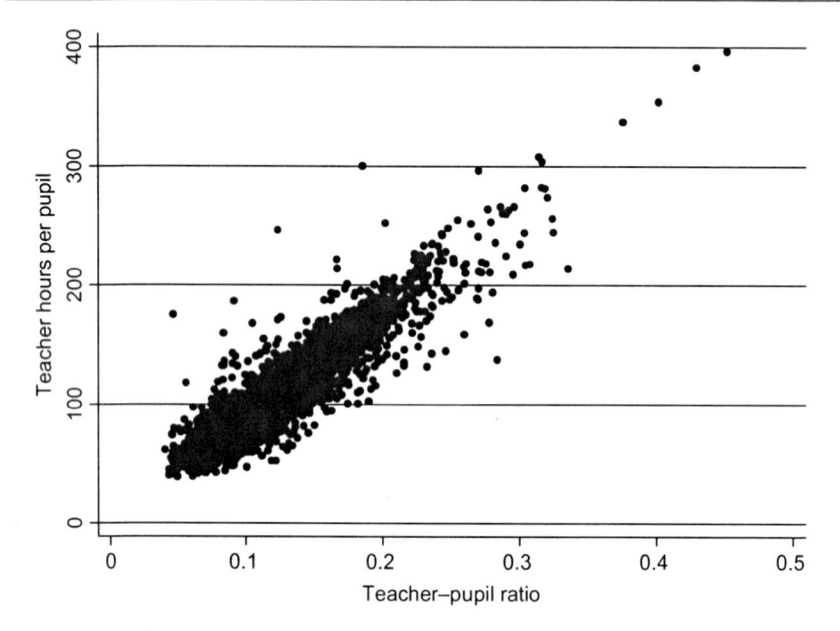

Fig. 11.1. The relationship between teacher hours per student and the teacher–student ratio.

The large variation in resource use per student across schools is related to variation in school size. The relationship between school size and resource use is illustrated in Fig. 11.2. In the figure, the first group of schools consists of schools with 10–19 students, the next group of schools has 20–29 students and so on.[8] The figure illustrates that Norwegian

---

[8] Schools with less than 10 students are excluded from the figure and the analysis below.

A Cost Model of Schools

compulsory schools are relatively small and that the largest schools have about 800 students. Only about 0.6% of the schools have more than 600 students, and average school size is about 200 students.

Figure 11.2 shows that the resource use per student is clearly negatively related to school size, but with a diminishing rate. Economies of scale seems to be most important for schools up to about 300 students, but the resource use is lowest for schools with more than 600 students.[9]

Table 11.2 presents descriptive statistics for the two variables of student composition we will focus upon. While the share of students with special needs is relatively stable around 6% in the empirical period, the share of minority students increases every year and is close to 5% in the school year 2005/2006. Only students with extra education in Norwegian language are included in our definition of minority students in the present chapter.

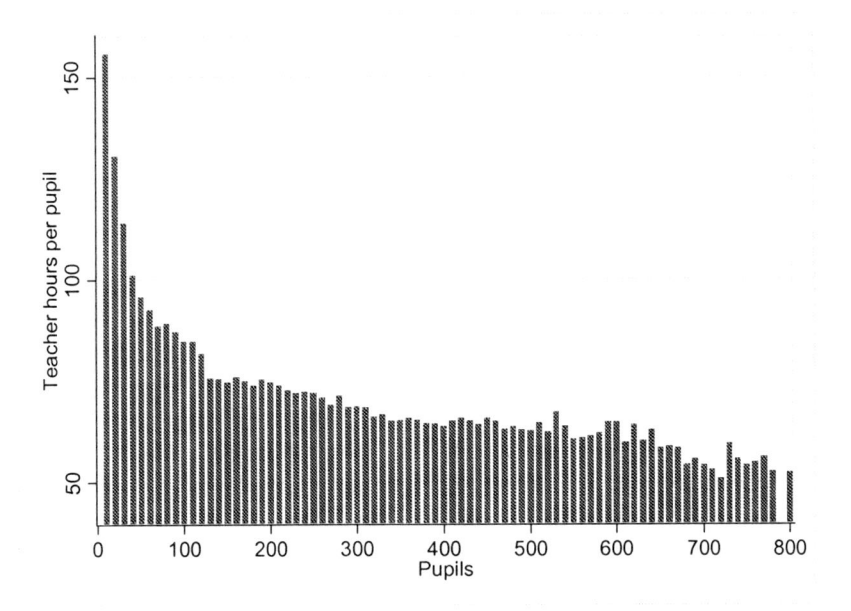

Fig. 11.2. The relationship between teacher hours per student and school size.

---

[9] Since there are relatively few schools with more than 600 students, Fig. 11.2 is based on data for all school years 2001/2002–2005/2006.

Table 11.2. Student composition

	Share of minority students			Share of students with special needs		
Year	Mean	Standard deviation	Observations	Mean	Standard deviation	Observations
2001/2002	0.039	0.071	3073	0.057	0.039	3065
2002/2003	0.041	0.074	3059	0.059	0.041	3060
2003/2004	0.043	0.080	3027	0.060	0.040	3028
2004/2005	0.045	0.081	2995	0.060	0.041	2995
2005/2006	0.047	0.085	2949	0.060	0.040	2949

In order to take into consideration that most resources may be delegated to students in lower secondary schools because they spend more hours at school per day than students at primary schools, we will include control variables for the share of students at the different grades. Variation in these shares will to a large extent reflect whether the school is a primary, lower secondary or a combined school, but dummy variables for primary school and lower secondary school will also be included in the model.

11.4. Results

We start out concentrating on the parameterization of the effect of school size. Columns A–D in Table 11.3 presents the results for different specifications of the relationship between resource use and school size, leaving out all other variables except the school district year-specific interaction effects. Considering the within-year within-school district explanatory power, the specification with the number of students squared (column A) performs relatively badly, while the specification with the logarithm of the number of students squared (column B) explains much more of the variation in resource use. The latter model indicates an optimal school size of about 400 students, which does not seem to be in agreement with Fig. 11.2. Thus, the next models presented apply functional forms without an optimum. While the explanatory power of the model using the inverse of the number of students (column C) is slightly lower than the model using the log of the number of students, that is not true for the model using the inverse of the squared root of the number of students (column D). However, the difference in explanatory power between these three models is small.

Table 11.3. Results of basic model formulations

Variable	A	B	C	D	E	F
Number of students	−0.256 (22.3)	–	–	–	–	–
Number of students squared/100	0.032 (15.3)	–	–	–	–	–
Log(number of students)	–	−82.0 (19.6)	–	–	–	–
Log(number of students) squared	–	6.87 (16.0)	–	–	–	–
Inverse of number of students	–	–	1171 (30.7)	–	–	–
Inverse of the square root of number of students	–	–	–	360 (35.2)	402 (38.9)	408 (45.9)
Share of minority students	–	–	–	–	64.3 (11.2)	66.2 (11.8)
Share of students with special needs	–	–	–	–	109 (15.0)	98.3 (13.7)
Classes at primary level only	–	–	–	–	−14.7 (19.9)	−14.4 (6.45)
Classes at lower secondary level only	–	–	–	–	−6.32 (8.11)	−4.30 (1.15)
R^2 (within group)	0.328	0.526	0.520	0.526	0.669	0.691
Observations	15,062	15,062	15,062	15,062	15,050	15,050
Variables for the share of students at each grade included	No	No	No	No	No	Yes
Year-specific local government fixed effects	Yes	Yes	Yes	Yes	Yes	Yes

Depended variable is the number of teacher hours per student
Estimated by ordinary least squares. The data covers all schools in Norway for the school years 2001/2002–2005/2006. t-values in parentheses are corrected to take account of within-schooling clustering of errors.

The predictive power of models B and D in Table 11.3 are presented in Fig. 11.3 together with the nonparametric results. The nonparametric results are obtained by using dummy variables for each school size. Both models perform well in terms of predictive power, but the model in column D seems to fit better the resource use in the largest schools.

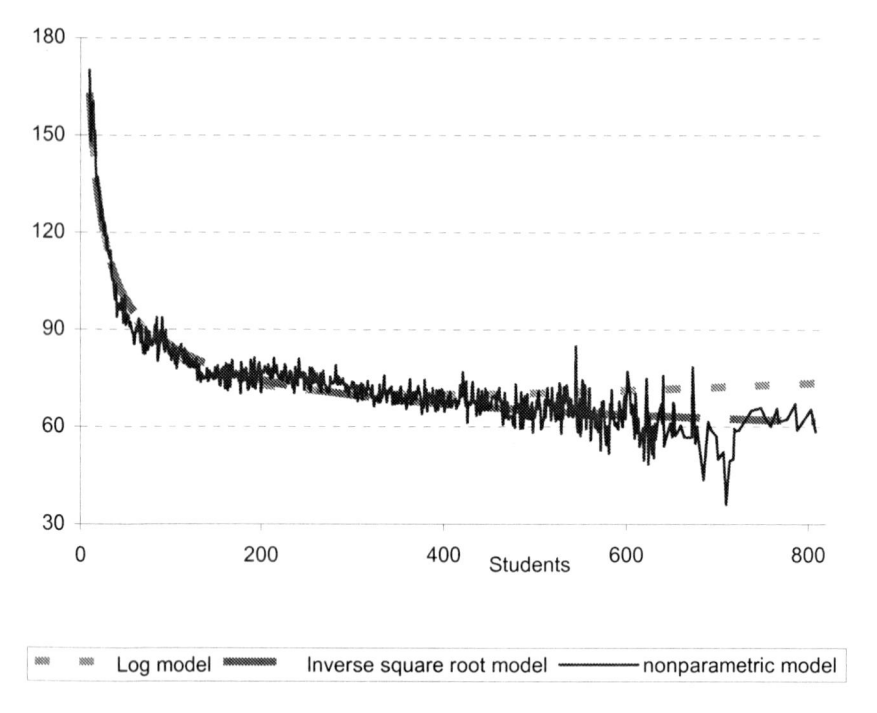

Fig. 11.3. Model predictions.

The lack of evidence of an optimal school size within our sample of relatively small schools is in accordance with findings for other countries. Andrews et al. (2002) review the literature on economies of size in the United States at the school district level and conclude that costs per student are minimized for about 2000–6000 students in the school district. For England, Taylor and Bradley (2000) use school-level data and find that the cost-minimizing school size is around 1600, which is about the size of the largest schools in England.

The estimated models imply large cost savings of school consolidation. The model in column D implies that the marginal effect of one new student when the school initially has 10 students is about −11. A reduction by 11 teacher hours per student is a large effect given that the average number of teacher hours per student is about 84. For initial school size of 200 (800) the marginal effect is still as large as −0.13 (−0.016). Further, the prediction of the model is that merging two schools with 50 (200) students reduces teacher hours per student by about 15 (7.5), that is 18 (9)% of the average resource use.

In the remaining analyses we use the specification regarding school size as in column D.[10] First, in column E in Table 11.3, we expand the model by including two measures of the student composition and dummy variables for whether the school is a primary school (1–7 grades) or a lower secondary school (8–10 grades).[11] All these variables have highly significant effects, but including them does not change the effect of school size to any large extent. The estimates indicate that a minority student costs on average about 64 teacher hours more than an average student, and a student with special needs costs on average about 109 extra teacher hours. Compared to average teacher hours per student, this is a major effect.

Primary schools have lower resource use per student than lower secondary schools, presumably because the students spend fewer hours per day at school. More surprising, lower secondary schools are slightly less costly than combined schools covering all grades.

Because the number of hours children spend at school per day increases with the grade, we include the share of students at each grade in the model in column F. This does not alter the results much, except that the dummy variables for school type are less precisely estimated as expected.

In Table 11.4 we undertake several robustness analyses. First, are the estimated coefficients stable across school types? In column A, we restrict the sample to include only primary schools, which is the largest group of schools. The estimated coefficients are close to the model including all schools, indicating that the results are reasonably stable across school types. However, there seems to be somewhat smaller economies of scale for primary schools than for other schools, and students with special needs costs about 10% more than estimated on the whole sample.[12]

One obvious reason for the economies of scale in teaching is the tradition to organize the students in classes. In Norway, as in many other countries,

---

[10] The results by using the specifications in column B or C are very similar.

[11] The reference group is combined schools (1–10 grades).

[12] We have also estimated the same model for the sample of lower secondary schools and combined schools, respectively. Regarding lower secondary schools, the model is sensitive to whether schools with 10–20 students are included in the sample or not, even though there are very few lower secondary schools of this size. Regarding combined schools, the economies of scale are slightly larger than for primary schools, which is not surprising given that, for given number of students, there are fewer students at each grade. The cost of students with special need is estimated to be about 20% lower in lower secondary and combined schools than in primary schools.

Table 11.4. Results for alternative model formulations.

Variable	A	B	C	D	E
Inverse of the square root of number of students	363 (53.6)	409 (39.6)	406 (40.9)	543 (16.3)	437 (59.1)
Share of minority students	65.7 (15.1)	70.2 (14.9)	64.3 (8.96)	45.3 (5.00)	57.2 (12.8)
Share of students with special needs	111 (13.9)	84.8 (9.17)	107 (11.6)	64.6 (9.06)	94.0 (14.4)
Classes at primary level only	–	−15.4 (7.08)	−13.3 (4.87)	−7.69 (−3.29)	−20.6 (10.1)
Classes at lower secondary level only	–	−5.50 (1.59)	−4.29 (0.92)	−0.51 (−0.09)	−4.33 (1.24)
R^2 (within group)	0.710	0.699	0.690	0.210	0.750 (overall)
Observations	9,606	6,112	8,938	15,050	15,050
Variables for the share of students at each grade included	Yes	Yes	Yes	Yes	Yes
Year specific local government fixed effects	Yes	Yes	Yes	No	No
School fixed effects	No	No	No	Yes	No
Year-specific effects	Yes	Yes	Yes	Yes	Yes
Sample	Primary schools, 2001–2006	All schools, 2001–2003	All schools, 2003–2006	All schools, 2001–2006	All schools, 2001–2006

Depended variable is the number of teacher hours per student
Estimated by ordinary least squares. The data covers all schools in Norway for the school years 2001/2002–2005/2006. *t*-values in parentheses are corrected to take account of within-schooling clustering of errors.

there existed a national determined rule of maximum class size. A class could not exceed 28 students in the grades 1–7 and 30 students in the grades 8–10. Then, of course, there will be equally number of classes on a school with, say, 10 students at each grade as a school with 25 students at each grade, even though the last school is 2.5 times larger than the first school.

In 2003, the maximum class size rule was terminated in Norway. To investigate whether the more flexible system changed the allocation of resources across schools, columns B and C in Table 11.4 present separate regressions for the school years before and after the reform. Surprisingly, the economies of scale estimated are almost identical in the two periods. Also, the effect of student composition does not change much, although students with special needs seem to be somewhat more expensive and minority students somewhat less expensive in the latter period. But all together, the estimated relationship seems surprisingly stable over time.

One may speculate why the termination of the maximum class size legislation did not have a larger impact. One reason may be that the parliament when making the legislative change recommended, and even assumed, that the resource use in primary and secondary education should not be reduced as a consequence of the more flexible rules. Many school districts and also the Directorate for Education and Training have interpreted this wording as a recommendation for the local governments to leave the allocation of resources to each school unchanged. Then the legislative change could change the internal organization of instruction within schools, and our available casual evidence clearly suggests it has, while leaving the allocation rule of resources across schools unchanged.

Even though we condition on all aspects common for all schools within a local government a specific year, the results may be biased if there are relevant characteristics of the schools that are not included in the model. Schools may use different shares of their available resources on teachers because they, for example, differ in the demand for computers and new textbooks. Such factors may be correlated with the student composition.

To check the robustness of our model, column D in Table 11.4 presents results from a model including fixed school effects. These fixed effects capture all unobserved time-invariant characteristics of the schools. The results indicate that some important school-level variables may be missing in our baseline model. First, the economies of scale are even larger than in our baseline model. This result implies that changes in the number of students within a school over time have larger impact on the costs than differences across schools. Second, the effect of student composition is lower in the fixed school effects model. One interpretation is that the effect of student composition is overestimated when we do not control for unobserved time-invariant variables at the school level. Schools with a large share of minority students and students with special needs are allocated extra resources not only because these shares are high, but also for some unobserved reason. Another interpretation of the findings, however, might be that there is simply too little variation within schools over time in student composition to isolate the effects of student composition in a model with fixed school effects.[13]

It may be interesting to consider the differences between the local governments. In the models presented so far, we have only utilized variation within local governments or within schools. The model in column E in Table 11.4 excludes all fixed effects from the model and utilizes all the variation in the data (except across years). Interestingly, the estimated coefficients do not change much compared to the previous models. Both the economies of scale and the extra cost of minority students and students with special needs are of similar magnitude. This indicates that the differences in local school district expenditure policy are not much related to differences in school structure and student composition across school districts.

All the results presented in this section have used the number of teacher hours per student as the dependent variable. Table 11.5 presents similar models with the teacher–student ratio as the dependent variable multiplied by 1000. By this multiplication the two dependent variables have about the same mean and variance, and the estimated coefficients are reasonably comparable. The estimated coefficients are very similar as expected because the two dependent variables are highly correlated.

---

[13] The within-school standard deviations for the shares of minority students and students with special needs are both about 0.02. The overall variation is 0.08 and 0.04, respectively. Notice in particular that changes over time within school for the share of students with special needs may be due to variation in the treatment of one or a few students. Students that are on the margin of being classified as special needs students will typically get only a small amount of extra resources and may get extra resources some years but not others. If changes over time in the share of students with special needs are driven by such marginal students, the signal to noise ratio in the within-school data is probably low and hence the estimated effect would be biased downwards. In any case, we would expect to estimate a smaller effect compared to the baseline model where the identification is based on both between- and within-school variation in student composition.

A Cost Model of Schools

Table 11.5. Results using an alternative dependent variable.

Variable	A	B	F	D	E	C
Log(number of students)	−84.2 (17.8)	–	–	–	–	–
Log(number of students) squared	7.13 (14.6)	–	–	–	–	–
Inverse of the square root of number of students	–	358 (29.2)	441 (45.6)	455 (36.6)	431 (40.6)	606 (15.2)
Share of minority students	–	–	71.7 (12.2)	80.8 (10.7)	67.4 (9.67)	28.3 (1.59)
Share of students with special needs	–	–	109 (12.5)	109 (10.4)	109 (10.3)	65.4 (7.55)
Classes at primary level only	–	–	−18.5 (8.01)	−23.4 (6.68)	−15.0 (4.55)	−9.22 (3.56)
Classes at lower secondary level only	–	–	−1.42 (0.37)	−1.42 (0.24)	−3.56 (0.64)	3.57 (0.84)
R^2 (within group)	0.390	0.389	0.668	0.675	0.670	0.216
Observations	15,046	15,046	15,034	6,117	8,917	15,034
Variables for the share of students at each grade included	No	No	Yes	Yes	Yes	Yes
Year-specific local government fixed effects	Yes	Yes	Yes	Yes	Yes	No
School fixed effects	No	No	No	No	No	Yes
Sample period	2001–2006	2001–2006	2001–2006	2001–2003	2003–2006	2001–2006

Depended variable is the teacher–student ratio times 1000
Estimated by ordinary least squares. The data covers all schools in Norway for the school years 2001/2002–2005/2006. *t*-values in parentheses are corrected to take account of within-schooling clustering of errors.

11.5. Conclusion

This chapter estimates an "allocation model" of school spending which describes how school districts allocate their school budgets across schools. We argue that this is the best possible way to analyze the cost structure of schools. We argue that it is inherently difficult to estimate a "cost function" that can predict how much it will cost to deliver a given level of student performance because researchers lack important information on school outcomes and the management and cost effectiveness of schools.

We focus on the effect of school size and student body composition on the amount of teacher resources allocated to schools using panel data on

Norwegian schools and local governments for the period 2001–2006. By using a fixed effect school district specification, we are able to estimate the model controlling for unobservable district variables that may affect the relationship via the demand for education and the political processes that determine school resource allocation.

Our results clearly suggest that the effect of school size is highly nonlinear. Thus, merging schools seems to be an important instrument in a cost-saving strategy in the school sector. However, the question of school consolidation also depends on the relationship between student performance and school size, a topic that has not been studied in this chapter. A positive (negative) relationship between school size and student performance would strengthen (weaken) the argument for a policy to stimulate school mergers. Our results coincide with studies from the United States and United Kingdom that cost-minimizing schools are large.

Our results also show a clear positive relationship between teacher hours per student and the share of students with special needs and the share of students from ethnic minorities. The point estimates indicate that on average 55–80% extra resources are allocated to minority students compared to "average" students, while 65–130% extra resources are allocated to students with special needs. The lower bond of these point estimates follow from a model including school fixed effects instead of school district fixed effects.

Finally, we investigated whether the removal of the maximum class size rule in 2003 changed the allocation of resources between schools. The evidence so far indicates that the reform did not have any significant effect on the allocation of resources. More future research is needed to determine whether the allocation changes in a longer run perspective and to which extent the reform affected student performance.

References

Andrews M, Duncombe W, Yinger J (2002) Revisiting economies of size in American education: are we any closer to a consensus? *Economics of Education Review* 21:245–262

Bonesrønning H, Falch T, Strøm B (2005) Teacher sorting, teacher quality, and student composition. *European Economic Review* 49:457–483

Bradford DF, Malt RA, Oates WE (1969) The rising cost of local public services: some evidence and reflections. *National Tax Journal* 22:185–202

Cohn E (1969) Economies of scale in Iowa high school operations. *Journal of Human Resources* 3:422–434

Downes TA, Pogue TF (1994) Adjusting school aid formulas for the higher cost of educating disadvantaged students. *National Tax Journal* 47:89–110

Duncombe W (2002) Estimating the cost of an adequate education in New York. Center for Policy Research, Working Paper 44

Duncombe W, Yinger J (1997) Why is it so hard to help central city schools? *Journal of Policy Analysis and Management* 16:85–113

Duncombe W, Yinger J (2005) How much more does a disadvantaged student cost? *Economics of Education Review* 24:513–532

Duncombe W, Miner J, Ruggiero J (1995) Potential cost savings from school district consolidation: a case study of New York. *Economics of Education Review* 14:265–284

Falch T, Rattsø J (1997) Political economic determinants of school spending in federal states: theory and time-series evidence. *European Journal of Political Economy* 13:299–314

Falch T, Rattsø J (1999) Local public choice of school spending: disaggregating the demand function for educational services. *Economics of Education Review* 18:361–373

Falch T, Rønning M, Strøm B (2005) Forhold som påvirker kommunenes utgiftsbehov i skolesektoren. Smådriftsulemper, skolestruktur og elevsammensetning. SØF-rapport 04/05

Fox WF (1981) Reviewing economics of size in education. *Journal of Education Finance* 6:273–296

Grob U, Wolter SC (2005) Demographic change and public education spending. A conflict between young and old? CESifo, Working Paper 1555

Hanushek EA (2002) Publicly provided education. In: Auerbach AJ, Feldstein M (eds) *Handbook of Public Economics*, vol 4. Elsevier Science BV, pp 2045–2141

Imazeki J, Reschovsky A (2003) Financing adequate education in rural settings. *Journal of Education Finance* 29:137–156

Kenny LW (1982) A model of optimal size with an application to the demand for cognitive achievement and for school size. *Economic Inquiry* 20:240–254

Ladd H, Yinger J (1995) The case for equalizing aid. *National Tax Journal* 48:211–223

Niskanen WA (1971) *Bureaucracy and Representative Government*. Aldine, Chicago

Poterba JM (1997) Demographic structure and the political economy of public education. *Journal of Policy Analysis and Management* 16:315–320

Ratcliffe K, Riddle B, Yinger J (1990) The fiscal condition of school districts in Nebraska: is small beautiful? *Economics of Education Review* 9:81–99

Roza, M, Hill PT (2004) How within-district spending inequities help some schools to fail. *Brookings Papers on Public Policy*, pp 201—227

Summers AA, Wolfe BL (1976) Intradistrict distribution of school inputs to the disadvantaged: evidence for the courts. *Journal of Human Resources* 11:328–342

Taylor J, Bradley S (2000) Resource utilization and economies of size in secondary schools. *Bulletin of Economic Research* 52:123–150

Part Four

Strategies to Encourage Performance and Equity

Chapter 12
The Potential of School Information Systems for Enhancing School Improvement

Ian Selwood[1] and Adrie J. Visscher[2]

[1]*University of Birmingham, Birmingham, England*
[2]*University of Twente, Enschede, The Netherlands*

12.1. Introduction

The ultimate criterion for "school improvement" is improved student achievement levels. This, however, does not mean that schools cannot improve in other important ways, especially when the preconditions for higher student achievement levels are influenced in a positive way (e.g. better teaching, more time for teaching, intensified student monitoring, higher student achievement orientations). These benefits in the long term may also improve student performance.

According to the British Educational Communications and Technology Agency (Becta) (2003) evidence that Information and Communications Technology (ICT) can lead to school improvement has increased over the last decade. When considering the impact of ICT on school improvement the focus is generally on the influence that ICT has had on pupil attainment, and there is mounting evidence that ICT can enhance learning, if used in certain ways in specific subject areas (e.g. Davis et al. 1997; Scrimshaw 1997; Stevenson 1997; Moseley et al. 1999; Trilling and Hood 1999; Cox et al. 2003; Ofsted 2004). The common factor in all these studies is that ICT's role is seen as being directly involved in the teaching and learning processes. Nonetheless, when considering the impact of ICT on school improvement we need to consider more than pupil achievement, and the direct involvement of ICT in the teaching and learning process. For example, research supports the beneficial effects of ICT in pupil motivation (Cox 1997; Pittard et al. 2003), pupil behaviour (Comber et al. 2002) and teacher workload (Selwood and Pilkington 2005).

Relatively few studies have considered the role of school information systems (SISs) in school improvement. Based on our experience with the design, implementation and evaluation of computer-assisted SISs we will focus on the degree to which such systems can be of value in promoting school improvement. We will do so by first defining the SIS concept and explaining the support they can provide in schools (Sections 12.2 and 12.3). Next, the benefits hoped for and achieved will be described (Sections 12.4 and 12.5) after which (Section 12.6) we will focus on what is known about the factors influencing the successful utilisation of SISs. In Section 12.7, the features and potential of a new type of information systems, so-called school performance feedback systems, is addressed, after which the balance sheet is drawn up in the final section.

12.2. What is a School Information System?

It is difficult to state precisely what a computer-assisted school SIS is, partly because the technology on which it is based is changing continuously, and the type of support that SISs offer and the applications that they consist of vary from system to system and are also continually changing. SISs are often referred to as management information systems (MISs); however, again we have the problem that there are many definitions of MIS and, furthermore, several authors (Thierauf 1987; Hicks 1993) agree that a number of information systems, such as decision support systems or executive information systems, fall under the umbrella of MIS. However, others (Bank and Williams 1987; Carter and Burger 1994) consider them as significantly different systems designed for specific purposes. A useful working definition coming from the former category of writers, which concentrates on the general use of MISs is probably appropriate for our discussion:

> ...an integrated user–machine system for providing information to support operations, management, and decision-making functions in an organisation. (Davis and Olson 1985:6)

This definition implies an interactive relationship between the user and the computer and a dialogue in which both are engaged. Furthermore, the definition stresses the need to support "management and decision-making functions in an organisation" and if the organisation concerned is a school, then this would appear to be an appropriate generic definition for a SIS.

Visscher (2001) specifies the activities SISs can support in schools when stating that a SIS is:

> ...an information system based on one or more computers, consisting of a data bank and one or more computer applications which altogether enable the computer-supported storage, manipulation, retrieval, and distribution of data to support school management. (p. 4)

This definition implies that the specific nature of a particular SIS is dependent on the number and character of computer applications (e.g. student administration, personnel management, student timetabling, etc.) included in the information system. As previously noted, SIS subsystems and their nature can vary considerably. Sometimes, they mainly support the routine recording of data and the production of standard lists. In other cases, the computer also provides policy-making information to school leaders and supports them in their strategic management activities.

The activities of school staff with the SIS hopefully result in a database containing up to date data on the school organisation and its environment, and this should enable the production of valuable managerial information (e.g. trends, patterns, forecasts). SISs are designed not only for assisting school managers, but also for clerical staff to record, process and output student, finance, personnel and other data for routine work. Indeed, the research has shown for some time (Selwood and Drenoyianni 1997; Visscher and Bloemen 1999; Visscher et al. 1999) that SISs are mainly used for clerical work, with managers failing to receive much benefit from these systems.

Although the term "school information system" has historically tended to refer to school-based computer systems that support clerical and managerial school staff, some new types of computer applications may also be regarded as SISs: student monitoring system for evaluating student progress (Gillijns 1991; Vlug 1997) and information systems designed for feeding back school performance data indicating schools' performance and other characteristics compared with that of other schools (Fitz-Gibbon 1996; Visscher and Coe 2002). The characteristics and potential of these "newer" systems will be discussed in Section 12.6.

12.3. An Overview of SIS Modules and Function

A detailed overview of a potential SIS, a SIS framework (Visscher 1992) is shown in Fig. 12.1. The framework is the result of an in-depth analysis of the clerical, administrative, and managerial work, outside the classroom, in Dutch secondary schools (Essink and Visscher 1989). The goal of the analysis was to identify all possible and valuable types of computer support,

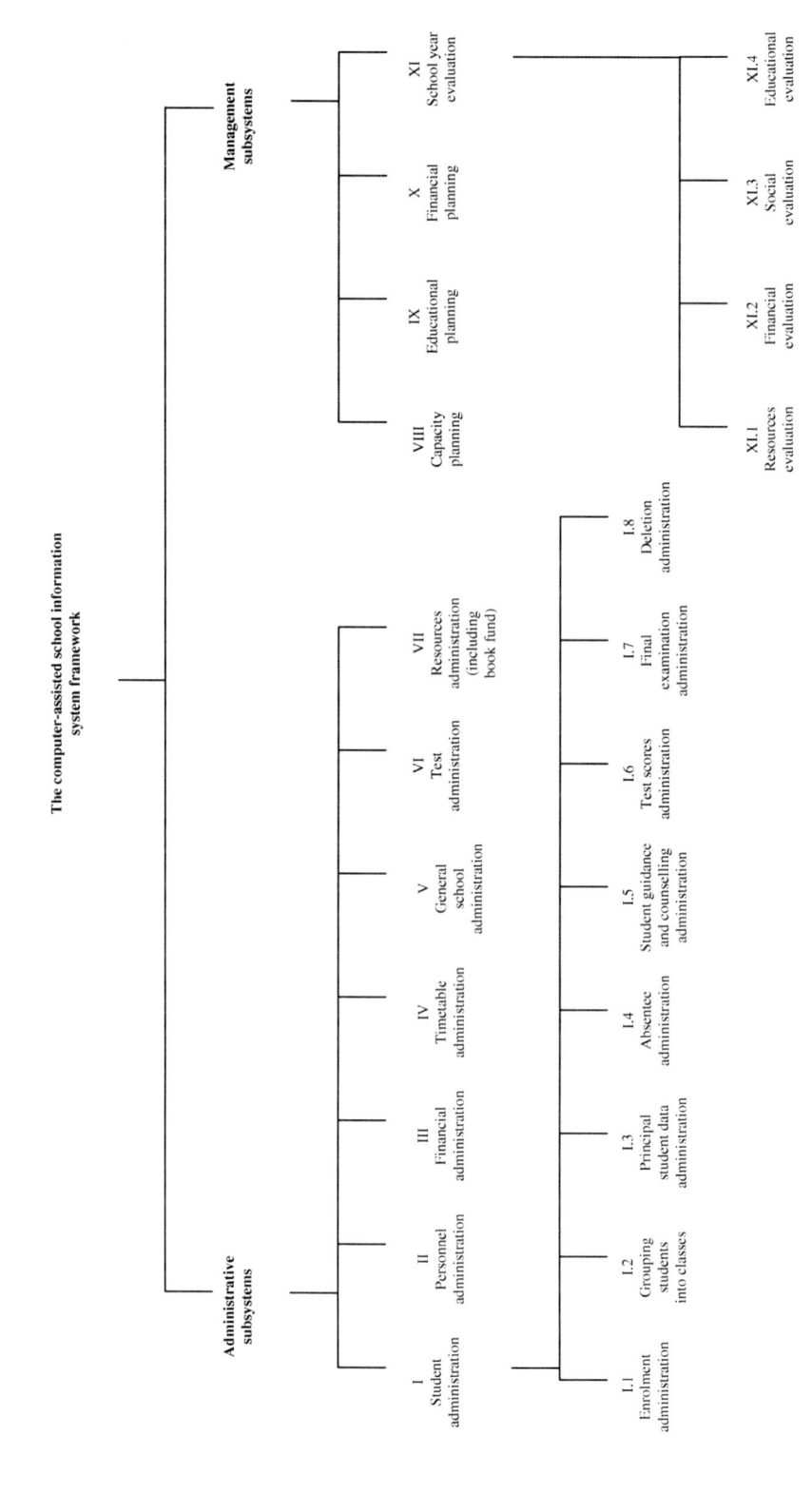

Fig. 12.1. Administrative and managerial subsystems of a computer-assisted information system for secondary schools. (*Source:* Visscher 1992.)

where the computer could replace existing manual work as well as assisting in new activities that have become possible as a result of the introduction of the computer. Visscher (1992) also describes the possible forms of support the computer can give within the subsystems of the SIS framework, in terms of elementary activities. These cannot be presented in full here for reasons of space but Fig. 12.1 shows that the SIS framework includes two types of subsystems/modules relating to administrative and managerial functions.

The administrative subsystems support various types of data handling activities concerned with student, financial, personnel and other school data. Logically, the student administration subsystem is the heart of the school office assisting in all data handling in the "life of a student", such as enrolment, attendance, counselling and assessment (report marks and central examination marks). In the same way that this has been done for the "student administration" subsystem, each of the other six school administrative subsystems can be elaborated into sub-subsystems, such as those supporting all stages of the life of a school employee (subsystem II), school budget (subsystem III), etc.

The management subsystems in Fig. 12.1 support school managers in activities they would carry out frequently and which are common to most schools (the latter makes the development of these modules cost-effective). The advantage of such modules is that school managers themselves do not have to define complex programming statements to obtain the management information they need. If the modules have been developed, then selection of an option provides the required information directly via a system menu.

Three of the management subsystems in Fig. 12.1 support school *planning* activities. The *capacity planning* module for example assists in the planning of:

- The number of lesson periods and task periods that will be allocated to teaching and non-teaching staff
- The technical infrastructure, e.g. computers for students and for school staff, photocopiers and other machines, school buildings

The *educational planning* subsystem is closely connected with the capacity planning subsystem as the results of the latter provide the starting point for the former. In educational planning, the available lesson periods are allocated to individual teachers, and the student, classroom and teacher timetables are constructed.

In the *financial-economical planning* subsystem, a school budget estimate is drawn up on the basis of financial data from previous years, expected trends, available finances and financial planning parameters. The subsystem can also provide support in forecasting the liquid assets of a school over a defined period.

The last management subsystem, *school year evaluation,* provides an evaluation of what has taken place within a defined timeframe in the school. The evaluation subsystem helps, for example, in retrieving the following evaluative information:

- The budgets spent in a school year (e.g. where did we spend more than planned, where less?)
- The personnel aspects (e.g. illness of staff) in a school year
- The academic results (e.g. the percentage of students in the final grades passing this year's final examinations in comparison with other school years; the percentage of students promoted to higher grades)
- The utilisation of other than financial resources (e.g. the classroom–student ratio)
- The percentage of students that have achieved the various school-type grades or that have passed an examination of a certain type
- The "bottleneck grades" in terms of student flow-through
- Per subject, per teacher statistics on final examination scores in comparison with previous school years and with school internal examinations
- The magnitude of student absenteeism after a school truancy reduction policy has been implemented
- Patterns in students' choices of subjects and school types
- Trends in cost types (the ones that increased, decreased or remained the same)

It is self-evident that such information can provide evidence, or otherwise, of school improvement.

Incorporated within these four explicit management subsystems is the potential for wide-ranging and contextualised managerial support. The questions of interest to school managers in performing their management tasks vary greatly between school managers because they operate in different schools and contexts. Thus the various information needs of all schools managers cannot be included in a standard information system menu. However, if the relevant school data have been collected in the clerical subsystems and if the database is of the relational kind that can be approached by means of modern query languages, then an enormous variety of interrelationships between the data can be analysed to support school managers in their work. It will, however, require particular skills to define these queries to satisfy this variety of information needs. These skills may be acquired in training courses where school managers can learn to exploit the wealth of information schools possess with modern, computerised SISs.

12.4. Aims of Introducing a SIS

The goals for the introduction of SISs into schools can be summarised by stating that it is expected that they can increase the efficiency and effectiveness of (the parts of) the educational institution they are introduced into. However, the ultimate goal for implementing a SIS must be that the education of pupils is improved – school improvement.

Efficiency is defined here as the ratio between input and output, for instance, the ratio between the manpower and time needed to produce a certain amount of information. A SIS should thus enable the storage, manipulation, production and distribution of the same amount or more data with the same or less manpower and/or time. The *efficiency* of school activities may be improved in the following ways:

- In the pre-SIS situation the same data may be collected separately and repeatedly at several locations which require much school staff time. The single entry of data in a central database saves time, facilitates the multiple usage of the same data by all staff and prevents errors which may have occurred as a consequence of the multiple data sources.
- The computer-assisted manipulation of data (e.g. making computations, sorting data, etc.), the production of lists and reports, etc. (for both internal and external consumption) saves time.
- The computer-assisted exchange of school data can be carried out more efficiently if the school database provides the data in a form acceptable to the recipient (e.g. local and/or central government, receiving school).

Improved school *effectiveness* is defined here as a better attainment of the school goals. Unfortunately, improved school effectiveness is difficult to prove in research. However, there are reasons for positive expectations:

- School managers often spend considerable time on clerical work. Because of the probable efficiency benefits described above, they can spend more time on other activities that may improve the functioning of the school – developing school policies and improving school quality assurance procedures. Hopefully, these activities will help schools to better achieve their goals.
- School staff can find better solutions for structured allocation problems (e.g. composing timetables, the allocation of students to lesson groups or the allocation of teacher–lesson group combinations to the timetable). The computer can compute alternative solutions for complex allocation problems from which the best one can be chosen and implemented (previously the first solution found was accepted). As

allocation results often influence daily school life (e.g. via a timetable) the SIS has an impact on the life and well-being of students and school staff and therefore impacts on the effectiveness of schools.
- The SIS is not just an automated variant of the card-index box in which data can be registered in computer files. The SIS can be set up to *signal* when certain aspects of schooling require attention. For example, a student's attendance is not up to standard or the achievement of a group of children is poor. This may improve process control, lead to more timely corrective actions and to a more effective school.
- If the SIS enables an investigation of the interrelationships between variables (e.g. between truancy and student achievement) then more informed school policy-making becomes possible (and by that, the reduction of uncertainty) and the effects of school policy can be evaluated, for example, whether the number of truants has been reduced after a school policy measure to achieve this was introduced. It seems likely that improving the conditions of school decision-making will affect the quality of school policies and, as such, the results achieved by schools.

The empirical research evidence for these claims, however, is still small. This does not mean that the opposite effects were found, just that it is very difficult to prove these benefits unambiguously (e.g. in pre-test/post-test comparisons). The research that has been done in this area consists mainly of studies in which SIS users are asked for their perceptions on the extent to which SISs have improved their efficiency and/or effectiveness (e.g. Visscher and Spuck 1991; Visscher and Bloemen 1999; Visscher et al. 1999). In general these self-reports are (very) positive; users usually report improved efficiency and effectiveness as a result of their use of SISs. However, whether their views reflect real improvements is unsure. Improved efficiency is very probable as the SISs are especially used for carrying out routine clerical activities. However, even today many SISs still provide relatively little support to higher order managerial activities, e.g. supporting managerial decision-making, but, as previously noted, improvement of effectiveness could result from improved efficiency (time saved by increased efficiency can be spent on activities promoting school effectiveness).

12.5. SISs Supporting School Improvement

In this section, we examine briefly two areas where the use of SIS by teachers can impact on school improvement.

12.5.1. Supporting Formative Assessment

Thus far, we have concentrated on the application of SISs by office staff and senior management in schools. Indeed with very few exceptions (Selwood et al. 2001; Selwood 2005) most research concerning SISs has focused on these users as SISs have mainly offered resources for use by clerical staff and senior managers rather than teachers.

In England, *formative assessment* is seen as one of the most powerful ways of improving learning and raising standards (Qualifications and Curriculum Authority (QCA) 2005) and thus a major contributory factor in school improvement. This view has been well researched and a clear link shown. Black and Wiliam (1998) undertook a meta-analysis of the research literature and concluded that formative assessment is an essential component of classroom work, and that effective use of formative assessment techniques could raise standards significantly. In addition, they stated that many of the studies they reviewed showed that improved formative assessment helped low achievers most and so reduced the range of achievement as well as raising achievement for all. In England, the approach of focusing on formative assessment in teaching is now known as "Assessment for Learning". The QCA on its website resources (2005) states

> Assessment for learning is the process of using classroom assessment to improve learning... In assessment for learning: teachers share learning targets with pupils; pupils know and recognise the standards for which they should aim; there is feedback that leads pupils to identify what they should do next in order to improve...

Kirkup et al. (2005) in a survey that looked at school uses of data for teaching and learning found that:

> the impact of data on teaching and learning operates at two levels: directly by means of interventions targeted at *individual* pupils; and indirectly by means of *whole-school approaches*. Commonly reported uses for data in all schools were: to track pupil progress; to set targets; to identify underachieving pupils for further support; to inform teaching and learning and strategic planning. (pp. 3–4)

and

> At the classroom or pupil level, effective use of data enabled schools to: highlight specific weaknesses for individual pupils; identify weaknesses in topics for the class as a whole; inform accurate curricular targets for individual pupils; provide evidence to support decisions as to where to focus resources and teaching. (p. 4)

Appropriately designed SISs could be key to helping schools manage formative assessment data, as it is apparent from the above that keeping full and accurate records of student progress and sharing these results and targets with pupils are essential.

ICT can be used in many ways as a tool to monitor and analyse pupil performance. NCET (1996) identified seven major areas of ICT usage related to this topic:

1. Recording and analysing progress
2. Reporting and recording achievement
3. Recording prior learning
4. Registration and certification
5. Testing and examinations
6. Integration with computer-based training, computer-based learning packages and integrated learning systems (ILS)
7. Initial and diagnostic testing

Some of these uses of ICT for assessment are in the main directly related to SISs (1–3), whilst others (5–7) may well supply data for the system but are not normally considered as part of it; and finally the fourth item – registration and certification – is normally considered as part of the examinations application of the SIS.

Taylor (2000) claims that assessment information will allow the teacher to answer many other questions:

– How is a pupil progressing in a subject, across the curriculum, over a period of time?
– What can we expect this pupil to achieve in his/her summative tests?
– Where are his/her weaknesses/strengths?
– Are there any areas where he/she is underachieving?
– Are there areas where he/she is near the boundary of a higher level?
– What specific targets shall we set?

(Taylor 2000:31)

If this process of analysis is extended to whole classes, years and areas of the curriculum, then whole school issues relating to school improvement and planning may be addressed by asking:

– Which areas of the curriculum are functioning well?
– Which areas need attention?
– What are our expectations in curriculum areas?
– How will this affect our assessment results?

(Taylor 2000:31)

12.5.2. Supporting Attendance

Another significant aspect of school life that is capable of computerisation and can lead to school improvement is the recording and analysis of pupil attendance. The pupil record system within a SIS could be used to print registers for registration groups or lesson groups. However, this is not utilising the full power of ICT. For example the process of recording pupil attendance can be streamlined by using direct data entry (DDE) systems such as optical mark recognition, bar coded registers, "swipe cards", networked computers and wireless networks.

All of these systems have associated advantages and disadvantages (Selwood 1996) but the introduction of ICT to the process of registering pupils has according to Selwood (1996):

- Raised the profile of registering attendance for both staff and pupils.
- Improved the categorisation and designation of absence by making the process more systematic and it has achieved greater consistency and reliability of data.
- Given schools greater confidence in the accuracy of their attendance data, and schools thus feel better able to confront parents of pupils with poor attendance patterns, and to designate absence as unauthorised. This, in turn, can reduce parentally condoned truancy.
- Tended to reduce unauthorised absence, because it is explained, and consequently the number of authorised absences may increase. However, a short-term decrease in overall attendance can actually occur.
- Possibly promoted a longer-term improvement in the attendance rates of most pupils, even if supplementary measures are not taken, as a prompt response to absence promotes higher attendance.
- Made it easier for schools to recognise improved attendance rates, to publish the data in required formats and to incorporate rewards for good or improved attendance into their policy.
- Identified the level of post-registration truancy and attempt to combat this.

12.6. Implementation Factors

Visscher (1996) presented a model portraying the assumed interrelationships between four clusters of variables and how they affect the usage and impact of SISs (see Fig. 12.2). The validity of the model has been proven in several instances (Visscher and Bloemen 1999; Visscher et al. 1999; Bisaso and Visscher 2005; Kereteletswe and Selwood 2005). Since the blocks in Fig. 12.2 are interacting with one another, a choice in one block has consequences for what happens in one or more of the other blocks. SIS usage (block E) is influenced by the SIS quality (block B), which results from the design strategy followed (block A). The nature of the implementation process (block C) and the characteristics of schools as organisations (block D) also influence SIS usage (block E). Finally, the degree of SIS usage and the way in which the SIS is used are expected to lead to both intended and unintended effects (block F).

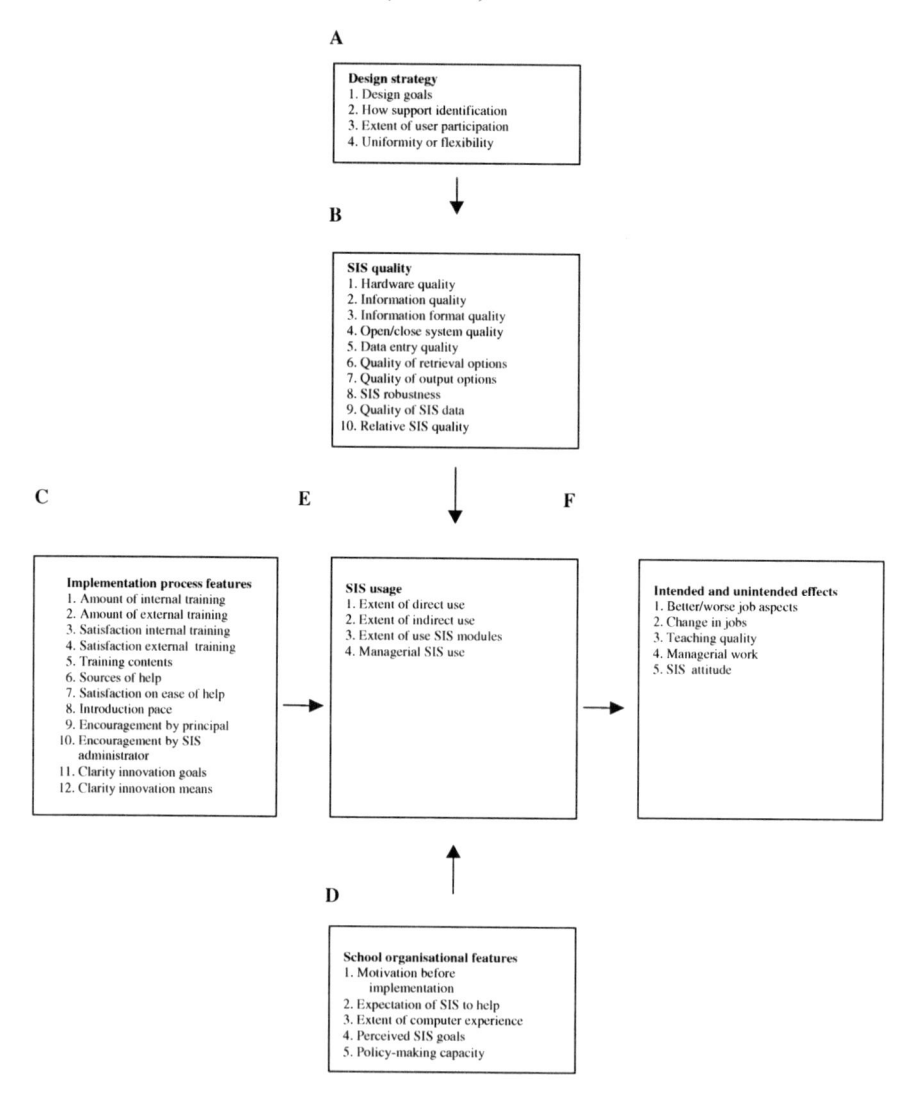

A

Design strategy
1. Design goals
2. How support identification
3. Extent of user participation
4. Uniformity or flexibility

B

SIS quality
1. Hardware quality
2. Information quality
3. Information format quality
4. Open/close system quality
5. Data entry quality
6. Quality of retrieval options
7. Quality of output options
8. SIS robustness
9. Quality of SIS data
10. Relative SIS quality

C

Implementation process features
1. Amount of internal training
2. Amount of external training
3. Satisfaction internal training
4. Satisfaction external training
5. Training contents
6. Sources of help
7. Satisfaction on ease of help
8. Introduction pace
9. Encouragement by principal
10. Encouragement by SIS administrator
11. Clarity innovation goals
12. Clarity innovation means

E

SIS usage
1. Extent of direct use
2. Extent of indirect use
3. Extent of use SIS modules
4. Managerial SIS use

F

Intended and unintended effects
1. Better/worse job aspects
2. Change in jobs
3. Teaching quality
4. Managerial work
5. SIS attitude

D

School organisational features
1. Motivation before implementation
2. Expectation of SIS to help
3. Extent of computer experience
4. Perceived SIS goals
5. Policy-making capacity

Fig. 12.2. The factors SIS use and their effects.

Table 12.1. Predictors of SIS use in three studies

	Hong Kong	Netherlands	England
Start motivation	x		x
Computer experience	x		x
Internal training	x	x	x
External training	x	x	x
SIS data quality	x		x
Clarity innovation goals	x		
Clarity innovation means		x	
Length personal use			x

Table 12.1 shows which factors proved to be predictors of SIS use in three different studies (Visscher and Bloemen 1999; Visscher et al. 1999; Wild and Walker 2001) that were all based on the theoretical framework presented in Fig. 12.2. In all three studies, training within schools (e.g. by the SIS administrator) and training external to the school in SIS use proved to influence the extent to which SISs were used: more training led to more intense use.

However, these findings generally relate to clerical use of SISs as this type of system use proved to be dominant in the three studies. The fact that school managers and other school staff involved in school decision-making processes had thus far benefited little from SISs does not mean that we should not try, where possible, to increase the degree of rationality in their behaviour.

Training school managers in a way that takes account of their specific characteristics can fulfil an important role here. Visscher and Branderhorst (2001) demonstrated, in a quasi-experimental study, that such training courses can change increase utilisation of SISs by school managers for decision support. They designed a training course with the following characteristics:

- Involvement of representatives of the target group in the design of the course.
- Voluntary participation.
- Potential participants should be informed on the main features of the course.
- Individual intake to determine the level and needs of participants.
- Set clear, specified and measurable training goals.

- Match the nature of the training course with the know-how and skills of participants, starting with problems that they face in their professional practice.
- Make the probability that participants will soon experience success as high as possible, by providing training content that they can apply immediately.
- Teach participants to determine what kind of information they need and how to select, retrieve, interpret and use it in school policy-making.
- Use various instructional strategies such as active learning, self-study, group assignments, etc.
- Explicitly pay attention to the various stages of a learning process with experiential learning, reflection, theory and experimentation.
- Transfer what has been learned to professional practice by having participants write an action plan, offer "on the job" support, involve their colleagues in the training course and guarantee follow-up training activities.

In addition to training school managers we also should design SISs that support the work of school managers. Simon (1993) stresses that information is not a scarce resource, and human attention and our information processing capacity are limited. If we let computers produce all the information they can produce, school staff will be unable to function efficiently as a result of information pollution. SISs should therefore operate intelligently, be selective and only output information that is interesting and that has the potential of supporting school improvement.

Computer output must also be appealing, easily retrieved, readily analysed and trigger actions. Current SISs rarely, completely, meet these requirements. It would therefore help if output is manipulated by school staff with the specific task of information handling, before it is distributed to other school staff, in such a way that it meets the "promoters of information use" criteria. Preferably we should build SISs that make it easy to retrieve all kinds of data and that produce information that is easily understood. The barriers for retrieving and processing valuable SIS data should be made as small as possible, and hence the probability that this information would be used is greater.

Finally, computer-assisted policy-making and evaluation touches the whole school organisation. In many schools, integrating SISs fully in their policy development requires fundamental *organisational development,* demanding a lot of energy from school staff. Organisational innovation and evolution should bring them to a level of organisational functioning that enables them to:

- Decide which SIS information they need for decision-making
- Retrieve (part of) the information they need from a SIS
- Interpret the data in such a way that it can be used for decision-making
- Use the information for developing, implementing and evaluating new school policies

12.7. School Performance Feedback Systems

During the last decade a number of different information systems have become available to schools that may well promote the improved functioning of schools. The so-called school performance feedback systems (SPFSs) provide information on various aspects of the functioning of schools, e.g.:

- Student performance
- Staff satisfaction
- The nature of instruction
- School management behaviour
- Cooperation among teachers

(e.g. PAT, PIPS, MidYIS in England, ZEBO in The Netherlands, The ABC+ Model in the United States).

Usually these systems provide information on how a class/teacher/school performs compared to a reference group (e.g. the national average). Some SPFSs provide the views of students and teachers or of teachers and school management on the same topic which can lead to interesting varying results. The idea behind school/teacher performance feedback is of course that the recipient, when necessary, uses the feedback and tries to improve performance.

There is good reason for investing in feedback. The meta-analysis by Kluger and DeNisi (1996) showed feedback's overall positive effect on performance. Nevertheless, although thousands of schools want this information and are prepared to pay for it, studies into their utilisation show that even under these circumstances utilisation proves to be far from easy.

In England the government has for some time provided schools, each autumn, with data on their performance and to enable them to better analyse these data produced the Pupil Achievement Tracker (PAT). This was sent to all schools in October 2003 on CD-ROM and regular updates have subsequently been available from the "Standards website". The PAT was built to enable teachers and senior managers to analyse performance data and generate information that can be used to support teaching and learning, identify pupil needs and set targets. It allows schools to look back at their previous performance and compare this to the results of pupils in other similar schools across the country. According to Kirkup et al. (2005) PAT users were generally positive about "the visual presentation of data and the ability to compare groups of pupils" (p. 2). However, they also reported that many questionnaire respondents and focus group participants found PAT difficult to use and "were confused as to how to input data" and incompatible with their SIS. Indeed Kirkup et al. noted that rather than use proprietary systems, school-based systems and Excel spreadsheets were the most popular data management tools as they were flexible in inputting internally generated data and allowed individual pupil tracking. It should be noted that PAT is being replaced by RAISEonline (Reporting and Analysis for Improvement through School self-Evaluation), a web-based interactive tool developed by Ofsted and the DfES to replace the Performance and Assessment (PANDA) report (an annual written report to schools) and PAT.

However, given the uncertainties teachers face when carrying out their jobs (e.g. "Do I use the correct instructional approach?" and "What is its effect on each individual student?"), knowing that they want the information and given the proven power of tailored training of school staff (Branderhorst 2005) it is worth investing in designing training courses that support school staff in utilising the information SPFSs provide for improving students performance and the functioning of schools. In doing so (which is our plan), it will be important to systematically evaluate the impact of a training course with specific characteristics on data utilisation and student performance.

12.8. Conclusion

As the use of SISs has reduced the amount of paper work that in former days had to be carried out by school staff manually, the efficiency of carrying out this work has probably improved. However, the availability of SISs may also have led to the recording of new data because the SIS enables the manipulation of these data which can produce new valuable information.

Furthermore, regarding the retrieval and utilisation of information that can be used in solving ill-structured problems we have not progressed very far as yet. As such, school improvement as an activity has not gained greatly from the SISs available in schools.

However, research has shown that training definitely can promote the attitudes and skills required for SIS use, as well as SIS use. If we manage to fulfil the preconditions for SIS use in school policy-making we can evaluate how this leads to improved school policy-making and greater school effectiveness.

If teachers are going to be expected to make use of formative data for improving pupil attainment then systems need to be developed that are integrated with the schools' main SIS, are easy to use and access.

Finally, much is to be expected from SPFSs as they can provide schools with very valuable information that directly relates to the quality of school functioning and leads to school improvement. As is the case with the "traditional SISs", the heart of the problem is how users who are really interested in this information can be supported in such ways that they use the information for the sake of school improvement. It is our belief that training and educating school staff in the utilisation of these information systems can have a strong impact here.

References

Bank A, Williams C (1987) The coming of instructional information systems. In: Bank A, Williams CR (eds) *Information Systems and School Improvement: Inventing the Future*. Teacher College Press, New York

Becta (2003) What the research says about ICT and whole-school improvement. http://partners.becta.org.uk/page_documents/research/wtrs_ws_improvement.pdf. Becta, Coventry, Retrieved August 30, 2006

Bisaso R, Visscher AJ (2005) Computerised school information systems usage in an emerging country – Uganda. In: Tatnull A et al. (eds) *Information Technology and Educational Management in the Knowledge Society*. Springer, New York

Black P, Wiliam D (1998) Inside the black box: raising standards through classroom assessment. *Phi Delta Kappan* 80:139–148. Retrieved August 30, 2006, from http://www.pdkintl.org/kappan/kbla9810.htm

Branderhorst ECM (2005) *What Is Wrong with MIS? Design and Evaluation of a Course in Using Management Information in Secondary Schools*. University of Twente, Enschede

Carter D, Burger M (1994) Curriculum management, instructional leadership and new information technology. *School Organisation* 14(2):153–168

Comber C, Watling R, Lawson T, Cavendish C, McEune R, Paterson F (2002) *ImpaCT2, Learning at Home and School: Case Studies*. Becta, Coventry

Cox MJ (1997) *Effects of Information Technology on Students' Motivation: Final Report*. NCET, Coventry

Cox N, Abbott C, Webb M, Blakeley B, Beauchamp T, Rhodes V (2003) *ICT and Attainment: A Review of the Research Literature*. LDfES, London

Davis G, Olson M (1985) *Management Information Systems*. McGraw-Hill, New York

Davis N, Desforges C et al. (1997) Can quality in learning be enhanced through the use of IT ? In: Somekh B, Davis N (eds) *Using Information Technology Effectively in Teaching and Learning: Studies in Pre-Service and In-Service Teacher Education*. Routledge, London

Essink LBJ, Visscher AJ (1989) *Een computerondersteund schoolinformatiesysteem voor het avo/vwo [A Computer-Assisted School Information System for Schools for General Secondary Education, and Schools for Pre-university Education]*. Faculty of Educational Science and Technology, University of Twente, Enschede

Fitz-Gibbon CT (1996) *Monitoring Education: Indicators, Quality and Effectiveness*. Casell, London

Gillijns P (1991) *Student Monitoring System*. Zwijsen, Tilburg

Hicks JO (1993) *Management Information Systems: A User Perspective* (third edition). West Publishing Company, St Paul, MN

Kereteletswe C, Selwood I (2005) ITEM system usage in the ministry of education in Botswana. In: Tatnull A, Visscher A, Osario J (eds) *Information Technology and Educational Management in the Knowledge Society*. Springer, New York

Kirkup C, Sizmur J, Sturman L, Lewis K (2005) *Research Report 671: Schools' Use of Data in Teaching and Learning*. DFES, Nottingham

Kluger AN, DeNisi A (1996) The effects of feedback interventions on performance: a historical review, a meta-analysis, and a preliminary feedback intervention theory. *Psychological Bulletin* 119:254–284

Moseley D, Higgins S et al. (1999) *Ways Forward with ICT: Effective Pedagogy Using Information and Communications Technology for Literacy and Numeracy in Primary Schools*. University of Newcastle, Newcastle

NCET (1996) *Information Sheet On: Assessment, Recording and Reporting*. NCET, Coventry

Ofsted (2004) *ICT in Schools. The Impact of Government Initiatives Five Years On*. HMSO, London

Pittard V, Bannister P, Dunn J (2003) *The Big pICTure: The Impact of ICT on Attainment, Motivation and Learning*. DfES, London

Qualifications and Curriculum Authority (2005) Assessment for learning. Retrieved October 2, 2005, from http://www.qca.org.uk/10009.html

Scrimshaw P (1997) *Education Departments' Superhighways Initiative (EDSI): Synoptic Report*. The Open University, Milton Keynes

Selwood I (1996) Information technology to record and monitor school attendance in education. In: The Second IFIP International Working Conference – Conference Proceedings. IFIP and HKBU, Hong Kong

Selwood ID (2005) Primary school teachers' use of ICT for administration and management. In: Tatnull A, Visscher A, Osario J (eds) *Information Technology and Educational Management in the Knowledge Society*. Springer, New York

Selwood ID, Drenoyianni H (1997) Administration, management and IT in education. In: Fung A, Visscher A, Barta B, Teather D (eds) *Information Technology in Educational Management for the Schools of the Future*. Chapman and Hall for IFIP, London.

Selwood I, Pilkington R (2005) Teacher workload: using ICT to release time to teach. *Educational Review* 5(2):162–174

Selwood I, Smith D, Wishart J (2001) Supporting UK teachers through the national grid for learning. In: Nolan CJP, Fung ACW, Brown MA (eds) *Pathways to Institutional Improvement with Information Technology in Educational Management*. Kluwer for IFIP, London

Simon HA (1993) Decision making: rational, non-rational, and irrational. *Educational Administration Quarterly* 29:392–411

Stevenson Committee (1997) *Information and Communications Technology in UK Schools – An Independent Enquiry (The Stevenson Report)*. Pearson, London. Rubble.ultralab.anglia.ac.uk/stevenson/contents.html

Taylor L (2000) Magic Markbook. TES Online. March 10, 2000, p 31

Thierauf J (1987) *Effective Management Information Systems* (second edition). Merrill, Ohio

Trilling B, Hood P (1999) Learning, technology, and educational reform in the knowledge age or "we're wired, webbed, and windowed, now what?" *Educational Technology* May–June:5–18

Visscher AJ (1992) Design and evaluation of a computer-assisted management information system for secondary schools, PhD dissertation. Department of Educational Science and Technology, University of Twente, Enschede

Visscher AJ (1996) Information technology in educational management as an emerging discipline. *International Journal of Educational Research* 25:291–296

Visscher A (2001) Computer-assisted school information systems: the concepts, intended benefits, and stages off development. In: Visscher A, Wild P, Fung A (eds) *Information Technology in Educational Management: Synthesis of Experience, Research and Future Perspectives on Computer-Assisted School Information Systems*. Kluwer, London

Visscher AJ, Bloemen PPM (1999) Evaluation and use of computer-assisted management information systems in Dutch schools. *Journal of Research on Computing in Education* 32:172–188

Visscher AJ, Branderhorst M (2001) How should school managers be traincd for managerial school information system usage? In: Nolan CJP, Fung ACW, Brown MA (eds) *Pathways to Institutional Improvement with Information Technology in Educational Management*. Kluwer, London

Visscher AJ, Coe R (2002) *School Improvement Through Performance Feedback*. Swets and Zeitlinger Publishers, Lisse/Tokyo

Visscher AJ, Spuck DW (1991) Computer-assisted school administration and management: the state of the art in seven nations. *Journal of Research on Computing in Education* 24:146–168

Visscher AJ, Fung A, Wild P (1999) The evaluation of the large scale implementation of a computer-assisted management information system in Hong Kong schools. *Studies in Educational Evaluation* 25:11–31

Vlug KFM (1997) Because every pupil counts: the success of the pupil monitoring system in The Netherlands. *Education and Information Technologies* 2:287–306

Wild P, Walker J (2001) The commercially developed SIMS from a humble beginning. In: Visscher A, Wild P, Fung A (eds) *Information Technology in Educational Management: Synthesis of Experience, Research and Future Perspectives on Computer-Assisted School Information Systems*. Kluwer, London

Chapter 13
School Autonomy and Financial Manoeuvrability: French Principals' Strategies

Yves Dutercq

Centre de recherche en éducation de Nantes, University of Nantes, Nantes, France

13.1. The Autonomy of French Public Schools from a Sociological Perspective

To avoid any possibility of misinterpreting this study, I would like to make clear that it is not intended to be the contribution of a financial analyst, but rather that of a sociologist whose findings are based on studies of how effectively French public schools are run, particularly in the context of their autonomy.

I would also like to specify that I have limited my study to public schools. The endowment of these institutions is provided almost exclusively by funds that are specifically intended for their use by their two supervisory agencies: the national ministry of education and the appropriate regional authority. I have excluded the case of private Catholic institutions, who receive the vast majority of the 20% of students who do not attend public schools, because the financial situation of these schools is quite different: their basic operational expenses are provided by the state and regional public authority just as they are for public institutions, but they also receive significant monies directly from families in the form of tuition.

In this paper I intend to outline the margins of manoeuvrability offered to the management teams of these institutions by the relative autonomy accorded to secondary schools (French *lycées* and *colleges*, i.e. high schools and middle schools) by various institutional texts since the early 1980s. Many principals feel that the autonomy they benefit from should be directed towards managing the restrictions imposed upon their activity. Some, however, meet with more success than others at this task and achieve a certain latitude of choice, at the financial level among others, for the benefit of their school. I shall attempt to demonstrate the current state of affairs before speculating about the future of this topic.

13.2. Autonomy and the Management of French Schools

The management of education systems like the French model that are basically publicly funded is divided into several different levels of a hierarchical organization. This distribution of power at different levels varies from one country to another, but the institution is always in an intermediate position between the system that is responsible for setting and regulating educational norms and the actual place where these norms are affected, in other words, the classroom (Simon 2004).

In its most limited function, the school may be only a cog in the machinery responsible for enforcing orders and instructions, but it can also have full power to decide how its resources are to be used. This is largely the case in the United States and Great Britain who have adopted the principle of school-based management (Leithwood and Menzies 1998).

The French system may be divided into three main levels. The decision-making power at each level is unequally distributed among the three divisions (Paul 1999):

- The central level (or "*la Centrale*"): due to the centralizing tradition of French administration, especially in the field of education, most power is weighted at this level where national education politics are enacted and operational guidelines for education system, including goals, programmes, or the allocation of resources (the focus of our interest here), are set. Most staff members are civil servants at the state level, recruited and assigned by the *Centrale*, despite the recent appearance of certain changes, like regionalizing technical staff or workers and managing teachers' appointments at the local rectorial level.
- Regional or intermediate levels: since the 1980s, the phenomenon of deconcentralization has conferred broader powers at this level. In the context of shared competencies, regional organizations have created, maintained, and continue to participate in the operation of schools (decentralization), while the local levels of national administration manage a portion of the staff and allocate resources (deconcentration).
- Schools: we must first distinguish between the different types of schools. At the primary school level, there is still relatively little autonomy, and their principal is only a figurehead who serves to

instigate policy. He/she is a local administrator, appointed by the national ministry of education, responsible for the pedagogical management of a school district that comprises several schools; their physical management is the responsibility of the municipality. Secondary schools (*collèges* and *lycées*) are primarily concerned with teaching; their teachers are minimally concerned with technical or economic considerations. This is certainly true at the college level and in *lycées* devoted to general education but is no longer the case for management teams.

Schools are the main area where the resources allocated to education are implemented. However, there is only a weak autonomy at this level when it comes to distributing these resources, since 80% of operational expenses go to fund salaries for staff. Regional authorities have also become landlords since the state transferred the facilities of these institutions to them in 1986.

On the primary school level, each school project addresses its cultural, sports, and extra-curricular activities, a fact which substantiates how much its freedom has been curtailed.

On the level of secondary education, schools have a budget and may rely on their own resources, thanks to operational subsidies granted by the state and regional authorities. Their total allocation of teaching hours leads in particular to choices that both depend on and affect the school's politics. As a consequence, the school's project may reflect ways of mobilizing resources that are relatively time-honoured and efficient. Recent reforms, however, regarding public financing have brought new demands (which we shall address later) to bear on these projects. As the case may be, we must now affirm that all these choices are forced by the significant impact of the overseeing authorities which is shared by state and regional organizations and the respective authorities of these two agencies; the same choices are also driven by the internal dilution of responsibilities that are shared by principals, a school council, and teachers, with all the ensuing tensions and conflicts of interest that one can imagine.

13.3. Towards the Conquest of Autonomy

School autonomy is at the centre of the debates on the reorganization of the French education system over the past 30 years (Pair 1998). The measures approved by vote during the 1980s led one to believe that this autonomy was in place: decentralizing education laws as well as the process that deconcentrated a centralized power down to different levels of regional administration succeeded in making room for extending the autonomy of secondary institutions. Some official decrees address this change directly, such as the creation of the local public institution of learning statute (EPLE in French) for these schools and the reinforcement of their school council's prerogatives, as well as the requirement that they present a school project. Other decisions led the same institutions more indirectly to make choices that sanctioned their differences, such as the aggregate allocation of teaching hours assigned to them.

This autonomy was soon recognized, however, as a mere enticement, since the margins of manoeuvrability made available to the institutions were apparently weak. In fact, what the schools had not been granted officially was the financial ability that would allow them real autonomy.

Consequently, when we met with elected members of the local political authority in charge of educational issues during a recent inquiry, we were told in no uncertain terms how weak the financial latitude of institutional directors actually was. Some of them began speaking as follows: "I think that their autonomy is limited. They make do with what they have been given, even if they have to defend and plead their request for any additional teaching or staff positions before the representative of national education…" or "They tell us that it would be a good idea for the regional political authority to become involved in this or that. We listen to them, and then we either investigate the problem or not, we move for or against it, but this is a way that some ideas take hold and allow us to move things forward" or else "Beside that, hmm, beside the *lycée*'s own solidarity fund [which accepts contributions from different sources for students who need financial aid], they have very little wiggle room."

At the same time, most of those interviewed put things into perspective as they went on, like this person: "They are given the means they need to run their institution, all that has to do with… Well, that being said, they really do have enough autonomy to do as they wish, and that's clear, because some do a better job than others, with the same means, so it's a management problem."

A management problem or a strategy problem? Insofar as the institutions' budgets are less and less pinpointed, if some principals do a better job than others, it is because they implement a deliberate strategy that is guided by priorities, which means that it is based on a specific project. Although they may have strong institutional power in dealings with their school council where they are appointed presidents, the financial decisions they are led to make must have been ratified by the council's authority. This presupposes that principals are able to convince their council members of the merit of the direction they have chosen to take.

As the upper echelons of the national education administration like to remind us, institutional autonomy does not signify the same autonomy for their principals, which leads these administrators to criticize those who tend to confuse the two.

13.4. The Impact of Decentralization

If institutional autonomy remains extremely weak, as we have just shown, economically speaking, this is the consequence and effect of decentralized, partnering operations on the attitudes and practices of management personnel. Of course, it is most important to note that this occurs despite numerous organizational changes brought about by decentralization. Management personnel tend to work more and more with partners outside the world of education and with agencies fortunate enough to have financial autonomy. This practice leads to evolving attitudes and occasionally to new ways of taking action (Dutercq 2000).

If it is not a matter of acquiring a financial autonomy that goes against the grain of official texts, one would expect principals to collect funds from different sources and no longer count on the generosity of only one lender. In any event, this is what all prospective financial backers from outside national education who represent organizations or businesses demand.

In the past, when a school had a developmental project, the process to be followed was bureaucratically laid out in advance: a request was made and presented through the appropriate hierarchical channels. This was a long and laborious process, requiring that the request be renewed often over a period of several years before it would have a chance of success. For instance, this was true whenever a new section, sequence, or elective course had to be opened. Today there is a new scenario, because of the growing number of prospective financial backers: not only must school board members call for support from different quarters, but these supporters do not have the same bureaucratic requirements vis-à-vis the requests that are submitted to them. A team must defend a specific project by developing an outstanding argument, demonstrating the importance of activating the project, proving the strength of its convictions, and delineating its requests for subsidies, even in a competitive context.

If a *lycée* would like to offer a new course as an elective, its headmaster must simultaneously make a request for the necessary teaching hours to the academic authorities, to his region for classroom space and any necessary equipment (or even to his town for complementary material aid), and in the case of professional vocational training, to appropriate companies in order to provide apprenticeships and job opportunities for his students and secure the donation of machinery, equipment, etc. One can easily imagine that all these different respondents do not speak the traditional administrative language of education, that negotiations by mutual agreement are more sought after than requests made by formal application, and that replies are faster and more direct: either "yes" or "no." As the applicant, the principal is expected to present his dossier on the project properly, indicating the diversity and complimentarity of the financial contributions he is seeking. This step permits him to play the competition between the different agencies being solicited. Sometimes it is necessary to obtain the support of only one agency for the others to follow suit. Ultimately this becomes a give-and-take process: each party, including the school, is expected to make a contribution to the extent of its abilities (which are recognized as limited), but partners outside national education always appreciate the effort made by someone who finds a way partially to fund his project out of his own pocket.

Here is the opinion of an elected official in a large city who was very critical of the national education administration's financial cowardice:

> National Education's real problem is not a problem with ideas or people but a problem of means. National education has few means available to it for carrying out independent projects beyond the tracks that are set by the ministry and the regional academic rectorship. As soon as there is a willingness to undertake projects autonomously, national education – whether it comes from the top or the ground level – always takes the same tack. They come before the organization and say "You have a great project – it's wonderful, but we have no money." National education never contributes a cent and we always have to make do with these non-cents. But in any joint project, each partner makes a contribution. That's the National education administration's real defence. And where does it come from? It comes from…it's no one's fault, it's the fault of the system, because local and intermediate education administrators and schools aren't given enough financial autonomy. Ultimately it's this negative image that does real damage to the work based on partnering.

This elected official is not targeting local authorities, principals and others, but rather the national education administration and its distrustful attitude towards money and anything that has to do with financial autonomy, especially if that autonomy means that schools would be able to seek their own funding. With the significant exception of the tax paid by businesses to professional and technological *lycées*, most initiatives that are submitted are disregarded or prohibited by the academic authorities. The only contributions that may legally be requested from parents are solicited on an optional basis and represent extremely small donations: the contribution to the social-educational centre, a kind of student union that manages extra-curricular activities, like after-school workshops, and extraordinary contributions as financial aid to students who need help, for instance, covering the expenses of their academic field trips and travel.

This last point, academic field trips and travel, deserves more attention as one of the most flagrant hypocrisies of the system. There are considerable differences from one institution to another: some schools have developed traditional exchanges with other schools in sometimes quite distant countries, like the United States, and annually offer a trip that is usually based on foreign language acquisition to their students. When these trips take place outside of class time, they are clearly not mandatory and are obviously intended for the élite of the student body. Of course some institutions do strive for a politics of fairness, which forces them to limit their offerings and do whatever they can to ensure that no financial obstacles prevents any student from participating in an activity along with his/her peers. However, there is a wide range of practices and some schools have staked their reputation on the breadth and vitality of their field trips and foreign language travel opportunities, with little or no regard for considerations of student equality. Also, the schools that attract a privileged segment of the public are most often the ones who maintain these programmes.

Thus the matter of principle that arises is the effectiveness of tuition-free education, which is recognized as a delicate subject in France.

13.5. Tuition-Free Education and Financial Autonomy

Let us return to the opinion developed by an elected official, vice president and chairman of the budget for a regional political authority:

> The ideal school principal is someone who could carve out his own financial autonomy for funding his projects. Knowing that he doesn't have much leeway in this area, I think he should carve out a margin of fiscal autonomy for himself from his budget. This could be extracted either from the institutional budget or by trying to sensitize students by showing them the cost of everything. Every action has its price, and if it is not supported by the students and the *lycée*, then it has to be supported by society and it would be a good idea to finance a portion of these projects through student participation, even symbolically say, by getting them interested in starting a kitty with the proceeds from bake sales or something like that.

So he suggests two ways of acquiring a margin of financial manoeuvrability at the school level: either by working with the budget that is allocated to him on a regulatory basis or by seeking his own funding. I would like to address the second point first, since we have already begun to see that he will encounter obvious problems at the institutional level.

The main problem from this point of view is the difference between public schools and private catholic schools (which contract with the state). Diversely from the catholic schools with which they compete in most areas, public schools cannot receive contributions from students or their parents, because they respect the principle of mandatory schooling that is free of charge. This principle extends to all primary and secondary schooling up to the leave-taking examination (*baccalauréat*).

One principal voiced his frustration with the arguments that are repeated every time a parental contribution has to be requested for one extracurricular activity or another as follows:

> We try to divide out the costs (across the board), but the problem is that everything costs, so we come up against the problem of the cost of transportation – an outing to a museum is a lot, we have a project on the Picasso show at the fine art museum in T., OK, that will cost 6–7€ per student. But when you have to go to battle with students' parents over free education, you have to argue with them every time in an ongoing and very repetitive way. Everyone has his or her standard and anticipated line, or else they say, "Well, we're not very much in favour of it, because we are for free schooling." And we reply that yes, school is still free, but this is an optional outing for those who want to go, everyone decides for themselves, right, so it has become a hollow debate by now and nothing is accomplished, but we can't spend our time asking for money...

Contrary to what happens in higher education, school is tuition-free at the first two levels of education in France. Families must still pay for school supplies, often at exaggerated prices. Especially in the past few years, a family's investment in education has grown significantly as educational support from the private sector has become inflated. This inflation undoubtedly corresponds to a certain expectation and parents' uncertainties about the quality of public education. It is also the direct consequence of recent fiscal prerogatives which are very favourable to this arrangement, since they allow parents who receive educational support to subtract half of the amount as a deduction from their tax return.

Because of the extension of this new expenditure in relation to school fees, some school principals adamantly insist that the principle of free education is constantly being chipped away, affirming that it would be more fair and advantageous to ask parents for a direct contribution that could be adjusted according to their financial status. This type of contribution would give each school the financial manoeuvrability we are looking at here. Others suggest voluntary contributions that would come from the profit taken from selling specific products, like snacks and drinks, following the model suggested by the elected official we cited above. Although there is no legal possibility of imposing a mandatory contribution on families, instances of profit seeking from sales have been recorded, but these are minimal and relatively insignificant.

Ultimately, principals can create a relative financial autonomy for themselves by working with their regular budget and certainly may make deliberate choices by sacrificing one budget heading in favour of another.

13.6. The Strategic Use of Resources

The leeway allowed by the total allocation of teaching hours that was decided over 20 years ago remains a topic of interest, although this is more a general matter of resources than a specific money matter. Under this arrangement, the larger the student body, the broader the span of teaching hours an institution receives. These hours may also vary depending on the school's scholastic performance level. On this basis, management teams may choose to inflate the number of elective courses which consume large quantities of hours since these options usually concern only small numbers of students, or else they may limit the electives offered as much as possible in order to concentrate on basic subjects. They may prefer to create classes with a balanced student population or else vary their numbers from one class to another or even reduce the number of students in classes at the most critical levels (for instance, the entry-level class for the *collège* or the *lycée*) to the detriment of other levels. These choices are rarely radical and more likely than not are the results of compromises that have been made, to the extent that some observers consider that principals are not capable of taking advantage of the potential autonomy that is being offered to institutions.

If they did so, principals could risk a confrontation either with their school council or with some of their teachers. The principal of a college where I was able to conduct a study in the mid-1990s did not hesitate to take such action. This case is so instructive that I would now like to present it in greater detail.

Mr L. was the long-time director of a difficult middle school (*collège*) located on the outskirts of a large city. With the support of part of his staff, he made his mark at the school by implementing an original project that was both pedagogically and functionally innovative. Basing his actions on the premise that entering *collège* is the most critical time for young students, Mr L. readily concentrated his efforts at this level: class sizes were highly reduced, which obviously made other levels overcrowded, but most of all, Mr L. deliberately eliminated certain otherwise mandatory classes, music education, art, and technology, in order to free up one afternoon per week in everyone's schedule that would be devoted to reading workshops. During these workshops, each volunteer staff member, teacher, technician, and administrator would depart from his/her customary role and lead a group of students through an original reading workshop experience where a text would be discussed, with multiple cultural and social goals. As a counterpart to the workshops, one or two light weeks at the end of the year were completely devoted to one of the classes that had been dropped. Students were allowed to choose the class which was designed as an activity focused on a specific project.

Mr L. also called upon the student of a business school in the neighbourhood and asked them to offer voluntary educational support to his college students. This activity, completely managed by a student association at the school, met with great success and allowed an incomparable variety of supervised studies and ancillary classes to be offered at no cost to the school or families.

Finally, Mr L. was a skilled communicator (not the least of his professional attributes) who knew how to publicize the initiatives being developed at his college. They were covered in the local and regional press, and Mr L. became the darling of elected officials. Consequently, he had no trouble finding additional subsidies, when he needed them, for realizing specific projects: businesses and organizations were always willing to lend a hand to finance educational activities, furnish equipment, or carry out any necessary labour or installations. It goes without saying that Mr L. was often "called on the carpet" by his academic authorities; he became the object of his colleagues' jealousy and was talked about behind his back by some of his teachers. But since he also received the support of parents, the media, and local public figures, he had little to fear. It should come as no surprise that his project did not outlive his departure to a new school after serving 13 years as a principal at his school.

13.7. Opportunities Generated by the Competition Between Two Supervisory Authorities

As we have seen, when Mr L. was challenged by representatives of the academic administration, he was able to rely on the support of his contacts at the regional supervisory authority. In the absence of any effective autonomy, school boards were quick to reap the maximum benefit that could be gleaned from financial supervision that was split between the deconcentrated agency of the national school administration and a regional political authority. The school is effectively situated at the crossroads of various networks that may provide educational public action: the national education network, the network of other administrations who participate in the action (for instance, the youth and health administrations), the network of various associations, the economic network, and certainly the regional political network (Dutercq 2005). Their position as an interface and necessary cross-over point (i.e. "obligatory passage point", according to Michel Callon 1986) for the two major authorities gives school boards unrivalled strategic power: the administrative agency and the political agency do not necessarily have bad relationship with each other, but they have shown a deficit or been a source of misunderstandings for a long while. The national education administration has been slow in adapting its work habits to the more direct and less bureaucratic work mode of the regional authorities.

In this fashion, the tensions or at least the misunderstandings between the two overseers have allowed skilful principals to play on this rivalry to increase their own autonomy and eventually their resources. As we have seen above, in the case of the hope of offering a new elective course at a *lycée,* a strategic approach was able to take advantage of the bureaucratic and hierarchical process. This approach concerns not only principals but affects administrative representatives who must keep track of new procedures if they do not want to find themselves outdone by partners who are accustomed to building balances of power and negotiating systematically. In most processes, the academic authorities have a few decisive advantages: the have uncontested legitimacy in matters of educational politics, and there is no getting around them at any procedural point. Unlike events in the 1990s, when regional authorities were in the vanguard of innovative procedures and believed they had unlimited spending power, while the representatives of national education were not yet used to working as a network (to the point of losing their credibility), the observation of what regional educational politics are able to accomplish reveals that academic authorities do know how to avail themselves of their expertise and willingly put themselves in the position of arbitrating local politics. The regional authorities sometimes find themselves called on the carpet, because of the discrepancy between the expectations they create versus the increasing difficulty schools have in working within their allocated education budgets. For instance, this is true in the case of the projected renovation of classrooms: a priority order must be issued and long-range planning put in place, but this means that some schools and those who use them – students and parents – are forced to express their dissatisfaction and wait several years before what they once perceived as an urgent need is actually met.

As for principals, they often take advantage of their position as an interface between the supply of education (in the broadest sense) – whose main purveyors are the national school board and the regional authorities – and the demands of families and students with whom they are in direct contact. When they want to press hard on a decision regarding financing, they can rely for support on the potential power of the request, to the point where some of them do not hesitate to threaten their oversight agencies with setting "their" parents on them if they are not given satisfaction!

13.8. Developing Contractual Arrangements

Since 2000, the education administration has adapted to its managerial role so successfully that it encourages a project-based approach and contractualization as preferred ways of doing business with schools and their boards.

Following a decision agreed upon by principals to re-evaluate their duties via their main union and the ministry of national education, any recently appointed principal would be expected to do a diagnostic study of his school in the first months of his appointment as a sort of general inspection that would be informed by a set of statistical data; a regional representative of the national education ministry would assist him in this task. The study would be confirmed by the academic rector, the highest authority of the national education administration at the decentralized level, and represents the starting point for the review of the new principal's decisions and actions. In phase two, after a certain amount of joint discussion and certainly with a view to the original diagnostic study, the new principal would receive a set of goals to be achieved in the context of a mission statement from the rector. The mission statement obviously represents a contract between the principal and his administrative superiors that forms both the basis of the review of his performance and will be decisive in the advancement of his career. For this reason, a school board member's career will be determined less and less from now on by academic degrees awarded before hiring, but it will be affected by their success in relation to the mission and goals that are set for them annually. This change of direction should logically motivate them to strive for outstanding performance or effectiveness, performative aspects that will be evaluated especially in terms of the best use of their allocated resources.

In so doing, they would no longer be subjected to an a priori controlled environment, whose basic criterion was the conformity to pre-existing rules. To this extent, priority would be given to actual results, in the spirit of an evaluation a posteriori. The autonomous management of the human and material resources available to them would then become much more significant, opening the way to the implementation of local priorities and strategic choices. The creative use of all their resources, including funding, is a key element here. Such a manoeuvre not only would certainly bring us to the outer limits of the institutional loyalty principals take so much pride in, but it also emphasizes the obvious and fundamental contradictions involved in running a school where old and new regulations co-exist on a regular basis (Dutercq and Lang 2002). The autonomy granted to schools is extremely limited and cannot be exercised in all areas: teaching programmes are nationalized, principals have no choice in recruiting their teaching staff (even if they do currently recruit their student supervision staff, budget allotments are almost completely consumed by unavoidable responsibilities, and the principal himself, according to rules and regulations, has only slight autonomy to take action). On the other hand, the evaluation of these same principals is based less and less on their respect for rules and their use of allocations, in favour of evaluating their ability to take action vis-à-vis their own school's mission and reap the greatest benefit from their allocated resources. In this sense, those who receive the best reviews make the distinction between old and new parameters of evaluation, which implies varying interpretations of the same official directives and different uses of the same resources.

The report of the commission presided over by Claude Thélot that was released in 2004 contains, among other suggestions, clear proposals in favour of increasing principals' power. For instance, it suggests setting up a more important steering committee, including representatives from each teaching level, and increasing the differences in the allotment of teaching hours (with a margin of up to 25% of these hours for schools of similar size and more freedom in the use of a portion of this allotment). The law on the future of the school (the Fillon law of March 2005), which is based on the conclusions of the Thélot report, was largely indifferent to the findings of the report; the only suggestion it upheld concerning the autonomy of the schools and increasing principals' responsibilities was that a pedagogical council be set up at each school, but any real result of this recommendation remains to be seen.

In the past few years there has been a clear trend towards personalizing or "tailoring" a principal's duties that marks a radical break with the old model that valued conformity to "good practice" as defined by official documents, programmes, and professional background above all else. The protocol signed with principals' representatives and the ensuing documents culminate the establishment of a regulatory mode inspired by management practices that encourages the expectation of results, a process that rationalizes professional activity on a technical level, and professional assessment.

Moreover, in 2001 the "organic law concerning financial laws" (referred to as the LOLF in French: the "loi organique relative aux lois de finances") changed the way it dealt with the management of public monies by giving preference to those who strive for outstanding performance. This means that administrators must define goals, assign proportionate means of accomplishing them, and evaluate the effectiveness of the action taken to fulfil these goals. In general, we could point to the greater role given to academic rectors in the context of the LOLF: in the field of education, it is the rectors who are responsible for the operations budgets for school programmes. Each school proposes an annual project based on its performance that combines national goals and regional specifications. In this sense, the rectors are the ones who call the shots when it comes to managing funds related to all scholastic education. On the other side of the fence, the school boards who receive these funds are severely limited in their discretion for using them, because the funds are earmarked at the academic level. In yet another way, it is easy to understand that the necessary link between national and local priorities forces principals to ensure that their school's project respects this connection. Moreover, the evaluation of the effectiveness of academic politics takes place at the level of the schools themselves, so much so that principals find themselves shouldered with heavy responsibilities that force them to be more attentive to the cost of decisions made at the local level, including pedagogical ones (Pouliquen 2005). This motivation to take into account the cost effectiveness of pedagogical decisions, such as the choice of elective classes or suggestions for student counselling (especially in the case of repeating a grade), is a completely new feature in the French educational system.

13.9. In Favour of a Controlled Autonomy

As we have seen, recent reforms enacted in France are less likely to support the emergence of local politics than to grant a school autonomy that would enable the enactment of national policy in a localized setting. We might qualify the French process as one of "delegation," the term used by Mark Bray in his critical vocabulary (2003). It is both the ambiguity and the goals of school autonomy that largely encourage principals' propensity to consider themselves autonomous.

This autonomy and its inherent responsibilities are certainly one of these principals' main professional interests: these officials realize that as a matter of fact – and contingent upon notifying their hierarchical authorities and conforming to regulations – they often do take action as they see fit and are encouraged on the whole to take the initiative. The LOLF has only served to emphasize this phenomenon. Consequently, hierarchical channels encourage this autonomy in an interaction that deconcentrates decision-making. As a result, the academic rectorate may perceive a certain degree of autonomy in how principals manage the financial means at their disposal, or even their human resources. Oppositely, regional representatives of national education deplore this blurring of the meaning of delegation. Their position as intermediaries explain this critique of the autonomy that some principals permit themselves to exercise: although regional inspectors are links in the hierarchical chain, principals, who are at the end of the same chain, handle the autonomy they need in order to act upon the directives handed down to them much more easily. As one headmaster of a *lycée* unabashedly confirmed:

> I have never felt insufficiently autonomous. If I lack autonomy, it's usually my fault. Early in my career, I would always ask permission from the regional representative of national education, but now *I* inform *him*. There's an important nuance here. But if I'm open about the autonomy, I had better not fall short. I hadn't realized before that by asking his permission, I could possibly be putting him in a compromising position. He could be tempted to say no. But if I simply inform him of something irreprehensible I've done by taking advantage of my leeway, it's OK.

Principals often conceive of autonomy as the equivalent of access to adequate resources, ones that are more plentiful and varied than the resources allocated on a standard basis. These new resources give them greater latitude in internal management and in managing their school, and also authorize them to take on local projects and try out new ideas. Even if more often than not financial autonomy corresponds more to managing restrictions than to a wealth of resources, it is important to note that this autonomy also has an educational and a pedagogical dimension.

Of course, schools still receive only a very limited autonomy. However, principals are evaluated less and less on how well they observe administrative rules and regulations and apply their allocations in favour of validating their ability to take action on their own projects and reap the greatest benefit from their allocated resources, however this may be accomplished.

Recent changes, especially in regard to the LOLF, give precedence to those who strive for outstanding performance and take into account, at the institutional level, the cost effectiveness of pedagogical decisions. Although these changes make their job more complex, French principals are universally in favour of them, since they are the flip side of a new autonomy – responsibility that is a badge of their credibility, both within the schools and beyond.

References

Bray M (2003) Control of education. Issues and tensions in centralization and decentralization. In: Armove R, Torres CA (eds) *Comparative Education. The Dialectic of the Global and the Local* (second edition). Rowman and Littlefield Publishers, Lanham, pp 204–228

Callon M (1986) Elements of a sociology of translation: domestication of the scallops and the fishermen of St Brieuc Bay. In: Law J (ed.) *Power, Action and Belief: A New Sociology of Knowledge?* Routledge, London, pp 196–233

Dutercq Y (2000) *Politiques éducatives et évaluation. Querelles de territoires.* PUF, Paris

Dutercq Y (2005) (ed.) *Les régulations des politiques d'éducation.* PUR, Rennes

Dutercq Y, Lang V (2002) L'émergence d'un espace de régulation intermédiaire dans le système scolaire français, Education et sociétés. *Revue Internationale de Sociologie de l'éducation* 8:49–64

Leithwood K, Menzies T (1998) Forms and effects of school-based management: a review. *Educational Policy* 12:325–347

Pair C (1998) *Faut-il réorganiser l'éducation nationale?* Hachette-éducation, Paris

Paul JJ (1999) (ed.) *Administrer, gérer, évaluer les systèmes éducatifs.* ESF, Paris

Pouliquen B (2005) La mise en œuvre de la LOLF. *Education et Management* 28:40–42

Rapport de la commission du débat national sur l'avenir de l'école présidée par Thélot C (2004) *Pour la réussite de tous les élèves.* La documentation française, CNDP, Paris

Simon J (2004) *Organisation et gestion de l'éducation nationale.* Berger-Levrault, Paris

Chapter 14
Finnish Strategy for High-Level Education for All

Reijo Laukkanen

Finnish National Board of Education, Helsinki, Finland

14.1. Introduction

Since the PISA surveys, the world has not been the same as it was. Decision-makers now have benchmarks for international competition in terms of the quality and performance of their educational systems. We have seen evidence and opinions that are external to our national jurisdictions. John Pratt has been a member of three international evaluation teams looking at polytechnic policy in Finland and he identifies five different areas that international evaluators may discuss. Evaluators may talk about: what you want to hear; what you don't want to hear; what you wish that you could say, but cannot or dare not; things that you don't know. They can also raise questions that you didn't know that you needed to ask (Pratt 2004:87–88). I am sure that when they see the PISA survey results, governments can see all these options. Some results were flattering, some came in time to facilitate change, some may have led to bad publicity (though hopefully not) and some came as big surprises.

The Finnish education system has received plenty of attention from all over the world because it came out on top in the first two PISA surveys. Finnish 15 year olds are number one in terms of skills in mathematics, scientific knowledge, reading literature and problem-solving (OECD 2001, 2004a). During the two and a half year period, approximately 15,000 people from German-speaking countries visited the Finnish National Board of Education or were present when Finnish lecturers visited those countries (Isotalo 2004). The Economist (2006) wrote that EU leaders should forget multiple priority areas and activity plans. Instead, "European governments should go back to school. In Finland." (The Economist 2006). Hundreds of newspaper articles about the Finnish education system have been published outside Finland. Recently, a book entitled "Zakaj Finci Letito dlje?" (Why do Finns Fly Further?) was published in Slovenia (Gaber et al. 2006). Such a high level of interest in the Finnish education system is a sign that confidence in PISA is high.

That confidence can be seen clearly and resulted in policy changes in some countries. Denmark, for example, spends more on education than most OECD countries, but the first PISA survey (OECD 2001) revealed that Danish results have been poor in proportion to the high level of spending. Denmark therefore asked the OECD (2004b) to carry out a special review of basic education in Denmark. I was involved in the review. The result was that the Danish Government took our recommendations concerning raising educational standards, creating an evaluation culture, etc. very seriously and is now aiming to make major changes.

Trust in PISA makes us think about two important methodological issues. The first one concerns the reliability of the PISA surveys. It is easy to say that there is high confidence in the reliability of results, because two consecutive surveys have ranked participating countries in a fairly similar order with just a few exceptions. Another issue concerns the validity of the contents of the tests. PISA assesses young people's capacity to use their knowledge and skills in order to meet real-life challenges, rather than merely looking to see how well they have mastered a specific school curriculum (OECD 2004a). Students have to understand key concepts, master certain processes and apply knowledge and skills in different authentic situations (OECD 2004a).

The tests used have been prepared as part of a consensus by international expert groups. That approach has also been challenged. The point is that PISA is not based on comparative analysis of curricula. Reijo Raivola (2006:19) cites a PISA critic from Hungary, who pointed out that Hungary performed well in IEA surveys unlike Finland, but the PISA survey brought the opposite results for these countries. He continues to cite the critique saying that the IEA approach is pedagogical and curricular while the PISA approach is political. As PISA results have been taken seriously across the world and as many countries try to develop their curricula in order to fit in the "framework" of PISA better, one possible impact is approaching a "world curriculum", says Reijo Raivola. He does not criticise PISA as such, but shows that it is not easy to explain the reasons for Finland's success, because PISA has not measured issues according to curriculum objectives.

As Reijo Raivola (2006) points out, one of the problems of surveys like PISA is that the unit of measurement is the individual student but national systems are the unit of analysis. Consequently, it is not possible to understand the educational performance of a system without understanding its social, cultural, institutional or historical context.

In the light of PISA success, it might look strange that, according to Hannu Simola (2005), Finnish teachers are politically and pedagogically rather conservative. That paradox is interesting. He says that "the Finnish 'miracle of PISA' no longer appears to be a miracle. To put it simply, it is still possible to teach in the traditional way in Finland because teachers believe in their traditional role and pupils accept their traditional position." (2005:465). Another issue that he mentions when explaining the success is that Finns have an authoritarian, obedient and collectivist mentality. Reijo Raivola's (2006) view is that one determinant of good success in reading literature surveys stems from the fact that the Finnish language is extremely phonemic in spelling.

Many scholars like Jouni Välijärvi (2004) also describe characteristics of the Finnish education system, saying that Finland's good results are largely a result of its education policies. It is interesting to note that PISA success has also been a "somewhat puzzling experience to all stakeholders in education in Finland" because "Finns are used to think that models for educational reform have to be brought from abroad" (2004:31). I would like to add to this by saying that PISA success has put Finnish decision-makers, researchers and teachers in a situation where they try to find explanations for such outstanding performance.

In this paper, I will show that a success story in education needs a long-term strategy that is followed up over time. In Finland, the most important objectives have been to enhance the equity and quality of education. This has meant that the aim has been to arrange high-level education for all. The policy actions taken have been incremental with the aim to get closer to the dream of high-level and equal performance as time goes by. Furthermore, I will highlight some education policy issues where Finnish experiences could be learned from.

Finland has built up an education system with characteristics made up of uniformity – free education, free school meals and special needs education – by using the principle of inclusion. Finnish basic education has been logically developed towards the comprehensive model, which guarantees everybody equal opportunities in education irrespective of sex, social status, ethnic group, etc. as outlined in the constitution. The focus has been on equity. In explaining all this, I will start with a very brief overview of the history of development of equal opportunities. It will illustrate Finnish thinking and will show that there have also been turbulent years as the Government has strived to reach the level that Finland is at today.

14.2. Via Unified Structure to Local Liberties[1]

14.2.1. Same Education for All

In 1968, it was decided that the parallel school system should be replaced by national 9-year basic education that would represent the ideology of comprehensive education.[2] As the government delivered its bill to Parliament in 1967, one of the arguments for the common 9-year education for all was that it was too early to judge individual capacities at the age of 11 or 12. They talked about losing the reserve of human resources that Finland would badly need in order to bring industry up-to-date. At that time, Finland was a poor country. At that time, decision-makers also had to deal with more and more private grammar schools being founded, because the state-run and municipal-run ones could not fulfil all the demand. Parents were voting with their feet. At the same time, there was an increase in ideology demanding equal education for all children: boys and girls, rich and poor, slow learners and fast learners (Hallituksen esitys 1967).

The legislation passed can be described as being framework legislation.[3] It laid the most important cornerstones of the new education system but left plenty of freedom for the Ministry of Education and the National Board of General Education[4] to confirm many of the details. That was justified by the fact that there was no advance knowledge of what kind of problems might need to be solved during the implementation phase. Legislation set a very clear target for the national administration stating that basic education should be developed to meet the criteria of comprehensive education.[5] This formulation is important. It was demanded that development should

---

[1] For extensive descriptions and analysis, see for example Lampinen (1998), Lehtisalo and Raivola (2000), Aho et al. (2006).

[2] Laki koulujärjestelmän perusteista (1968).

[3] See note 2.

[4] See note 8.

[5] In order to develop, a new unit for research and development (Research and Development Bureau) was founded by the National Board of General Education in 1969. That unit was in a strategic position, because it was responsible for planning, steering and reporting of pilot projects. According to the legislation, it was possible to deviate from legislation and national rules at that time with the permission of the Ministry of Education. For example, solutions for getting rid of streaming and introducing school-based liberties when forming teaching groups flexibly were piloted for a long time. I myself joined that office in 1974 and was responsible for several basic education pilot projects up to the beginning of the 1990s.

lead to ideals and it was not made clear that the ideal had already become clear in practical terms. Parliament and the government saw that there was still a way ahead to the ideal.

Implementation of the new basic education system was carried out in stages between 1972 and 1977, starting in the northern part of Finland and finishing in the southern part of the country.[6] It was the end of the parallel education system that labelled students as being "talented" or "untalented" after only 4 or 5 years at elementary school. That meant an increase in educational optimism.

Responsibility for basic education was given exclusively to the municipalities. The grammar schools that had been privately run until then were incorporated into municipal education systems. Only a few special needs schools for severely handicapped children and university teacher training schools remained under state control.

Schools had to follow the very detailed, nationally authorised curriculum including 700 pages in very small font meticulously. Ability grouping was introduced in teaching of mathematics and foreign languages at lower secondary level. That was a compromise so that the new education system would be acceptable for various parties. However, the national committee that had prepared the national curriculum for basic education stated that the government should find a way to get rid of such streaming (Komiteanmietintö 1970:139). The lowest ability group curriculum did not offer general eligibility for upper secondary general education.

School teaching was inspected by the state's school inspectorates that were founded in all counties. Each school had to be inspected at least once every 5 years. Furthermore, all schools had to submit their very detailed yearly school plans for approval by the inspectorate. That was natural and important because state funding for municipalities was based on the real costs of the schools. School books were inspected in advance by the National Board of General Education.[7]

14.2.2. Decentralisation of Decision-Making

Since the 1985–1986 academic year and after lengthy political debate and pilot projects lasting many years, the ability group system (streaming) at lower secondary education level was abolished and eligibility for further

---

[6] The curriculum of basic education was applied in all municipalities at all grades by the beginning of the 1981–1982 academic year at the latest (Hallituksen esitys n:o 30 – 1982 vp., see in Koululait 1983:17).

[7] See note 8.

studies became open to everyone (Koululait 1983). The legislation changes at the same time provided extra resources for schools at lower secondary level guaranteeing fairly small teaching groups for the whole age group. Schools were given freedom for flexible grouping of pupils and further freedom in terms of how to use resources. All rules about sizes of teaching groups were removed from legislation. That was a natural consequence of a given total frame of resources.

You could say that 1985 was a culmination point in the search for a more equal education system but also in terms of decentralisation. The status of the then new national curricular guidelines was to create a framework for curriculum design in municipalities (Kouluhallitus 1985). Municipalities did not have much room to deviate from the national mainstream, but that was an important step towards broader local liberties. Before that change, the curriculum had been the same in all municipalities. At the end of 1980s, municipalities were also given more and more opportunities to decide how to organise their own administration of education.

Ten years later, in 1994, a significant change came about in order to reduce the role of central administration in deciding the contents and aims of teaching (National Board of Education 1994). The National Board of Education[8] only gave very broad aims and contents for teaching different subjects. The municipalities and, ultimately, the schools set up their own curricula on the basis of the national core curriculum. As part of these plans, local needs could be taken into consideration and special characteristics of schools could be taken into account.

At the beginning of the 1990s, the system of national preinspection of textbooks was discontinued. By the beginning of the 1990s, the system of state-run school inspections had also been discontinued. The same applied to the state inspectorates' approval of schools' annual plans. As a result of strong decentralisation, those institutions were no longer needed.

Systematic national evaluation of learning results began. The first reports were published in 1995. These evaluations were (and still are) used for development purposes. The Finnish basic education system does not have any high-stakes external tests, nor does it have any final examination run external to the schools in basic education.

---

[8] The National Board of Education was formed in 1991 from two former Boards, the National Board of General Education (founded in 1869) and the National Board of Vocational Education (founded in 1966). The National Board of Education is a central administration educational agency reporting to the Ministry of Education. Since 2004, it has been known as the Finnish National Board of Education.

In Finland, school administrators really do cooperate with teachers and their union and associations. That openness has been applied to preparation of changes in the national core curricula (since the 1990s). As the latest national curriculum started to be drafted in 2000, a network of 500 schools from nearly 200 municipalities was formed that actively commented on draft versions of the new core curriculum. The core curriculum was drafted in several working groups of the National Board of Education representing municipalities, teachers, teacher educators, researchers, textbook publishing houses and people from different areas of society (Halinen 2005). Such open cooperation with schools and society has increased the sense of realism in national guidelines and has enhanced general ownership of the required changes.

In order to understand the big change that happened in the 1990s, it is advisable to know that the two successive ministers of education in the 1990s came from the National Coalition Party (liberal conservative) that was eager to remove the remaining burdens of state control. Development had already been heading in the direction of decentralisation, but this political change speeded up local liberties (Laukkanen 1998). Vilho Hirvi, then Director General of the National Board of Education, talked about the rhythm change in education. He argued that in the era of net economy and self-directing organisations, it was important to free the personal capacities of those working in the education system and to take these capacities to use in development of the quality of education. He said "[l]et us allow education to change more in line with the conditions of people, according to their skills and knowledge, than in line with the condition of the system" (Hirvi 1996:56).

The development history shows that strong central steering was needed to develop a uniform educational structure and that the government then loosened its grip in order to achieve better results. In this respect, it is easy to agree with Andreas Schleicher who wrote: "In the past, education systems could claim that they achieve equity when all schools are operating in the same way. Now equity must be assessed by the extent to which schools achieve equitable outcomes" (Schleicher 2006:14). He also points out that equal inputs to schools do not automatically lead to better outcomes. The development history of Finnish basic education clearly proves that.

During the years when the new education system was being implemented, many critics claimed that government rules would lead to a reduction in standards compared with those that were in place in grammar schools (Rinne and Vuorio-Lehti 1996). Those critical voices were very loud from the 1970s to the mid-1980s as the government tried to find ways to abandon streaming in teaching of foreign languages and mathematics. Streaming came to an end in 1985. This was because the choice of lower level courses led to significant differences in results between pupils, and this then set the scene for further studies in upper secondary education. The government wanted to make all options available to everyone up to tertiary education.

14.3. Some Preconditions for Good Performance

14.3.1. Resources for Those Who need them Most

As streaming was abandoned in the mid-1980s, the government was aware that the benefits of that change could not be reaped without increasing financial resources for lower secondary education.[9] If you assess the annual expenses per student in Finnish educational institutions, you will find that it is unique in terms of how the total amount of educational spending (including all education levels) is allocated between different levels of education. This is different from the situation in most countries. Figures detailing average expenditure on primary, lower secondary, upper secondary and tertiary education in OECD countries show that expenses increase evenly from one level to another. In Finland, expenses increase up until the end of basic education, followed by a decrease for upper secondary education and a further increase in tertiary education (Table 14.1).[10] Finland has wanted to focus resources on lower secondary education where there are the most problems.

Table 14.1. Annual expenditure on educational institutions per student in 2002, US $ (OECD 2005:172)[11]

Countries	Primary education	Lower secondary education	Upper secondary education	Tertiary education
Finland	5,087	8,197	6,455	7,332
United States	8,049	8,669	9,607	18,574
OECD average	5,313	6,089	7,121	7,299

---

[9] The increase in teaching resources for remedial education included from the beginning of the 1985–1986 academic year was 14.6%. It increased the amount of teachers at lower secondary level by around 1700. At the same time, resources in special needs education were increased (Koululait 1983:21, 23–24).

[10] The profiles of spending in Iceland, Italy and the Netherlands are similar to Finland (see OECD 2005).

[11] Tertiary education expenditure does not include R & D costs.

At the same time (1985), legislation was changed to include no more rules on minimum or maximum sizes of teaching groups. As a result of this change, schools received complete freedom to decide on how to form teaching groups. The prerequisite for that was to move to formula-based state funding in basic education instead of the criterion of real costs that had been used up until then (Koululait 1983).

14.3.2. High Standards and Support for Special Needs

The curricular changes resulting in the removal of streaming that were implemented in the mid-1980s meant that education standards were raised (Koululait 1983:15; Kouluhallitus 1985). All students in basic education began to have the same goals also in mathematics and foreign languages. In so doing, of course, the Finnish government was realistic. The reality is that such goals are reached by individuals with different levels of success. However, with extra support for the weakest students, we can considerably raise the performance of the whole age group.

Finland offers a significant amount of remedial education in schools.[12] Remedial education was broadened at the beginning of the 1970s. Finnish authorities have found it important for those with learning difficulties to receive special extra support. If you look at the OECD (2003:16–17) review comparing 12 countries, you will find that 19.7% of Finnish pupils receive extra support because of learning difficulties.[13] The median percentage in that international comparison was only around 6%. That difference does not suggest that Finnish people have more problems and that they have more learning difficulties than people in other countries. Instead, it explains the Finnish way of understanding equal opportunities. That is a democratic way of evening out differences in the social background of students and a way of increasing the overall educational performance of a country.

Remedial education is mostly provided for those with very normal learning difficulties, e.g. reading, writing and speech. Needs in those three difficult areas are met by teachers specialising in university programmes. Their help in those three issues concentrates on the first 2 years of primary education. It is important that those basic difficulties are taken care of at the very beginning of basic education, because these communication skills

---

[12] See Blom et al. (1996).

[13] The latest statistics show that 21.9% of students in basic education have received part-time special needs education between 1995 and 2004 (Statistics Finland 2006:35).

are fundamental for any further personal growth. A major review showed that the focus of remedial education from the third grade onwards is to take care of other learning difficulties, mostly in mathematics and foreign languages.[14] That support is given throughout basic education for those who need it.

14.3.3. Qualified Teachers

In order to cope with a heterogeneous teaching group, a teacher has to be a highly educated pedagogical expert. Finnish teachers are well acquainted not only with various teaching methods but also with educational research. That is one of the benefits of the fact that teacher education is carried out in university departments of teacher education within faculties of education. Pertti Kansanen explains this by arguing that "[t]he basic aim of every teacher education programme is to educate competent teachers and develop the necessary professional qualities to ensure lifelong teaching careers for teachers" (Kansanen 2003:89). This means that teachers must have a good basis for lifelong learning within their profession. Therefore, teacher education is research-based in Finland. "The aim of research-based teacher education is to impart the ability to make educational decisions based on rational argumentation in addition to everyday or intuitional argumentation" (Kansanen 2003:90).

Since 1974, teacher education for all teachers in basic education has been arranged at universities. Before 1974, primary school teachers were educated at teacher training colleges. In 1979, primary school teacher education was also upgraded to the level of a Master's degree. Competition for teacher education is really hard because only around 15% of applicants are accepted (Kansanen 2003:86–87). Thus, it is fair to say that teaching work is popular. Lately, we have seen that a career as a teacher in Finland is the most popular choice amongst those leaving upper secondary education. This was confirmed in a poll carried out by the biggest newspaper in Finland (Liiten 2004).

However, there are a few subjects that have ongoing problems attracting enough applicants for teacher education. These subjects are mathematics and physics. Another problem is the low application rate of men. Many male teachers also escape from the education sector to work in other sectors of society. That tells us about the high academic level of teacher education but the loss of competent teachers is a problem for the education sector (Kansanen 2003:87–88).

---

[14] Blom et al. (1996).

Why is the teaching profession so popular? Teachers' salaries in Finland are only at the average level in international comparisons, so this cannot be the explanation (OECD 2004c:390). My own guess is that the high popularity is the result of three things: (1) All Finnish teachers in basic education complete an academic Master's degree either in education or in one or two teaching subjects. Academic education is respected. If teachers' education was still based at colleges, it might not be so popular. (2) Finnish teachers enjoy significant autonomy in organising their work. Due to decentralisation, Finnish schools do have plenty of autonomy in terms of the organisation of instruction, personnel management, planning and structures and deciding on the use of resources. Teachers are fairly satisfied with their position (Simola 2005). That is not the case in many countries. (3) In Finland, education has been respected through its history. Thus, teachers have also enjoyed considerable respect.

14.3.4. Evaluation of Education[15]

From the point of view of the government, evaluation is one component in the whole structure of education policy. You could therefore say that evaluation policy is a method within the methodology of education policy. (Laukkanen 1998). As we define evaluation policy in such a way, it also implies that evaluation should support education policy choices. Some researchers have stated that evaluation can take back from the local level what decentralisation has given to it (Lundgren 1990). The Finnish government has tried to avoid that phenomenon. In Finnish national evaluation practice, it is respected that teachers are accountable to the municipalities, not to the state.

Since the mid-1990s, the Finnish National Board of Education has conducted national assessments of learning outcomes mostly in the ninth grade of basic education. Regular assessments have been carried out in mathematics, mother tongue (either Finnish or Swedish) and literature and occasionally in other subjects as well. National assessments produce information about the quality and results of education and training in relation to objectives stated in the national core curricula. Assessments are sample-based and thus do not cover the whole age group. This is because results are used for development of education. Recently, evaluations have also been started at the end of the second grade, for example. The purpose of this is to enhance the use of evaluation for formative purposes.

---

[15] Development of evaluation policy in Finland, see Laukkanen (1998).

All schools in a sample of an assessment receive an individual feedback report (see for example Lappalainen 2006:21; Mattila 2002). These reports are delivered to schools as soon as possible after assessment data has been collected, as fresh results are more interesting for schools than results that are months old. Recently, feedback has been received as quickly as 2 months after the data were collected.

Individual feedback reports present national profiles and the profiles of an individual sample school. In mathematics, for example, it shows how many points the whole sample received on average in numeracy, geometry, statistics, functions and algebra and the averages of those in an individual school. As you present results in this way, it is important and interesting to look at differences in performance between the whole sample and the sample of an individual school. If the average performance level in a school is lower than in the sample as a whole, it is obvious that the school should take a look in the mirror. That makes teachers think once again about what to demand of their students and how to teach better. That will gradually lead to the positive use of tests run from outside the school. Linda Darling-Hammond (2005) encourages the use of "tests worth teaching". The Finnish practice of individual feedback supports her opinion in a way.

National assessments also collect background data through enquiries sent to head teachers, teachers and students. Figure 14.1 compares the average correct answers with the latest school report marks that students got in the sample and at school "z".[16] The example is very revealing and the data could have been collected in any country. The figure shows that teachers at school "z" have on average given lower marks than teachers at other schools.

Similar findings have been attained over the years. They tell us that teachers are setting their teaching objectives (i.e. standards; performance levels expected of students) at different levels. Teachers at school "z" in our example set higher standards than teachers at other schools. School "z" is very demanding. The same problem is that there are schools that set their performance standards low. That finding has led to changes in the latest version of the national core curriculum.

The national evaluation reports by the Finnish National Board of Education never publish data municipality by municipality or school by school, but they scrutinise the performance of the whole sample. As a result, ranking lists

---

[16] The marking scale in Finnish schools is from 4 to 10, with 10 being the highest mark and a mark of 4 being a failure.

Line of marks

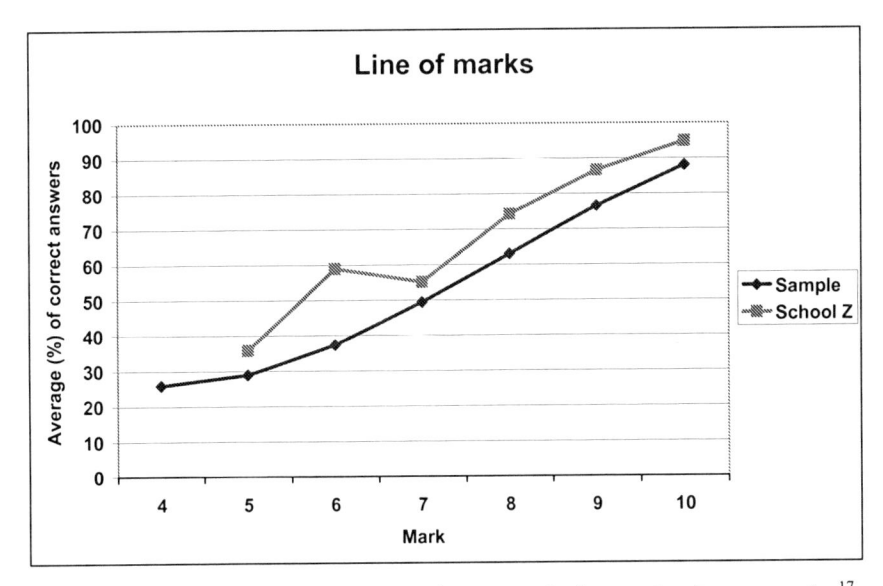

Fig. 14.1. Example of feedback for schools: test results/latest school report marks.[17]

are not published. Ranking lists would also not be fair, because schools participating in an assessment are randomly sampled. Use of them would also not respect the division of roles and powers between local and national levels. Schools are accountable to the local level (municipalities/parents) and not to the state. The Finnish thinking is also true in that publication of school- or municipality-specific test results and ranking lists produces more problems than benefits for individual schools.

These evaluations increase the level of information about education both for the purposes of national and local educational development. As a result, the authorities know where we stand, but Finland still faces the major challenge of ensuring that these evaluations have a real impact on everyday school practices.

14.3.5. Balancing Decentralism and Centralism

After implementation of the 1994 national framework curriculum, central steering of the education system was perhaps the lightest in the world. It is worth knowing that the 1994 national core curriculum only included some 110 pages (National Board of Education 1994). That was all that the cen-

---

[17] This is a fictional example. For more examples, see Mattila (2002: 144–150).

tral administration wanted to say about all subjects for the whole 9-year long basic education. The document outlined the general objectives of various subjects for the whole of basic education. For mathematics, for example, teaching the core curriculum only took up 3.5 pages and 6 pages for foreign languages.

In the latest change to the national core curriculum, implemented by the municipalities at the beginning of the 2006–2007 school year at the latest, steering is more detailed (Finnish National Board of Education 2004). The national document concerned contains around 320 pages. It devotes 9.5 pages to mathematics and 18.5 pages to foreign languages. A big change compared with earlier national guidelines is that educational objectives have been set not just for the whole 9 years of education, but for the second grade, sixth grade and the ninth grade, for instance. The cutting points (grades) for objectives in different subjects have been chosen differently. These objectives have been set in the form of criteria for good performance.

The reason for this change can be understood by looking at the points raised about "school z" (Figure 14.1). The variance in marking explains differences in standards setting. The national criteria of good performance have been set for school mark 8. The rationale for that is to calibrate teachers' setting of objectives at different stages of basic education. Another reason for the new approach is the fact that students use their final school reports in basic education when applying to upper secondary education institutions. Thus, the new rules also safeguard the equality of students.

Wilmad Kuiper and Jan van den Akker (2006), who have studied the move between centralisation and decentralisation in nine education systems, notice that Finland has taken a step backwards towards centralisation. By comparing curricular policies, their position is that the Finnish model describing good performance would produce more favourable expectations for increasing performance than setting attainment targets.

It is important to notice that Finnish PISA success was gained just at the time when education was nationally ruled by the very liberal curriculum guidelines of 1994. In the future, we will see if Finland manages to enhance educational performance and narrow the performance differences by the move towards centralisation that it has taken.

14.4. Important Policy Issues

A very basic issue in the political arena is to determine who should receive benefits. In education policy too, it is fundamental to have a clear understanding of what we mean by high-level education for all.

In basic education, there are two traditions. The first one represents the parallel education tradition where students are divided during basic education in different schools or in study lines within a school according to their earlier performance. That option definitely leads to different competences. Another tradition is the comprehensive education model, as I call it, where all students have the same objectives and opportunities. By implementing that policy, it is possible, as Finnish experience shows, to raise the quality of educational performance for the whole age group. In terms of education, governments want success for everyone, but as they decide between those two traditions, they also decide what kind of success (benefit) would be seen and by whom. Finland represents the comprehensive model.

International comparisons are important. Individual countries can use them as mirrors in which to reflect their own performance and policies. Although it is not wise to import policies from other countries as such, countries can benchmark their own products with products from elsewhere. Countries can also learn from each others' good practices.

In terms of education, countries represent different traditions, values, institutions and systems depending on social and economic pressures in their own countries. As a result, their strategic choices also differ from each other. Having said that and understanding that political realities determine what can be done in an individual country, I would like to make some statements. Taking the Finnish experience seriously, I see the most important issue for all educational systems as being:

1. Making a profound change in education requires strategic objectives, time and patience. The Finnish example shows that, after setting detailed objectives at the end of the 1960s, successive governments have made incremental changes to basic education in order to meet the original aims set for 1968. There has been national consensus that education is important. I would say that this is rare. In many countries, government change means radical changes to education policy that can at the same time reverse the effects of the earlier policy.

2. Empowerment of the teaching profession produces good results. Professional teachers should have space for innovation, because they should try to find new ways to improve learning. Teachers should not be seen as being technicians whose work is to implement strictly dictated syllabi, but rather professionals who know how to improve learning for all. All this creates a big challenge for initial teacher education around the world. That certainly calls for changes in teacher education programmes. Teachers are ranked highest in importance, because educational systems work through them. Therefore, their opinions should be taken as advice when changes are planned.

3. A supportive ethos of education is essential. If we want success for all, we must understand that slow learners drop away from the pace of others without appropriate extra support. That support should be given to anyone as soon as his/her learning difficulties become apparent. The whole ethos of schools is important to support a feeling of safety. The Finnish central administration has reacted to that issue in the latest national core curriculum stressing that schools must take care of the physical and psychological safety of students. If students are not relaxed, they do not learn well.
4. High standards for all encourage and enable students to do their best. If a teacher sets low standards, he/she will see low performance and vice versa. That was why Finland stopped the process of "streaming" in lower secondary schools.
5. Education policy and educational practices are never at their peak. Thus, development of education must continue and it is essential to set new challenges for all stakeholders.

14.5. Concluding Remarks

In Finland, long-term development objectives for basic education were set almost 40 years ago. The main goal was to develop basic education to meet the criteria of the comprehensive education system. PISA shows that Finland has succeeded in its policy to enhance the equity and quality of learning. Finland is on top and, at the same time, only a very few students fall within the lowest PISA categories. Likewise, differences between schools are small.

At the beginning (in the 1970s), basic education in Finland was not like that. Several changes were thus implemented over the years. The most important ones were: (1) discontinuation of streaming, (2) strong allocation of affordable educational resources to lower secondary education and (3) decentralisation of decision-making powers. (4) Primary school teacher education was also raised to MA level. (5) Support for weak students was taken care of. (6) Different stakeholders were invited to express their opinions. That is the Finnish strategy and it shows that it has taken a long time for the strategy to mature and that it is composed of several interrelated issues; that was noticed by an OECD review team looking at equity in the Finnish education system. The team writes, "This is a complex of practices that has emerged over time, but it must be maintained since any weakness in one component will undermine other practices" (OECD 2006:48).

From the top it is easy to fall down, so Finland has a challenge to maintain its position in international comparisons. There are many reasons for saying this. One issue is increasing international competition that forces countries to find ways of increasing knowledge and competences. Another issue is that certain problematic developments can already be seen and Finland will have to solve these in the future. In this respect, I do not want to consider everyday problems that can be found across the world, but instead I want to focus on two major issues.

One big issue is that the population of Finland is ageing very rapidly. That presents a challenge for the educational system in two ways. Firstly, the impact of demographic changes is that sizes of age groups currently in basic education are falling very rapidly (OECD 2004c:50). At the same time, there is strong internal immigration that adds to the problems. Consequently, the educational infrastructure needs to change. In Finland, people have become used to having schools close to where they live and the government also wants to strengthen that principle (Ministry of Education 2004). However, adjustment of the school network to demographic realities is in the hands of decision-makers and cannot be achieved easily. Another impact of the ageing population is that the education sector will face increased competition for qualified workers in the near future as will other public sectors and the private sector. In Finland today, there are no problems attracting bright young people to teacher education, but the future may be very different.

Another concern that might be crucial for the education sector concerns municipalities' abilities to deliver equal welfare services. In a country of 5.2 million inhabitants, there are 431 municipalities, many of which have small populations and have financial difficulties in arranging high-standard welfare services, especially in terms of not only health care but also education. The OECD review team on equity in the Finnish education system noticed that the distribution of special-needs or, more specifically, of fully qualified teachers is uneven among municipalities. Therefore their "concern is that efforts to achieve equity in [Finnish] comprehensive schools, as good as they are in theory, may be unevenly distributed in practical terms" (OECD 2006:48).

There is no perfect education system. That is the ideal image and the reality is that we do not know how such a system would look and work in practical terms. Finnish education policy is a very good example of the very nature of the search for excellence. What policymakers can do is to set long-term objectives based on the values that society wants to support and to try constantly to meet the criteria of those objectives step by step. In doing so, policy-makers have to meet new challenges all the time.

References

Aho E, Pitkänen K, Sahlberg P (2006) *Policy Development and Reform Principles of Basic and Secondary Education in Finland Since 1968.* World Bank, Washington, DC

Blom H, Laukkanen R, Lindström A, Saresma U, Virtanen P (1996) (eds) *Erityisopetuksen tila [The State of Special Education].* In Finnish. Opetushallitus, Helsinki

Darling-Hammond L (2005) Constructing schools for competence: teaching, assessing, and organising for student success. In: Kanako M (ed) *Core Academic Competences: Policy Issues and Educational Reform.* University of Tokyo, Tokyo, pp 73–93

Finnish National Board of Education (2004) *National Core Curriculum for Basic Education.* The Finnish National Board of Education, Helsinki

Gaber S et al. (2006) *Zakaj Finci letijo dlje? [Why do Finns Fly Further?].* Educa, Ljubljana

Halinen I (2005) The Finnish curriculum development processes. Paper presented at the Finland in PISA studies conference, October 10–11, 2005, Helsinki

Hallituksen esitys (1967) Hallituksen esitys Eduskunnalle laiksi koulutusjärjestelmän perusteista [Government bill to Parliament on legislation for foundations of education system]. In Finnish. Helsinki (1967 vp. – HE n:o 44)

Hirvi V (1996) *Koulutuksen rytminvaihdos. 1990-luvun koulutuspolitiikka Suomessa. [The Change of Rhythm in Education. Finnish Education Policy in the 1990s].* In Finnish. Otava, Helsinki

Isotalo T (2004) Kaikki tiet vievät Suomeen. Selvitys Suomen PISA-menestyksen aiheuttamasta mielenkiinnosta saksankielisissä maissa. Lehtiartikkelit ja vierailut 12/2001–6/2004 [All roads lead to Finland. A report on the interest caused by Finland's success in PISA in German-speaking countries. Newspaper articles and visits between 12/2001 and 06/2004]. In Finnish. Moniste 7/2004. Opetushallitus, Helsinki

Kansanen P (2003) Teacher education in Finland: current models and new developments. In: Moon M, Vlăsceanu L, Barrows C (eds) *Institutional Approaches to Teacher Education Within Higher Education in Europe: Current Models and New Developments.* Unesco-Cepes, Bucharets, pp 85–108

Komiteanmietintö (1970) Peruskoulun opetussuunnitelmakomitean mietintö I. Opetussuunnitelman perusteet [Comprehensive School Curriculum Committee Report I. The Basics of the Curriculum]. In Finnish. Komiteanmietintö 1970:A4. Valtion painatuskeskus, Helsinki

Kouluhallitus (1985) *Peruskoulun opetussuunnitelman perusteet 1985 [Framework Curriculum for Comprehensive Schools in 1985].* In Finnish. Valtion painatuskeskus, Helsinki

Koulujärjestelmälaki (1968) Laki koulujärjestelmän perusteista [Principles of the Comprehensive School Act]. In Finnish, 467

Koululait (1983) *Koululait. Lakikokoelma 13 [School laws. Law collection 13].* In Finnish. Valtion painatuskeskus, Helsinki

Kuiper W, Akker van den J (2006) Curriculum policy and practices in a European comparative perspective: finding a balance between central structure and local autonomy. Paper presented at the Second World Curriculum Studies Conference, 21–24 May 2006, University of Tampere, Finland

Lampinen O (1998) *Suomen koulutusjärjestelmän kehitys [Development of the Finnish Education System]*. In Finnish. Tammer-paino, Tampere

Lappalainen HP (2006) *Ei taito taakkana ole. Perusopetuksen äidinkielen ja kirjallisuuden oppimistulosten arviointi 9. vuosiluokalla. [Skills Are Not a Burden. Assessment of Performance in Mother Tongue and Literature in Basic Education Grade 9]*. In Finnish. Opetushallitus, Helsinki

Laukkanen R (1998) Opetustoimen keskushallinnon evaluaatioajattelun kehitys Suomessa 1970-luvulta 1990-luvulle. Development of conceptions of evaluation in central educational administration in Finland from the 1970s to the 1990s. In Finnish. University of Jyväskylä. Koulutuksen tutkimuslaitos. Tutkimuksia 5

Lehtisalo L, Raivola R (2000) *Koulutus ja koulutuspolitiikka 2000-luvulle. [Education and Education Policy up to the 21st Century]*. In Finnish. WSOY, Juva

Liiten M (2004) *Opettajan ammatti nousi abiturienttien ykkössuosikiksi [The Teaching Profession Became the Favourite of Matriculation Examination Candidates]*. In Finnish. Helsingin Sanomat

Lundgren UP (1990) Educational policymaking, decentralisation and evaluation. In: Granheim M, Kogan M, Lundgren UP (eds) *Evaluation as Policymaking*. Jessica Kingsley, London

Mattila L (2002) *Peruskoulun matematiikan oppimistulosten kansallinen arviointi 9. vuosiluokalla 2002 [National Assessment of Performance in Mathematics in Basic Education Grade 9]*. In Finnish. Opetushallitus, Helsinki

Ministry of Education (2004) *Educational Research 2003–2008*. The Ministry of Education, Helsinki

National Board of Education (1994) *Framework Curriculum for the Comprehensive School*. The National Board of Education, Helsinki

OECD (2001) *Knowledge and Skills for Life. First Results from the OECD Program for International Student Assessment (PISA)*. OECD, Paris

OECD (2003) *Education Policy Analysis*. OECD, Paris

OECD (2004a) *Learning for Tomorrow's World. First Results from PISA 2003*. OECD, Paris

OECD (2004b) *Denmark. Lessons from PISA 2000. Reviews of National Policies for Education*. OECD, Paris

OECD (2004c) *Education at a Glance. OECD Indicators 2004*. OECD, Paris

OECD (2005) *Education at a Glance. OECD Indicators 2005*. OECD, Paris

OECD (2006) *Equity in Education Thematic Review. Finland Country Note*. www.oecd.org/document/3/0,2340,en_2649_34531_36296195_1_1_1_1,00.html

Pratt J (2004) Finland reviewed: a view from a foreign evaluator. In: Laukkanen R (ed) *OECD: n teema- ja maatutkinnat*. The Ministry of Education, Helsinki, pp 87–92

Raivola R (2006) How far can we learn anything practical from the study of foreign systems of education? Finland and the PISA model. *Comparative and International Education Review* 6:11–23

Rinne R, Vuorio-Lehti M (1996) *Toivoton unelma? Koulutuksellista tasa-arvoa koskevat toiveet ja epäilyt peruskoulun synnystä 1990-luvulle [A Hopeless Dream? Hopes and Doubts in Terms of Quality from Establishment of the Comprehensive School Through to the 1990s]*. In Finnish. Opetushallitus, Helsinki

Schleicher A (2006) *The Economics of Knowledge: Why Education is Key for Europe's Success*. Lisbon Council, Brussels

Simola H (2005) The Finnish miracle of PISA: historical and sociological remarks on teaching and teacher education. *Comparative Education* 41:455–470

Statistics Finland (2006) *Education in Finland 2006*. Statistics Finland, Helsinki

The Economist (2006) *Some Remedial Lessons are Needed for European Leaders. Back to School*. From the Economist printed edition 23rd March, http://www.economist.com/displaystory.cfm?story_id=E1_VGVVTSN

Välijärvi J (2004) The system and how does it work – some curricular and pedagogical characteristics of the Finnish comprehensive schools. *Educational Journal The Chinese University of Hong Kong* 32(1), 31–55. See also (2003) 31(2)

Index

Academic oligarchy, 42
Academic self-governance, 4, 37, 38, 41–44, 46, 47, 49, 51
Additional educational needs, 209, 210, 222, 225–227
Additive policies, 8, 9, 13, 14, 18–20, 27, 28, 64, 264, 321
Administrative discretion, 206, 207, 209
Administrative subsystems, 272, 273
Allocation, 7, 8, 10, 42, 51, 206–209, 211, 215, 216, 218, 219, 222–224, 231–233, 236–239, 242, 249–252, 261–264, 290–292, 297, 298, 301, 303, 320
Assessment, 116, 132, 165, 169, 179, 207, 216, 228, 229, 233, 273, 284, 301, 316, 317
 for learning, 277, 278, 291, 315
Attendance, 9, 89, 231, 273, 276, 279
Austria, 3, 4, 35, 40, 41, 43, 44, 45, 47, 50, 91, 93, 95, 96, 98, 99, 102, 103, 123, 242
Autonomy, 9, 15, 17, 18, 20–23, 25, 27, 30, 31, 43, 51, 138, 139, 141, 175, 179, 181, 232, 236, 238, 239, 289–293, 295, 297–299, 301–303, 315

Basic education, 100, 139, 307, 308–321
Belgium, 3, 13, 14, 16, 20, 24, 27, 86, 91, 92, 94–96, 98, 99, 101, 102, 123

Budget, 2, 6–9, 42, 45, 47, 137, 140, 141–146, 148, 150, 190, 205–208, 212–214, 216, 218–224, 226, 229, 231, 232, 236–242, 248, 249, 250–252, 263, 273, 274, 291, 292, 295–297, 301, 302
Bulgaria, 90, 96, 99, 101, 205, 219

Capital expenditure, 216, 218, 219, 222
Classification scheme, 236, 237
Class size, 4, 6, 62, 69–71, 78, 123, 138, 143, 150, 169, 178, 180, 182, 199, 200, 206, 212, 219, 247, 251, 253, 261, 264, 297, 298
Clerical, 271, 274, 275, 276, 277, 281
Competition, 1–4, 9, 18, 23, 24, 26, 29, 30, 38–41, 44, 46, 48, 49, 50, 58, 199, 232, 239, 294, 298–300, 305, 314, 315, 321
Compulsory schooling, 68, 74, 82, 100, 149, 221, 224, 251
Computer, 7, 169, 196, 197, 261, 270, 271, 273, 275, 276, 278, 279–282
 network, 279
 support, 270, 271
Continental systems, 50
Contractualisation, 23
Conversion rule, 206, 207, 209, 225
Coordination, 3, 13, 22, 23, 29, 35, 39, 51, 60, 66

Cost(s), 7, 8, 40, 70–75, 77, 80, 82, 126, 138–140, 157, 158, 207–230, 232, 237, 241, 242, 243, 244, 251–253, 255–264, 273, 274, 295, 296, 298, 302, 303, 309, 313
    function, 8, 248–250, 263
Cyprus, 90, 95, 96, 98, 101
Czech Republic, 91, 94, 96, 98, 99, 102, 123

Data, 5–8, 58, 61, 63, 64, 70, 72, 73, 74, 76, 79, 80, 82, 85–89, 92, 94, 95, 98, 99, 101–104, 108–123, 132–149, 163–165, 169, 170, 172, 181, 192, 227, 229–232, 238, 240, 243, 251–253, 257, 258, 260, 262, 263, 271–284, 285
Database, 95, 98, 155, 165–168, 179, 188, 194, 230, 271, 274, 275
Data envelopment analysis (DEA), 7, 187–189, 191, 194, 195, 197, 198
Decentralisation, 1, 10, 17, 19, 20, 27, 30, 309–312, 315, 317, 318, 320
Decision-making, 4, 10, 17, 24, 30, 38, 42, 44–47, 66–68, 72, 73, 250, 252, 270, 276, 281, 283, 290, 291, 309–312
Democracy (direct), 2, 6, 137–150
Denmark, 91, 93, 95, 96, 98, 101–103, 123, 230, 242, 306
Deregulation, 40, 43, 44, 45, 47
Direct data entry, 279
Direct legislation, 137, 138, 140, 141–143, 150

Economic downturn, 1
Economic growth, 2, 5, 109, 114–117, 120, 131, 132

Education
    administration, 6, 9, 45, 60, 64, 65, 82, 141, 142, 146, 272, 291, 293, 294, 298, 299, 300, 310
    policy, 59, 66, 70, 72, 73, 75, 80, 81, 82, 122–127, 134, 318–321
    structures, 94–104, 161–171
Educational planning, 271–274
Educational programme, 6, 165, 172–182
Educational quality, 5, 8, 22, 23, 41, 47, 70, 71, 74, 76–78, 81, 82, 126, 127, 131–134, 137, 138, 144, 155–182, 187, 223, 237–244, 305, 307, 311, 315
Effectiveness, 36, 40, 66–82, 85, 86, 94, 104, 122, 156–182
Efficiency, 2, 7–9, 21–23, 40, 41, 45, 47, 67, 70, 71, 77, 80, 134, 157, 158, 163, 187–195, 197–201, 205–208, 212, 217, 218, 223–227, 230–233, 236–239, 244, 275, 276, 284
    behaviour, 238
Elite universities, 48
England, 3, 4, 8, 13, 14, 16, 17, 18–20, 24, 25, 27, 28, 31, 35, 40, 41, 42, 50, 213, 214, 216, 218, 220, 225, 228–232, 236, 237, 242, 258, 269, 277, 281, 283
Equality, 2, 26, 85–101, 295, 318
Equity, 2, 4–10, 67, 68, 85–88, 94, 103, 104, 162, 164, 182, 194, 205, 206, 209–211, 213, 217, 218, 225, 232, 239–242, 244, 247, 270–285, 289–303, 307, 311, 320, 321
Estonia, 90, 96, 98
Europeanization, 36, 37

Index

Evaluation, 3–7, 17–31, 35, 38, 40, 43, 44, 45–49, 57–68, 82, 86, 100, 115, 121, 175, 192, 201, 270, 272, 274, 282, 284, 300–303, 305, 306, 310
  of education, 67, 86, 115, 315–317
Evaluative state (evaluative state model), 14, 20, 21–31
Excellence initiative, 48
Expenditure(s)
  administrative, 6, 142, 143, 150, 206, 207, 209
  instructional, 142, 143, 149
  sub-federal, 137, 139, 141, 142, 150
External stakeholders, 2, 10, 42, 48, 51, 74, 209, 307, 320

Federalism, 182
Feedback, 121, 270, 277, 283–285, 316, 317
Financial autonomy, 9, 232, 239, 293–297, 303
Financial planning, 271–274
Finland, 8, 87, 89, 90–92, 96, 98–100, 102, 103, 123, 213, 214, 225, 236, 305–321
Fixed effects, 181, 250, 252, 257, 260–264
Formative assessment, 277, 278
Formula, 8, 49, 221, 253, 257, 260, 308, 309
Formula based funding, 205–233, 237–244, 313
France, 3, 9, 13, 14, 16–19, 24, 26, 27, 29, 91, 96, 98, 99, 101–103, 123, 242, 295, 296, 302
Funding, 7, 8, 19, 36, 38, 41, 48, 49, 70, 208, 294–313
  criteria, 8, 205–208, 222–229

Germany, 3, 4, 35, 40, 41, 43, 45, 47–49, 91, 94–96, 98, 99, 102, 103, 123, 133
Globalization, 36

Governance, 1–9, 13–31, 35–52, 57–65, 69, 73, 79–82, 85, 237, 239, 240, 244
  equalizer, 3, 35–40, 50, 52
  systems, 1–12, 35–50
Greece, 91, 96, 98, 99, 101–103, 123

Horizontal equity, 209, 241, 242
Humboldtian tradition, 45
Hungary, 3, 13, 14, 16–20, 26, 91, 93, 96, 98, 99, 102, 103, 123, 306
Hybridisation, 27–31

Iceland, 8, 89, 90, 92, 96, 98–103, 123, 213, 214, 220, 224, 236
ICT, 224, 269, 278, 279
Implementation, 5, 15, 28, 29, 31, 35, 44, 46, 51, 94, 104, 159, 270, 279, 280, 301, 308, 309, 317, 318
Incentive system, 240
Indicator, 4, 5, 18, 42, 49, 52, 57, 59, 61–82, 85, 87–89, 92, 94–104, 144, 168, 170, 180, 206–209, 212, 216, 217, 225, 227–230, 236, 237, 240
Individual earnings, 5, 109, 111, 131
Inefficient allocation, 236
Information, 2, 4, 9, 18, 24, 58–64, 65–82, 89–117, 133–138, 143, 150, 164, 165, 170, 194, 196, 201, 212, 213, 250, 263
  Communications Technology, and, 9, 269
Internationalization, 36
Ireland, 91, 97, 100, 101, 102, 103, 123
Italy, 91, 93, 95, 97, 99, 101–103, 123

Latvia, 91, 97, 98, 99, 101–103
Leviathan, 6, 143, 146, 150
Liechtenstein, 91, 97, 98, 99, 101, 103
Lithuania, 90, 97

Local
  authority, 213–219
  government, 141, 216, 217, 221–224, 249–252, 257, 260–264
  politics, 298–303
Long-term strategy, 9, 40, 58, 240, 269, 307, 320, 321
Lump sum budget, 7, 8, 43, 205, 208, 236, 238, 241, 244
Luxembourg, 91, 97–103

Malta, 90, 97–101
Management, 1–3, 6–9, 15, 18, 20, 22, 23, 28, 30, 36, 40, 42, 43, 48, 52, 57–59, 69, 73, 79, 80, 82, 159, 160, 163–165, 169–182, 192, 205, 212, 217–220, 223, 226, 231–233, 236, 240–243, 263
  by objectives, 48
  Information Systems, 270, 271
  self-governance, 38
Market-like competition, 40
Market-type behaviour, 44
  subsystems, 272–274
Mathematical literacy, 165–168, 179, 182
Median voter, 146
Minority students, 8, 225, 253, 255–257, 260–264
MIS, 270, 271
Monitoring, 4, 57–83
Multilevel analysis, 155, 156, 163, 164, 181
Multi-level multi actor
  governance, 35
Municipality, 213, 215, 221, 222, 290, 291, 316, 317

National reporting, 59
Neo-liberal ideologies, 35
The Netherlands, 3, 35, 40, 43–45, 50, 98, 99, 101–103, 123, 212, 213, 220–222, 225–227, 232, 233, 236, 283, 284

Network governance, 35, 36
New governance, 36
New public management, 1, 36, 37
Norway, 8, 91, 95, 97, 98, 100, 102, 103, 123, 247, 249–253, 257, 259, 260, 263

OECD, 2, 6, 58, 61, 76, 82, 85–87, 95, 98, 101, 103, 123, 138, 144, 145, 147, 150, 155–157, 161–182, 187, 192, 208, 305, 306, 312, 313, 315, 320–321
Optical mark recognition, 279
Output, 6, 7, 8, 40, 43, 62, 73, 77, 79, 80, 124, 132, 157, 160, 161, 167, 168, 188–217, 230, 231, 237–242, 248–250, 271, 275, 280, 282

Paradigm, 1–3, 57–59, 236, 237, 241, 242
Participation in university decision-making, 47
Partnerships, 42
PAT, 283, 284
Peer review, 4, 38, 49, 51
PISA, 1, 6, 7, 9, 60, 61, 72, 73, 80, 86, 89, 92, 94–96, 98, 102, 107, 108, 123, 134, 168–182, 196, 305–318, 320
PISA 2000, 137, 138, 139, 140, 144–150, 187, 192, 193, 197, 198, 200
  mathematics, 144–148, 165–168
  natural science, 144–148
  reading, 144–148
  Swiss sample, 144–148
Planning, 46, 48, 127, 160, 206, 272–278, 299, 315
Poland, 8, 91, 95, 97, 98, 102, 103, 123, 213, 214, 236
Policy-amenable school
  characteristics, 156, 168, 169
Political institutions, 140

Index 329

Portugal, 3, 13–30, 91, 95, 97, 98, 100–103, 123
Post-bureaucratic regulation (or regime), 3, 13, 23, 24
Primary school, 10, 82, 139, 142, 166, 215, 220, 223, 226, 227, 241, 252–260, 290, 291, 314, 320
Production function, 6, 131, 132, 138, 143, 144, 146, 157, 231, 232, 243, 249
Professional bureaucracy (professional bureaucracy model), 15, 143, 144
Public discussion, 72, 150
Pupil Achievement Tracker, 283, 284
Pupil performance, 193, 194, 278

Quality, 21–29, 41, 42, 47, 48, 70–78, 81, 82, 107–118, 131–134, 155–182, 237–239
Quasi-markets (quasi market model), 38, 41, 49, 51, 209, 210, 232

RAE, 41, 42
Ranking, 77, 78, 92, 101–103, 132, 198, 316, 317
Reasons for rethinking governance, 36
Reduced form, 249–251
Referendum, 140
Regional authority, 289
Regulation, 1, 3, 4, 13–31, 35–51, 58, 100, 120, 140, 206, 208, 211–217, 240, 301–303
Research Assessment Exercises, 41
Resource use, 8, 249–251, 253–261
Romania, 90, 97, 99–101
Russian Federation, 123, 213

School
  administration, 6, 9, 142, 146, 272, 299
  autonomy, 31, 169, 179, 181, 232, 291–297, 302, 303
  based management, 8, 232, 233, 290
  budget, 6, 137, 143–146, 148, 208, 214, 218, 219, 221, 223, 250, 251, 263, 273
  context, 161–182, 232
  effectiveness, 156–181, 275, 276, 285
  improvement, 9, 117, 269, 270, 274–279, 282, 284, 285
  management, 9, 30, 163, 164, 165, 169, 171, 172, 175–177, 179, 181, 271, 283
  managers, 9, 219, 271, 273–275, 281, 282
  performance feedback systems, 270, 283
  principal, 165, 168, 169, 209, 222, 295–297
  project, 24, 82, 291–293
  resources, 6, 148, 149, 157, 162–172, 174–178, 181, 182, 247, 251, 252
  size, 7, 8, 169, 178, 198, 200, 211, 217, 247, 248–252, 257–259, 263, 264
School Information Systems (SIS), 9, 269–270
  aims, 275–276
  implementation, 279–283
  modules, 271–274
  subsystems, 271–274
  usage, 281–283
Secondary education, 95, 96, 100, 101, 166–171, 221, 223, 253, 261, 291, 309, 312, 314, 318, 320
Secondary schools, 7, 13, 19, 72, 121, 126, 187, 188, 200, 201, 216, 223, 227, 232, 252, 253, 256, 259, 271, 272, 289, 291, 320
Segregation, 5, 88–90, 92–94, 99, 101–104
Slovak Republic, 91, 97, 98, 101, 102, 123
Slovenia, 90, 97, 306

Socio-economic class-composition, 172–174, 182
Spain, 91, 96, 98, 101–103, 123
Special educational needs, 209–211, 226, 227
Special needs, 8, 19, 94, 96, 210, 215, 219, 222, 226–228, 241, 248, 251, 255–257, 259–264, 307, 309, 312, 313, 321
SPFS, 283–285
Stakeholder guidance, 37, 38, 40, 43, 45, 48
Standard cost accounting, 236–237, 242, 243
State regulation, 3, 37–39, 43, 45, 47, 50, 51
State-university relationships, 44
Steering from a distance, 43
Student
   composition, 8, 247, 248, 250–252, 255, 259, 261, 262
   performance, 6, 116, 119, 122–124, 138, 144–149, 177, 179, 182, 248–250, 263, 264
Sweden, 8, 90, 93, 95, 97, 98, 100, 102, 103, 123, 212
Swipe cards, 279
Switzerland, 6, 59–83, 90, 95, 98, 102, 103, 123, 133, 134, 137–150, 155, 165, 166, 172, 182, 187, 192, 236, 242

Teacher
   education, 127, 314, 319–321
   hours, 253, 254, 257–260, 262, 264
   qualification, 124, 138, 144, 147–150
   quality, 107, 108, 124–127, 131, 144
   salaries, 123, 220, 222, 224, 237
   wages, 143, 149
Test scores, 107, 109, 116, 119, 121, 131–134, 144, 145, 147, 148, 171, 193, 272
Training, 20, 23, 48, 66, 74, 75, 81, 88, 139, 141, 143, 146, 147, 148, 150, 196, 261, 274, 278, 280–285
Transparency, 8, 46, 208, 241, 244
Truancy, 274, 276, 279
Turkey, 91, 95, 97, 98, 102, 103, 123

United Kingdom, 91, 97, 98, 102, 110, 116, 216, 229, 264
USA, 109, 110, 115, 116, 119–121, 123–127, 143–144, 146, 150, 312

Variance
   between classes, 171–176
   within classes, 171–173
Vertical equity, 209, 210, 225, 226, 232, 239, 241

Wireless network, 279

Printed in the United Kingdom
by Lightning Source UK Ltd.
123680UK00007B/115-147/A